THE
TROUBLE
WITH
CANADA

WILLIAM D. GAIRDNER

D0595954

Published in 1991 by
General Paperbacks
30 Lesmill Road
Toronto, Ontario
M3B 2T6

First published in hardcover 1990 by
Stoddart Publishing Co. Limited

Canadian Cataloguing in Publication Data

Gairdner, William D. (William Douglas), 1940-
The Trouble with Canada

Includes bibliographical references and index.
ISBN 0-7736-7311-3

1. Canada - Social conditions.   2. Canada - Politics
and government.   I. Title.

HN103.5.G34 1991   306'.0971   C90-095877-4

JACKET DESIGN: Brant Cowie/ArtPlus Limited
JACKET ILLUSTRATION: Al Wilson
INDEXING: Heather Ebbs
TYPESETTING: Tony Gordon Ltd.

Printed and bound in the United States of America

*For my family
and all who cherish
freedom and responsibility*

Contents

Preface

A FAMOUS WRITER, WHEN asked what he thought of a certain situation, replied, "How do I know what I think, until I see what I say?" For me, this sums up the process of discovery inherent in any creative project. A book is the product of the writer's struggle to give a coherent shape and substance to strong thoughts and feelings.

Like so many citizens of this country I became upset over the past two decades to see this great country rush headlong into the embrace of sweet-sounding but inherently destructive political, economic, and social policies. Like them, I felt helpless. How, after all, can one person affect the course of the nation, especially when the three major parties are all but identical in their political and moral philosophies? One ballot once every four or five years is important, but feeble. No sooner had I begun my search for some other way than I discovered I was pregnant with a book. From that point on, I felt like the book was writing me.

A month into this process, through one of those delightful accidents of life, I found myself surrounded by an enthusiastic and understanding publisher and his capable team. He said that Canada was a country of such uniform and unexamined opinion that an individual with strong contrary views could no longer make himself heard — except through a book. And that's why he wanted to publish *The Trouble With Canada*.

Such words are music to a writer's ears. From that day I resolved that this book would not be aimed at academics or specialists but at the everyday reader searching for answers to our troubles. Further, I was convinced that the language, like my feelings, had to be passionate and caring, and that if it was judged excessive on occasion, then at least it would be judged so for an excess of truth. My purpose, in short, was to reach out and touch every reader's feelings, not just to make argument (a dry fare, at best).

Further still, I wished to depart from the general Canadian view that we are a calm, compromising, pragmatic people — a view I have always taken to be a false compliment which, to our great national detriment, might very well camouflage a spiritual dullness and a certain lack of intellectual vigour. Surely a cavalry charge from an unexpected quarter would stir us from our slumbers?

So there was the formula: passionate language; caring argument; a determination to get at the root problems; a reluctance to couch divisive matters in compromised terms (as my grandfather said, even if you're going to be wrong, "speak up!"); a readiness to take the heat this book is going to generate; and above all, a vision. It was important that *The Trouble With Canada* not only expose the political, economic, and cultural lacerations on the national body, but also that it provide the cure. Implicit and explicit in this book, therefore, is a sustained moral vision spurring the reader and the country on to a healthier life.

During the writing of the book, in sometimes surprising ways, Canada and the world have changed. At the beginning, I could not convince anyone that our national debt was a major problem (it was not even an election issue in 1988); now the debt is on everyone's lips. Then the Meech Lake Accord was barely a reality; today it is poised to disrupt the nation. In my early chapters, I wondered why so few seemed able to see that the blandishments of the social-welfare State were a moral danger to us, and to the whole world — that socialism was sick and would die of internal wounds because it was politically, economically, and morally unsound; today, as if in a dream, we see its astonishingly rapid demise in Eastern Europe, with more convulsions yet to come there and elsewhere. My hope is that this book will help us to bring down political, economic, and cultural walls of our own making, paid for by us and put in place by governments eager to encircle and restrict us as we sleep.

I wish to thank a number of people for their help, for no book ever sees the light solely from the author's efforts. It is the result of a whole network of personal and professional relationships, advice, expertise, warnings, encouragements, and work from others.

In particular, for serving as a mentor and fount of knowledge, and for early editing and research, my friend Kenneth McDonald, a successful author himself who sounded the alarums long ago, and is still doing so. My wife, Jean, who early alerted me to the crucial difference between *telling* the reader how upset I was and clearly *showing* what is going on so that the reader would be in turn upset. Christine, Emilie, Ruthann, Billy, and Franklin, for putting up with their father's obsessive interest in "the book" for two years. My mother for her interest, and my father for his patient reading and criticism of early drafts. And much is owed to those who took the time from their own busy lives to provide material, or to read various chapters and criticize, redirect, or nudge, as the case may have been, including Alphonse Juilland, Lowell Cohn, David Steen, Michael Bliss, Michael Walker, Jean Sparling, Alex Alvaro, Phil Gold, Don Elliott, Bill Allen, Ken Murray, Allan Carlson, Gwen Landolt, David Cole, Lionel Weinstein, Patrick Hewlett, Bill Goodman, Brian Rogers, and Kay Sommerfeld.

Introduction

ON THE WHOLE, Canada is a great place to live. It's beautiful, wealthy, politically stable, does not make war, and is rarely subject to natural disasters. What more could we hope for? What we see on the surface is a healthy, harmonious picture.

But despite their outward appearances, countries, like biological organisms, bear within themselves the seeds of their own health, or decay. Just as there is within each of us a constant, ever-present struggle between healthy and unhealthy cell life, so there is within all countries a constant, ever-present struggle between the political, economic, and cultural forces that lead to strength, and those that lead to weakness. Once unhealthy cells or unhealthy political, economic, and cultural policies get the upper hand, an organism or a nation can sap itself of vitality until it is unable to function. While Canada still seems relatively healthy, the signs of illness have been present for some time, visible to those prepared to see them, and if the illness isn't treated properly, Canada could get very, very sick.

This book was written for all Canadians concerned about the future of this great and beautiful country. But it is not an academic study or research document — there are too many of those available already on every subject in this book. For the most part, no attention is paid to them, or they preach to the converted, or they are countered by further research, equally ignored. So I'm not trying to add to the academic uproar by writing a book in which the risk of offending is reduced to zero. That can result in a dull book and endless equivocation. Rather, this is a book meant to change minds. For at bottom, what is truly lacking in our overstudied society is a basic commitment from the people of this nation to fight actively for the core values that made Canada great in the first place. Instead, we seem content to sit passively and watch our society evolve — for the worse, I believe — in the vague hope that some day a guiding truth will arise as if by magic and appear on the front page of the *Toronto Star*. Of course, that's not going to happen. But we have grown so used to hearing "experts" tell us how we ought to live that we lose sight of the fact that strong, cohesive societies are based on even stronger belief systems sustained by the people as they make their daily fundamental political, economic, and cultural choices. Over the ages, people creating strong civilizations made such choices not because they felt they could be "proven" correct (science barely existed), but because they believed their choices were right and arose naturally from their common belief system. Today, however, we seem to have abandoned the idea that a common belief system is necessary at all — a result, in part, of a general decline in faith, and the moral strength derived from it. Instead, we like to think that all values are equal or "relevant" — that just about anything goes. This attitude has arisen not from any deeply honest confrontation with past or present values but from a flight from values altogether. Moving away from any coherent moral code, Canadians have turned to science for direction, to the extent that misplaced respect for science now overrules our best instincts. If, say, the importance of traditional family life hasn't been substantiated by research, we fail to resist government policies that lead to its decay. Or if research can't prove that babies are harmed by the impersonality of third-party daycare or that the poor are harmed by give-aways, then it must be all right for them. But society can't make choices based only on scientific observation because most of the important moral choices in life lie beyond the reach of objective data. Society must therefore base its choices on a common moral vision sustained by the hearts, minds, and beliefs of the people, and no more. Such a vision underlies the evolution of any society, but if that vision fades the society will slowly fragment. With no common moral vision, political, economic, and social life becomes a war of all against all, in which interest groups contend for ever-diminishing tax dollars to fund their morally conflicting causes. The rules of the game no longer ensure fairness; they favour those with power.

Will we be a nation guided by a philosophy of individual freedom and responsibility, or will we become increasingly socialized and turn responsibility for ourselves and our families over to the State? That is a question about values, not facts, and it's time we faced that fact! Unless we do, and do it soon, we will watch, immobilized, as our own society sinks slowly beneath the waves. Such common visions work best if they rise from the bottom up (from the people), rather than being imposed from the top down (by the government). Most of the evil of the twentieth century has resulted from this latter form. The important thing is for the people to have values, to articulate them, live by them, and defend them. To attempt, as we Canadians have done, to accommodate every pressure group in the country with a pastiche of government-promoted political, economic, and cultural hand-outs from overextended budgets leads only to long-term deficits, social fragmentation, and more unproductive research. This book is one man's effort to define and speak for a specific set of values and for the social choices that necessarily arise from them.

Almost imperceptibly during the past few decades, all the political parties of our nation have embraced, to a greater or lesser degree, the twin philosophies of *collectivism* and *egalitarianism*. Collectivism is an elitist political philosophy which insists that the central government ought to control and engineer the condition of society. Egalitarianism, a close cousin, is the inevitable outcome of a democracy controlled by the idea not simply that everyone should have the same *opportunities*, but that everyone has the *right* to the same *results*, regardless of natural differences, effort, or personal choices. The unfortunate effect of these twin philosophies, as we shall see, is to erode individual freedom and responsibility by granting the government extraordinary powers of coercion so that it can engineer social outcomes in favour of some, and to the detriment of others.

What this all boils down to is that all societies must choose between two radically different methods for organizing society: either (1) they must insist on *the same rules* for everyone and let all social outcomes evolve according to natural and freely expressed individual differences, or (2) they must impose an *equality of outcome* that can be achieved only by creating different rules for different social groups.

Unfortunately, we have allowed our government to adopt the latter method. Through countless judges, administrators, commissioners, regulators, and inspectors, governments at all levels launch all sorts of programs that openly discriminate against all sorts of people who are not beneficiaries of these programs, while they claim to promote nondiscriminatory practices. The consequent erosion of our basic freedoms through this and many other kinds of social engineering eventually leads to a further breakdown of traditional values such as the primacy of honesty, freedom, and hard work; respect for society, authority, and private property; and all related matters built upon these values. I believe that there is a silent majority of Canadians who are deeply upset by the present trend and who feel that their values and

wishes are not being defended by any of the political parties or promoted by the so-called opinion-makers in our society. Neither do they
see any reflection of their values in the media, the government, or the
special-interest groups they are forced to support through their tax
dollars. These people are not going to march in the street every time
they see something they don't like. Neither have they the time to
become experts in the field of political economy. But they know what
they think and feel. And my experience tells me they're fed up, they're
cynical, and worst of all, they're totally distrustful of the political
process — a dangerous climate for any democracy, because it leads to
political and moral apathy, which in turn leads to an "elite vs. the
people" style of government — and the end of real democracy. They
can't do anything about this situation short of giving up their livelihoods
and entering a political game for which they have lost all respect. So,
from a sense of futility, they do nothing. Given this situation, we must
ask how such a problem — or illness — can be cured. Naturally, we
must understand the illness (Part One of this book) before agreeing on
the cure (Part Two).

Over the years I have slowly become more alarmed that the average
business or professional person has only the vaguest idea of the basic
differences between, say, a truly conservative viewpoint and a modern
liberal or socialist one. I have become further alarmed by the discovery
that such people frequently vote, unknowingly, against their own best
interest. Cynical politicians, social engineers, and of course many
career bureaucrats are keenly aware of this. They manipulate to their
advantage the confusion that exists about the real meaning of political
concepts and political language. One of the aims of this book, therefore,
is to provide a key to the real meaning of these terms. That's why, in
the first chapters of this book, I will clarify some basic political and
economic concepts and language. Only a proper understanding can
arm us effectively against political dissemblers from any party. It's like
cracking the politician's secret code; once you know it, it's harder for
him to fool you.

But more than by language, clear understanding of political, economic, and cultural matters is made difficult by what I have called the
"popular illusions" that operate as a kind of inarticulate ideology at the
heart of society, and in which the clash between the traditional values
of a free society and the reaction to them can be seen. Once commonly
accepted, these popular illusions generate damaging policy directions
for Canada, and a resentful, dependent society. For confusion over
concepts like "rights" and "opportunities" become intermingled, like

the ropemaker's continuous red threads, in the attitudes of our teachers, in daily newspaper columns, and in the speeches of politicians. These illusions are seductive traps for the unwary, devices that allow those in positions of power to tap into the public purse in the name of noble-sounding but misleading ideals.

Once such deceptive ideas are put aside there will naturally arise from any society that energetically promotes what I call "the Bonus System" (Chapter Four) *a definable set of values and institutions, which, once effectively put in place and supported with the right cultural attitudes, will produce freedom and wealth almost anywhere on earth.*

A crucial moral consequence for those who gain this knowledge, therefore, is that at long last a solution to the twin problems of oppression and poverty — the oldest and most fundamental problems of all — is at hand. We now have not only an intellectual interest in persuading others that the tools of freedom and wealth creation are available, but also a *moral obligation* to work toward helping others in the world to understand and use them.

Of course, having the tools is one thing; using them properly and maintaining them is another. For there is just no question that such tools, once developed, can become inefficient and useless to the very societies that prospered from them. For more than a century and a half, these tools have been under attack by those who promote — knowingly or unknowingly — what I call "the Handicap System" (Chapter Five), or the socialist reaction to democratic capitalism. This reaction has always been easy to see in the works and writings of the international socialist movement itself, and it is far more radical than what we normally see in Canada. Here, the socialist reaction is less open and certainly less revolutionary in tone because it hides its own face. In this country, adverse reactions to democratic capitalism range from apathy, to unwitting support for socialist policies by well-intentioned people who are simply unaware of the ideological consequences of their thinking, to well-orchestrated efforts to lobby for programs and legislative measures destructive to our nation's success.

Of course, it is the political parties that attempt to steer the nation's course, and once their ideological strains are revealed (Chapter Six), we see graphically (Chapter Seven) exactly what has happened to Canada over the past few decades. It's one thing to be told that government spending has increased substantially. It's another to see a chart that dramatically illustrates the inexorable trend.

In Part Two of the book I will deal with "the issues" — welfare, affirmative action, immigration, pay equity, our medical crisis, foreign aid, radical feminism, the Meech Lake Accord, official bilingualism, multiculturalism, the criminal-justice system, and many other subjects that are dividing our nation. These are but expressions of the underlying philosophical and ideological tensions highlighted in Part One, and there is no end to the number of possible subjects one could cover. The aim here will be to bring clarity to the resolution of these issues and to show that all Canadians must take a more active role in deciding what the common vision of our life as a nation should be, and then ensure that public policies reflect this vision. There will be a lot of fireworks in this section, and I certainly don't expect everyone to agree with all the views expressed, nor could I cover every angle of every question. And I know that those with a vested interest in egalitarian collectivism will be swarming over this book like angry bees. Nevertheless, I believe that the neglected majority of Canadians who are upset by what is happening to their country will share most of these views and values.

Finally, the book closes with a Call to Action — a prescription for a limited number of measures that would surely bring an end to the trouble with Canada.

Part One

Through The Looking Glass

1

A Question Of Styles
What Should Be Our Method Of Government?

As a nation, we have failed to articulate and defend the basic principles and values that underlay our founding, and because we have abandoned any honest search for new ones, our social and political conflicts can never be more than temporarily patched up. In the absence of first principles, politicians are forced to appease ever-noisier special-interest groups. Inevitably, new groups arise in opposition to these, and at that point the social-policy "issue" of the day begins once again to disrupt our society. After all, how can a people agree on a matter like free trade, when they can't even agree on the principle of freedom itself?

Freedom, Virtue, And Authority

The deepest question facing our nation has little to do with the precise legal meaning of some word in our Charter, or how much tax money we give to universal daycare, but everything to do with our system, or style, of government. The real concern, as I shall try to make clear, is how we should work out the problems of *freedom*, *virtue*, and *authority*. How much freedom should Canadians be allowed? What is the nature of the social good, the virtue, for which we strive? How should these matters be controlled by the State? For these three concepts are of timeless and universal concern to every nation, and the way in which they are worked out dictates the framework within which we exercise power over each other, earn our livings, use our manners, treat our

criminals, and otherwise build our moral lives. As it happens, the
relationships between these concepts have traditionally been deployed
in two conflicting patterns throughout the modern world.

The roots of these two patterns, or styles, have been traced to ancient
times, and their more recent modern expressions to the conflicting
French and Anglo-Scottish Enlightenments of the eighteenth century,
specifically to Henri Saint-Simon and John Locke. Perhaps the most
lucid modern writers on the impact of these two styles are the American, Irving Kristol (*Reflections of a Neoconservative*), and the French-
man, Alain Peyrefitte (*The Trouble With France*).[1] Because these two
styles of moral and political authority have found a home in Canada, it
is extremely important for us to understand the difference between the
so-called "French" and "English" visions, for they have been at war
since the birth of our nation. The present turn of events with the Meech
Lake Accord, and Quebec's trampling on language rights, are but
surface manifestations of the underlying — and irresolvable — clash
between them.

The terms "French" and "English" are, of course, but convenient
labels. The former could as easily have been termed the Swedish, or
European, style, and the latter the American style. But these two very
different methods of social and political organization happened to find
their earliest homes and most complete theoretical expression in
France and England, respectively. As a visitor, I could not choose
between my affection for either of these two nations; but I know under
which style of government I distinctly prefer to live. What is the crucial
difference between these two visions?

THE "FRENCH" STYLE

THE "FRENCH" STYLE, or model, has distant Roman origins, but as
practised by modern governments it has become a prototype for
bureaucratic collectivism and is chiefly concerned with power. Rooted
in the belief that people basically need to be looked after and controlled,
this style results in an effort to create order and keep anarchy at bay by
ensuring that an elite political class is maintained with the instinct and
the power to instruct the people in social virtue. (In modern France,
for example, would-be civil servants are trained at special schools.) It
is therefore a "managerial" concept of society that rests on a utopian
vision bent on social perfection — by force, if necessary. Characterized
by a basic distrust of the people, it inevitably sets the governors against
the governed, the politicians against the people. (The Gallup profile,

"The Government vs. The People," in Chapter Seven illustrates this dramatically.) At bottom, it is a collectivist, authoritarian vision that gives rise to a New Class, based on tax money and political power, a class of entrenched and privileged civil servants, politicians, and other functionaries who feed on the body politic and who will do everything they can to preserve and enlarge their privileges.

The extreme modern form of this concept is to be found in all highly socialist nations, particularly in the communist states. The astonishing rate at which such states are crumbling — of which there was barely a hint when work on this book began — is vindication of the book's argument in its entirety, and a warning to Canadians. Not surprisingly, this style of controlling freedom and instilling virtue tends radically to depress the wealth-creating instincts of the people by removing incentives for personal and family advancement, and at the extreme, substitutes for those instincts an all-pervasive dependency on the State, a labryinth of regulation of commercial and social life, a fear of authority, and a consequent clamouring for political power. After all, in such a system most of us would rather govern than be governed.

THE "TOP-DOWN," OR "HANDICAP," SYSTEM

AN EASIER WAY TO CONCEIVE of the French style of government is simply as a top-down concept that exerts a broad control through elitism, government coercion, and social engineering, *all of which are upheld by granting the State special rights to abrogate freedoms.* (Canada's Constitution grants the State this right.) The essence of this style lies in its willingness to design different rules for different social groups in the interests of engineering an equal result for all. Its ideological imperative lies in *forcing* different people and groups to be the same. It therefore must operate on the "handicap" theory of government, whereby the strong are handicapped in the hope of benefitting the weak. We shall see that such a method ends up handicapping the entire society, for more forced equality always requires more government, and absolute equality requires absolute government. Top-down governments hold power through autocracy and fear and are bound eventually to crumble as the powerful benefit and the people increasingly suffer. We are today witnesses to extraordinary examples of reaction to this phenomenon in the *glasnost* of the U.S.S.R. and the hunger strikes and nationwide demands for freedom in East Germany, Poland, and the Baltic states — and to its hardiness when the top-down system prevails utterly, as in the tragic slaughter of students in China's Tiananmen Square.

THE "ENGLISH" STYLE

THE TERM "ENGLISH STYLE" is used not because the English are inherently better, but because from the creation of Magna Carta, to the development of a system of parliamentary sovereignty, to the invention of checks and balances on power in American (and to a degree in Commonwealth) government, they were the first to entrench in the Common Law a clear legal and philosophical protection of the individual against the power of the State. For example, the ancient English Common Law writ of *habeas corpus* that protects the innocent from unlawful confinement is worth any number of glorious-sounding written constitutions from other nations. But such guarantees, we have seen, are fragile, for even in Britain, until Prime Minister Margaret Thatcher appeared, a succession of English governments spent about fifty years eroding many such ideas and protections.

Rooted in the ancient concept of "natural rights" and further developed in the eighteenth century by John Locke, the English style emphasizes free will, individual responsibility for one's deeds, and political and economic freedom with all the contractual rights and legal protections attached thereto. Its dominant feature is not power, but liberty. From a purely pragmatic point of view, the English realized very early that the simplest, least expensive, most tolerable way to build a virtuous society was to think of every individual as a kind of moral agent, adding to or subtracting from the moral fabric of society.

With this respect for the individual comes the idea that the role of government is not to control the people and manage their morality, but to create an environment in which each, subject to the same rules, will control himself. Suffice it to say that such moral agents function best in a politically decentralized society in which the fullest expression can be given to personal and family needs, free enterprise, and local interests. Authority under this method is obtained through the strength of family, church, town, and hundreds of other spontaneously organized social groups, each with its own constraining traditions. Such a society is noninterventionist, nonmanagerial, nonegalitarian, and promotes political and economic freedom under limited government. People are allowed to become whatever they wish, to express all their natural differences as long as they obey the law — which is the same for all. Any economic atlas of the world will show that the wealthiest nations on earth are those that have recognized, and incorporated to some degree, such political and economic tools.

THE "BOTTOM-UP," OR "BONUS" SYSTEM

THE "ENGLISH STYLE" may be thought of as a bottom-up system, a spontaneous local order that arises from the actions of millions of individuals exercising freedom and responsibility under a "Rule of Law" (this exists when a country upholds laws that protect and apply to all equally — with no exceptions for the governors, or the governed). Natural differences are nurtured and allowed to flourish, and self-fulfilment through striving for excellence is encouraged and rewarded, resulting in a spontaneous "bonus system," for rewards are the natural objective of striving. A bonus system is always in deadly conflict with a handicap system, for the two have utterly different goals; and wherever they are forced to co-exist, unnatural political, economic, and cultural results will always occur. In the end, this will always be manifested in constitutional disputes.

CANADA: THE STYLES CLASH

AS IT HAPPENED, these two rival visions were available at the birth of the Canadian nation. England was enjoying the fruits of parliamentary democracy during and after the Victorian period, while France suffered the aftermath of revolutionary and imperial despotism and then endured about sixty different governments in the forty years preceding World War II. To some extent, English stability and productivity were the reason a great majority of Canadians until recent times believed fervently that the British-derived political, economic, and cultural institutions of Canada were of inestimable value. Many Canadians still believe this, even though they are now fighting a rearguard action. Their sentiments are perhaps best summed up by the great English historian, Paul Johnson:

> *Virtually all the ideas, knowledge, techniques and institutions around which the world revolves came from the European theatre and its ocean offshoots; many of them quite explicitly from England, which was the principal matrix of modern society. Moreover, the West is still the chief repository of free institutions; and these alone, in the long run, guarantee progress in ideas and inventions. Powerful societies are rising elsewhere, not by virtue of their rejection of western world habits but by their success in imitating them . . . The sober and unpopular truth is that whatever hope there is for mankind — at least in the foreseeable future — lies in the ingenuity*

and the civilized standards of the West, above all in those western
elements permeated by English ideas and traditions. To deny this is
to surrender to fashionable cant and humbug.[2]

Onto this stage — one on which both styles struggled to co-exist for
more than a century, the English style gradually giving way — marched
Pierre Elliott Trudeau and his colleagues, in 1968. At that point he
began, as he put it, to spin the wheel slowly, so that without realizing
the change of direction, Canadians would find themselves disembark-
ing at a different island than the one they thought they were sailing for.
Fundamentally, all that he did was clearly and resolutely to substitute
the French-collectivist for the English-individualist vision at every
opportunity. By the time he was finished, Canada had changed from a
fiscally stable, relatively free, mildly socialized nation under limited
government, to one bending under, proportionately, twice the U.S.
per-capita debt, highly centralized and managerial, and much more
thoroughly socialized in its institutions and social commitments.

The collectivist vs. individualist tension described above sets out a
basic philosophical context in which policy can be considered in Canada. In effect, whenever someone offers a political opinion you have
only to decipher which of these two conflicting visions of social governance is being promoted, and then the opinion falls more easily into
place.

Usually, the person will be either a top-downer (a collectivist, or
handicapper), who distrusts the masses and therefore favours a coercive egalitarian State, or a bottom-upper (an individualist, favouring a
bonus system), who respects the spontaneous order that results from
millions of very different individuals exercising freedom and responsibility under common rules of law.

The clash of these two styles has been the constant theme, everywhere felt if not everywhere seen, of Canada's struggle to govern itself
and establish its institutions ever since the Battle of the Plains of
Abraham in 1759. However, one of the impediments to a clear focus on
the nature of this ongoing struggle is the existence of what I call the
"popular illusions," and it is to these that we now turn.

2

The Popular Illusions
Eight Unnecessary Obstacles

THE ULTIMATE DECISION to align with a top-down or bottom-up system, or with something in between — lurching blindly at great social and financial expense between competing political visions — is made all the more difficult by the presence of what I call the Popular Illusions. To swing from outright left-wing unionism under David Barrett in British Columbia to pseudo-evangelical conservatism under Vander Zalm, or from socialism in Saskatchewan to staunch conservatism under Grant Devine, is more than an expression of political fickleness or favouritism. It is a sign of moral and philosophical weakness on the part of the electorate. To vote for a conservative or a liberal because it seems to be the fashion is a poor reason for anyone to vote. Those of us on the "right" or "left" of the spectrum may cheer when we see things lurching our way. But the lurching itself is the real weakness, for it bespeaks a lack of grounding in the core values, beliefs, and principles that really do create a properly functioning society. When, through erosion of such principles or traditional belief systems, voters are left to elect the most attractive face, or the best shopping list of electoral goodies, the lurching begins. The basic ideas most fundamental to the success of the nation go out of focus and may be entirely forgotten, only to be replaced by political, economic, and moral illusions.

IDEOLOGY IS DESTINY

IF YOU BELIEVE THAT ideas (when we are thinking clearly) and assumptions (when we are acting, but not necessarily thinking) shape government policy, then you will surely agree that it is of the utmost importance for a society to get its ideas and assumptions right — to have an appropriate ideology. By "ideology" I mean *the structure of interdependent ideas that results in the formation of government policy.* In such matters, however, Canadians are largely an inarticulate people. This leaves us exposed, if not to immediate political disaster then to gradual social stagnation, simply because we have constructed conflicting political assumptions that contain too many contradictory principles. As they say, "If you don't know where you're going, you'll end up somewhere else!" My continuing argument will be that if Canadians do not equip themselves to see clearly how political ideologies work, however inarticulate these may be, they will be vulnerable to the processes of decline, victims of political expediency. Unless we master our destiny now, future generations will read how it mastered us. In this respect, *ideology is destiny.*

Even now, whether we realize it or not, we all subscribe to ideologies that affect our daily lives. A businessman speaking about share-equity, a neighbour objecting to a disturbance, a child guarding the last lick of his ice-cream cone — they are all acting from ideological motives. In these cases, the actions are based on principles concerning private property that conform with our notion of common law, and show that ideology is no mere abstraction. It is communicated to every citizen by teachers, judges, priests, workers, or simply wise citizens. Their sayings, writings, actions, daily judgements, poems, and lessons to children are like beacons that serve to keep the whole society on course. In most societies, however, the light fades at some point. The highly articulated and avidly defended core ideology — the belief system — that has served as a social foundation is taken for granted, then ignored, and finally replaced by other, less articulate values, which exist in tension with vestiges of the original core values. In the end, as few are left who care to defend basic principles, society enters a long, wave-like decline.

The first sign of this is the inevitable collapse of institutions and policies that have slowly descended into moral and philosophical contradiction. Examples are the erection and then crumbling of "sacred trusts"; the creation of Constitutions that give the government the legal right to discriminate; charitable unemployment "insurance" plans that become welfare "rights" paying people not to work; and egalitarian state auto-insurance schemes that reward those at fault and penalize good drivers. In short, the level playing field with the same rules for all (the basis of our original core values, and the bonus system) becomes a field with different rules for different groups. This is guaranteed eventually to tear society apart. But few see the root moral and philosophical causes.

So all the popular illusions embody the *counter-ideology* of the whole society. If they are at a long, steady, and unchallenged variance with the *core ideology*, they will prevail. They will *replace* the core ideology. Policy will be based on them. Then a slow process of decline will triumph in all areas of society.

In what follows, each illusion is described as *a popular belief without foundation, running counter to the original core ideology of the nation*. These illusions appear to ensure that our society is just, but if followed to their logical end they become the basis of a new, unjust society, in which all are to blame or all are blameless — it's all the same thing. Each in its own way, these illusions have the effect of substituting the collectivist "French" style for the "English" one at every turn.

The popular illusions are presented early in this book because they constitute *obstacles to seeing clearly*. They inhibit the creation of a moral society because they stand in the way of the truly hard work of thrashing out core social principles and values that will work together as an interdependent, coherent moral system. All of them are normally discernible in the ordinary experiences of everyday life and can be discovered with minimal effort in any daily newspaper. Once aware of them, you will be able to spot them — the way a horticulturalist identifies common weeds — in the ideological garden of our country.

1. THE FREE LUNCH ILLUSION

(How the government's sleight of hand fools us into believing it really has money of its own.)

THERE IS A WIDESPREAD and unfortunate illusion afoot that the government has its *own* money, that what we get from government is "free." Too few understand that government *has no money of its own*, that the only money government can possibly have is never earned through its own productive work and comes from only three sources. Government either *takes* the money from us (creating a tax burden), or it *borrows* it from us or from foreigners (creating a debt burden), or it *prints* money for itself (creating an inflation burden). In this sense, the game of government, once it goes beyond establishing and enforcing the rules for a level playing field, is truly a "zero-sum" game. *What it gives to some, it must first take from others.* As Michael Novak points out, *advances in the desire for equality and security within Western nations, as in Great Britain, appear to bring with them the "zero-sum game" . . . descending on the United States. Socialism is a zero-sum game. Democratic capitalism is not.*[3]

This point can be illustrated to students, or your own children, simply and dramatically. The lesson begins this way. First arrange for two students (Mary and John) to come to class with ten one-dollar bills, representing their annual income. Then tell the whole class that you will represent government (you want them to see how it works). Then ask both students what they feel is the most important thing the government ought to provide. Mary will say something like, "I think a good government ought to give us all free police and free daycare." John will say something like, "I believe every Canadian should be guaranteed free health care and a pension." Then ask each to come to the front of the class with his or her money. Hold up your empty hands and ask Mary to give you five dollars. Put three in your pocket (the cost of government), and hand two to John, saying, "Here's your health care"; then take five from John, pocket three, and hand two to Mary, saying, "Here's your free daycare." Repeat the process to "fund" Mary's free police and John's free pension. They will each end up with four dollars, and a firm lesson in government. (You will end up with six.) Properly executed, this will be the most memorable and effective political education of their young lives, for they will quickly see that government money is an illusion; that the government's power and influence increase with the wealth it takes from the people; and that we are duped by the free-lunch mentality. Most of all, they will realize that by demanding a free service from government they are really demanding it from their neighbours, and that when others demand something free from government, it is first being taken from them. Whenever we say "the government ought to do so-and-so," we really mean that the government ought to take the necessary money from everyone else and provide us with what we want.

Leaving aside for the moment the "production" of Crown corporations (which are largely uncontrolled, and net debtors to boot — about $32 billion by 1988!), government creates nothing. It merely provides government services. But in order to render these, it first has to take resources from the people. Since, by definition, government services are anywhere from 10 to 150 percent less efficient than the same services rendered privately (see Chapter Five for the figures on this), the net productivity result is always a loss. But here's the real moral rub: *Government cannot confer a benefit upon one person or group without penalizing another.* What it gives to one, it must get from another. Even if it prints money for itself, it is virtually taking it from future generations who must pay for the hidden tax of inflation. That's an iron law of economics. The social-welfare State is therefore a great fiction, by which everyone tries to live at the expense of everyone else.

2. THE FIXED-PIE ILLUSION

(How misunderstandings about the process of wealth
creation lead to resentment of success.)

So WHEN THINKING about *government*, it is correct to label it a fixed-pie or a zero-sum game. Even when government succeeds in priming an activity that might not otherwise have been started (but that may subsequently be sold and run profitably), it is not operating efficiently — the whole process is too costly and too slow.

Government enterprises discourage commercial efficiency and entrepreneurial risk, since they are political, bureaucratic entities and lack a basis for economic calculation. Debt that would have bankrupted normal private operators is often forgiven and excluded from the reported financial "success" of the operation. Our railways are an example. I have been told that before its sale to private buyers, CN Route (a public transport trucking company formerly owned by CN) spent more on annual maintenance of its vehicles than the total asset value of those vehicles! In short, there is no good economic or even policy excuse for state enterprise, simply because, whether an operation is run by government or private interests, it is subject to the same laws of economics: if the return on investment is there for government, then it's certainly there for private operators, who are at least risking their own funds, and not the public's. It may be true that *some* government entities are necessary to safeguard our way of life, but surely not the five or six hundred we have created since 1970!

But the world of the so-called "private sector" is just the opposite of government. First, it's misnamed. It should be called the "productive" sector, for this is its most beneficial feature. Properly considered, all successful entrepreneurial processes worldwide are *growth* processes, in which the economic pie gets larger all the time because they are continuously creating new wealth.

So to think of the productive democratic capitalist world in fixed-pie terms — which is how people in the middle ages thought about all commercial activity — is wrong. If an individual, such as your neighbour, gets wealthy, it doesn't mean that he has taken wealth you otherwise might have had. The same applies to the economic activity of nations. Third World economists eager to receive more from First World countries — and First World spokesmen of the welfare mentality who press for such donations to be made — constantly use this fixed-pie argument in an effort to persuade us that our "greed" is depriving the world's (unproductive) poor of wealth they could have had — an argument we will debunk in Chapter Nine. But don't believe it for a minute. Nations grow in wealth over time only if they consume less wealth than they themselves generate, thus producing savings for investable capital. Such growth can be accomplished without depriving any other nation, as it is accomplished internally, through savings and productive efficiency. Of course it is also possible to grow and spend the proceeds at the same time. But then the growth is being used to pay back money — debt — that was borrowed to finance the growth, and not for expansion or capital refurbishment — a cycle that must soon end because the cash is going out the door while the machinery wears out. Soon a society caught up in this illusion has to decide between (1) cutting back its consumption (especially of social-welfare services) in order to buy new machinery (of all sorts, soft and hard) in order to grow again, or (2) continuing with debt and stagnation. There's the rub. It's that basic. The choice is an obvious one now facing Canada, a country that is borrowing money to pay interest on borrowed money!

Despite the calamitous misunderstandings about how growth is achieved (as a group, Third World nations, too, have experienced stunning increases in GNP), the modern world trend is growth — very slow, but ever upward. The productive pie is increasing in size almost everywhere. Consider Max Singer's book *Passage to a Human World*, in which we read that by World Bank calculations the percentage of the world's nations living in poverty will have fallen from 50 percent in 1960 to 16 percent by 2,008.[2] Singer shows how even very low, but steady annual growth can produce tremendous results. England ruled the world after a steady average annual growth of only 2 percent over a hundred-year period! So the answer to wealth creation is steady annual growth so that investible capital increases. Singer's formula for calculating this phenomenon is: 72, divided by the average rate of growth, which equals the time needed to double net wealth. For example, with a growth factor of 2 percent per annum, a nation could double its net wealth in $72/2 = 36$ years. Not bad! Of course, net growth means a bigger pie for all concerned — including the government.

However, the piece of the pie government gets to spend will always be fixed by what it takes from us, or borrows (for us to pay back). If we grow, it grows too (unless, like the Swiss, we limit government spending by legislation). *However, if we don't grow, government may still grow!* It can do this because it knows that *deficits are just deferred taxes.* Whereas private enterprise can grow by increasing productivity and through savings, government can grow only by *taking more of our wealth by force.* Even if it borrows from other sources, we or our descendants will have to pay the debt back through taxes. So remember this the next time someone tries to fool you with the fixed-pie argument. It's true for all governments and tends to be true for socialist states, because their system creates a dampening effect on wealth production — but it's not true for democratic capitalism, under which all boats go up on a rising tide. The secret to successful wealth production is to create the wealth-producing machine (see Chapter Four) and limit government's ability to paralyse it at the same time. To do the former without the latter is an invitation to disaster.

3. THE RIGHTS ILLUSION

(How rights to act freely become claims against the State
for specific goods.)

THERE IS RAMPANT public confusion about "rights." Let us explore the meaning of this word for a few moments. What do we mean today when we say that someone has a "right" to something? I suggest we mean he has a *claim* against another person, an institution, or the State itself. He can throw a tantrum and "demand" his "rights."

But that is not the traditional, or classical Liberal, concept of rights, which referred to *an envelope of general legal protections* surrounding every citizen equally. For example: the right to walk on a public beach meant that, legally, no one could throw us off it. These traditional rights — the ones on which Canada and the free world have been based — are labelled "negative rights" because they protect our right *not* to be interfered with unless we break a law.

Today, however, the term "rights" has been transformed into one with a very different — and dangerous — new meaning: today, many would say it means the "right" to demand *a bundle of specific goods, services, money, or privileges* from the State. Such rights are called "positive rights" because the person declaring them wants much more than to be left alone: he wants something specific to be provided for him by the State. I submit that this radical change — so common to welfare states — is a net subtraction from the moral quality of our national life. Why should this be so? Simply because as a free person with the protected right to walk, think, speak out, and so on, *you are undertaking these actions yourself.* No one else is being forced to *do* anything for you. Others are simply being *restrained* from preventing you from doing these things for yourself. That arrangement is a healthy situation for any society. But during the past thirty years this noble idea has deteriorated rapidly into the perverse notion that a right is a *claim* against others (represented by the State) for goods to be supplied by them (not by you). Instead of protecting our *freedom*, the state is trying to enforce *fraternity*. When, in 1850, the French statesman Alphonse de Lamartine said that his philosopher countryman Frédéric Bastiat's idea of government was inferior because it stopped at *liberty*, while Lamartine's own system went on to *fraternity*, Bastiat replied, *"The second half of your program will destroy the first!"* That is exactly what is happening in Canada today. The law, as an instrument of justice, has been perverted into an instrument of injustice — an instrument not of protection, but of coercion (often disguised in humanitarian garb).

Now this has led to a wholesale "rights fever" in this nation, such that there's almost nothing left to which someone doesn't claim some right or other. Why, I have even heard someone argue that he had a "right" to marry! I pointed out, to his embarrassment, that this meant that someone else had an *obligation* to marry him. A moment's reflection reveals that these are *reciprocal* notions. So these modern positive rights, as claims against the State for goods and services, are really claims against other citizens, now or in the future. (Don't forget, the State has no money of its own.) The government of the day just happens to be the broker, who takes a sizeable commission for arranging all this feasting on each other. Unfortunately, the gluttony does not end there. The real moral sin inherent in this is that through massive debt financing of our social-welfare programs we will be borrowing from future generations for a long time to come. Our grandchildren will rightly look back on us as selfish people who lived beyond our means and saddled them with the consequences. For we have broken our contract with the future — a contract based on the moral principle that each generation will look after its own needs and will not burden future generations with its debts. Indeed, under democratic capitalism, each generation will *invest* in the future of the next!

Somehow, as dependence on the State has increased, a terrible and immoral chain-reaction has become established, which looks like this:

WANTS > NEEDS > RIGHTS > CLAIMS

From *private* wants, to *public* needs, to *legal* rights, to moral *claims* against society. This is the destructive "rights illusion" at work in our society, and in the whole world. If you take one look at "The Universal Declaration of Human Rights," largely drafted by a Canadian, John Humphrey, who still teaches law at McGill University, and was honoured on December 10, 1988, on the fortieth anniversary of the Declaration, you will feel good all over. Who wouldn't? It reads like a cornucopia of the good life — especially articles 24 to 30, which basically say that everyone on earth has a right to the nicest, most secure, and most enjoyable life possible. There is nothing imaginable in this Declaration to which the individual does not have a "right," many of which are to be provided "free"; and all these wonderful goods, services, and benefits are to flow from the simple *declaration* of these rights. In short, it is an inspired piece of misleading fantasy which ought never to have confused the provision of equal *protections* by the State with the *provision* of goods and services by the State (other citizens), for this is an illusion.

I believe that future historians of Canada will say that we gobbled ourselves right up by falling for this illusion. There is no need to look very far for a clear example of it at work right now. On the cutting edge of welfare-state policy is the national effort being exerted to convert the *want* of some for subsidized daycare, into a "right" for all. In fact, the *specific* and purely ideologically based complaint of the proponents of free daycare is that it should not be a welfare good (only for the needy), but a "right" of all Canadians. "Money Squeeze Makes Day Care into Welfare," trumpets the *Toronto Star* (Oct. 16, 1988): "We brought daycare out of the welfare system and now the province through its gross underfunding [read: refusal to take more money from other people] is telling us to put it back there," said Scarborough Alderman Brian Ashton. And Toronto Councillor Roger Hollander said: "Our objective is to move child care out of the welfare system and into a public service."

To the extent that such generalized claims for goods to be provided by others are successful, the private sphere of individual responsibility is diminished, liberty is defeated by enforced fraternity, and the wealth of the nation redirected toward yet another unproductive transaction of decline.

4. The Discrimination Illusion

(About our national fear of preferences.)

THERE IS AN UNFORTUNATE but telling anecdote about a black man who goes to the Canadian Broadcasting Corporation to be interviewed for a job as a radio announcer. Half an hour later, he emerges, downcast, to meet his friend, who says: "What's wrong? Didn't you get the job?" The applicant replies: "N-n-n-o. Th-they d-d-didn't h-hire m-m-me, b-b-because I'm b-b-black!"

Of course, anyone would feel sorry for the fellow, who obviously applied for the wrong job. But the telling feature of the story lies in the way it illustrates the discrimination illusion. That is, it clearly separates the difference between acts that should be called *prejudicial* (they prejudge something before all the facts are known) and those that are simply normal discriminating actions, or preferences. The first kind are mindless generalizations based on limited experience or on "stereotypes," which are intended to harm in thought or action others of whom we unjustly disapprove. Of course, some stereotypes are extremely useful, because they spare us a lot of grief. I like the humorous example the well-known U.S. economist Walter Williams uses about a man walking in the jungle who hears a lion roar. Well, rest assured it was only his preconception, or stereotype, about the behaviour of lions that spared him his life as he jumped into a tree before ever seeing the lion! In the CBC story told above, the hiring supervisor rightly discriminated against stutterers, about whom he held a stereotype: all stutterers stutter.

A general problem in our present society is the confusion between prejudice and preference — a confusion that is damaging because it vulgarizes meaningful distinctions by mixing them with hurtful ones. Human-rights activists have imposed on us a certain moral terror that makes us afraid to let our ordinary preferences be known. But if the idea behind this is to rid society of bigots, it can't be done by driving useful distinctions underground. Bigots love such confusion. This problem needs more distinctions, not fewer. When Walter Williams says he fully intends to discriminate in taking a black wife (because he has black parents, wants black kids, and thinks black is beautiful), well, he's dead serious, and rightly so. But can you imagine a white Canadian saying publicly that he fully intends to discriminate in taking a white wife? Why, he'd probably be hauled before the Human Rights Commission in record time!

If Canadians don't want to become a nation of sheep, they must learn to distinguish between acts of prejudice and normal, discriminating acts, or preferences; between actions the intention of which is to avoid or to harm others and those that arise from simple observation or personal experience. But what I have called the egalitarian-collectivist mentality, so eager to erase all differences, has cowed us into either immediate mental erasure of our normal discriminating thoughts and preferences or into making only positive remarks about people not like us — which amounts to a childish and servile form of flattery. The egalitarian philosophy suffusing our society therefore has the effect of suppressing not only bad distinctions, but good ones too.

The second crucial feature of the discrimination illusion is the confusion between *cause* and *effect*. We have been brainwashed into seeing discrimination where none exists. For example, it is true that, statistically speaking, all Canadian women as a group earn about 60 percent of the income of all men as a group. The conclusion of the uninformed is that therefore women are discriminated against in Canada's workforce. But a bit of scrutiny reveals how misleading this judgement is. The fact is that *most* women and *most* men get married. When they do so, *most* women quit their jobs, take part-time jobs, or reduce their work hours to raise families. *Most* men, on the other hand, quickly worry about how they are possibly going to support that family, pay for a home, education, and so on. So they take better jobs, go for promotion, work harder and longer, or even take on two jobs. The result? As a group, the total wages of all married women drop, while the total wages of all married men rise. If all you do is compare the two groups without taking into account this phenomenon of choice, or preference, on the part of married men and women, you indeed will find a 60 percent average difference. However, this is a reflection not of discrimination but of life choices that are obscured by statistical aggregation. Even a first-year statistics student would be embarrassed by the sloppy conclusions the feminists have so shamelessly drawn from these facts of life.

Interestingly, bachelors in all age groups show average wages 60 percent (actually 48 percent in 1988) of married men's for the same reason: no family to support. But guess what? Never-married women and never-married men in Canada, at all ages, earn the very same wages, and where differences exist, they tend to favour women. So the differences we see are real and understandable, but they are a result of preferences; they do not result from "discrimination." This is a typical example of the discrimination illusion at work. Inevitably, advocacy groups have exploited the public confusion between cause and effect that underlies so many policy matters like this. It's a bit like assuming that because drownings and ice-cream sales are highest in August, ice cream causes drowning. Canadians should challenge irresponsible allegations of discrimination aggressively before yielding to intimidation.

5. THE EQUALITY ILLUSION

(How the idea of equality is a logically impossible dream.)

WHEN I WAS A CHILD, it struck me as peculiar that whenever the whole school was required to run a foot race, the general result was always the same. The few fast and strong ones always finished up front somewhere, followed by a growing crowd of runners, which then tapered off into a few stragglers at the end. When we went to watch a regional championship, the pattern was the same. And it held true even for the Olympic Games. In other words, no matter how narrowly defined the band of measurement, the spread of abilities always showed the same pattern.

However, I also felt it a truism that no two things are the same, that everything is in flux and, as the Greek philosopher Heraclitus said, "You cannot step into the same stream twice." Little by little, the conflict between these two observations grew in my mind until I realized that although everything in the universe might be *different* from every other, the *patterns* formed by large numbers of these different things might be quite predictable — whether those different things were people, sea shells, intelligence, or physical skills. Later in life, I discovered what statisticians call the "normal curve." This scientific vindication of my childhood perception seemed to me as miraculous and strange as my first reading of Old Testament stories, for I had thought these were stories my grandmother had invented and was stunned to discover that someone had written them down. So it was with the normal curve, which looked like this:

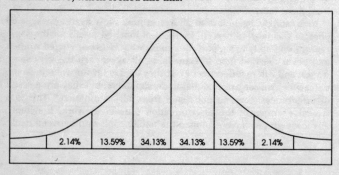

It was the pattern of the foot race, on paper. Some universal law must be at work! Further, it was even divided into precise percentages! I immediately drew several jarring conclusions:

• If the law holds, then people can never be equal in anything.

• Equality, or sameness in things, is necessarily an illusion — an elusive quest.

• Subdivisions of measurement, provided the sample group is large enough, will always produce the same curve.

• Therefore, regardless of how good or bad something may actually be, some people will always be at the bottom or middle or top of no matter what we are measuring.

Here's a simple example of this reality at work. It can be applied to poverty, wealth, education, intelligence, weight, money-earning ability, mathematical skill, strength — whatever you wish:

Let us imagine the pattern formed by a measurement of the height of *all Canadian males*. (I have made up round numbers for purposes of the exercise; they are not actual numbers.) The pattern would look something like this:

One Foot Difference:

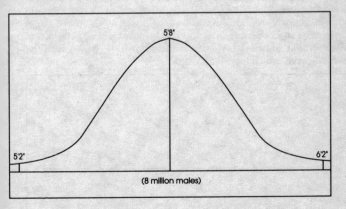

5'8"

5'2"   6'2"

(8 million males)

However, when we narrow the measurement, it looks the same. We again see a normal curve:

Six Inches Difference:

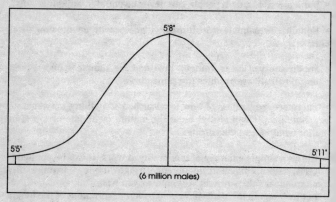

This can be repeated once again for an even narrower band of heights — and it still looks the same, with the same percentage allocations from one end to the other:

Two Inches Difference:

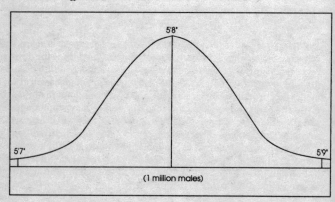

Theoretically, this exercise could be repeated infinitely, provided we were willing to make infinitely fine measurements (the 100-metre race was first measured in fifths of a second, then tenths, and now hundredths) — and we would always get our normal curve. The "law of variations," which predicts this "normal curve" behaviour of large groups (but not of individuals), is at work, and therefore to the extent that measurement is meaningful, *equality is impossible*. Now, how does this fact affect social policy? Very simply, it strongly reinforces the idea that *liberty* and *equality* will always be mutually exclusive, if by equality we mean (and this is what social engineers mean) striving for equal social results or outcomes (wages, incomes, material resources, intelligence). It means that modern social policy, in striving for State-enforced equality, is striving for an unattainable goal. It means that once, say, subsistence level is reached by everyone in a population, there will still be "poverty." In fact, "the poor" in Canada are defined "distributionally," so that by definition they will always be here, even if the lowest income group earns $100,000 per year. Despite massive efforts to "redistribute" income in Canada since 1951, the per-quintile share of income (income received by the five groups from lowest to highest) has held steady as a rock (see Chapter Eight). And the distribution of individuals in terms of their income-earning ability results in a normal curve. According to Statistics Canada, "This means that although each group's income has increased substantially, there's been no movement toward greater equality between the groups."[3]

6. The Determinist Illusion

(How we are encouraged to blame our environment for everything.)

THOSE UNFAMILIAR WITH the debate might be surprised to learn that scholars, philosophers, and theologians have argued since the dawn of recorded history over the issue of *determinism* and *free will*. These are dry-sounding terms, but anyone used to the history of ideas will always detect this debate overtly or covertly at work throughout history in all civilizations. Are individuals the result of causes they cannot alter or are they masters of their own destinies? (Do they have free will?) Aristotle and Plato, all their students since, and all Christian theologians have worried about this. You might even say it is the core issue of modern philosophy. The famous philosopher Jean-Paul Sartre wrote a seven-hundred-page book on free will, then turned around and wrote an even longer one trying to negate the first!

It is crucial for any society to resolve the debate on determinism and free will because social policy is developed as a result of the changing outcome of this debate over time. It is of the utmost importance that any society decide — no, *declare* — whether we are free agents or whether we are determined by our social circumstances, our personal history, and so on. Since personal actions have consequences, *no society can be just if it cannot decide who is responsible for individual actions*: to whom, to what party, what institution, what *cause* should consequences be allocated? Is the drunk a drunk because his father was? (Then how about his brother, who is *not* a drunk because his father was?) Is the criminal guilty and to be fully punished or will the defence win the case by saying, "It was true, my Lord, that he held the gun, but history pulled the trigger"?

So there it is. The whole determinism – free-will debate turns on the matter of the just allocation of consequences. And it so happens that whole civilizations have risen and fallen, depending on how this matter got settled. One thesis of this book is that the social-welfare mentality actively pushes public opinion in the direction of determinism, while democratic capitalism does the opposite. The former seeks to allocate consequences to the social environment (examples are our soft-headed criminal-justice system, and the writings of most behaviourists and sociologists); the latter to the individual (the Protestant work ethic, positive thinking, the human-potential movement, and so on). For most societies, most of the time, this is an ongoing debate. Young, dominant cultures tend to be aggressive and achievement-oriented, and allocate consequences individually (the best example is the U.S.A. until this century); but as cultures age, one of the weakening agents is the gradual shunting of this allocation to the environment (fate, etc.), or to other social groups (class warfare, the soak-the-rich mentality), or to the factional warring of political interest groups.

My personal twist on the whole matter is that this decline cannot be avoided unless the determinist illusion is settled by first realizing that the debate is circular, and that it must be set aside in favour of the following propositions.

PROPOSITION #1

HUMAN AFFAIRS IN RELATION to the environment are in fact hopelessly intertwined, and as good a logical (not moral) argument can be made for one side as for the other. It is as easy to argue that life consists of infinite free possibilities as it is to argue that life is determined in its every minute aspect. For this reason, no scientist or philosopher will ever logically settle the debate to everyone's satisfaction. Therefore,

PROPOSITION #2

EVEN IF SCIENCE were to prove, logically and irrefutably, that our lives are determined, we would simply have to ignore this conclusion. Why? *Because any society that intends to be moral* (freedom is a necessary precondition for moral life) *must make a fundamental decision to opt for free will* in order to conduct its affairs. In short, human moral — and therefore social — life is not possible without clear support for the individual allocation of consequences. So there you have it. There is a high correlation between the freedom of a society and its insistence on free will and individual responsibility, just as there is a high correlation between the lack of freedom in a society and its insistence on determinism, or social causality.

My concern for Canada — for the West — is that we have forgotten this bit of truth, to our great peril, and this has loosed upon us what I call "the psychology of excuse." Through this, we will slowly become a dispirited people, blaming our history, our genes, our families, our social class, the rich, the bureaucrat, the privileged, illness, mental torment, some food we ate — and so on — for our condition. There is actually a murder case in which the defence lawyer won acquittal using the now-famous "Twinkie defence." He claimed that his client had consumed a whole bag of Twinkies and was sugar-overloaded, and therefore not responsible for the murder of his victim! When whole societies start falling for things like the Twinkie defence, or let a murderer go free because he claims he was "sleepwalking" (he may have been, but for goodness' sake, lock him up!), or allow cases like a liability suit against a beer company because the plaintiff drank too much of the company's product before his car accident — when such things occur without public outrage, the foundations of an ordered society cannot hold much longer. When individual morality crumbles, society itself crumbles. The fundamental problem here arises from our failure to distinguish between physical states or feelings and moral actions. After all, two people may be in exactly the same lifelong turmoil or pain, so that both may wish to kill someone. But the decision of one to go to a therapist to cope with this urge and of the other to murder his father is a moral decision, not a physical one. "The psychology of excuse" is just one outward manifestation of this transfer of responsibility — so common in the welfare-state mentality — from the individual to society itself, in a self-consuming "war of all against all." The psychology of excuse is an obvious illusion because we are all part of the very society we are trying to blame. To the extent that we put in place methods — legal, cultural, or moral — allowing us to shuck off our responsibility to others, we create a circle. Others bear the weight of our actions and we, the weight of theirs.

The concept of fairness based on individual responsibility that has always lain at the root of our civilization may not be a perfect principle, but it is so far the fairest discovered, for it allocates consequences accurately, based on an identifiable perpetrator. It refuses to look beyond this to physical determinants precisely because this would destroy the general moral tenor of society. After all, it is not a great leap from blaming other individuals, to blaming our family life, to blaming our genes, to blaming society in general, to having no society left at all. We must disabuse ourselves — and our legislators and judges — of the determinist illusion, in order to preserve our national moral health.

7. THE POVERTY ILLUSION

(How we have destroyed the meaning of "truly needy.")

IT IS DIFFICULT to discuss "poverty" when you have always been well off — and the vast majority of living Canadians, compared with most in the world, have always been "well off." In fact, any Canadian earning over $50,000 annually is officially declared "rich." Despite this, there is a "poverty illusion" which is, I fear, promoted with particular enthusiasm and carelessness by today's so-called "liberals." For example, we are commonly asked to accept the idea that "the poor" are a fixed class of people to whom we ought to be transferring more wealth. The wealth is supposed to "cure" their poverty (if you think of it as an illness) or at least provide them with a dignified reclassification (if you think statistically).

Now, I cannot remember ever seeing a newspaper article in Canada seriously questioning the idea of "poverty," let alone asking what the term *means*. But a bit of general reading in this area will suffice to persuade the average reader that there is a good deal of chicanery afoot. It turns out that very little is known about "poverty," and even less is agreed upon (despite the harmonious, almost beatific confidence of the media in their own views on this subject). And so we, the public, are quite vulnerable to being told anything a propagandizing journalist may want us to hear. The poverty illusion in Canada says:

- Poverty is defined by the presence or absence of material resources.

- We have a class called "the poor."

- They suffer because they have fewer material resources (money, goods) than those who are not poor.

- If we don't give them a hand-out, their condition will worsen.

Canadians are owed some fundamental insights on this matter. Not that we should ever lose our capacity for sympathy with the truly needy. Far from it. We need more of this quality in our materialistic world. But let us at least attempt to avoid being witless victims of poverty propaganda. Let us protect ourselves against being browbeaten into shelling out for a trumped-up abstraction, an illusion. What, if anything, do we know about poverty? For an answer, I will be drawing chiefly from Charles Murray's two fascinating books, *Losing Ground* and *In Pursuit of Happiness and Good Government*. Murray dispels the poverty-equals-misery illusion. He tells us, first, that the main objective of human beings the world over is "the pursuit of happiness," which everyone more or less reduces to: a "justified satisfaction" with one's life. Second, he says that in order to pursue happiness, we have to satisfy certain basic needs, as outlined by Abraham Maslow in his famous "Hierarchy of Needs." First we need food, shelter, and clothing; then we go after security, then love, etc.; and ultimately we pursue "self-actualization" (at least in the West). Third, he points out that the first, or "subsistence," level is the cut-off point for happiness. People the world over report great unhappiness if they fall below this point. But almost the moment they exceed this point, their self-reported happiness skyrockets — *and is not appreciably increased by greater and greater amounts of money, or things*.

Murray's analysis is revolutionary because it insists that *after subsistence level is reached, material resources have little or nothing to do with degree of happiness*. In other words, he has had the boldness finally to extricate the idea of happiness from the solely material framework in which it has been confined for over two hundred years. Murray also gives us a clear idea of how difficult it is to determine who is really poor, who makes up the class called "the poor." He points out that even the poverty experts have an awful time deciding what they mean, or how a poverty-line income is to be calculated (defined in most of the world — but not in Canada — as three times the amount of income needed for an adequate diet). Here's why. He is speaking of the United States, but his comments, summarized below, provide a valuable general message.

1. Poverty measures are insensitive to local differences in the cost of living; for example, between expensive big cities and inexpensive rural areas or small towns.

2. They do not capture the "nonmonetary differences in quality of life." For example, how much money would it take to persuade a poverty-level city family to move to "the sticks," and vice-versa?

3. The definition of poverty is too relative. As long ago as 1940, when government was lamenting poverty in Harlem, New York, Harlem already "had a per-capita income that would have placed it fifth among the countries of the world!"

4. No one can definitively decide on rather crucial matters, such as: Should we be counting individuals or families when defining poverty? Much of the world considers it natural to count the total family unit. Is a student over eighteen living at home "poor"? Is a working woman who stops going out to work to raise a family "poor"? No attempt is made to explain these differences.

5. Even worse — how much money do the poor really have (as opposed to how much they officially say they have)? It is well known that even legal income is wildly — up to 73 percent — underreported.

6. What about the "cash-only, please" underground and the "contra" economy? Figures suggest that from 20 to 75 percent of the income of the poor is underground.

7. Finally, Murray tells us that "as of 1980, the many overlapping and in-kind benefit programs had made it possible for almost anyone [in the U.S.A.] to place himself above the poverty threshold."[5]

Just so that we do not continue as victims of the poverty illusion — here are two more recent comments meant to unseat the prevalent opinion that "the poor" is a fixed class of human beings. First, from the internationally respected magazine, the *Economist* (Aug. 6, 1988): "Although 13% of Americans are officially poor, an American has under a 1% danger of staying long among them, provided she or he does three things: completes high school, stays more than a year in a first job even if at minimum wage, gets and stays married." (The *Economist* article refers to many of the poor who cannot manage these three things as "self-manufactured.") Next, from *National Review* (Oct., 1988), we read:

> *A University of Michigan study that tracked the year-to-year eco-
> nomic vicissitudes of five thousand American families found that
> only 48.5 per cent of the families who were among the wealthiest
> 20 per cent in 1971 were still there in 1978; 3.5% of them had fallen
> into the lowest 20% bracket. Conversely, 44.5% of the families in
> the poorest fifth in 1971, were no longer there seven years later. Six
> per cent had actually risen all the way to the highest fifth . . . !*

All of which suggest the following conclusions about the poverty illusion: after subsistence, "poverty" is a very subjective, very *relative* concept. Official definitions and statistics are grossly unreliable, and even when we can pin down who the "poor" are, they are generally not the same people year after year (except in cases where the government is paying them to stay that way).

8. THE SOAK-THE-RICH ILLUSION

(The real shock is that the "rich" don't have as much as
we like to think.)

I HAVE COME TO BELIEVE that the governments of welfare states like ours promote the idea of more "progressive" (punitive), "soak-the-rich" tax rates in order to seduce the people to "accept complacently a burden of government expenditure and taxation that they would not otherwise tolerate."[6] In other words, *the welfare state encourages public envy and resentment in order to divert attention from its own plundering activities.* If it successfully persuades us that it is going to "soak the rich," its hand can slip deeper into the pockets of the middle class, and below, where the *real* tax money lies. This is the conclusion arrived at once you realize that *there aren't very many people who are rich* in Canada and they don't have as much income as we believe. As the famous economist Henry Hazlitt once said, it is patently an "illusion in the overwhelming majority of taxpayers that the 'rich' — meaning the people in the brackets above them — are really paying for most of the benefits that the majority gets from the government."[7]

When you stop to think about how much power and coercion are exercised under the banner of the illusion that wealth will be taken from the rich and redistributed to the poor, the truth comes as a great shock (as it did to the middle-class Frenchwoman who voted for President Mitterrand because he promised to soak the rich, and then discovered: "We were the rich!"). We learn that in 1985, 690,753 Canadians filed tax returns reporting annual incomes that classed them as rich — $50,000 or more. Even this quantity of "rich" people, however, could not underwrite government's expenses. If government had taxed their incomes at a rate of 100 percent, "total tax revenue in 1985 would have been $8.5 billion higher than it actually was. Redistribution of this increased tax revenue to those [15 million people] with incomes less than $50,000 would yield an average annual payment of $566 for each person submitting a tax return."[8] Since many spouses, children, and dependants do not submit returns, this amount could probably be cut to less than $150 for every Canadian. And that would be a one-time payment. *For after one year of such total confiscation of wealth, there would be no "rich" left.* Neither would their businesses be left, nor the jobs they provide, and so on.

In the same vein, Hazlitt estimated in 1965 that total confiscation of the income of all the rich in the U.S.A. would not be enough to run the U.S. government for one day![8] So much for soaking the rich, for the philosophy of progressive taxation, and for the "redistribution" that this is supposed to accomplish. Even a casual study of the matter suggests an elaborate shell game, wherein by the maintenance of such illusions the people are being forced to part with more of the fruit of their labours. (Although the Consumer Price Index has risen only 340 percent since 1961, total consumer taxes have risen over 1,105 percent in the same period! See Chart 19, Chapter Seven.) They think their government is soaking the "rich" and paying the "poor." But they are really soaking each other and paying each other while the New Class of bureaucrats and politicians act as highly paid managers of this elaborate, self-defeating, and expensive performance, raking off a large commission at all three levels of government in the process.

How The Illusions Mask The Truth

ONCE THEY ARE EXPOSED for what they really are, it is incredible that any of us could have fallen for the free-lunch illusion, the soak-the-rich illusion, and all the other popular illusions that are now an integral part of our social philosophy. For these illusions are obstacles to clear moral and political understanding, have become entrenched, particularly since the sixties, and are now part of the reaction to the philosophy of democratic capitalism. Unfortunately, once such popular illusions take hold of a society, they soon become the unexamined basis for policy. What they all have in common is a tendency to pass the moral — and fiscal — buck to others, thus encouraging a general clamour for rights and increased resentment from those who do not receive what they have been taught to expect is theirs.

Government, in turn, cannot possibly afford to satisfy the growing hunger for rights, even though demands for government or the rich to pay get louder. This leads to a populace alienated from government, splintered into interest groups feeding at the trough, and divided against itself, which in turn leads to an increasingly litigious society (Canada now has about twenty times as many lawyers per capita as has Japan), as the people increasingly pursue their "rights" under the Charter. Lying behind all this is the general adoption of a top-down, collectivist style of government that encourages the surrender of freedom and responsibility to the State, and to the governance of its New Class of academics, politicians, bureaucrats, regulators, supervisors, commissioners, and committee members, who are among the chief beneficiaries. They are paid with security, power, large salaries (with which the private sector often cannot compete), tenure, indexed pensions, generous expense accounts, free travel, and so on. If it is true that the chief motive of commercial activity is *profits*, it is equally true that the chief motive of governments and those who run them is *size*.

These two motives — the first, which creates wealth; the second, which spends it — are always contradictory. I fear that we will never reverse this drive to ever-larger government until the popular illusions become unpopular. This will happen only through a public resolve to return to the traditional sense of freedom and personal responsibility that beats at the heart of wealth creation and a free society, the complex, interwoven aspects of which will be covered next.

3

Democratic Capitalism
Breaking The Chains Of Economic Stagnation

Social forms are constructs of the human spirit.
Michael Novak, *The Spirit of Democratic Capitalism*

THE EVOLUTION OF THE English bottom-up style of government, or "bonus system," with all its venerable institutions, has been long, and not without difficulties. Its present health is the result of its struggle to escape, like a person caught in quicksand, not only from the millennial bog of destitution and disease, but more importantly from the resentment and attitudinal stagnation by which it is always haunted. So let us step back a bit in time, not merely to refresh our memories of the past, but also to recognize how very much of the past is still with us.

Anyone who looks at history dispassionately, in its simplest aspect, can see that it is basically a record of the outcome of power relationships within societies and between them. If you stop for a minute and ask yourself who has power over you in your daily life, you will be amazed how many officials and agencies could fine you or throw you in jail. An easy test of this might be actions like charging market rent for a "rent-controlled" apartment, or offering a potential employee less than a certain wage, or fishing without a licence, or making and selling your own beer. Not so long ago, you were free to do all these things. But today, any one of them could get you into deep trouble.

The history of any society at any time can be described in many different ways, but at bottom there is always the question of who has power over whom? Once that question is answered, and you realize that it costs money to exercise power over others — a lot of money! — you have only to ask how the power and the money are obtained. For make no mistake: *There is a direct and absolute relationship between the amount of money a government takes from its people and the degree of power it exercises over their lives.* In 1950, total government spending in Canada was barely 25 percent of GNP. Today, it is more than 52 percent. Accompanying that increase is a doubled burden of red tape, legislation, and regulation, and the creation of whole classes of people, industries, and regions now dependent on the State, its protection, and subsidies.

In ancient times, when societies were first exposed to the problem we now call "scarcity" (the lack of sufficient food and other resources), the stronger groups simply exercised power over the weaker, especially in cases where a stronger tribe or nation had conquered a weaker one. Rules governing the distribution of resources, including labour, then developed over time. As such structures were hardened by custom and then by law, power became vested in the military or, more commonly, in the police, and the money needed to support the activities of government was taken from the people by legislation, usually in the form of taxation. Today, we like to think that taxes are paid voluntarily, in the sense that by voting for our preferred candidates during elections we thereby consent to the legislation that created the taxes. But this consent is only theoretical. From a practical point of view, we cannot, as individuals, alter such laws; we cannot change or reduce the amount of money taken from us, nor can we refuse to pay without incurring a severe penalty. Practically, we are helpless. The decision to take what is ours is made by others.

Given this situation, one might expect discontent or revolt, and we surely must wonder how a government that consumes more than half of its citizens' income can maintain order. It so happens that most governments that are not outright police states maintain order through a dubious kind of "contract," or understanding, with the people. In other words, the people get something they want in exchange for their taxes — such as protection from external enemies or, more commonly today, "free" education or "free" health care or some other desired service. As long as such promises are made, believed, and carried out acceptably, the political party that makes them has a chance to stay in power. Other parties, sometimes with different ideologies, then compete to acquire this power for themselves. But what holds all this together in most of the world and what most contract theories fail to take into account (it's really a one-sided contract) is plain old naked fear of government power.

What follows is a thumbnail history of such power relations from precapitalist times to the present. Readers may wonder why a book about contemporary Canada includes descriptions of early systems of government such as feudalism. The answer lies in the fact that almost every current social or political policy, while important in itself, is also usually the expression of an ideological force that sustains it. To use a biological analogy: we don't think much about what appears to be an innocent blemish on our skin. But if we are told that it is a sign of cancer and that the disease may be spreading, our concern for the blemish changes considerably, despite the fact that we can still see nothing more than we did at first. In exactly the same way, political, economic, and social policies often signify much more than we think they do, and cannot be fully understood unless we know what lies beneath them.

Early Capitalism

Capitalism has existed in a primitive way ever since people began trading goods, but it did not begin to appear as a distinct economic system until the end of the Middle Ages in Europe, during the greater part of which feudalism prevailed. In terms of power relationships and the dominance of one class over another, feudalism could be defined as an arrangement whereby vassals exchanged their labour and their freedom for the right to work the lord's land, from the produce of which they paid him a portion as a tax. They also owed him military service in the event of war, and he owed them protection from invaders and other enemies. Such was their "contract." We will see that some of the very economic policies that rigidified mediaeval society and helped to keep it poor are coming back today in only slightly different guise.[1]

Capitalism was straining to be born during this period in Europe, especially in England, but could not fully emerge for a number of reasons. Feudal life was overwhelmingly agricultural; economic and political authority were not yet separate (the lord was both); custom and law determined the terms of exchange according to which a "just price" had to be paid for something purchased and a "just wage" paid to labour (wages were set by political decree, not by the market, which is exactly what we see happening in minimum-wage and so-called "pay-equity" legislation today). Contributing to this extreme rigidity were the absence of free exchange, minimal use of money (goods were bartered for other goods), and the fact that the authorities (especially of the Church), considered supply and demand irrelevant to daily life. Most importantly, the Christian Church forbade the charging of interest, which was considered immoral, following Old Testament scriptures, and because it constituted material gain without visible work. The same attitude can still be seen in our own government's use of the phrase "unearned income" to refer to investment income. Both then and now, this attitude portrays a misunderstanding of the "work" done by capital when it is put at risk. Few people in mediaeval times could acquire money or put it to work through lending, even if they had it. Investment was therefore minimal, because "capital" could be accumulated only with difficulty. But early merchants eventually avoided the interest sanction: instead of charging illegal interest, they lent "discounted bills of exchange." That is, they were allowed to lend someone ninety dollars in exchange for a note guaranteeing repayment of one hundred. The difference was considered their insurance against the possibility of default. This was a fascinating and clever invention and one of the crucial tools of wealth creation during the early stages of the development of capitalism. It was also an early example of commercial inventiveness in the face of man-made obstacles.

Largely as a result of such creative use of capital and despite the obvious limitations of mediaeval commercial life, capitalism developed rapidly and spontaneously, especially in England where, thanks to early emphasis on what I have called the English "style," economic rigidity was less pronounced than on the European continent, where it took until the nineteenth century to achieve the same degree of political and economic freedom acquired by the English more than two centuries earlier. Along with increasing wealth came rapid growth in population and a shift from economically static country life to dynamic city life. With this vastly increased volume of trading relationships came the division of labour and the need to use money, instead of goods, as the means of exchange. This, in turn, necessitated the creation of a social climate that would honour future contracts and all the instruments and conventions that accompany an honest and predictable trading culture. Finally, there came a loosening of political and Church restrictions on prices and wages, and a yielding to the forces of the free market. Feudalism eventually faded away, largely because most legal rights formerly controlled by the local lord gradually became national rights established between each citizen and the realm. In short, in the final years of the European mediaeval period were created all the political, economic, and cultural tools for the emergence of full-blown democratic capitalism.

"Capitalism" And What It Means

As CAPITALISM IN THE Western world began to flower fully during the eighteenth and nineteenth centuries, and as its prodigious influence spread, the word "capitalism" came into common use. Formed from the Latin root *caput*, meaning "head," "capital" originally referred purely to capital stocks of money and funds carrying interest. But in retrospect, the term *caput* is especially suitable as the root for "capitalism," because its most powerful contribution to mankind has come not from its emphasis on the material production of wealth, but on the products of the head: the intelligence, organization, innovation, and cultural and spiritual values that have made such wealth production possible. Unfortunately, the remarkable development of capitalism was given a bad name by its opponents — especially by Karl Marx, in his book *Capital* (1867) — and it has never lost the negative connotation he gave the word.

For two reasons, then, the use of the term "capitalism" is unfortunate. First, it now has a negative connotation, and second, it is imprecise. For the fact is, *all nations of the world, no matter what their type of political system, employ capital.* The telling question is to what degree that capital is employed by free individuals, or by the State on their behalf. In the first and I believe best case, free people employ it on their *own* behalf. In the second (the case in all highly collectivist nations), it is employed *for* them by politicians who think they know best what is good for others — and, incidentally, for themselves!

The distinctive feature of true democratic capitalism (as distinct from despotic capitalism), wherever it is employed successfully, is not that it uses capital, but that *it is inextricably linked with human freedom and the institutions of freedom.* Rightly speaking, capitalism should therefore be called "the freedom system," because at bottom it is truly about freedom, and though it has managed to survive in despotic surroundings for brief periods, it cannot function for long without freedom and it is manifestly a "system." As early as 1776, in his groundbreaking book *The Wealth of Nations*, Adam Smith called this phenomenon "the natural system of liberty," and the 1976 Nobel laureate Milton Friedman wrote *Capitalism and Freedom* to illustrate the power of this connection between wealth creation and freedom. But there is little likelihood that this term will come into common use.

Therefore, in this book I have used the term "democratic capitalism," which at least neatly sums up the interdependence of these two features — a usage inspired by Michael Novak's moving book, *The Spirit of Democratic Capitalism.*

A Moral Imperative For Our Time

ONE OF THE MOST TELLING points Novak makes in a book rich with insights is that while throughout history moral people have always felt a responsibility to help the needy, that feeling has always been accompanied by a sense of frustration. Famines were the rule. Wealth seemed elusive except for the few. Misery has been the lot of two-thirds of mankind. But what I call "the tools of freedom and wealth creation" have never been so clearly understood as they are today. Because they are now available to us, *we have a new moral obligation to ensure that the principles from which such tools are derived are spread as far afield as possible.* Novak's vision is that once and for all, human material suffering can be ended if we have but the will. What was once wishful thinking is now within our grasp because we now know how to create wealth. The only thing stopping us is politicians and ideologues who, while they may often be well intentioned, are plainly wrong-headed. Such people are generally oriented toward centralist, interventionist government control, and tend to push their societies to enter into what the economist Jane Jacobs calls "transactions of decline."[2] Much of this book will therefore touch upon the many ways in which the tools of wealth creation are stifled in our own Canadian society. But first, let us look at the effect created in the world by the very first and most famous burst of wealth in human history, now called the Industrial Revolution, which is continuing to this day as a general modernization and technological revolution.

The Industrial Revolution

MODERN OPPONENTS OF DEMOCRATIC CAPITALISM, loosely characterized today as "the Left" (they are not all conveniently confined to a particular party), are not hard pressed to find horror stories they are pleased to quote regarding the evils, indignities, and social dislocations created by the Industrial Revolution. There are whole libraries of documents on this grim and still controversial subject. Child labour, insanitary conditions, long hard hours of backbreaking work, and early death are on the not always unbiased record. In fact, such abuses have been on the record for most of human history, and, in much of the world, according to the Anti-Slavery Society, still exist.[5] UNICEF estimates that there are currently more than 80 million known child workers between 10 and 14, and probably double that when clandestine child labour is included (the *Toronto Star*, May 27, 1989). The Industrial Revolution, it turns out, accelerated and multiplied not only the process of wealth creation, but also enough social difficulties to require reforms. While no right-minded person would today consider the working conditions of those times desirable, our indignant criticisms are softened when we stop to remember that for the vast majority of the nineteenth-century poor, such conditions were a measurable improvement on their alternatives — which were frequently starvation, begging, or crime. As for child labour, it was (and still is) for the most part their own parents who willingly sent children to work in factories and mines because such families needed the money. Home life for the poor was, for the most part, a sordid experience, and even the famous Dr. Gaskell, who opposed child labour at the time, wrote:

> *The employment of children in factories ought not to be looked upon as an evil, till the present moral and domestic habits of the population are completely reorganized. So long as home education is not found for them, and they are left to live as savages, they are to some extent better situated when engaged in light labour, and the labour generally is light which falls to their share.*[4]

Although at the time the banning of child labour seemed socially just, it also caused both real hardship for many families and a shortage of labour. This was satisfied by importing Irish factory hands, who then sent English capital to Ireland; the reformer's social justice was a two-edged sword. Although mostly absent in wealthy Western nations today, in much of the world child labour is still widely used because to outlaw it would bring real hardship and therefore resistance from the people. I am persuaded that the only way to end true child labour among the poor (as distinct from casual child labour performed by the children of the well off) is through a combination of legislation and economic activism leading to increased national wealth. Legislation alone will not succeed.

Also on the record, yet unfortunately rarely mentioned, are the benefits that the great majority of the people derived from the Industrial Revolution. In other words, it now appears that many certainly suffered, but many more benefitted, and impressively so. In fact, it would not be an exaggeration to say that the Industrial Revolution gave such an economic lift to a large segment of mankind as had never been seen in all of human history. That statement, today, is not much in dispute. The argument is about the price that was paid, and by how many, for this stunning success.

A DISTORTED RECORD

VAST AMOUNTS OF ENERGY have been spent by generations of critics to characterize the Industrial Revolution as a time of "exploitation" by cruel and greedy capitalists. But this criticism is misdirected. After all, when we really stop to think about it, most people the world over could be accused of greediness of one sort or another, regardless of their political philosophy. What was unique about the Industrial Revolution was not that it was based on self-interest, but that *at long last there had been combined with this self-interest, for the first time in human history, a set of definable, repeatable, transposable political and economic techniques which had the spontaneous effect of benefitting large masses of people.* It may have been caused by the self-interest of capitalists, but it was successful only because that self-interest was inherently *other-directed.* For capitalism could not possibly have succeeded unless it gave large masses of people exactly what they wanted, of the right quality, in the right quantity, and at the right price. As Adam Smith pointed out, the revolution succeeded in providing silk stockings not for princesses, who had always had them, but for the common folk, who had never had them — and at a cheaper and cheaper price.

Despite this success, modern businesspeople can still be seen to cringe when the subject arises, because most of them simply accept as true the dismal picture that has been drawn for them. At the extreme they see themselves cast, quite wrongly, I believe, as modern but more humane equivalents of early exploiters. But it remains one of the mysteries of human life why so many have spent so much energy to vilify the first event in history that succeeded in dragging mankind up by its bootstraps from the millennia of slavery and poverty that had theretofore been its lot. Even today, when the resulting success ought to be manifest, our university courses characterize this period as one of darkness and misery. For example, a section from one of the most widely used literary texts, *The Norton Anthology of English Literature*, has the following to say about the Industrial Revolution. When I first read this passage more than twenty years ago, I accepted it at face value and, like all the other students around me, nodded my head in agreement:

For the great majority of the labouring class the results of [the Industrial Revolution] were inadequate wages, long hours of work under harsh discipline in sordid conditions, and the large-scale employment of women and children for tasks which destroyed both the body and the spirit. Reports by investigating committees on conditions in the coal mines, with male and female children of ten or even five years of age harnessed by the waist to heavy coal-sledges which they dragged by crawling on their hands and knees, read like lurid scenes from Dante's Inferno.[5]

Such ritual readings, written by literature professors who can hardly be said to have studied the subject from an economic point of view, are guaranteed to ensure that students leave the classroom appropriately inflamed against the heartless system oppressing them. But the point here is to understand how much is truth and how much is myth that has been swallowed whole, and often promoted, by writers and historians who either have not checked the facts or are set upon attacking democratic capitalism. Even today, many academics and journalists promote without question the theory of "immiseration," which says that under capitalism the rich get richer and the poor get poorer. What they don't tell us, however, is that throughout the two centuries of the Industrial Revolution real wages and real standard of living (wages and standards after subtracting inflation) rose handsomely indeed. In fact,

the invention of the market economy in Great Britain and the United States more profoundly revolutionized the world between 1800 and the present than any other single force. After five millennia of blundering, human beings finally figured out how wealth may be produced in a sustained, systematic way. In Great Britain, real wages doubled between 1800 and 1850, and doubled again between 1850 and 1900. Since the population of Great Britain quadrupled in size, this represented a 1600 percent increase within one century.[6]

In addition, mortality rates dropped sharply, the price of manufactured goods plummeted, life expectancy jumped, and unemployment was never greater than 8 percent. Canada soon followed suit. It further turns out that the government reports referred to above were highly inaccurate and politically motivated, that doctors who gave evidence during the famous Sadler's Committee hearings on child labour had not so much as been inside a single factory, and, furthermore, refused to testify under oath. Further, the inflammatory writings of Marx on this subject were derived not from personal experience (Marx never set foot inside a factory), but from highly unreliable and often intentionally distorted secondary sources. Marx, whose scholarship was more polemic than factual, relied almost entirely on Engels's *The Condition of the Working Class in England in 1844* — a work written in haste after twenty months in England. It described bad conditions reported by the Factories Enquiry Commission of 1833, without mentioning the Factories Act of the same year, passed to eliminate those conditions.[7]

I don't think much more needs to be said to suggest that the standard view most of us have imbibed has been the weak-kneed version fed to us by our mentors from the elite class of teachers and media experts, most of whom have not bothered to research the facts themselves. Someone who has is Friedrich Hayek, the brilliant 1974 Nobel economist, who tells us:

> *The truth is that economic conditions were highly unsatisfactory on the eve of the Industrial Revolution . . . The factories freed the authorities and the ruling landed aristocracy from an embarrassing problem that had grown too large for them. They provided sustenance for the masses of paupers. They emptied the poor houses, the workhouses, and the prisons. They converted starving beggars into self-supporting breadwinners. The factory owners did not have the power to compel anybody to take a factory job. They could only hire people who were ready to work for the wages offered to them. Low as these wage rates were, they were nonetheless much more than these paupers could earn in any other field open to them. It is a distortion of the facts to say that the factories carried off the housewives from the nurseries and the kitchens and the children from their play. These women had nothing to cook with, and to feed their children. These children were destitute and starving. Their only refuge was the factory. It saved them, in the strict sense of the term, from death by starvation.*[8]

Enough said. I do not wish to suggest that there were no rascals in such times. There certainly were. There was an adequate share of business rascals, government rascals, and all other sorts. There always have been and there always will be. But today's businessmen and women should understand that the unprecedented economic revolution to which they are heirs and which they continue *created a crucial trade-off*. It indeed generated its share of misery, as will any revolutionary human endeavour, the total significance of which can be grasped only after its good and bad effects are experienced and weighed. Nothing can be done about that now. But this same revolution created the conditions under which a new and still growing wealth was created by great numbers of people in quantities never dreamed of before. The final lesson of the Industrial Revolution is that the rich indeed got richer, but so did the poor. Canada itself is an example of this, for per-quintile shares of total income have not changed in the past century, yet real income (adjusted for inflation) for all given quintiles has multiplied many times over.

THE MODERNIZATION EFFECT AND THE KUZNETS CURVE

EXHAUSTIVE RESEARCH HAS been done on so many aspects of capitalism and industrialization that a consensus is now emerging. What seems to be clear is that it is almost impossible to separate the effects of democratic capitalism and the Industrial Revolution from the effects of what is now called "modernization." In other words, over the past two and a half centuries, there has been a modernization effect which has spread, at different rates, over the entire world, *regardless of the political ideology controlling any particular country*. Whether a country is socialist, a dictatorship, or a representative democracy, there are certain common dislocating social effects of modernization, and it is wrong simply to blame these on the political system. Rather, they are effects of scientific discoveries and technological inventions on culture in general — of change — and they will occur wherever such modernization is introduced. It is also clear today — and this has been forcefully spelled out by Peter Berger in his book *The Capitalist Revolution* — that democratic capitalism, the free-market system in general, and the tools and institutions of wealth creation it developed have had a powerful *accelerating effect* on modernization. In other words, the *rate* of modernization is powerfully increased if democratic capitalism is also present. As Berger says, "capitalism provides the optimal context for the productive power of modern technology."[9] I would add that it also provides most of the ideas and inventions.

If you want to see the effect of modernization in a country *without* democratic capitalism, you have only to visit the socialist nations of the world. Despite the fact that they, too, use "capital," they tend to exhibit what Swedish economist Sven Rydenfelt has called "a pattern for failure" in his now ominously prophetic book by that title,[10] which examines just how socialist economies set about undermining their own wealth-creating potential. The standard response to this revelation is that the *distribution* of wealth in socialist nations is "fairer," so it doesn't matter if as a whole their economies are not more robust, and that it is legitimate to surrender freedom for such equality. But we will see in Chapter Eight that this argument does not hold up. The socialist nations are no more "fair" than democratic capitalist ones, and from a pure "equality" of income point of view (what percentage of income is held by each fifth of the people?) the socialist nations do no better than the democratic capitalist nations. Not only do they do no better than we do, they do no better at a far lower economic level.

The next chapter will survey "the tools of freedom and wealth creation," both conceptual and practical, without which it is unlikely that any nation will be able to develop a sustainable tradition of wealth and progress. While all these tools may not be found in any one country, in most of the wealthy modern nations of the world, most of the time, most of them can be found. By their very nature, such tools are unstable and subject to promotion or extinction by ideologues in power. Lenin, Stalin, Hitler, Mao, Pol Pot, Castro, Nkrumah, and many other tyrants succeeded in extinguishing them, along with millions of their own citizens. After inheriting a legacy of unparalleled domestic massacres in his own country, the Soviet leader Mikhail Gorbachev is now bravely attempting to reintroduce such tools, and thousands of students in Communist China have been martyred as they clamoured for basic freedoms our children take for granted. What a pathetic but stirring thing it is to see such powerful, self-conflicted nations groping for the basics of wealth creation outlined as long ago as 1776 by Adam Smith in *The Wealth of Nations*!

On our own side of the fence, we are today witnesses to a remarkable transformation. From the turn of the century to the 1970s, under the rule of a collectivist, top-down mentality, Great Britain was driven from its position as world leader to a pale shadow of its former self. Today, regardless of how her foes may wish to quarrel with particular policies, they must admit that Margaret Thatcher has led the British, in a period of only ten years, from the brink of economic dissolution to a new economic prominence among the nations of Europe. Such are the real and, it is to be hoped, enduring effects of first understanding, then forcefully implementing, not only a definite — in this case a revived "English" — style of government, but also of recognizing and implementing the tried and true tools of freedom and wealth creation.

4

The Bonus System
The Tools Of Freedom And Wealth Creation

A man owns two cows:

Under communism, the government confiscates both cows, and sells him back some of the milk.

Under socialism, the government takes one of the cows and gives it to his neighbour.

Under democratic capitalism, he gets to sell one of the cows, and buy a bull.

By NOW IT IS OBVIOUS, as Max Singer points out in *Passage to a Human World*, that over the past two or three centuries we have been undergoing a transition, or "passage," from an inhuman, poverty-stricken world to a human, or wealthy, world.[1] At the turn of this century there were only a handful of "wealthy" countries. But today there are more than thirty-five, and many more approaching wealth. In every nation that has become wealthy, money has been the means to higher ends. Wealthy countries create new standards of health care, education, nutrition, quality of work, professionalism, transportation, and communications, the sum total of which raises the general standard of living to levels never before achieved. So this is not a chapter about wealth in the narrow sense of money-getting. Rather, it shows that countries can become wealthy (or poor) according to their willingness to create and use (or destroy) certain proven political, economic, and cultural "tools of freedom and wealth creation," which will launch them on the road to success more surely than anything ever tried before in human history. Considered as a whole, these tools amount to a "bonus system" that will almost always produce a wealthy and successful society. What does such a system do? Very simply, it establishes one clear set of playing rules binding on all with respect to how freedom is used, thus nurturing the natural expression of differences, and it openly rewards success.

In view of this, nothing is more surprising to an observer of democratic capitalism than the discovery that this most powerful system of wealth production has never really had a prophet, has no simple central document or manifesto of the kind important to all other social and religious revolutions and movements, and has no international organization to promote its beliefs. The reason for this is that democratic capitalism is a bottom-up system which has evolved from general principles, not from a top-down theory imposed on the people. Nevertheless, the need for simple self-awareness and self-preservation suggests that democratic capitalism ought to protect itself by articulating and defending its beliefs, values, and principles. What is even more surprising, until you realize just how deeply our educational establishment is imbued with the social-welfare mentality, is that while an important function of the educational system in most nations of the world is to ensure that the young appreciate and defend national cultural values, it doesn't work that way for us. If anything, democratic capitalism is usually presented as a malign alienating force in society by teachers who do not understand it and who have no direct personal experience of the way it works. In other words, democratic capitalism in Canada struggles to survive within a society that begrudgingly accepts its benefits.

Future generations will be hard pressed to explain the psycho-social perversity of a society that literally erodes itself, and finances this suicidal act with tax money generated by the wealth-creating system that built and supported the society in the first place. The only way such a self-annihilating trend can be reversed will be through a commitment on the part of all first to understand and then thoroughly promote the principles, tools, and institutions responsible for our strength. This is likely to be a long and daunting task, as collectivists in the West have long since captured the prime means of media communication plus the vast majority of schools and universities. (Peter Desbarats, Dean of the Graduate School of Journalism at the University of Western Ontario, has often underscored the "leftism" of Canada's journalists [*Financial Post*, July 13, 1985]).

There are three crucial points to be observed about the system itself before we take a detailed look at the practical everyday tools that make it work.

1. WEALTH IS NOT NATURAL, BUT CREATED

To BE BLUNT, nothing has economic value unless someone is willing to pay for it, a point made clear with a simple question. Does a large vein of pure gold that is completely inaccessible five miles beneath the earth have any economic value? Most people would say, Not as long as it stays in the ground. In fact, if in trying to mine it we spend more than we can sell it for, it has a negative value. At best, we can say it has only potential value until a method is created to extract it from the ground at a cost less than its market price.

This example serves as a case in point for the whole of democratic capitalist activity, and the need for profits to ensure its continuation. Obviously, none of us would bother to do the backbreaking work to get gold out of the ground if doing so cost *exactly* the same as the yield from the sale of the gold. We would do so only if we were relatively certain that after paying wages, rents, utilities, taxes, and so on, we would be left with *more* value in revenues than the sum of all our direct expenses and could still expect to replace worn-out machinery, put some money aside for recessions, strikes, and so on. It is this margin of revenue over expenses, normally called "profits," which is so misunderstood by the opponents of democratic capitalism. For without the possibility of gaining this marginal excess over expenses, no business, and no individual, can do anything but decline economically, bereft of both motivation and reward.

So no country, regardless of its "natural resources," has any wealth at all until one person creates a product which another is willing to buy. It all boils down to getting the gold out of the ground, smelted, and on the shelf, or the car out of the factory and into the showroom. As Julian Simon has pointed out so clearly, what he calls "the ultimate resource" is not natural at all, for it doesn't matter what a nation has in the ground if it doesn't care or doesn't know how to get it out, or if no one wants to buy it.[2] At best, we can say that a nation has *potential* wealth. Japan is not rich in natural resources. Neither does Switzerland grow chocolate. Neither did Taiwan, a tiny beleaguered island of immigrant Chinese, one two-hundred-and-fiftieth the size of mainland China, ever have great resources; yet it outproduced mainland China economically until the 1970s, despite the latter's size, and its population approaching one billion people. The lesson in this is that *all countries are potentially very rich* in what economists call "human capital": innovation, the entrepreneurial spirit, the work ethic, the individual desire to succeed, and other such complex human factors are what form the most important part of any system of wealth creation.

Finally, history has already provided us with an enormous and dramatic continent-sized human experiment to prove convincingly the main contention of this book: that countries that recognize and use the tools of freedom and wealth creation will be better off than those that do not. I am referring to the experiment of the North and South American continents. Even though they were discovered by Europeans in the same historical period and arguably have comparable "natural" resources, it is only the North that has developed those resources, both natural and human, so as to give it a pre-eminent economic position in the world and the highest standard of living for the greatest number of humans in history. Why is this so? Very simply, because *the North Americans got the system right.* They implemented and further developed the ideas and institutions of their British forefathers. The historical result of this experiment is that whereas Canada and the United States are at the very top of the economic success charts, no South American nation places in the top twenty-five in the world.[3]

2. "THE NATURAL SYSTEM OF LIBERTY"

WHEN ADAM SMITH characterized democratic capitalism with this phrase, he did so with the understanding that no system of political economy would ever be perfect. But above all, he felt, let it be *natural*. The entire subject of his innovative book on the causes of the wealth of nations could be said to be how this natural system works. He liked it, not because he felt it was at all times high-minded (what system is?), but *because* it worked. And he reasoned that it worked because it was natural. Most importantly, *the unintended beneficial consequence of this natural system of liberty is that it serves the common good of the greatest number of people, and does so by forming a "spontaneous order" (not a phrase Smith used) which is based on voluntary exchange, free from coercion.* A key factor, therefore, in the success of the tools of freedom and wealth creation is that they are not top-down tools, imposed by government planners or intellectuals. They are natural, bottom-up tools that have evolved from centuries of trial and error, and that survive in free nations because they are naturally successful and benefit all who use them. So the use of the word "system" here does not imply a consciously created or imposed set of regulations or methods. Just the opposite. The "system" arises naturally from the human actions of free people, who develop it and use it as naturally as they use their own language, in the creation of which none of them has played a conscious part.

Government has only one legitimate role to play in this: to create and protect a climate in which the system can flourish with justice.

This role — one government has vastly exceeded today — is like that of a referee who regulates and adjudicates a game, but does not play it. Rather, he creates a just and fair environment in which the same rules are established equally for all players, who can play as hard or as lazily as they wish. The one and only thing that makes societies (or sports) based on this system possible is that they are acknowledged as absolutely fair for all, with no exceptions.

3.   A Clever Splitting Of The Systems

Finally, as Novak has so carefully pointed out, a key feature of the complex natural system we are discussing is that it works best when its three most important areas of influence — political, economic, and cultural — are kept apart. Perhaps one of the greatest achievements of democratic capitalism during its emergence — one might say escape — from the rigidity of the mediaeval feudal system, was the splitting apart of these three spheres of influence (which had been controlled up to that point by a central authority) and their separate but interdependent flowering as a pluralistic system. One of the greatest threats to wealth production under democratic capitalism today is the threat of abandoning that pluralism and returning to a modern form of feudal stagnation by driving these three realms together again through collectivist and egalitarian coercion.

The Political Tools

INDIVIDUAL FREEDOM AND RESPONSIBILITY

It would be difficult to find anything more important to the development of democratic capitalism than the long, primarily British tradition of individual freedom and responsibility, many versions of which have sustained the free world since its beginning. Scholars are still at work on the origins of this tradition, which was first written about in religious texts of the thirteenth century. But whatever the origins, it is now clear that the idea of relying on individual freedom of choice and personal responsibility as the moral bedrock of a nation was and remains an extremely radical and powerful idea, one which has always been — must be — in direct and irreconcilable conflict with collectivism.

Part and parcel of the philosophy of individual freedom and responsibility is the right of everyone to do anything that is not prohibited by the law. In other words, a mainstay of this idea is that we are all born free. Our freedom is a *natural* right which cannot be given to us by any government (since we have it already), nor can it be taken away by legislation (although it can be so limited as to be practically nonexistent, as when we are jailed for a crime). Essentially, our freedom precedes the existence of government and is basic to our humanity. If there is no choice, there is no personal responsibility, and therefore no moral society is possible. It is this rigorous chain of interdependent ideas — from freedom to choice to responsibility to a moral society — that constitutes the foundation of democratic capitalism. In the long run, without this moral chain of ideas firmly in place, democratic capitalism cannot survive.

FREEDOM TO ASSOCIATE OR TO SECEDE

An essential adjunct of individual freedom is the right to associate with others or to secede by refusing to associate with others. Obviously, this is a moral right inherent in the meaning of democratic capitalism, and to override it by law, for the purposes of social engineering, is plainly coercive and immoral. Unionism is a case in point. No one could oppose the right of free individuals to associate to form unions. But objections can be made when the government grants unions coercive powers that force individuals to support them. So-called "forced union dues," which require workers to pay dues to a union at their place of work even if they refuse to join it, are just one such immoral force in society, as are all the other union regulations that make it extremely difficult for the members to dissolve a union once it has been established. A country's workers cannot be said to be truly free until workers have the right to join or quit union membership at will, free of coercion from the union itself or from government. In the U.S.A., "right to work" laws protecting workers from union coercion are stronger than in Canada, and private-sector unions there are correspondingly weaker (12 percent belong to private unions in the U.S.A., 37 percent in Canada).

The right of any individual to associate with or secede from any lawful group in society must be enshrined in the country's constitution. Governments that prevent the exercise of this freedom far exceed their role as referee of equal rights for all, for the ref suddenly becomes a player.

THE RIGHT TO OWN AND ENJOY PRIVATE PROPERTY

Caring. Why is the concept of private property so important to the free world? After all, as long as we have a right to use things, why should we care if we own them? But unless we own them, despite our best intentions, we simply do not care as much about the condition of things we use. After all, caring well for something takes effort, and most human beings naturally undertake tasks with the least effort possible. One could even say that when people spend effort on something they own, the effort is stored up, or invested, in the objects they care for. So to spend effort beyond what common decency requires for something that belongs to or is rented from others is like conferring a benefit upon them that becomes theirs when they reclaim the object, resulting in the feeling that we have wasted our work. Our labour was spent on others instead of ourselves. Aside from charitable works, this is an objectionable feeling, especially if the people to whom we return the rented thing are lazy, or somehow pride themselves on the free work they got from us. These natural feelings explain why private family garden plots in the Soviet Union, which total only 3 percent of all cultivated land, produce an astonishing 27 percent of that country's total farm output.[4] They also explain why virtually all commune experiments eventually fail, or transform into property-based organizations.

Trading. The next reason for the importance of private property follows from the first. If we are forbidden to own a thing, then even if it is improved with our work, we cannot sell it for more than it was originally worth. So we do not try to improve it. In other words, without the right to own things, we have no enduring incentive to acquire greater wealth for ourselves or our children. The fundamental engine of wealth production *depends on the voluntary exchange of goods and services between two parties, each of whom considers himself better off after the exchange than before*. But this most basic of human actions is just not possible without the concept and right of ownership, and without voluntary exchange, economic growth is not possible. Thus the cycle of stagnation begins. Everything depreciates. Without the physical and emotional fuel of private property, the engine of democratic capitalism cannot work.

A natural outgrowth of the right to private property is therefore the idea of free contracts between free individuals. It is easy to see just how these first two building blocks of wealth creation — freedom (in this case, to make contracts) and property — fit together to form a structure, in the sense that neither one means much without the other and would crumble without the other. What's the point of being free if we can't *do* anything with our freedom — if we are not allowed to acquire anything or create things that have value? Conversely, what is the point of having a right to own property — books, shoes, homes, or anything whatsoever that could be considered "ours" — if we cannot freely decide what to do with them?

That is why so many Canadians were upset when the right to own private property was intentionally left out of Canada's Constitution Act of 1982. The government, apparently at NDP leader Ed Broadbent's insistence, felt such a right would hamper the government's ability to expropriate our property. Precisely. Despite whatever protection for ownership the common law might nevertheless provide, many saw the omission as an attack upon our system that can be staved off only by the entrenchment of this right in our Constitution.

Protection from the State. Finally, private property, often criticized as the advantage of the rich over the poor, is really the last bastion of protection for everyone from the long arm of the State. If even the poorest citizen has a right to own property and this right is protected by the Rule of Law, then even the State will have difficulty wresting his property from him. *If the State cannot easily take property from individuals, then it cannot easily make them do its will.* But once your home, land, money, and goods are confiscated by the State, what else is left with which to protect yourself from such power? Nothing. You are bereft of all defence. A mere plaything of the State. With property rights protected by the law, however, a single citizen within his rights can defy the government. Collectivists are aware of this fact of life. That is why the very first thing an outright collectivist government will do is to strip people of property through total taxation or by "nationalizing" industry, banks, transportation and, at the extreme, by forcibly relocating large masses of people to areas of the country in which the government wants them to live. When property rights are strong, this cannot be done easily. But in nations without such rights, like the Soviet Union, Cuba, Romania, Tanzania, and Ethiopia, it is done regularly to millions of ordinary citizens. In Tanzania, Julius Nyerere, an avowed socialist, tried to attract his people into collective communities with incentives. But only 20 percent responded. When his plan had obviously failed, he forced the peasants to relocate to his *ujamaa* communes. Thirteen million people — equal to half the population of Canada — were forced to abandon their ancestral lands and homes and were powerless to resist because they had no legally protected property rights. To ensure the "success" of his plan, Nyerere then resorted to burning the homes they left behind! If we need a chilling reminder of the socialist models for the recent restructuring of Canada, it can be found in Richard Gwyn's *The Northern Magus*, in which he describes Pierre Trudeau's admiration for the socialist leaders Nyerere, Manley, and Castro.

In Canada, at the stroke of a pen during World War II, more than twenty-five thousand Japanese Canadians were deprived of their property and locked up, although they had committed no crime: their property and other fundamental rights were simply taken away by summary legislation. There are other, less obvious but no less damaging examples: the Trudeau government's National Energy Program was a forced transfer of wealth from western Canada to central Canada in the order of $60 billion. One of the underlying reasons for the Left's opposition to the Free Trade Agreement with the United States was that it would render future collectivist policies of this magnitude impossible. Of course, the most insidious form of dispossession, or legal plunder, is the growth of personal, corporate, and consumption taxes at all levels, against which the citizens have no defence, nor any means to measure their gradual and inexorable effect. Without the minimum of a constitutional protection for private property, Canadians will continue to suffer from the usual, and occasionally the unusual, legal plunder. Without a court of appeal based on a constitutional right to own and enjoy property, what could possibly prevent it? In a stunning about-face, the chief Soviet economist is now urging the legalization of private property, to end "decades of state exploitation of workers" (*Toronto Star*, Oct. 4, 1989).

THE PRIVATE CORPORATION: A MIGHTY ENGINE OF WEALTH CREATION

THE IDEA OF THE FREE corporation is a young one.[5] In mediaeval times, the king owned everything, including enterprises, in that he granted groups wishing to enter into a venture a "concession" which required a "royalty," or payment to the King. Such royal extortion was felt everywhere. In this sense, the early corporations were a creation of the State and could not operate without its permission. In effect, they had "charters" from the Crown to operate, often as monopoly businesses.

But after the Glorious Revolution of 1688 in England, which spawned the Bill of Rights and repudiated the Divine Right of Kings, such special charters from the Crown were eventually replaced by "general laws of incorporation" (the first in 1844). This change marked the open recognition that businesspeople had already found a multitude of ways to act as free businesses without first seeking the permission of the Crown. They did this by forming partnerships, trusts, and other similar contractual arrangements to get on with business. The change from Crown charters to general laws of incorporation was revolutionary because it meant that whereas formerly permission from the State was required to operate as a corporation, individuals now only needed to register with the State their intent to form a corporation, in the same sense that we today register a marriage. In effect, during this long evolution, the State ceased to be a grantor of corporate privileges, and became merely a registrar, with a few refereeing powers.

As a crucial tool of wealth creation, corporations have certain essential features: They are considered to be a person, or "entity" under the law, separate from their owners; thus they can sue and be sued, just as a person can. They also have the privilege of limited liability, so that shareholders can be liable only to the extent of their interest in the company. And finally, they have by law a perpetual life, which is to say that they have the legal right to continue beyond the death of the owner(s). In treating the corporation as a person, we can see how its very shape and function essentially mirrors the idea of individual freedom and responsibility, and the right to private property.

Yet today, three hundred years after the end of the Divine Right of Kings in England, we read with amazement that the U.S.S.R. has finally granted Soviet families the right to form private corporations! From a commercial perspective (if this amazing right is permanent and not something to be snuffed out by the next power shuffle in the Kremlin), this seemingly minor change in Soviet life is really much more. It is the Eastern equivalent of the early emergence of the West from its mediaeval condition of State-controlled concessionary enterprises. It means that the Soviets are finally recognizing one of the basic tools of wealth creation, and its superiority to centrally planned economic measures. This change may well prove to be the thin end of the wedge for the Soviets, simply because free enterprise cannot be truly free without the right to private property, individual freedom, contractual rights, and all the inevitable cultural attitudes that accompany these traditions. For these are the tools of liberty, and they are hell-bent on a collision course with the whole idea of the centralized State, which only understands the tools of power.

At bottom, it is really the energy, flexibility, and innovative power of the corporation that is the engine of production in the free world. It is the corporation, and the entrepreneurs who take risks in running it, that serves the whole economy of the nation as a kind of testing ground, not just for good ideas — which are not so difficult to find — *but for good ideas that also work and make economic sense.* In essence, hundreds of thousands of private corporations bear the risk of failure (around 40 percent fail every year), or reap the rewards of success, and in this manner spread over millions of individuals a total economic risk that would otherwise fall only upon the State and therefore on the taxpayers who support it. Private corporations thus relieve the State not only of the impossible task of operating effectively as a single corporation, but also of the risk of going broke. If we were assigned the task of teaching some new country how to create wealth, one of our most essential tools would surely be the development of the private corporation.

THE CONCEPT OF LIMITED GOVERNMENT

The absence of government results in chaos and barbarism. Total government results in slavery. The history of mankind's efforts to avoid either of these extremes has resulted in every possible combination in between. But a historical scorecard would show that the overwhelming pattern for most civilizations has been heavy-handed government control, by which the few exercise nearly total power over the many. But the modern, basically Anglo-American realization that civilizations could in fact achieve more by *reducing* the power and influence of government is unique in human history. In this respect, it is truly revolutionary. Yet we are now living at a time when this unique experiment is being severely threatened by the new barbarians of collectivism. A simple indicator of this growing collectivism is total spending expressed as a percentage of GNP. In recent years, Canada's level has exceeded 50 percent. (See Chapter Seven, Chart 24A.) Because we live within the bosom of our own system, it is especially hard to notice its gradual erosion. In order to help us, Freedom House, an American institution, makes an annual practice of ranking the world's nations by their "degree of freedom."[6] Unfortunately, what the list does not show is the slow movement toward or away from freedom *within* nations like our own. For me, a good starting point to think about government is Henry Thoreau's remark, "That government is best which governs least." As a baseline guide for readers, therefore, here is a brief list of the defensible functions of a limited government:

• The defence of the people against external and internal threats to person and property.

• The maintenance of representative, democratic government.

• Protection (not regulation) of the people's political and economic freedoms, through the establishment of rules of just conduct, equal for all, accompanied by a Rule of Law, equal for all, for the adjudication of any disputes arising therefrom.

Those wearied by the growth in the power and influence of our government at all levels will read this list, and weep. For the distance we have travelled from this noble standard is indicative of far more than the power-lust of politicians and the indifference of the people. It fairly cries out the terrible loss of confidence in our own moral capacities as a free people, resulting from the weakening of our old fierce will to order our own lives freely. Plainly and simply, we have lost the fearless courage of our forefathers, who would have objected violently to the impudence of any paid bureaucrat who tried to tell them how to live.

In truth, the only condition required for the triumph of evil is that good people do nothing about it. When Thoreau was in jail for refusing to pay a tax he considered unjust, Ralph Waldo Emerson visited him, and approaching his cell, said, "What are you doing in there?" To which Thoreau replied, "What are you doing out there?" But enough of the mourning. Let us at least recognize that the concept of a limited government is one of the greatest tools of wealth creation because it leaves the people's resources in their own hands where more wealth creation can take place through the interactions of freedom, responsibility, the right to private property, and voluntary exchange. Limited government is another crucial cog in "the system of natural liberty."

REPRESENTATIVE PARLIAMENTARY DEMOCRACY

REPRESENTATIVE PARLIAMENTARY democracy — the system in which freely elected representatives of the people make laws in a parliamentary setting against the check of an elected Opposition — is a crucial political tool of wealth creation. Both democracy and capitalism have evolved as "other-directed" systems intended to respond to the wishes of their users — whether voters or consumers. A democracy that does not respond to voters becomes a tyranny; an enterprise that does not respond to consumers goes bankrupt. When we set one of these systems *against* the other, we will have problems: a collectivist political system obstructs the efficiency of a free-market economic system at every turn, every decision point, and it *must* do so because in both method and spirit it has quite different aims. One system *controls*, the other *responds* — they inevitably erode each other in the way that sandy beaches disappear, not all at once, but one grain at a time.

We Canadians have witnessed the creation by our government (not by the people) of a Constitution specifically designed to encourage government to interfere with the democratic capitalist system in order to achieve egalitarian goals. Financial and distributional controls on economic life such as capital-gains taxation, minimum-wage laws, pay-equity laws, agricultural marketing boards, affirmative-action laws, international-banking-privilege laws, and so on, are just a few among thousands of ways the political system controls the economic system. If Montreal and Vancouver can't compete with Toronto to attract international banking, well, the State laments, let's either slap a penalty on Toronto or grant a privilege to the others, and equalize everyone! This appalling piece of intervention ignores the fact that if your team has a star you are unlikely to win by handicapping him just to make the other players feel better. All will lose.

A representative parliamentary democracy is an important tool of freedom and wealth creation *only if it is that*; it is counterproductive to pervert it into a social-engineering agency.

CHECKING THE POWER OF THE STATE, AND PROTECTING OUR RIGHTS

THE MOST IMPORTANT CHORE once the political tools and rights have been created is to protect them from witting as well as unwitting attacks by interest groups, politicians, and legislators whose goals are collectivist in nature, and reliant on government coercion and interference. For our rights and institutions are not inherently stable, precisely because they are based on liberty, not on power; on leaving people alone in their freedom, not on controlling them.

To the degree that government interferes, to that same degree the millions of arrangements it interferes with become less efficient and productive. Decisions affecting millions of lives are made for political, not economic, reasons. Economic signals become confused, and contracts become complicated. Worst of all, everyone becomes wary of that unpredictable and invisible partner — the government. In effect, government becomes the largest competitor to enterprise, *not because of its productive capacity, but because of its capacity to stifle production*. It is therefore imperative that once the right tools have been put in place they be protected by a rule of law. Normally such protection in the West has been assured by our long tradition of legal precedents, otherwise known as the Common Law. That is to say, hundreds of years of legal decisions now serve as legal precedents that protect our traditional freedoms. However, in 1982 we had imposed upon us, by politicians with no mandate to create it, who did not consult us, a Charter of Rights and Freedoms. And in it, what have always been our inherent inalienable rights as protected under the Common Law, are such no more. For at the same time that the Charter "guarantees" our rights and freedoms, it *specifies* and therefore *limits* them, and subjects them "to such reasonable limits as can be justified in a free and democratic society." In short, it grants appointed judges the right to erode or even eliminate those freedoms.

So we now have a Charter that is set against our traditional freedoms as provided in the English mode; set against them, not because it does not recognize them, but because it reserves for itself the power to withdraw or modify them — something which under our English-style Common Law no court or government could legally do. The courts can now limit or eliminate our freedoms whenever the political mood suggests this would be a popular thing to do. Our rights will be controlled by the whims of judges. They will no longer stand alone, and above judges, in the Common Law tradition, or entrenched in an unqualified Constitution. In Ontario this was recently witnessed when the courts ruled that our right to be protected against search and seizure did not apply in the case of the province's "RIDE" program, which basically hauls drivers off the road at random and forces them to submit to breathalyser tests, confiscates their cars, and so on. The courts ruled that this was indeed a breach of our freedoms and rights, but that it was "reasonable" and therefore could be allowed. In other words, every time a new set of judges comes along with a particular set of personal beliefs and biases, we'll get a new opinion of what "reasonableness" is. This means, of course, that political parties are going to fight like mad to ensure that judges of their own persuasion are on the bench everywhere possible.

Let us consider another scenario for such pre-emptive suspension of rights: let us suppose that kitchen knives are involved in a significant percentage of deaths by murder. Does this mean that it would be judged "reasonable" for the police to enter our houses without warrants and confiscate all kitchen knives? Murder, after all, is a far more vicious and serious social problem than road accidents. Does this example seem far-fetched? If so, just ask yourself what the difference in the reasoning is, for I can find none whatsoever, except "reasonableness." If this question ever arises, then, it will be determined by the attitude of the judge. One person. Not by the Charter, which offers no absolute protection, or by parliament, which is now subordinate to the Charter. Without a firm and inviolable rule of law, equally applicable to all, to sustain and protect the political tools of freedom and wealth creation, we have no guarantee they will survive simply because, as everyone knows, we need a fox to watch the chickens . . . but who's watching the fox?

THE ECONOMIC TOOLS

ONCE THE POLITICAL TOOLS are in place, a country can embark on truly long-term economic growth protected from tyranny, at the kind of growth *rates* experienced by the West in the past two centuries. Strictly speaking, these economic tools might be called financial tools, because many of them are about methods of structuring financial arrangements. But while finance is about *particular* financial transactions, economics is about the general effect of all such transactions. What is important to any country is the long-term economic effect of these forms of financial action. Another way to say this is that finance deals with the way we communicate with each other through money transactions, and economics represents the grammar, or laws, of those communications.

ECONOMIC FREEDOM

THE FIRST AND MOST important economic freedom is the right to contract fully with another person on any legal and mutually agreeable terms. Trading your old bicycle for your neighbour's old ladder is a form of contract, which can work only if each party first checks out the goods and then agrees to take them. Physically, once you accept his ladder and he takes your bicycle, the contract has been consummated without recourse, should either change his mind. The principle of *caveat emptor* (let the buyer beware) is at the basis of such an exchange, as is the principle of fair value received.

We are only now beginning to realize that all economic value is *subjective*, in the important sense that it is based on free choice and personal responsibility for those choices. It is not only ludicrous for government simply to *declare* that something has a specific economic value, like a job (minimum-wage laws and "pay-equity" laws) or a month spent in your apartment (rent control), but worse than this, it is a measurable and distinct interference with the free choice and responsibility of the two key partners to an economic agreement. The new "third party" (the government) will generally produce a diminution of this relationship because its method is based on coercion and the least knowledge of the three parties. In this sense, such interference is immoral, because if one of the two true economic partners decides to withdraw, as when a discouraged developer decides to get out of the rent-control game and invest his money somewhere else, the tenant who relied on the government to help him is left with no apartment to live in at all. Similarly, when the shirtmaker must close up shop because so-called "pay-equity" legislation has forced him out of the market, the government is unlikely to hire his jobless workers. Instead, it will shift that burden to the hapless taxpayers through an unemployment "insurance" program, which has degenerated into another form of welfare.

A further deleterious effect of ever-present government is that Canada is rapidly becoming an ever more litigious society. Today, an individual of sound mind and body over twenty-one years of age can find so many ways to wriggle out of the most straightforward contractual commitment, and there are so many judges and lawyers out there waiting to help him, that the whole idea of a simple contract between consenting adults has become almost a joke — if it were not so serious! As a result, there are as many interpretations of a fair contract as there are lawyers to write them, and Canada has twenty times as many lawyers per capita as Japan — clearly a burdensome situation for any business, and for society, since most legal work is not economically productive. We are rapidly creating a distrustful society in which one's word is no longer accepted as one's bond, where cleverness is measured by legal tricks, and honesty is for fools.

Certainly there is a need for a lawyer, and perhaps a court if the parties are intractable, but if economic freedom is to mean anything our society must insist on the integrity of simple contracts once again, and the assumption that people of sound mind know what they are thinking, reading, and agreeing to. This process of reversing our increasing litigiousness will help get the nursemaid State and parasitical legal and accounting professionals out of the lives of adults involved in free exchange and free contracts unless called upon by the contracting parties. We may think that the story about a drunken man slipping on a banana-skin in his own home, then successfully suing the fruit company that imported the banana for a million dollars, is a good joke. But I think it is sadly symptomatic of our mentality, and it could grind our economy to a halt in short order. Only a strong public awareness leading to a legal and constitutional emphasis on freedom, *caveat emptor*, and the assumption of fair value received will achieve the renewal required to put responsibility back where it belongs.

THE USE OF MONEY

MOST OF US NEVER STOP to consider the strange properties of money, because we are so used to it. But the development of money as a general instrument of exchange has been crucial to the evolution of democratic capitalism. In ancient and mediaeval times, exchange was achieved primarily by barter. Under the barter system, trade was restricted to one person's need for the physical goods of another. I would gladly trade you my saw for your dinner plates. But if I needed only six dinner plates and I felt my saw was worth twelve plates, the likelihood of a trade was diminished. What to do? As often as not, I would end up taking a few items thrown into the deal that I didn't really want and then would be faced with the job of trading those with someone else, and so on. Trading was burdensome because it was restricted by the problems of inventory, distribution, and what today is called "shelf life."

But money changed all that. Its use as an instrument of exchange meant that each party was free from the problems of barter. It also meant that whereas a man could not accumulate, say, a large quantity of perishable goods in exchange for something he owned, he could accumulate any amount of money, which was easy to store and would not perish. The use of money as a universal means of exchange meant that the hard-working, wise, and frugal now had an opportunity to become rich, and the foolish and improvident might become poor, according to how much money they made or lost, and not simply according to how much they had inherited or what class they had been born into. This was one of the greatest tools of freedom in that it enabled the lowly to liberate themselves from bondage to the material world of their superiors.

Before the widespread use of money, trade was cumbersomely restricted to the immediate "usage" value of the items traded. But with the advent of money, usage value didn't matter as much any more. Money could be exchanged for anything, regardless of the usage value of the thing itself. From this point forward, things acquired an "exchange" value, which took the place of their usage value in the minds of both parties.

This subtle transformation has troubled all socialist thinkers, especially the Marxist opponents of democratic capitalism. In the next chapter this will be dealt with more fully, but anyone who wishes to understand the primary reason for the socialist/Marxist antagonism to capital accumulation need only look to this usage vs. exchange value conflict. Anyone who follows the development of Marxist thought carefully will notice that one of its foundations is this very animosity toward money and the change in values Marxists say its use brings about. In his challenging and comprehensive critique of central economic planning, Professor Don Lavoie tells us that classical Marxism, the ultimate form of socialism, had as its serious aim the complete abolition of the use of money, as well, of course, as that of markets, prices, and property.[7] And in his major work, *Capital*, Marx comments on how he felt money destroyed true human values. Money, he says, "has . . . deprived the whole world, both the human world and Nature, of their own proper value."[8]

Although many of us as young students were duly impressed by this convenient symbol of oppression, it was impressive only because convenient, and because nothing is quite as strong as a symbol for oppression powered by envy. Today we can see that, as the economist and social critic Georg Simmel argued many years ago, "the development of the capitalist money economy went hand in hand with the liberation of the individual — or, perhaps one could say more accurately, with a whole set of liberations of the individual."[9] For it was the very abstract and universal quality of money which Marxist socialists hated that in fact freed mankind from its bondage to concrete things. Examples abound of immigrants to the West who arrived devoid of assets save for their native wit and readiness to work. The money they earned and saved enabled them to buy the property or things they wanted and to climb in status in a way that once and for all broke the heavy chains of class and blood bondage. We must therefore be struck by a contradiction: socialists, who say they despise money and yet claim it is their mission to help the poor, have never acknowledged that more than any other single physical reality, *it was the universal exchange qualities of money that finally freed the common man.*

Despite this fact, and in a less strident but no less worrisome form (because many are unaware of its consequences), the very same spirit that underlies the Marxist dislike of private money also underlies the preference of our own New Democratic Party for government control of financial policy and government ownership of the means of production. Forms of socialism such as those promoted by the NDP (and often supported by the other parties) aim at many of the same ends as did Marx, but by much less revolutionary means. In this respect, Marx was far more straightforward, for he declared that he wished to slaughter the capitalist bull and replace it with an angel. The NDP and its fellow travellers declare no such thing. They are all going to ride on its back until the bull collapses, feasting all the while on the fruit of its labours — and then scurry off to find another. Although Marx was utterly utopian, he at least had a rigorous philosophy to support his vision. And you have to admire that sort of commitment. But our modern socialists, none of whom could carry Marx's intellectual briefcase, enjoy the comforts our democratic capitalist society affords them, even as they mount confused and parasitical efforts to bring it down.

Finally, money is a dreaded threat to socialism because it is a form of property that can be traded at will by its owners. The daily buy-and-sell choices made by millions of individual citizens constitute a form of "dollar democracy" that makes tyrannical State control of individuals and the economy almost impossible, for money is *a means by which the people themselves vote on national economic policy on a daily basis.* Collectivists understand that *central economic control is inversely proportional to the volume of money controlled by the people.* In a country like our own, where the total government tax burden on the average income is greater than 50 percent, the government has effectively appropriated half our freedom.

If money in the hands of free individuals is threatening to collectivists, pooled money is even more so. We now turn from money as an instrument of voluntary exchange to its pooling power as a tool of wealth creation.

THE INVENTION OF DEPOSIT BANKING

ONCE MONEY BECAME POPULAR as an instrument of exchange and individuals and corporations began to collect sums larger than what they needed for daily transactions, the problem arose of what to do with the excess money. Without banks, people hid surplus money under the mattress. But money that was merely stored at home could be lost or stolen, so people looked for a safe place not only to store it, but to put it to work earning interest for them. Commercial deposit banking arose as a free-market solution to this dual problem of providing both security and earning power for the savings of the people (originally in the form of gold, later in currency).

Today deposit banking is a formidable tool of wealth creation because the very process of depositing (buying) and lending (selling) money generates an increase in the money supply. This increase is then loaned out for further investment, which creates more wealth and thus more deposits, which are in turn loaned out, and so on. In other words, deposit banking creates an upward spiral of new wealth in a process that is central to any nation's economic well-being.

If we imagine Bank A with initial holdings of $1,000,000, we can see the upward spiral. Bank A, as required by law, holds back a portion in reserves (for convenience, we'll say 20 percent), and lends out the rest. These borrowers in turn deposit at their own banks (Bank B) where, if their ventures are successful, they will deposit even more. Bank B, in turn lends out its money to still others, who deposit these smaller amounts in their banks (Bank C), and so on, in a long chain reaction.

	BANK A	BANK B	BANK C
(1)	$1,000,000 (initial capital)	→ $800,000	→ $640,000, etc.
(2)	$200,000 (a 20% reserve is held back)	160,000	130,000
(3)	$800,000	640,000	510,000

((3) = amounts available for loans to individual customers of each bank)

- Money borrowed from Bank A is dispersed, through new payments to suppliers, etc., to Bank B, and so on.
- Borrowers of funds from Bank B repeat this process by depositing in Bank C, and so on.

So there it is: by the facility of deposit banking, after a reserve is maintained by law as security against deposits, the balance is loaned out to create new wealth. So long as the flow of deposits and loans is predictable, reserves maintained, and loans secured, the system works. After the loans and cheques written on them have travelled to only two other banks (the process could in principle continue to many others, each smaller in scale than the one before), the original $1,000,000 has become $1,950,000! (If readers are wondering where the banks get the money they start with or new money to accommodate growth, the simplified answer is: they get it from the nation's Central Bank, and they give the Central Bank a note in return.)

Leaving aside for the moment some valid criticisms of the entire banking system, we can see that compared with leaving our savings under the mattress, deposit banking is a powerful tool of wealth creation. We can easily imagine how nations that either do not have such a system or are bent on government control of all banking functions vastly reduce the entrepreneurial use of money and are prone to stagnate financially.

In Western society, the new wealth created by the banking system can be used by entrepreneurs to the benefit of their communities. But a standard method of accounting is required so that traders will not confuse financial apples with oranges. Such a system accurately tracks the creation of new wealth — or losses — in any financial entity.

DOUBLE-ENTRY BOOKKEEPING

The development of double-entry bookkeeping was an important tool of wealth creation that enabled buyers and sellers to track the integrity of financial transactions in a way that isolated each one from any connections to prior financial transactions. The idea of determining assets and balancing them against liabilities at all times meant not only that each engine of production could be studied as such for greater efficiency, but also that it could now be bought or sold on universally understood terms. The important balancing feature for all corporations in comparing total assets with total liabilities became the value of the shareholder's "equity"; the rise or fall in this value was now easily quantifiable. By this means, the market value of an enterprise could be reliably determined for private owners, or "earnings per share" for public owners.

The ability to construct a historical record of value in this way (and for that matter the simple ability to determine profit and loss in a universal accounting language) is essential to wealth creation. Combined with the price system, it provides businessmen and economists with an objective basis for determining economic value. The foundation of this value, under our bonus system, is decision-making man, to whom, through shareholder's equity or cumulative deficits, profits or losses will be precisely allocated in accordance with the individualist principle of responsibility. This very methodology has the effect of discouraging statist economists from meddling in economic matters they do not understand. In socialist economies, this ability to assign value and determine profit and loss does not exist because their buy-sell decisions are coerced and not freely made. In this sense, their economic "values" are artificial because for them supply and demand operate not through clear economic signals, but through confused political ones. Their financial planners are therefore faced with an irrational balancing of assets and liabilities based on political considerations, rather than on objective measures of value. You can't run a business for very long without reliable numbers. Nor can a country's finances be controlled for long without them.

So much for the condition of the numbers. What about the condition of the workers under these two systems, and how are they affected by the revolution called the "division of labour?"

DIVISION OF LABOUR

THIS IS ONE OF THOSE extraordinary themes of history which has served as a political watershed for half of mankind. As the Industrial Revolution developed increasingly specialized and machine-based forms of production, early socialist thinkers such as Saint-Simon and Karl Marx strongly felt that the spectacle of men doing the same mindless task all day, one only part of a larger, more complex assembly process, was dehumanizing. Socialist opponents of free enterprise still think so today. Obviously there was some truth in this. I've done such work myself, and didn't like it much. But what Marx failed to acknowledge was the fact that the division of labour was, and remains, one of our most basic methods to increase productivity, and without increased productivity (output per hour, of work, per worker), a country — especially one growing in population — cannot increase its wealth. (Savings, or keeping more money than we spend, is the other key to increased wealth.)

We tend to believe that new wealth is a result of people's working harder today than in the past. But this is not necessarily so. In fact, it would be very difficult to match the workmanship and labour of, say, mediaeval craftsmen, who had very high standards, and worked about twice as long per week as we do. Rather, what has caused our fabulous increases in wealth is the new savings/new investment/new machinery cycle, combined with the division of labour. Contrary to Marx, division of labour, except in totalitarian countries, is not exploitive, but freely assumed by workers. In this sense, it is a contract, like any other, by which the worker sells his skills on a labour market, trying to get the highest price he can, and an employer buys that labour for the lowest price he can. Why would either do otherwise? Such contract labour is a marvellous invention of the free world, because the worker gets a fixed return with low risk, and the freedom to bid up his wages, while the employer may increase his return by accepting more risk. Ultimately, of course, all wage and price levels are determined, not by owners of capital, or of economic entities, or by workers, but by all the consumers who make the final decision to buy or not to buy the commodity produced. This is dollar democracy at its best. In an effort to bring the labourer his highest wage, the owner his highest return, and the consumer the lowest price and highest-quality product, labour tended naturally to divide itself.

This division springs from a natural human tendency, or law, not of history, as Marx thought, but of conservation of energy. For any man going out to cut wood with another will be unwilling to cut and then carry each piece home. One will cut and one carry, or both will cut and then both carry. Their labour will be divided in the interests of efficiency. More importantly, while one man might build a car in two years, a thousand men, with all their different skills, can build tens of thousands of cars in two years. Fundamentally, one of the oldest divisions of labour in history, one much reviled by feminists today, is the division between the work of men and women, whereby in the greater part of the world the men agree to provide and protect, and the women to nurture and process. Whether it is fashionable to say so or not, this simple and very specialized division of labour — still the world's commonest — has been an enormous engine of wealth production, and remains so to this day.

Those with socialist leanings object that the division of labour is tedious and dehumanizing because the worker is cut off, or "alienated," from the natural end-result of his work. The person installing car-bumpers may never see the end product — the finished car. But this is hardly more dehumanizing than labour under collectivist regimes. After all, most basic human labour, whether in a rice paddy or a factory, is tedious. But at least in a free nation, those who dislike such work can save what they are able and leave for other work, or they can group together and start their own business. In a free society, where individual circumstances are not fixed by law, a high degree of mobility is afforded to everyone, especially to those who innovate and take risks. Through division of labour, *democratic capitalism has developed one of the most powerful and flexible modes of economic — and therefore social — cooperation known to history*. Simply put, labour is divided both by task and by ability. Not only are tasks divided into sub-specializations, but millions of human beings of different levels of ability do forms of work that depend for their success on finely co-ordinated voluntary co-operation with those above them and below them. The new wealth this has created more than offsets any tedium in the work itself, and is often preferred by working people to more interesting but less well-paying jobs, or no job at all, or a risky job with high potential returns but no guarantees.

Of course, division of labour according to skill means that some people will receive higher wages than others. The Left is fond of arguing that where wages are low by Western standards, workers are "exploited." But this is an invalid accusation. Even if an employer is greedy, unprincipled, or of distasteful character, no worker is forced to work for him. Unless a gun is held to the head of an employee, forcing him to accept the conditions offered, there can be no "exploitation." In fact, the use of this term, in the absence of such force, is sloppy. An employer is under no obligation, financial or moral, to offer more in wages than the least required to induce people to work for him. After all, most people who shop seek out the best they can find for the lowest price. Buying labour is no different. And the quickest and most foolproof test of whether or not a wage is "enough" is its acceptance by the employee. For he can always refuse, and then the employer must raise the wage, find another employee, or close up shop. If there is no other work available, it is not a legitimate criticism to say that the employee is exploited because he "has no choice," for before the employer brought the job to market, there was no job at all. In many situations in the world, the only alternative is starvation, compared to which any kind of wage is a blessing. This calls to mind situations in which multinational companies employ Third World labour for rock-bottom wages. We can deplore this all we like, but the wages *will not* go up until the employees refuse to work for the going rate, and the wages *cannot* go up if higher wages raise the price of commodities so high that no one buys them. Between these two crucial and free decisions (to buy and sell labour, and to buy and sell the product of that labour), lies the wealth-creating process itself. In a free society, individual choice does not always mean we will be able to change the world we see in our own favour, but it does mean that we are always free to choose for ourselves the best of the available alternatives, and take the sometimes unpredictable consequences.

INSURANCE

THROUGHOUT ITS HISTORY, commercial life has been shot through with risks which, if great enough, can prevent transactions from taking place. In the long run, many financial transactions amount to a form of sophisticated high-stakes gambling in a game with few rules and lots of unpredictables, where fortunes are made and lost at the margin. For those who stand to win or lose their own money, it all comes down to "risk and return," regardless of the amount at stake. Most people involved in such transactions therefore search for a means of avoiding, transferring, or spreading their risk. One of the most important tools of wealth creation has therefore been the invention and subsequent evolution of insurance to spread risks sufficiently to enable ventures both physically and financially dangerous to be undertaken.

Certain forms of insurance such as marine insurance have been available since ancient times, and were designed to protect against physical loss or danger. The insurer would receive a huge premium from the insured if a voyage was successful, and nothing at all if it failed. But this was too risky for most, and was therefore left to specialists. Over time, therefore, general insurance evolved to cover all sorts of ordinary merchant risks. As Birdzell points out, this enabled the merchant-marine business to attract investors who would otherwise have been too cautious to enter such a risky market.[10] This, in turn, created capital flows previously unavailable, and at one stroke took away from the adventurers some of the risk of loss and provided enormous injections of new investment into commercial ventures once considered hazardous. The beauty of such a sophisticated insurance technique, in which small investors felt safe, had a parallel among the insurers themselves, who "co-insured" with other insurance companies or with pools of investors unconnected with the venture itself, in order to further spread their own risk.

FREE MARKETS AND JOINT-STOCK COMPANIES

A NATURAL EXTENSION of insurance and co-insurance strategies, which in effect spread risk to nonparticipants in financial ventures, was the evolution of joint-stock companies, which in effect spread risk — and reward — to a multiplicity of *owners*. No one really could have foreseen the phenomenal rise in popularity of joint-stock companies that has taken place over the past two centuries. Another in the long list of flexible financial instruments based on individual freedom and private property rights, such companies could not have developed without these two political tools of wealth creation. The most conspicuous and creative feature of such companies is that they are able to raise money for expansion through the issue of various classes of debentures or shares, some with preferences as to the receipt of dividends, redemption, or convertibility, and in addition offer the protection of limited liability. In collectivist nations that do not recognize private property, a corporate entity with individual rights cannot be created and therefore ownership in the entity cannot be divided — nor can the risk or reward of owning that entity be shared. Again, these tools are "structural" in the sense that a change in one necessarily entails a change in another; they are interdependent. Such structural interdependence exists in all ideological systems. Gorbachev is wrestling with this fact of life at this very moment in the U.S.S.R., where his *perestroika* policies have, like a key to Pandora's box, unintentionally let all sorts of ideological beasties loose upon his empire.

When the history of the evolution of democratic capitalism is finally written, the joint-stock company will be recognized as one of its proudest institutions, a device that spurred wealth creation in the West and spread that wealth to large masses of people at the same time. To the chagrin of socialist ideologues, this effective tool of free enterprise has even succeeded in creating a more "progressive" allocation of wealth to the people than any single political scheme to achieve the same end. The most dramatic example of this sharing of real wealth with the people is Margaret Thatcher's program of "privatization" in Great Britain. This program, unlike most, aims not to sell public corporations to private ones — a mere transfer of assets from a government corporation to a private corporation — but to sell off the majority of shares to a broadly based mixture of workers, management, and the general public, thus achieving a truly progressive spreading of real wealth to shareholders who really do "own a piece of the action," as the saying goes. Thus, when our own government fatuously argues that a company like Petro-Canada is "ours," we are being misled. Petro-Canada is not ours at all, because individual Canadians do not personally own shares in it, in the way that the British own shares in British Airways. For when you own something, you can sell it, and we have nothing to sell. All we really "own" of Petro-Canada is its debt, which our government will force us to service by raising our taxes.

The second, and by no means insignificant, way in which the joint-stock company contributes to the distribution of wealth is by its payment of corporation taxes, much of which ends up in the social-welfare system. Another way of looking at this is to say that while the government triple-taxes, or triple-handicaps, us (through personal, corporate, and consumption taxes), democratic capitalism triple-bonuses us (through salaries received, dividends earned, and equity gained on any shares owned)..

THE CULTURAL TOOLS

AS A YOUNG BOY, I asked my father what it felt like to see a dead person, and he answered that it was "like being in a house with nobody home."

Just so, all the political and economic tools discussed so far are of incalculable importance to the success of democratic capitalism. But unless they are vivified by the living will of the people to sustain the ideas and values that shaped those tools, they are like a house with nobody home, a mere dead structure. So when I talk in this book of "cultural" tools, this has little to do with our preferences in literature or music. I am using the term in a very broad sense to capture the whole set of ideals, morals, values, concepts, and traditions that sustains any unified nation or people. For the real threat to civilization arises from the simple fact that laws are made by mere mortals and are therefore changeable. If good values drift to bad, though the noblest legal institutions remain in place, the worst villainies may be carried out in the name of those institutions.

Paul Johnson's insightful book, *Modern Times: The History of the World From the Twenties to the Eighties*, eloquently demonstrates this point. In it, he traces the history of despotism in the twentieth century and shows clearly how if the will of the people to protect their freedoms is absent, those with a greater will can pervert even the strongest institutions of free societies and turn them to their own destructive purposes. Once again, all that is required for this to occur is for good people to do nothing. When they have finished doing nothing, they are a beaten people, subject, like slaves, to the new tyranny. "It is a commonplace," writes Johnson, "that men are excessively ruthless and cruel not as a rule out of avowed malice but from outraged righteousness. How much more is this true of legally constituted states, invested with all the seeming moral authority of parliaments and congresses and courts of justice! The destructive capacity of the individual, however vicious, is small; of the State, however well-intentioned, almost limitless. Expand the State and that destructive capacity necessarily expands too."11

He shows in detail how Germany under Hitler suffered this very sequence of events, as did the Soviet, all the Eastern Bloc nations they subjugated, the Italians, the Chinese, the Tanzanians, the North Vietnamese and Cambodians, and so many others in this century who have been destroyed, pillaged, starved, or murdered mostly in battles between and within what Churchill called "the mighty educated states."

At present, Canada is in the process of endangering its very existence as a nation at the hands of successive governments that have wilfully undermined our core values and traditions and replaced them with a set of alien values from the collectivist-egalitarian tradition. In a de-mocracy, this process can be stopped only by the people, and only then when the people realize what is happening, and then have leaders to express their will. But modern Canada is ruled not by the people, but by a government elite that propagates many values alien to the long-term interests of the Canadian people. It does this by camouflaging its agenda, or by simply proceeding with that agenda in opposition to the will of the people. ("The Government vs. The People" chart in Chapter Seven — showing Gallup poll results and government decisions — illustrates this point.) The people want capital punishment restored? The government bans it. The people want lower taxes? The govern-ment raises them. The people want to reduce government and the national debt? The government borrows more. The people do not want official (forced) bilingualism? The government forces it on them. The people want to slow immigration and favour traditional British-European stock? The government increases the flow, and disregards country of origin. The people want a better climate for free enterprise? The government increases the regulation of business. And this is government by the people, for the people? This list goes on and on. One reason the government elite gets away with this so easily is that the people are no longer sure what values they cherish, so they cannot speak out with one voice. The importance of individual freedom, responsibility, family, hard work, self-reliance, local government, good manners, personal success, and so on are no longer emphasized in our schools; and on television, on radio, and in the daily newspapers they are under steady attack. In short, they are everywhere replaced by their opposite, the popular illusions of our time.

If the political and economic systems outlined earlier are to be supported by Canadians who hold corresponding cultural values, we need to know what those values are. They are described below.

PERSONHOOD

"PERSONHOOD" IS AN AWKWARD word for an important concept. Each of us is not *merely* an individual unit, but more profoundly a *person* in the sense that we are "an originating agency of insight and choice."[12] In this very important sense, *the values of the nation cannot simply be handed down from on high, but must be created daily in the hearts and minds of the people who freely choose them, sustain them, defend them, and propagate them.*

This concept of what it means to be a full person is utterly alien, even actively repressed as a threat to communal life, in many societies, and in socialist political theory is constantly under attack. This is because the whole idea of actively fulfilling oneself as a person is "designed to frustrate the totalitarian impulse."[13] At the heart of all socialist/collectivist systems you can always find a strong philosophical and political effort to eradicate the idea of the individual, or the person-as-value-creator, from the thinking of the people. Nobel laureate Friedrich Hayek summed this up nicely in *The Counter-Revolution of Science* when he said that "consistently pursued collectivism must lead to a system in which all members of society become merely instruments of the single directing mind and in which all the spontaneous social forces to which the growth of the mind is due are destroyed." This form of attack on personhood and on the idea of individual conscience first took definite form in the early nineteenth century, most notably through the work of two Frenchmen, Henri Saint-Simon, and his student and collaborator, Auguste Comte, both of whom had strong socialist-authoritarian views. It was Saint-Simon who saw "more clearly than most socialists after him that the organization of society for a common purpose, which is fundamental to all socialist systems, is incompatible with individual freedom."[14]

At root, it is this idea of the importance of individualism and the possibilities of personhood for each such individual that supplies the foundation for all other social institutions of free societies. With this one cultural value in place, a society is ready for the "bottom-up" system of government. Without it, a society is ripe for the "top-down" authoritarian formation so typical of collectivist systems of all stripes.[15]

If the first protection against tyranny is love and respect for individuals and their creative and ever-evolving personhood, the second is the veneration of the family as cradle and shelter for the growth of individuals.

THE FAMILY

"BLOOD IS THICKER than water," we were told as children. And sure enough, the same brother or sister who enraged us could, if suddenly attacked by an outsider, spark in us the strongest passions of courage, love, and protection. The "family" is a natural presence in our lives, and especially when we are children, it is the absolute centre of our world. As adults, we have a crucial moral responsibility for the strengthening or weakening of this institution, whether we wish it or not. How we build or destroy our own families, and how we defend the institutions set up to protect them, multiplied by millions of Canadians, will determine the stuff and fibre of the family for generations to come. If the first building block of democratic capitalism is the individual and his personhood, the second is the family, which nurtures and creates this reality. Practically speaking, however, we could reverse this order, and say that the family is first, for it is in the bosom of the family that the crucial values, disciplines, and standards of individual behaviour are formed, and transmitted from generation to generation. In the same way that private money is a threat to the economic theory and policy of the homogenizing socialist State, so the traditional family is a threat to state efforts to inculcate collectivist values and standards in the people. This was well observed by the Soviet writer Igor Shaferevich in *The Socialist Phenomenon*. He said that "at least three components of the socialist ideal — the abolition of private property, the abolition of the family, and socialist equality — may be deduced from a single principle: the suppression of individuality." This phenomenon is also at work in all socialist revolutions, kibbutzims, communes, and similar experiments. In the popular and moving film *The Killing Fields*, during a brief, chilling scene in which the communist Khmer Rouge are holding a "re-education" class for villagers, a young child is told to come forward to a drawing on the blackboard of a mother and father and rub out the linked hands of the whole family.

This eradication of the idea of the family is not limited to times of war, but has been occurring in peacetime in many Western nations, especially in Sweden, where collectivist/egalitarian social policies are more widespread than here (though we are gaining fast). Young architects from Sweden's "Directorate of National Planning," for instance, try to mould collective feeling through architecture. One of them, Mr.

Jan Stromdahl, says, "The political climate helps us . . . I am interested in collective living and want to see it spread . . . By removing amenities from the home and moving them into communal premises, you can force people to live communally . . . Once they see the advantages of the new kind of life, they will *want* to change." And one of his professors at the Directorate tells us that "environment has to be planned so that the family situation can be corrected. Children have to be socialized at an early age, in order to eradicate the social [family] heritage." The author of *The New Totalitarians*, journalist Roland Huntford, from whose alarming book these quotations were taken, tells us that "It is an acknowledged aim of Social Democratic ideologists (and others) in Sweden to break up the traditional family, because it fosters individuality and because it fosters class distinction and social disability."[16]

At least the Swedes have the merit of openly declaring their political and ideological agenda! In states like Canada, however, where ideological thinking is no less present but a lot less codified and lucid, the State does not dare to attack the family *explicitly*. Astonishingly, it may even promote the idea of the family in words, while providing funds to special-interest groups that promote perverse anti-family sexual "orientations" (for example, Ontario's Bill 54, which has the unfortunate effect of giving homosexuality the status of normal behaviour); or staggeringly expensive State daycare programs (no one yet has even an inkling of the extent of this burden on the people's pocketbooks — or of the burden of such impersonal care on the minds and hearts of the nation's children); or extensive State support for single parents, the most disastrous model for which is the American AFDC program (Aid to Families With Dependent Children), which even left-wing politicians now agree has amounted to a State incentive program to lure poor, single (mostly black) women out of their parents' homes to have babies without husbands (if they marry, they lose support!). Finally, there is the deadly equation: more government = more taxes = more inflation = the necessity for two incomes. Politicians seem impervious to the basic and time-honoured economic lesson: if you *subsidize* something (like illegitimacy or laziness) you get *more* of it — that's basic reward-and-punishment theory. At any rate, egalitarian and collectivist government programs have the effect of directly or indirectly undermining the traditional family by subsidizing dependence on the State instead of the family at all ages, through its public schools, its insurance schemes, welfare plans, old-age homes, granting mechanisms, and tax policy — all of which cause citizens to turn to the State for help instead of to the family.

In short, by failing to protect and promote the traditional family aggressively and by actively encouraging social policies inimical to it, the State has become an unwitting midwife to the stillborn family of the future. In the absence of doctrinaire anti-family policy, this can be explained only in terms of political expediency, and the philosophical and ideological sloppiness by which it is always accompanied. For this is the crucial mixture of which pressure groups are keenly aware. If our politicians were in fact ideologically and philosophically brighter and stauncher, then all lobby groups would have a much tougher go of it.

The success of groups that have lobbied for policies destructive to the family unit is perplexing, for to speak only in terms of economic success, it is clear that the traditional heterosexual marriage and family is an enormously effective spur to economic growth and wealth creation for the entire nation, and *on every imaginable social and physical scale married people do better than others.* They have fewer emotional problems, less disease,[17] and make far more money than singles. And yet, in his book *Men and Marriage,* George Gilder writes of the sad state of government policy in the United States, that "everywhere in America unemployment, illegitimacy, divorce, and separation find fuller favor in the laws of the land than does raising children in an intact family."[18] We are nearing a similar stage in Canada. Gilder's description seems to vindicate Joseph Schumpeter's early warnings about the capitalist system. He said that "its very success undermines the social institutions which protect it, and 'inevitably' creates conditions in which it will not be able to live and which strongly point to socialism as its heir apparent."[19]

Personally, I believe that Schumpeter was right about the process and wrong about his conclusion that there is an "inevitable" result. Democratic capitalism is both strong enough and flexible enough to triumph. And clearly (and perhaps surprisingly to some) the most important arena for the playing out of the struggle between socialism and democratic capitalism is not the school or church or neighbourhood, but the traditional family. Even though schools may be filled with left-liberal teachers who try to normalize sexual "orientation"; though mainline Churches may preach against democratic capitalist values, as they are now doing in an ever more strident and vocal way; and though a child's neighbourhood peer group may chip away at community morals — to all this a child has a chance of immunity if the family is strong, for this is the one place and the last place where cherished values can be kept safe from all who would threaten them.

This has been so for all persecuted peoples, whether Protestants who fled from England or France in the early seventeenth century, or the Jews who were persecuted by Hitler. Despite seventy years of State effort to stamp out Christianity and Judaism in the Soviet Union, it is the family unit that has kept the faith there to this day.

For these reasons, we must publicly recognize the family, once and for all, as our prime transmitter of values from generation to generation; our most basic economic tool of wealth creation; our final sanctuary, through the laws and institutions that protect it, from the anti-family forces of radical feminism and fashionable sexual liberalism; our most important tool in the fight against poverty and a barbaric society (married men are involved in far less violent crime than unmarried men); and our last bastion against State interference in the intellectual and moral lives of the people. All of these values are now under attack and cannot survive unless they are proudly promoted and defended by us all, in particular by our political representatives. Once such freedoms and traditions are secure, a society can become tolerant and open to voluntary (not coercive) pluralism.

PLURALISM OR AUTHORITARIANISM?

ONLY WHEN WE HAVE established a clear rationale for the importance of individuals and the families that nurture them can we ask what kind of society is best suited to the growth of these two primary institutions. The choices available to us range from societies that are more or less open to those that are more or less closed. Openness refers to a morality according to which individuals are largely self-governing. It implies tolerance or pluralism — that is, openness to a huge variety of alternatives co-existing under a general rule of law. General rules of law — *the only sort that parliaments were originally meant to pass* — encourage and permit the natural flowering of differences and are typical of open societies. But closed, or authoritarian, societies go far beyond this to create "imperative" laws of the social-engineering variety, in an effort to equalize the results, or outcomes, of their societies.

It is obvious, nevertheless, that all societies require some basic mechanism of authority, and they have to decide where — that is, in what body or bodies — this authority shall reside. Dictatorships, or totally closed systems, solve the problem by vesting absolute authority in one person; totalitarian regimes, by vesting it in a group, or a controlling elite, like the Communist party. Social-welfare states like Sweden vest authority in their thousands of bureaucrats, many of whom have police-like powers. This last is the model Canada now seems to be following, as made obvious by our many bureaucrats in our many ministries, commissions, and agencies, with their many police-like powers.

So how do the more open societies associated with democratic capitalism prevent any one group from seizing power and exercising tyranny over the whole population?

The answer is: first by a thoroughgoing separation of the major spheres of human action (the political, economic, and cultural), and then by a self-regulating system of checks and balances so that the fox who watches the chickens will be watched, and will watch himself. Although far from perfect, the American system of checks and balances seems so far the best invented, as its intent from the start was to set up institutions like an elected Senate *specifically to counteract the human tendency toward monopoly power*, in the interests of creating a free, democratic capitalist system. By contrast, our Canadian system has very few restraints or checks on political power. Our Senate, for example, is filled not with the elected, but *appointed* members — pure patronage!

We can see how all these cultural values begin to tie together now. Individuals are basically trusted to govern themselves according to a common set of rules, within which their individual differences are allowed and *expected* to flower. Families are openly promoted and protected as society's most important moral-cultural institution for nurturing this flowering. Because we acknowledge that mankind is inherently capable of tyranny, checks and balances are set up to prevent any one group from monopolizing power. And finally, preference is necessarily declared for a pluralistic, open society, stressing freedom, the natural expression of talents, and co-operation between its self-governing parts.

Once again, we are reminded that ideological systems are "structural," in the sense that the ideas that form them are linked, and support each other, like a building. Attacks on the foundation, or too much substitution of parts that don't belong, may eventually bring the whole thing down. Democratic capitalism, and all forms of socialism, are very different buildings based on different principles. They can't be mixed. A tidy metaphor for this is two children each building a house from sets of blocks based on different interlocking principles, one with Lego and the other with Duplo. As many parents will know, these two types of blocks cannot be fitted together, because each has its own structural system, or integrity. It so happens that political-economic systems have the same kind of internal integrity, which must at all costs be protected.

But the bureaucrats who try to build with them don't know that, and they tinker around for the longest time mixing the two kinds of blocks. They may succeed in getting the house off the ground, but only by gluing, Scotch-taping, or balancing one piece against the other. In the end, this ideological and structural confusion succumbs to its inherent instability, and can be held together only by constant surveillance, coercion, and force. That is, by bureaucrats, supervisors, commissions, by — let's face it — labour police, pay police, rent police, liquor police, and the many other people with police powers such societies require in order to be propped up and kept running, all financed by us and our neighbours.

Nevertheless, democratic capitalism, despite witless efforts to ruin it, has so far managed to stay together through its own structural integrity. In Canada we have very few outright revolutionaries who want to destroy the one system and replace it with another. Instead, we have legions of social-welfare promoters who take pieces of Lego out of the system and substitute Duplo for them, which will result in a structure requiring so much interventionism to keep it together that it will eventually fail to function efficiently.

What we read daily in our newspapers about the Soviet Union is a living example of this metaphor. For more than two generations, the spirit of capitalism (not yet democratic) has flourished in the Soviet underground. Even though the Communist system has held authoritarian sway over the Russian people for more than seventy years and taken an estimated 11 million or more of its own citizens' lives through forced starvation and labour camps, the forbidden system of capitalism has always co-existed within it and is now struggling to get out, like a sprig of fresh grass pushing its way through barren pavement. What we see taking place there now is the patched-up mess composed of the Lego of capitalism and the Duplo of Communism, crumbling because it obviously can't work, so the will of the authoritarian State to hold the dispiriting mess together has dwindled. In the end, because the will to maintain even the existing level of repression and coercion is waning, the natural system of democratic capitalism will arise, because it *is* natural. These two systems will then have to be separated, and the socialism put on the shelf, or else there will be no structural integrity to what remains. This is a lesson the Soviets will have paid a lot to learn. As they head toward democratic capitalism, we slide toward socialism!

THE BONUS SYSTEM

INHERENT IN A SYSTEM that encourages the flowering of individual differences and the free expression of our humanity under the rule of law is the idea of rewarding excellence. While everything described in this chapter is a specific tool of freedom and wealth creation within what I call "a bonus system," the actual idea of rewarding people for excellence is nowhere carved in marble. It is cultural, in the sense that it has been carried for generations in the hearts and minds of the people of free nations. For them, rewards or the lack thereof are intuitively linked to the idea of personal success or failure. Once the rules are set, everyone has to play by them. Infractions are punished; success is rewarded. Such societies have been borne forward on the intuitive belief that any conception of reward or punishment other than one indelibly linked to personal responsibility is morally unworkable — that a society that encourages the blaming of our circumstances for our lack of success becomes morally bankrupt. Despite, say, bad luck, uncaring parents, or illness, *a moral life cannot be built without personal accountability for success or failure.*

Conversely, and dreadfully, once a society chooses to swallow what I call "the determinist illusion" through which the environment is seen as the cause of everything, it is doomed, simply because the environment is impersonal. For then there is really no one to blame for failures except our history or each other. As each group within the whole then attacks, blames, and demands "rights" from society, the idea of responsibility disappears via "the Rights Illusion." When a society reaches this point, it becomes overly litigious, cranking out more lawyers, accountants, and court settlements instead of more buildings, factories, and higher-quality products. Furthermore, even though some may not think it "fair," *the idea of individual responsibility is an all-or-nothing principle.* It cannot be applied to some people, or groups, and not to others — or there would be no end to the no-fault claims. We may choose to help criminals, the poor, or the disadvantaged all we like, but *as a society* we cannot exempt them from moral responsibility.

On a broad political scale, whole nations are typified by this type of behaviour, or its opposite, or something in between as they struggle to balance justice with liberty. If we spread an economic atlas of the world before us, we will see that the wealthiest nations have bonus systems imbedded in them from bottom to top (tyrannical nations have them at the top, but never the bottom), and that the poorest are either outright tyrannical or "redistributionist" — based on the philosophy of the handicap. These latter take property in the form of land, assets, and ever-increasing taxes from those who are productive, and give them to those who are not. (In the case of tyrannical nations they claim to do this, but in fact keep the tax — and the foreign aid harvest — mostly for the governing elite.) In less tyrannical social-welfare states, a huge commission is skimmed off for the bureaucratic establishment by means of the tax harvest. *Ironically, this commission, rent, or fee amounts to a bonus system in the form of secure jobs, salaries, and special privileges for those who are inventing and administering the handicapping system!* Their idea is that the stronger you are, the bigger the load you carry. This leads logically to the penalizing of excellence, to underground economies, and to the skewing of natural human values.

Obviously, there is an inherent conflict between the *bonus* and the *handicap* systems, and in Canada we have, especially since Trudeau, slowly de-emphasized bonusing and emphasized handicapping. This can be seen in daily life right from school athletic programs that tend to emphasize co-operative mediocrity, to instituting "quotas" which by their nature overlook excellence, to major government "affirmative action" programs which use the force of law to discriminate officially. A girl like Justine Blainey of Toronto may win a "right" to play on a boys' hockey team, but a boy may not play on a girls'. Internationally, the most famous test of such "reverse discrimination" was the *Bakke* case in California, in which a white student everyone admitted was better qualified for medical school was turned down in favour of a black student because there were not enough blacks to fill the ethnic "quota" for the program. It turned out that the favoured black student had scored below the 50 percent level on the same test on which Bakke scored over 90 percent. Bakke sued the university, and won. Then, one year later, in the separate but equally famous *Weber* case, the U.S. Supreme Court upheld the principle of racial quotas! This was a case of the handicap system beating out the bonus system, and it resulted in society's getting a lower quality product that it would otherwise have got. If you were a patient with an operable brain tumour, which doctor would you prefer? I suspect you wouldn't care what colour the doctor was, as long as he, or she, was the best! Quota thinking, however, always results in what economist Jane Jacobs calls "transactions of decline," because such transactions inevitably end up by lowering standards, production, and quality in everything, everywhere they are applied. Most of all, they lead to the creation of a cynical populace which grows to expect "tokenism," and a double moral standard that accepts mediocrity in some but pretends that it's excellence. The result? A black may be granted a PhD. But did he really earn it? The cynicism that thus flows from quotas does no favour to the black. Rather, it misleads him, and creates a two-tiered value system in society. And our politicians are cynical, too. They know that many of their programs are transactions of decline — but why should they care, if we are blind enough to pay them in votes for such programs? In the long run, all transactions of decline cause such social cynicism, and everyone suffers — especially the poor and the disadvantaged — because as the whole system goes down, they sink the lowest.

Bonus systems are based through and through on inherent support for personal success; handicap systems are based on support for interpersonal resentment and the failure-claims this generates against the body politic.

From an economic point of view, the bonusing attitude eventually results in something the socialists lament, which is the commercialization of every aspect of society, simply because where freedom and the urge to success reign, there are no limits to what can be turned into an achievement. So we get our share of "unnecessary" products like "pet rocks" and Rubik's cubes. Well, why not? To a socialist, these are essentially frivolous items whose production ought not to be permitted or rewarded. But to a culture based on the bonus system, they are just a manifestation of individuality in search of reward, and they occur alongside such inventions as silicon chips. Obviously, productive, achievement-oriented cultures as well as handicap societies also turn out some products later discovered to be harmful, such as Styrofoam (which apparently harms the ozone layer). These, better science, better tort law, and legislation must cope with.

But in the end, probably nothing is so glaringly absent from the whole collectivist/socialist scheme as its failure to consider innovation and risk-taking as factors of production. Take Marx, for example. In *Capital*, he considers labour, rents, and capital as factors of production, but totally leaves out innovation and entrepreneurial risk, as if these would just occur automatically! But of course they don't. In a free society, these are the crucial factors that drive the "creative destruction" (Schumpeter's term for the innovation process) that enables economies to transcend a lower condition and evolve to a higher. Without them, economies decline into stagnation because they are subsisting on dead ideas and produce citizens who shun any form of risk and only buy bonds.

The simple modern proof of this lies in a direct comparison of the U.S.S.R. with the U.S.A. Although the U.S.S.R. has a larger population, and is two and a half times as large in area as the U.S.A., with correspondingly vast resources, it has the most entrenched handicap system in the world, and the results show. The United States, with the most vibrant bonus system in the world, is by far the world's largest food exporter, while the Soviet State cannot provide bread for its own people. It is just a huge Third World country with an impressive army (its chief claim to superior status). The lesson to be learned from all this is that even when a country admits a bonus system, there must be a *structural alignment* between a country's political-economic philosophy and its bonus system, or else it will fail. It will fail if its political and economic system is based outright on handicapping (as in the U.S.S.R.) or, less dramatic but no less fatal (Canada beware!), if there is an inherent conflict between the moral philosophy that made the nation strong in the first place and the subsequent imposition of a handicapping philosophy intended to engineer a "fairer," coerced result.

ECONOMIC ACTIVISM AND THE IDEA OF PROGRESS

IT IS A TRUISM THAT WE ARE all largely captives of our own time, and the most difficult thing is to see outside the encasement of opinions that surrounds us, to see the world as others see it now or as it was seen in the past. It comes as a surprise, therefore, to learn that the ancients, particularly the Greeks and Romans who so influenced the Western world, had generally a static, cyclical notion of history. In other words, the idea of "progress" would have been alien to them, for they imagined the universe around them as a circular, recurring phenomenon, in which the life and death of people, the seasons, and all worldly events succeeded each other in a noble, but endless and interlocking round, governed by the powers of their gods and the special ceremonies of their societies.

This world view was — and remains in many cultures — a primordial response to the awesome power of nature, which held such dominion over men and their world, and served as a mythical and religious fortification against the threat of ceaseless change. At any rate, this static world view led to material pessimism and economic stagnation, for the thought of hoping for "progress," in the sense of change for the better, was contrary to everything such cultures held sacred. (Yes, Greece and Rome created vast empires through power; but simultaneously they spread their secure notion of a timeless, repetitive world.) Here, for example, are a few lines from *The Consolation of Philosophy*, written in A.D. 524 by a famous Roman named Boethius. It was a work that influenced every learned person's attitude toward wealth creation (among other important things) from its publication until the end of the Renaissance a thousand years later! Lady

Philosophy, one of his characters, in what is in effect a teaching dialogue with Boethius, is talking about wealth, and tells him that

> *if all the money in the world were acquired by one man, everyone else would be penniless. The sound of a voice can be given equally to many hearers, but money cannot be distributed among many persons without impoverishing those who give it up. Riches, then, are miserable and troublesome: they cannot be acquired by some without loss to others.*[20]

The modern equivalent of this thinking, so very influential in its time, became the title of a best-selling French book a few years ago entitled *Le Bonheur des uns, fait le malheur des autres* (the happiness of some creates the misery of others). But what such thinking boils down to is what we today call "zero-sum" thinking: the idea that the economic pie is fixed in size, and therefore no one can gain without hurting someone else. Such people never stop to ask themselves how, if this were true, so many nations have become wealthy over the centuries, or what an annual national economic growth of 4 percent really means.

While such an attitude might seem remote from us we should not be fooled. It is very much present in many countries today, and although we say we believe in "progress," it is manifest in our own society. And there is a great difference between this world view and the belief in progress — a difference that has a host of ramifications for the political economy of any nation. Importantly, the idea of progress and the economic activism it implies was slow in coming to centre stage in the West, but this crucial cultural tool of wealth creation was recognized by early traders and entrepreneurs who found their commercial lives — and sometimes their lives themselves — put in jeopardy by the vested interest of the State and ancient religions that propagated the view of a static world.

The way in which Christianity participated in this is well known, so that whereas today it is not unusual to find devout Christians at peace with the values of capitalism, this has not always been so (and the modern Church is increasingly anti-capitalist — see Chapter Thirteen). In fact, there existed a fierce tension between traders and the Christian Church for centuries before the Reformation, for the Church preached against material wealth, riches, pricing for profit, and in particular the charging of interest on money loaned. In mediaeval times, the static idea of history was not outwardly different in its effects on society from that of ancient times, but the combination of Christian beliefs, a static world view, and feudal control of all aspects of society was particularly deadening. This effect, visible in modern socialism, inevitably results in what has been called the rigidification, or the "militarization," of society. (Each was assigned his role in the economic and social structure. A microcosm of this today is "featherbedding" in government institutions and union shops.) This rigidity is only slowly broken down, and then primarily by the concentrated effects over time of economic freedom. The dramatic mirror-image of this today is the breaking down of Soviet-style socialism from the inside out, through the same slow workings of its own primitive capitalism — yet to become democratic. These events are like birthing procedures in which a whole society of caterpillars slowly evolves into a society of butterflies through economic activism.

Historically, the idea of progress seemed to take hold of our imagination during and after the Reformation, in which so many forces in society struggled against government and Church and finally broke free, achieving that all-important separation of the political, economic, and cultural realms of which Novak so eloquently speaks. It was the subsequent joining together of this belief in progress with the dominant values of a Christian society that gave a final and still accelerating burst of energy to the creation of wealth. In other words, once Christians (rightly or wrongly) began to believe that the creation of wealth was an acceptable activity, things really began to take off. The result of this crucially important attitudinal change to a belief in progress was first grasped, as Novak reminds us, by Max Weber in his seminal essay, "The Protestant Ethic and the Spirit of Capitalism," and belief in the *possibility of progress (of all kinds) through economic activism* is now seen as the one crucial factor without which a nation simply cannot successfully raise itself from poverty to wealth.

Examples abound, and here's a personal one. I have a friend who invested heavily in a silver mine in South America (where the mediaeval, static world view still permeates economic life, as it did for three centuries in Quebec until very recently). He calculated everything except the attitude of the people toward work and personal or social progress. He failed, lost a lot of money, and came home. The reason, he explained, was that he knew all the workers in his little town earned only ten dollars per week. He would pay them fifteen to work his mine! The result? They came to work on Monday very happy indeed. He immediately imagined his future success. But on Thursday, no one came to work. Horrified, he discovered that in their view nothing much could be changed with more money, they were going with what they had, and if he was going to pay them more, they were going to work less. He never succeeded in changing something so fundamental. The lesson here is simply that our attitude toward "progress" is a reflection of our attitude toward mutability in general: whether we want to alter our condition as part of an evolving, improving world, or settle for repeating an endless round of materially unproductive (but in themselves perhaps quite satisfying) activities.

THE PRODUCTIVE POWER OF FAITH

I AM USING THE WORD "FAITH" in both its religious and its general sense, because long after a culture has openly ceased to centre itself on religious or spiritual ideals, its life continues to unfold from them, although often in a quite distorted form. Such roots run deep, having grown in the same soil for millennia. So this section is not about churches or organized religion. It is about faith (albeit shaky) and the spiritual attitudes (however distorted) that serve as the source of the majority of our actions and, in a world untethered, still manage to keep us together. It is possible that the success of democratic capitalism *requires* such soil in order to be ultimately successful. Even though the recent success of "the four little dragons," as Hong Kong, South Korea, Singapore, and Taiwan are called, might appear to refute this, they were all formed on Western institutions in their modern period, before which they were exceedingly backward nations.

Also, there are some interesting parallels between Eastern spiritual asceticism and Western Calvinism, which to some extent may account for the East's easy digestion of the economic activism of the West. Weber labelled this aspect of Western thought "inner-world asceticism," in part to explain how those basing their ideals on (Calvinistic) Protestantism went about "earning" goodness.

One of the most interesting requirements of any faith before economic activism can be successful relates to the people's view of the nature of God and His presence in the material world. In cultures like India's, where people essentially believe that God is everywhere present in the material world, we see a reluctance to manipulate that world to material advantage. If you believe that God is present in every blade of grass, or tree, or housefly, you do not harm the grass, cut the tree, or kill the fly easily. This is called "immanentism" by theologians, and cultures where it is found believe that God is everywhere present (is immanent), or indwelling, a part of the entire universe. Such cultures (like those of many of our own North American Indian peoples) in which this belief is strong tend to remain static economically, in part for this reason. They are content with spiritual wealth, and economic activism would threaten the foundation of that spirituality virtually by disturbing the order of God's world. The economic lethargy this encourages is further accentuated if such people also hold beliefs such as reincarnation, or other sorts of fatalism that basically teach them they have no control over their destiny.

Although there is also a distinct tradition of immanentism in the West, it is by and large secondary to our common conception of God and how He may be regarded. We tell our children in Sunday School that "God knows everything," but not that He is part of the chair we sit in, or the beef we eat. Even the prayers of Christian children are imagined by them to be a sort of magical telegraph system to God, who is "in heaven," and who will answer our prayers through symbols (they hope), or (if they are very good) directly. For the Judeo-Christian tradition has evolved from a notion of a God who is everywhere felt, but nowhere seen. He is what the ancients called a "Deus Absconditus," or a not-present God. (Jews believe the Messiah is yet to come, many Christians that he has come and will come again.) Essentially, we communicate with Him through prayer, and we get to *know* Him not directly, as for example an Indian knows his God, but indirectly, through revelation. Ours is a religion of conversion, in which we strive to know God, and then (if at all) experience Him in a sudden spiritual manifestation. (Converts say they are "born again.")

An advantageous feature of such a faith is that it does not implicitly prohibit us from exercising our will upon the material world for our own betterment (environmentalists might say our own ruination). In fact, we have worked out our everyday theology in such a way that we say God expects us to use the world for such betterment and, by extension, for the betterment of others (see Matthew, "Parable of the talents," 25: 14-30). Such a conclusion has not been arrived at easily, and having evolved over two thousand years has resulted in a commingling of the creative energies of Western man with the natural resources of the earth (the "subdue the earth" theme) in such a way that our actions feel consistent with our faith. Thus we believe we labour in a direct or indirect sense *for* our God, and not against His will. A fascinating example of this hangs on the wall of a business friend's home. His family, devoutly Christian, develops large office buildings. On the wall is a picture of one of their forty-storey towers, and superimposed on the photograph is an image of Jesus. I was stunned by the picture because of the way it so neatly summed up the idea of working for God. The difference between the Indian view in which God actually *is* the inviolable tree or plant before us, and the Christian view in which we *transform* such material things to His glory, means everything if you are thinking about economic activism. It's tougher for those who find God already there before they even think of economic activity. But we don't. So we make offerings to Him with the work of our hands, hoping to please Him. You can make the point — difficult to sustain — that this has led to a rape of the environment or, conversely, that it has nourished and fed millions of people who would otherwise have starved, as they are doing daily in many countries without such beliefs in economic activism.

A further aspect of faith well presented again by Novak (who is also a theologian) in his books *The Spirit of Democratic Capitalism* and *Will It Liberate?* is the manner in which Christianity supports competition among friendly rivals, the net effect of which is to raise up everyone through the increase in human excellence, output, and wealth. His is a theological version of the "trickle-down" theory in economics, or rather (an image from another Christian, George Gilder, in his fine book *Wealth and Poverty*) of the idea that "all boats go up in a rising tide."

The reason why Christianity ties in to the promotion of competition is that although it is very interested in "community," it is particularly interested in the individual, and the moral worthiness of individuals, *as earned by those individuals* (through good works, repentance, etc.). This has enormous importance for understanding social policy in the West. For worthiness is not, as under socialist regimes, decided by an elite, or imposed, or only material in nature. In fact, unlike the socialist tradition, the Christian tradition denies the possibility of true community without a focus on individuality. Why? Because Christian values are consonant with the ideas discussed in Chapter One of this book: that each of us must act as a moral agent in life, and that a truly moral society must be formed from the bottom up, not the top down. A society of free individuals, each coming to moral fulfilment in his own right, then supports a full community of similar individuals who are held together, not by some coercive, collectivist ideal and the fear this implies, but by an uplifting common faith in a strong community of values individually and freely upheld. This is the link through Western Christian faith to the idea of competitive self-improvement as the true ground for the creative individual. Even Karl Marx, the most hardened enemy of democratic capitalism, realized that "political democracy is Christian in nature because man in it — not man in general but each man separately — is considered a sovereign and supreme being."[21]

Finally, this in turn is intimately associated with the Christian idea of fallibility, or sin, and the consequent search for future betterment. (Whether or not this is an accurate reflection of these theological grounds is another matter.) Cultures that do not believe in future betterment simply do not believe in the future. They believe in an ever-recurring present. Some of them don't even have a word for the future. But we do, and this, combined with a deep desire to better ourselves as we strive toward that future, provides us with an enormously powerful motive for economic activism. (That some Christians believe in predestination, or some Eastern religions that we are already perfect, does not affect this powerful cultural force in the West.) This is quite a different form of optimism from that found in the minds of socialists, for it finds its expression in concrete personal achievements, quite unlike the abstract utopian concepts of socialism.

One final point to be raised as to the effect of faith on economic activism is the matter of self-denial. To the extent that no nation can accumulate capital for investment and productive expansion without savings, and that savings are a result of consuming less than we produce, wealth comes about in part through *our willingness to postpone present pleasures for future gains*. This is in pointed contrast to the socialist idea that capitalism thrives on greed for profits. For it is only profits that can produce savings, as all else is consumed by expenses. And only savings put aside from corporation or personal profits can supply individuals or corporations protection against emergencies, funds for research and development, or the many other tangible benefits of a successful operation. When the economic activities of entire cultures are informed by such an attitude, as they are especially in Protestant societies, the result is an extremely powerful cultural tool of wealth creation that is threatened by State-imposed disincentives, in particular by social programs that remove the incentives to work, earn, and save.

SUMMARY

HAVING EMERGED WITH difficulty from ancient and mediaeval roots, the bonus system subsequently evolved with characteristics that have been identified, institutionalized, and defended as productive tools of wealth creation. These appeared with particular force during the period now called the Industrial Revolution in Europe. Since that time, these tools of wealth creation have been employed to transform most of the world, through a process now called "modernization." While only some of these tools may be present at any one time or place, the majority will tend to be present in a democratic capitalist system — and necessarily so, for the existence of one depends on the presence of many of the others. This philosophical and structural — we might say "architectural" — integrity cannot remain if certain principal trusses are removed. An attack on the idea of private property, for example, will undermine the entire structure of democratic capitalism — a realization not lost on its enemies.

The thrust of this chapter has been to make apparent the necessary relationship between the ideas, values, and practices that are the tools of freedom and wealth creation, for in the next chapter we will turn to what I have called "the socialist reaction" to democratic capitalism, or the "handicap system," which has its own structural integrity, and thus is enormously dangerous to democratic capitalism. Paradoxically, democratic capitalism, which is successful wherever it has been tried, has millions of practitioners, but as an ideology it has failed to capture a strong following. It has been an ideological failure. Socialism, on the other hand, has been an ideological success, but a practical failure wherever it has been imposed. But this has not prevented utopian thinkers from promoting it vigorously, for their standard response to revelations about this failure is that it has never been properly tried. So we must keep in mind that in the next chapter we will be comparing a system with a practical, measurable, proven record to one which in the minds of its own proponents is imaginary, or utopian, in character, and therefore not falsifiable.

5

The Handicap System
The Socialist Reaction To Democratic Capitalism

If you're not a socialist by the time you're twenty,
you haven't got a heart;
If you're still a socialist by the time you're forty,
you haven't got any brains!

Old European Saying

WE DO NOT FANCY OURSELVES to be an ideologically sophisticated or politically strident people. Rather, we like to think we are "pragmatic." But I fear that pragmatism — the search for practical solutions — may also be a self-congratulatory label camouflaging a national intellectual laziness. I would go even further and say that our pride in pragmatic solutions to political and social problems makes it especially difficult for us to see beneath the surface, and thus we are vulnerable to the *gradualism* relied upon by social engineers. They know that we can be easily distracted by the din and uproar of the game — while they quietly change the rules. With pragmatism as a national philosophy, you can certainly win a lot of short-term battles, but without a solid set of commonly upheld national values, standards, and institutions, you risk losing the war.

The first reason for including this chapter is that I think every Canadian should be able to recognize collectivist policies clearly and early (the better to resist them) as the main threat to democratic capitalism. This act of recognition is made all the more difficult by the fact that such wolfish policies are normally presented to us in sheep's clothing.

The second reason is that so many competent people have told me, first by the frustrated look in their eyes when we touch on this topic and then openly, "I would really like to have a simple grasp of what collectivism or socialism is, so that at least I can converse on the subject, or give my children a decent answer if ever they ask; but I haven't really got the time to take a course . . . " and on it goes. I hope this chapter will meet their personal need, because Canada, as a nation, badly needs people conversant with the main lines of these arguments (although Eastern Europe may currently be teaching us all we need to know).

Of the various forms of collectivist thinking, the one that ought to concern us most deeply is socialism. This is because its whole founding purpose — *the specific, openly stated intention of all honest socialists*, whether revolutionary Marxists or peace-loving dreamers — is to *replace* democratic capitalism with a better, more "just" system of social organization. This has been the ongoing, worldwide struggle of socialists for the past 150-odd years, and is the expressed intent of the Socialist International.[1]

What Do We Need To Know About Socialism?

THERE ARE ONLY FOUR questions anyone living in a democratic-capitalist society ought to be able to answer in order to understand the workings of the system that was specifically designed to replace our own.

- Where has socialism come from?

- Why do socialists complain about our society?

- What are the solutions socialism offers?

- Why is it that socialism doesn't work?

Where Has Socialism Come From?

TO BEGIN WITH, there is an endless variety of socialist views out there, many of which are intellectually interesting in their own right and therefore tend to supply a lot of academics with full-time work. However, although all forms of socialism differ in the *means* they choose, they tend to agree on the *goal* of striving for a better social system than the one that exists in democratic-capitalist countries. But no one has ever created a better system than our own. On Remembrance Day, 1947, Winston Churchill rose in the House of Commons and said wisely, "Democracy is the worst form of government — except all those other forms that have been tried from time to time." It is this utter absence of an attractive real-world alternative that marks all forms of socialism as "utopian." They are only able to complain about our system as compared to a utopian one they insist is possible in the future. Somewhere. Down the road. Financed by others (bring your chequebook). And so it goes. To me, this flimsy basis for social change is the next thing to religious fanaticism and is therefore most dangerous. In fact, many serious scholars suggest that socialism, in this time of declining religious faith, is just a secular mirror of the other-worldly spirit found in all religions. So my aim here is to arm Canadians, through enlightened awareness, against the natural enemy of their traditional values and institutions. To do this, I will have to simplify a good deal.

The term "socialism" as used here will therefore include its other variants, such as "Marxism," "democratic socialism," and "Communism," a generalization for which there is much precedent. As the influential political economist Joseph Schumpeter wrote in his widely praised book *Capitalism, Socialism and Democracy*, "I have not separately defined collectivism or communism . . . but if I had to use them I should make them synonymous with socialism."[2] And this is echoed more recently by one of the world's most lucid writers on political economy, Thomas Sowell, who says, "In the late years of their lives, Marx and Engels used the terms 'socialism' and 'communism' interchangeably . . ."[3] The difference between these two terms, as G.D.H. Cole, chairman of the Fabian Society, pointed out in 1941, "is one of tactics and strategy, rather than objective."[4] In short, the difference is one of degree only. Communists want the same thing as socialists, but they are prepared to get them by revolutionary means. A convenient distinction useful to Canadians who are so shy of the word "socialism" is that the only real difference between the "social-welfare State," which is distinguished by thorough *control* of society, and socialism proper, is that the latter is careful not only to control, but also to *own*, all property. These two terms will be used interchangeably in this book.

But just so that we don't get stopped on such academic niceties, and on the grounds that you can get as badly burned by a campfire as a bonfire, the position I have taken in this book is that *there is a gradation of ideas*, from simple, everyday notions of social justice which make everyone feel warm all over, such as "Everyone should be treated equally," to more complex plans to bring about social justice through outright socialist dictatorship, or even revolution. Because of this *gradation*, it is quite legitimate to refer to an idea such as "universal daycare" (just to pick one of our own hot national topics) as a *socialist idea*, because you can find it alive in Canada today, as well as in most socialist regimes, even though (don't bet on it) the people promoting it may insist they merely want "free" daycare and may be incensed to hear this idea characterized as "socialist." However, it so happens that some of the most blatantly socialist policies in our society have been promoted by so-called "liberals." One such policy is Ontario Premier David Peterson's "pay-equity" debacle, which at first sounds very fair to most, because they think he's talking about "equal pay for equal work." But he's not (this brand of reverse discrimination, courtesy of the State, will be exposed in Chapter Ten). Others are promoted by so-called "conservatives" (Mulroney's government has promoted both the daycare plan and the coercive bilingualism law, Bill C-72). And, of course, almost everything the NDP offers us is intentionally socialist in origin and design — though they try to cover up this fact.

Sometimes all three federal parties even collude in establishing collectivist policies. For example, one thing common to all collectivist governments is the stifling of dissent (whereas open, democratic societies understand its importance). But on October 25, 1983, all three federal parties, after only forty minutes of debate, unanimously passed Bill C-169, which basically threatened all Canadians with $5,000 fines and imprisonment if they so much as dared to publish their personal political views supporting or criticizing any political party during an election period. Introducing the bill, Privy Council President Yvon Pinard said, "Under the bill before the House today, all election expenses shall be made solely by the parties and the candidates who are running."

Although this bill may have been well-intended by its designers, Pinard basically told the people they would be muzzled if they tried to comment on politicians attempting to represent them! This bill was subsequently challenged in the courts by the National Citizens' Coalition *and declared unconstitutional* — yet it was in effect throughout the 1988 election (though not enforced). Even though such obviously collectivist assaults on our system are taking place all the time, most of the people responsible (who parade themselves as liberals or conservatives) would not take kindly to being labelled socialistic for their plans to soak the taxpayer for universal daycare or to interfere forcibly in business life with the most draconian "pay-equity" scheme in the free world, or for colluding to muzzle voters, or co-opting the entire energy resource of a province under a National Energy Program. Nevertheless, especially in the absence of clear ideological positions, it is the *sum* of such political and social changes, gradually introduced, that can result in the complete socialization of a nation like Canada, *without anyone ever using the world "socialism"*!

I am not suggesting that we will succumb to authoritarian, one-party socialism such as exists in communist states. But we may end up with the same dispiriting mess anyway, because our real problem here is that all three parties agree on most of these policies! Therefore, we the people have no choice or alternatives. There is no debate. There is no way out for the voter who disagrees with the way his money is spent. We are disenfranchised. Certainly, our official socialist party, the NDP, avoids the word like the plague. Bob Rae, leader of the Ontario NDP, has even publicly refused to call himself a socialist, despite the fact that his party is a paid-up member of the Socialist International and the long-time federal NDP leader, Ed Broadbent, one of its vice-presidents. Can you imagine? Both Rae and Broadbent refuse to use this label because they know very well that Canadians don't like the word "socialism" or what it stands for. They know that if they call it something else — such as "fairness" or "a policy for ordinary Canadians" — we won't recognize it for what it is and might vote for it.

THE ORIGINS OF SOCIALISM

IT SEEMS THAT ALMOST everything can be traced to the dawn of recorded history, and socialism is no exception. After all, men have always been rightly concerned that their societies should be just and well ordered. And, of course, Christianity itself (like many other religions) supplies us with plenty of concern for the meek of the earth. Warnings against the accumulation of wealth abound in parables about the difficult time any rich man will have getting into the Kingdom of Heaven.

But modern socialism only emerged as a direct alternative to democratic capitalism during the success of, and I'm sure mainly because of, the social dislocations created by the Industrial Revolution. Just before this, around the time of the French Revolution (1789-1803), there were many social theorists who were outraged by what they saw as centuries of privilege, feudalism, aristocracy, and government tyranny. In general, this outrage spawned two distinct philosophies.

The first, we would call "libertarian" today. Libertarians wanted to get *all* government out of the people's lives. This movement is still very much alive today. In fact, in the United States, it is the third-largest political party, and ran 125 candidates during the U.S. election of 1988. It is also alive in Canada, but has a much less significant following here. We will see that many, but not all, of its ideas are shared with classical Liberalism, and true Conservatism — terms I am using carefully, because they've been bent all out of shape today. (See Chapter Six for clarification.)

The second philosophy was that of "socialism," which called for social justice for the masses and intended not to get rid of government but, on the contrary, *to use the coercive power of the State to guarantee social justice*. This decision by socialists to use State coercion to achieve their goals is one of the most telling features of this political movement. It has resulted in a paradox that haunts socialists to this day, because the combination of a religious type of utopian ambition, with the right to use force to achieve social goals, has been devastating for humanity. In short, the very methods of socialism raise the fundamental moral question: How can you achieve justice by unjust methods? You don't need a PhD to know that you can't. But this is the "pact with the devil" that socialists of all stripes have made. They have agreed among themselves to use the force of law, not to *protect* us from tyranny, but to *promote* their own social goals, which can be brought about only through legal tyrannies, small and large. They all agree that it is legitimate to sacrifice freedom for equality. Now, let's turn to how it all began.

THE ROOTS OF THE FRENCH STYLE

THE MOST INFLUENTIAL early socialist thinker was surely Henri Saint-Simon (1760-1825), the first to lay the intellectual foundations of the French style of government outlined in Chapter One. It was primarily under Saint-Simon's influence that the libertarian ideal of establishing a just society for all, free of the evils of the past, quickly became perverted into the ideal of "setting up an elite for the rational *control* of society."[5] Fancying themselves empowered by the authority of rationalism, logic, and the scientific method, Saint-Simon and his followers had a pervasive fear of the dangers they felt were inherent in free societies, with their competitive free markets. Free enterprise struck them as irrational, out of control, and driven only by individual economic greed. They didn't see that the capitalist who tries to please only himself loses, whereas the one who pleases consumers wins; that democratic capitalism is other-directed before being self-directed. To replace capitalism, he "sought to institute a complete monopolization of economic activity under a unified plan."[6] In effect, "it was the chief exporters of the Saint-Simonian system . . . not Karl Marx, who first clearly articulated the goal of a comprehensively planned society: a hierarchical organization of the whole world's industries into 'a vast workshop, labouring under a common impulse to achieve a common goal.' "[7] This is beehive thinking at its best. For it was Saint-Simon who "saw more clearly than most socialists after him that the organization of society for a common purpose, which is fundamental to all socialist systems, is incompatible with individual freedom and requires the existence of a spiritual (meaning political) power which can 'choose the direction to which the national forces are to be applied.' "[8] By this, Saint-Simon meant that such societies would need an elite, educated class to steer their destiny. Welcome to Ottawa, the idea of pervasive central government, and the creation of a new Constitution designed legally to permit and encourage our government to engineer social outcomes!

The growth in government required to bring about such social engineering is staggering, and a typical alarm that signalled this binge was sounded in a 1983 book entitled *Governments Under Stress* by Colin Campbell, who surveyed many governments and many world leaders, but had a field day when he got to Trudeau and his colleagues. Trudeau, he informs us, built an administrative monstrosity, replete with twice the per capita number of advisers used in the U.S. and five times the number in the U.K. Further, between 1975 and 1979, he put Canada through "perhaps the most furtive expansion of central agencies the world has yet experienced."[9] He did this by creating new government agencies like the federal-provincial relations office, the office of the comptroller-general, and the ministries of state for economic and regional development and for social development. That's just one indication of where Saint-Simonian centralist thinking leads. Although Canada's population between 1910 and 1984 only tripled, the number of federal civil servants swelled from 20,000 to a staggering 250,000.

Not to be forgotten (for the English socialists were far from idle when Saint-Simon was at work), across the channel another well-known founder of socialism, Robert Owen, was busy advocating "a national system for the formation of character."[10] But whether English, French, or German socialist, the conclusion historians have reached is that "by about 1840 Saint-Simonian ideas had ceased to be the property of a particular school and had come to form the basis of all socialist move-ments."[11] Other scholars have reached the same conclusion on this archetypal French-model thinker. Historian Leszek Kolakowski refers to Saint-Simon as "the real founder of modern theoretical socialism," and the great historian Elie Halévy called him "the great precursor" of Marxism. Even John Stuart Mill said that he "sowed the seeds of nearly all socialist tendencies which have since spread so widely in France."[12]

When we hear Trudeau, Ed Broadbent, or David Peterson commiserating about the need for a "national industrial strategy," we are just hearing echoes of the Saint-Simonian ideal and the French model. In our government's insistence on constitutionally promoted "affirmative action" programs (Charter — section 15(2)), we hear echoes of Robert Owen's desire for "a national system for the formation of character" or, at the least, for legislation to coerce standardized moral behaviour from the people. Trudeau, like Owen, spoke of "the need to develop new values, and even change our institutions." This is an example of the elite socialist's top-down, dial-a-culture mentality in full flight.

GRADUALISM

ALTHOUGH VERY LITTLE of what passes for "social policy" in Canada can be said to have the sort of clear ideological foundation attributable to socialism proper, a summary glance at the underlying aim of true socialism will certainly help us to spot its weaker, but no less damaging, cousin here in Canada. For the most part, such objectives are achieved here through a process political theorists call "gradualism." In this slice-by-slice technique, the salami of freedom is reduced to nothing over time. The method took its name from the Roman general Quintus Fabius Maximus, who harassed his opponents mercilessly, but never joined them in all-out battle. The socialist Fabian Society in Britain adopted this strategy as a matter of principle in its effort to "permeate" existing institutions with such thinking, thus hoping to achieve socialism without revolution. Wherever gradualism is at work, there is no marching, no manifesto. Instead, objectives are achieved through such things as a pervasive bias toward social welfare in the media, often achieved simply by neglecting the other side of the story as "not newsworthy." An example would be the difficulty experienced by the likes of Professor John Crispo of the University of Toronto when he tried to get the excellent book of which he is editor — *Free Trade: The Real Story* — properly reviewed by the media in this country. Why the difficulty? I suspect because the media didn't want to hear about much that supports free trade, and in particular, they didn't want *us* to hear about it, despite the fact that the book contains serious pro-free-trade contributions from twenty established experts. This is the Saint-Simonian elite controlling the formation of our opinion by controlling the information we receive.

The elite further achieves its objectives through highly vocal interest-group influence, through strategic political placements (Trudeau loaded the Senate with like-thinking collectivist Liberals before he gave up power), and not least through government grants for leftist social policy groups. (There has always been lots of money for the strident "left-wing" feminist group called the National Action Committee on the Status of Women — more than $550,000 in 1987 — but until 1989 not a thin dime for the "right-wing" group REAL Women, which, after endless refusals, finally secured a grant for $21,000.) This is gradualism at work; nice, well-intentioned, effective, and utterly dangerous to popular democracy.

UTOPIA: THE IMAGINARY GOAL

ALL SOCIALIST DOCTRINE is united in expressing dissatisfaction with the existing social order and is pervaded by a near-religious desire for an ideal future society. In this sense, the socialists have an advantage over everyone else. Completely enamoured of an attractive imaginary society, they are at liberty to complain about everything that falls short of this ideal — which everything must do. Until the end of 1989, the most unreported fact of our era was the death of socialism. But this does not bother them. Far from being disappointed, they reply that it hasn't really been tried yet, and get renewed conviction from failure. Such people are termed "teleological," or abstract-goal-oriented thinkers, and they share a quasi-religious mentality in that, like astrologers and parapsychologists, they are attracted to doctrines that are unfalsifiable. You can't beat them with the present facts, for they will plead the future. Democratic capitalist nations measure themselves by achievements; the socialist nations by promises and dreams. The very last words of NDP leader Ed Broadbent before resigning were: "Utopia must be our guide" (*Globe and Mail*, Sept. 29, 1989).

WHAT IS THE SOCIALIST COMPLAINT?

SOCIALISTS DON'T LIKE INDIVIDUALISM

THE SOCIALIST FINDS the philosophy of individualism abhorrent; the idea of a "community of individuals" a contradiction in terms. Individualism of the "enlightened self-interest" variety found in the tradition of democratic capitalism he thinks of as simple, naked greed. The idea of the individual as a moral agent forging a community of freely upheld values he sees as creating moral chaos, a ship with no rudder, or rather a flotilla of ships with no chart. He prefers instead a centrally controlled agenda of political, economic, and moral values designed to permeate society under the stewardship of an elite. If the elite can't reach these socialist goals by moral persuasion, then it achieves them through the courts under a Constitution designed to allow it the extraordinary privilege or overriding the freedoms of other individuals.

The socialist doesn't understand that the *community* of values he prefers can be morally authentic only if it's formed in a bottom-up fashion and freely upheld by individuals. But it is exactly for the reason that all socialist doctrines reject individualism that they are forever committed to other linked philosophical positions. For example, we saw earlier that underlying the belief in individualism, so strong in the West, is the idea of personal responsibility and the moral values inherent in that ideal. But since socialists reject individualism, their idea of responsibility is necessarily social. We therefore find throughout socialist thinking and, I'm sorry to say, in much of Canadian society, something like a rampant "psychology of excuse," promoting the idea that if there is anything wrong in us, this must be blamed not on ourselves, but on our environment.

SOCIALISTS DON'T LIKE THE FREE MARKET

THE SOCIALIST SEES the free market as an extension of all that is loathsome in individualism. For him, it is a free-for-all of competing material desire that can only result in wasted resources and lead to the sort of "business cycle" expansions and contractions he feels are typical of an inefficient economy. He avoids considering the possibility that the greatest cause of such cycles, as we now suspect, is interventionist government policy. The resurgent Chicago "fresh-water" school of economists, as they are called (because they work near Lake Michigan), maintain convincingly that government policies can never react to market crises in time to solve market problems. Only individuals, especially those at risk — whether for a paycheque or for a corporate debt — and intimately involved in market transactions, can do that. With rare exceptions, government efforts to "correct" market conditions are inevitably bureaucratic transactions made for political, not economic, reasons, which therefore send faulty signals to buyers and sellers, and thus function as salt in the wounds of an economy that is otherwise self-healing. Worst of all, government central "planning," with its power gained in proportion to the wealth taken from the people, results in a loss of the "dollar democracy" freedoms exercised by the people under democratic capitalism.

SOCIALISTS DON'T LIKE THE DEMOCRATIC CAPITALIST'S
SENSE OF SOCIAL JUSTICE

FUNDAMENTALLY, ALL SOCIALISTS are united in believing that present social arrangements are inequitable. Some people are born rich; some are born poor. Socialists delight in saying with a cynical smile that under our system "the rich and the poor are both free to sleep under park benches." They will generally argue that the conditions of our lives are for the most part not of our own doing, that wealth tends to end up in the hands of too few, and therefore the State should play a strong and permanent role in redistributing it. They are careful to ignore the fact that, with the exception of the very top level of earners, whom we reward handsomely for their leadership and for taking the risks they do, democratic-capitalist societies have a record for wealth distribution as good as or better than that of any socialist nation (see Chapter Eight). Nor do they consider it important that the wealth created under democratic capitalism is freely exchanged between sellers and buyers, whether individual or corporate; that consumers gladly make certain people wealthy by eagerly purchasing what they have to offer.

Importantly, the lack-of-justice charge of socialists is the most convincing because we are all, without exception, in general sympathy with the truly needy. The crucial difference, however, is that the democratic-capitalist solution to this dilemma of justice is to acknowledge openly that although life may not be inherently *fair* in the sense that we are not all born into the same conditions, let it at least be *free*. For democratic capitalists do not believe that we can achieve greater fairness by stifling, or possibly destroying, the very tools of freedom and wealth creation that have lifted society up by its own bootstraps. The problem is not simply one of equity, but one off overall social well-being. For it helps no one to have a completely equitable but wretchedly poor society; whereas it helps everyone if we have a wealthy even if less equitable society, in which the poor, relatively speaking, are very well off.

The reason for this depressing emphasis of socialists on redistribution of wealth, of course, is that *no socialist has ever produced a practical theory of wealth production.* Marx didn't have one. Saint-Simon certainly didn't. Ed Broadbent doesn't. There isn't one in existence. *Socialists have theories only of wealth distribution.* This sad truth leads us to the conclusion that all forms of socialism are little more than vast parasitical schemes for the redistribution or transfer of the wealth created by democratic capitalism into the hands of those who fancy themselves to have a right to administer or partake of that wealth.

THE ECONOMIC TOOLS OF SOCIALISM

CENTRAL PLANNING

IN 1975, AS IF PROMPTED directly by his intellectual predecessor Saint-Simon, at a time when Canada enjoyed a standard of living among the highest in the world, we heard with astonishment our own Prime Minster Pierre Trudeau say, "We haven't been able to make it work, the free market system. The government is going to have to take a larger role in running institutions . . . It means there is going to be not less authority in our lives, but perhaps more" (CTV year-end interview, 1975).

There you have it. For those sensitive to the subject, this speech might as well have come through a loudhailer from the Socialist International. The primary socialist solution to what they regard as the dog-eat-dog chaos of the free market is *comprehensive State planning* (State-eat-dog). The socialist desires a society that will produce only what government bureaucrats decide people "genuinely" need, instead of what a strong or wealthy producer tells them (through advertising and the like) he has made for them and hopes they will buy, just to make himself richer. It's the *motive* for commercial activity that so irks the socialist. He hates the fact that people buy for what he thinks are artificial reasons (such as vanity, acquisitiveness, power, status, personal hobbies), instead of for reasons that conform to his vision of the social good (helping others, equalizing the goods of society, etc.).

But more to the point, socialists consider all economic activity to be amenable to rational "planning." In a later section of this chapter we will show why this concept is naive. Nevertheless, the idea of rational central economic planning is attractive to many, especially to intellectuals, *because of the efficiency implied in the notion of matching production precisely to consumption* and, by extension, leaving advertising (the lure to false needs) and even profits (the pay-off for greed) out of the picture. Curiously, socialists never ask themselves on what grounds anyone would work hard, invest, take risks, and so on, without profits as a reward. Or how any enterprise can survive without the margin it saves over costs — its profit — to finance research, innovation, and renewal. Of course, some people will produce, sometimes at very high levels, for short periods of time, under the influence of *moral persua-*

sion (socialism pins its hopes on this), especially when lured with promises and dreams of future satisfaction. Revolutionary zeal produces such effort, as do all wars regarded as just struggles by those involved. That's how the Afghans beat the Soviets, despite the latter's calculated savagery. And, of course, there are millions of companies threatened with failure whose managers and employees rally round the cause and achieve remarkable economic recovery.

The only other method that results in a lot of effort expended without material reward is labour under the *threat of force*. (Most socialist, and certainly all totalitarian, systems end up falling back on this after the moral persuasion wears thin.) If you add up all the collectivist systems the world has ever known, this stacks up as the world's most popular method for getting work done. Of course, it also shows up in armies and prisons and in "production quotas" under "five-year plans" in Eastern Bloc nations. But the result, as the Russian people say, is that "they pretend to pay us, and we pretend to work."

Despite its obvious failures worldwide, socialists still plug away at the idea of central planning, an ideological necessity in which they are trapped by virtue of their primary beliefs. The cure for any attraction to this idea is to read a compelling survey of this economic and social disaster — such as Sven Rydenfelt's *A Pattern for Failure*. And if you want a more detailed, complex, and fascinating treatment, try Professor Don Lavoie's *National Economic Planning: What Is Left?*

OWNERSHIP OF THE MEANS OF PRODUCTION

ALL TRULY SOCIALIST SOCIETIES insist that because the root of the modern capitalist evil is private property — in particular properties that produce wealth, such as factories and other large concerns through which they assert that money ends up in the hands of the few — such concerns must be owned by the State, not by individuals. There you have it. By their logic, it all makes sense. Ignoring the crucial role of profits in the production process, they prefer to set up "nonprofit" agencies, for which the burdensome taxes levied to cover administrative and regulatory costs are a form of profit-taking that allows the State to expand.

Trudeau and his cohorts pushed for the nationalization and regulation of major sectors. Canada's energy production was almost destroyed through his disastrous National Energy Program (NEP) — estimated to have cost the nation about $15 billion directly and between $100 and $200 billion in lost entrepreneurial activity — and investment in general was stifled through his counterproductive Foreign Investment Review Agency (FIRA). He established hundreds of other agencies, commissions, and Crown corporations, all designed to control Canada centrally. The present conservative-oriented government (far from truly conservative, as we shall see) abolished many of these programs, has attempted to decentralize government through the Meech Lake Accord, and is slowly privatizing even such "national symbols" as Air Canada. (There is talk Canada Post or Petro-Canada may be next.)

As the pendulum swings from socialism or its ilk to democratic capitalism or its ilk, the Canadian people are swung through repeated rounds of institutional change, enormous confusion and cost, social strife, and perplexity, all because they have never confronted the ideological grounds on which their belief system stands, and truly declared their preference. If they had been more alert, Canadians would have recognized Trudeau's policies as socialist, for their intent was to take the economic means of production or, for that matter, anything of social or economic importance, out of the hands of individuals and turn it over to the control of the State, while taxing us more to pay for it.

REDISTRIBUTION: THE HEART OF SOCIALIST POLICY

AGAIN, ALL SOCIALISTS are united in their desire to redistribute society's wealth so that everyone has equal resources at his command. That's how the vaunted "fairness" is to be arrived at. We must all start the poker game of life with the same hand. But they do not say much about the *differences* between us after the game has begun! They cope with any emergent differences by constantly reshuffling and redistributing the deck as soon as anyone gets ahead — which, of course, ruins the game. If men get ahead of women, or whites ahead of blacks, richer ahead of poorer, stronger ahead of weaker, hard workers ahead of lazy ones, or the educated ahead of the uneducated, that's the government's signal that it's time for a reshuffle. In general terms, the reshuffling technique boils down to handicapping those who are ahead in whatever the race might be.

TAX FREEDOM DAY

IN PRACTICAL ECONOMIC TERMS this reshuffling is achieved through so-called "progressive" taxation, meaning: as you work progressively harder, take progressively larger risks, and earn progressively more money from people who freely pay for your product or services, the State progressively takes more of it away from you. In Canada today, if you calculate the *total incidence of all taxes* on individuals, you will arrive at what is called *"Tax Freedom Day,"* which fell on July 7 in 1989!

This is the first day in the calendar year that the average Canadian finally stopped supporting the government and started working for himself and his family.[13] Canadians ought to be seriously alarmed at the inexorable advance of this date. (We had no income taxes at all before World War I.) At the present rate, a child born today will arrive at Tax Freedom Day about September 15 of his or her first paycheque year! In the socialist scheme of redistribution, it does not suffice simply to *take* money from the rich and *give* it to the poor (although there is talk of this through a so-called Negative Income Tax). The preferred technique is to give the wealth taken from the "rich" to the "poor" not as money, but in services deemed "good for them."

No one keeps track of the enormous cost of this pernicious scheme, which, incidentally, supports civil servants on three levels of government and consumes billions of dollars. John Raymond reported on the disturbing result of the redistributionist mentality as outlined in the Burns Fry Economic Outlook in the *Globe and Mail* (Aug. 26, 1988): "Federal expenditures on various social programs totalled almost 60 billion dollars this year, representing 60% of non-interest expenditures" of our federal government. Of this enormous amount of money (Canada's GNP in 1987 was only $537 billion), "less than 17 billion will go to the poor." And here's the corker: Raymond says that "if you exclude the 6 billion dollars that the government contributes to welfare, *76% of social spending will go to middle and higher income Canadians.*"

THE POLITICAL TOOLS

INTERVENTIONISM: THE MILITARIZATION OF SOCIETY

FROM EVERYTHING WE HAVE said, it follows that in order to achieve its objectives, the socialist-style State must resort to programmatic intervention on a regular basis (thus, a "militarization" of society). There are *economic* interventions such as wage and price controls, rent controls, minimum-wage controls, agricultural marketing boards, and literally hundreds of other specific controls on (and warranted protections for) free enterprise, in the form of regulations, by-laws, licences, taxes, and so on. Then there are *political* interventions such as energy programs, affirmative-action programs, quotas, and pay-equity programs, bilingual programs, medicare programs, and a host of regional-parity measures designed to "equalize" parts of the country that are inherently unequal. Then there are the ubiquitous *cultural* and moral interventions designed to align the people's behaviour and attitudes with State-approved ethnic, sexual, linguistic, and mostly unworkable cultural ideals such as "the great Canadian mosaic" — unworkable not because Canadians are not tolerant, which they seem to be, but because these programs promote foreignness among Canadians. The socialist-style State is proud to intervene, and even considers itself to have a social and moral duty to do so, as it strives to enforce the equal distribution of money, property, and its view of morality.

It is hard for us today to understand that the democratic State was not originally designed to intervene in this fashion. In fact, it was set up by "classical liberals" precisely to *prevent* such meddling in the lives of citizens. For this reason, our philosophical godfather, John Locke, "made it very clear that in a free state even the power of the legislative body should be limited in a definite manner, namely to the passing of laws in the specific sense of *general rules of just conduct equally applicable to all citizens*." [14] We would all do well to memorize that phrase and measure our society against it at every opportunity.

WELFARE AND UNIVERSALITY

SOCIALISM IS NOTHING if it does not help the poor and the downtrodden, for then it would be a failure in its own eyes. In a relatively prosperous society like our own, socialists are thus driven to define ever greater classes of "needy" people. In fact, *socialism needs the needy in order to survive as an ideology* and therefore takes pains to avoid absolute standards of need. Suffice it to say that the continuous generation of more and newer social-welfare programs has become the moral justi-fication of socialism, without which even its most ardent promoters would have to question its naked use of power to extract the wealth of producers for indefensible purposes. In short, *socialism needs welfare far more than society needs socialism*. And what socialism shrinks from admitting is that coercion underlies its morality. It seeks ever greater justifications, the chief of which in our time is the idea of "universal-ity." This is the idea that because the distinction between rich and poor, capable and incapable, lazy and industrious, bright and stupid, moti-vated and unmotivated, honourable and dishonourable, worthy and unworthy, is deemed to be odious — then the handouts go to all, without distinction, under what Brian Mulroney has termed "a sacred trust."

Remember that socialism abhors differences, individualism, compe-tition, or distinction. Everything is calculated to create equality where none would naturally exist. So all mothers will have access to daycare without regard to their need or wealth, and the wealth of families that look after their own children will be generously taxed to provide daycare for those that don't (as distinct from those who truly need help with daycare). It is always possible to define the truly needy. But such distinctions have no part in the universalist philosophy for social programs. (See the *Toronto Star* article, "Money Squeeze Makes Day Care Into Welfare," Oct. 16, 1988, for an example of this whining after "free" social programs.) For socialists today are very "nice" and shun any effort to define the "truly needy," arguing that such an act would deprive the needy of their dignity. But what kind of dignity can be left when we promote the basic dishonesty involved in taking something for nothing? Rather, those who take from others must be defined if they are to be discouraged from dependence, especially on the State. At least this would enable us as a society to help them and not get bled to death by all the well-off feeding at the trough at the same time!

We will see graphically, in Chapter Seven, that this "sacred trust" is well on its way to becoming a "sacred bankruptcy," and that the guaranteed "social security" the social-welfare State is supposed to be providing is resting on financial quicksand. The government attempts to deal with this through so-called "clawback" programs — a round-about bureaucratic way of undoing the initial absurdity. For now, we merely need to know that welfare and universality are two ideological concepts — intellectual necessities, so to speak — of any socialist program, which can be and have been put in place by political parties of all stripes. And thus, as the Fabians say, does socialism "permeate" our institutions.

The Cultural Tools Of Socialism

ATTITUDINAL UNIFORMITY AND THE DENIAL OF DIFFERENCES

Under socialism, enormous amounts of effort and money are expended to ensure attitudinal uniformity, a fundamental requirement of any ideology that sets itself against differences. The more thorough-going the socialism, the more propaganda one is exposed to in this regard. Under National Socialism in Germany, it was everywhere, and resulted in powerful advertising programs orchestrated by Hitler himself to ensure that there would be uniformity of thought and behaviour at all levels of society. In February 1941, he declared, glossing over some important differences, that "basically national socialism and Marxism are the same."[15] One of his most famous posters said, "One People, One State, One Leader." It is this age-old appeal to unity and uniformity on which he played so well, as all such nations and movements do. They must, for their ideologies are built upon this need.

In Canada, we privately abhor such monolithic thinking, while public cultural policy encourages it. For example, even though most Canadians don't want it or need it, they are legally forced and socially stigmatized into promoting the official national use of two languages (with the exception of Quebeckers, whose official language is French only!). This flawed and failing strategy to appease and win votes from Quebec under the cheery guise of national unity is an outright fraud, for it reaches far beyond the simple good manners of allowing Québécois to use French in Parliament and the federal and Quebec courts. Yet to speak out against forced official bilingualism in Canada today immediately invites a volley of unsavoury adjectives. Not one major newspaper speaks out against this intolerable double standard, even though there is just no sense to a national bilingualism policy — for if we were all bilingual, why would we need two languages? But our leaders, all of whom crave the Quebec vote, consider it politically expedient, and use not only shame but also the force of government to compel conformity. (This is quite unlike Switzerland, which is a confederation of unilingual provinces.) In the same fashion, we are forced to use only the State's medical care system (Canada is the only Western nation to outlaw private care), and our doctors are shamed publicly into adherence. No doctor can be paid more than the legislated rate for his services, no matter how much better a practitioner he is than another.

Robert Heilbroner, one of America's clearest socialist thinkers and writers, who has the great merit of honesty, had this to say about how socialist societies create a pressure for conformity of all kinds:

> *Because socialist society aspires to be a good society, all its decisions and opinions are inescapably invested with moral import. Every disagreement with them, every argument for alternative policies, every nay-saying voice therefore raises into question the moral validity of the existing government . . . Dissents and disagreements thereby smack of heresy in a manner lacking in societies in which expediency and not morality rules the roost.*[16]

I think he's got everything right, except his implication that morality rules the socialist roost. For in my view, although the "morality" of socialism is always *verbally* present, it is merely part of the incantatory process of socialism, a chant of moral-sounding phrases to sway the faithful. It is present in language only, and is contradicted by the great immorality of general coercion. Desperate to ensure the denial of differences, and despite its protestations to the contrary, socialism inevitably creates the opposite of the pluralism welcomed by and necessary to democratic capitalism.

STATE-SPONSORED CULTURE

A MATTER OF OBVIOUS IMPORTANCE to all centralist or top-down collectivist regimes is control of the media and of the important cultural avenues of expression. In the absence of complete authority over such matters, democratic socialism seeks to control society through financial control of culture. Furthermore, democracy evolves a spontaneous order, while socialism requires central planning. The phrase "democratic socialism" is of course a contradiction in terms, because once an elite has been "elected," it's game over. Here's a sobering revelation from one of Canada's successful authors, John Metcalf, who once sat on a Canada Council jury. Commenting on the state of culture in Canada, he complains that

> the big commercial publishing houses are subsidized. The smaller literary presses are subsidized. The still smaller regional presses are subsidized. The writers are subsidized. The literary critics are subsidized. Translation is subsidized. Publicity is subsidized. Distribution is subsidized. More bizarre than perhaps anything else, the Writers' Union of Canada is subsidized.[17]

In Metcalf's view — and my own — "the acceptance of subsidy means that consciously or unconsciously the writer is joining the State's enterprise. However arm's length the relationship, the writer is entering into a partnership with the State." And of course, when it comes to the State's motive in offering money gifts to artists, Canada's motive is the same as that of any other social-welfare State. The money is not given to promote literature. It is given, Metcalf continues, "to promote Canadian literature, books which the government vainly hopes will foster a greater sense of national unity and will forge a national identity."

What Metcalf has to say about literary culture holds for every other cultural activity in Canada, much of which is largely an instrument of the State's effort to embellish itself and to give visible justification for what it takes from the people. But what our artists really need, as Metcalf insists, is "to be free from culture," so that they can be free from the State. Literature must be taken away from the State and given back to individuals. Alas, even the noblest souls can be purchased — and it turns out that there are thousands of them: the Writer's Union of Canada has 4,000 members.

There are three basic reasons why socialism does not and cannot work: faulty theory, faulty execution, and faulty morality. Each of these is fascinatingly intertwined. But my only purpose here is to supply readers surely too busy to research the field themselves, with such reasons in a readable and hopefully useful form.

FAULTY THEORY: "THE KNOWLEDGE PROBLEM"

IN A REMARKABLE BOOK on this subject, Don Lavoie lays out in unimpeachable detail the reasons why what he calls "comprehensive national economic planning" can't work. I will be drawing heavily from his important third chapter, entitled "The Knowledge Problem," which I think ought to be required reading for all federal and provincial finance ministers. His basic thesis is that central economic planning can never be successful because it is impossible for any central planner to have at his command the incredibly detailed and intricate "knowledge" (as distinct from the "data") necessary for such a plan. Further, Lavoie states that "it is impossible to achieve simultaneously advanced technological production and comprehensive planning." What he calls "the knowledge problem" is the contention that "a central planning board, even if well-intentioned, would lack the knowledge to combine resources in a manner that is economic enough to sustain modern technology."[18]

THE CHESS GAME

ONE IMAGE LAVOIE USES to drive this point home is based on the game of chess. In a thought-experiment, he asks us to imagine teams of thousands of chess players at a competition. What would happen, he asks, if a coach suddenly asked all players to move the same piece at the same time? Of course, it would be chaos. Every game of chess, just like every market exchange, is different, and though the rules are the same for all players, it's a competitive transaction with infinite possibilities. Only the players are in a position to know best what their next move should be, because only they can complete the game by taking the hundreds of calculated risks necessary to win. The analogy is a good one, because each citizen, *operating under fixed rules of just conduct, equal for all* — our standard for good government — surely must know his own situation most closely, has his own self-interest at heart, and wins or loses each of life's manifold games accordingly.

PRICES ARE KEY SIGNALS

IMPORTANTLY, AFTER MAKING SOUND arguments for complexity, Lavoie then argues that "the function that prices play in a market is a cognitive one. It is to reduce for each decision-maker the otherwise overwhelming number of *technologically* feasible ways of producing things to the relatively much smaller number that appear to be *economic* — that is, those that appear to more than repay their costs."[19] Any political, merely data-based decision that intervenes between buyers and sellers therefore cannot clarify but can only confuse such knowledge-based signals.

KNOWLEDGE VS. DATA

AS HE REVEALS THE UNDERLYING fallacy of centralized planning, Lavoie stresses that data and knowledge are not the same thing. The assumption that mountains of data loaded into our computers constitute knowledge is a booby-trap. It does not, and cannot, for

> *the truly relevant "data" that a planning organization would need . . . resides deeply embedded in and dispersed among the separate minds of millions of people. In the relevant sense of the term, the data do not exist. The knowledge relevant for economic decision-making exists in a dispersed form that cannot be fully extracted by any single agent in society.*[20]

In short, he says, "the Market is the source of that knowledge which rational activity requires; it is thus indispensable."[21] And he adds that even the more modest efforts to guide or steer the market toward particular outcomes (as agricultural marketing boards attempt to do) "are really blind and dangerous obstructions of the very source of that knowledge which is essential to rational economic decision-making."[22] Such interventions inevitably end up subsidizing inefficiencies and penalizing excellence, thus dampening growth and vitality (although such protectionist measure may indeed secure needed votes).

SUBJECTIVE VS. OBJECTIVE KNOWLEDGE

DATA ARE OFTEN MISTAKEN for knowledge because we have uncritically accepted "objectivist" assumptions about knowledge: the view that knowledge is a set of proven, unambiguous facts "completely detached from the particular persons who articulate them."[23] In fact, Lavoie argues, "knowledge is inextricably connected to the knowing subject and crucially dependent on the subject's values and beliefs . . ."[24] This, of course, is particularly true in the fields of business, and economics, where so much of judgement, after the facts are gathered, is based on experience and intuition. Most businessmen are confronted daily with what I call the "conflict of expertise," whereby they gather all the "data" to make a decision and find that the two alternatives are about equal. They then have to rely not on the data, or facts, but on their intuition and personal acumen. The famous scientific writer Michael Polanyi argues that this is true of all fields of human knowledge — even, or perhaps especially, of hard science. This observation ties in directly with the whole bottom-up nature of free activity under democratic capitalism, in which the mass of the people (rather than some elite) is considered the cradle of social and economic intelligence, generating and sustaining values spontaneously in billions of daily transactions, groups, and associations. The amount of knowledge thus generated is simply not available to the central planner. As Lavoie says, "it would be impossible *in principle* [for the central planner] to obtain the sort of knowledge that is required for rational planning."[25]

ARTICULATE VS. INARTICULATE KNOWLEDGE

A FURTHER DIFFICULTY which we have conveniently hidden from ourselves is that the most important knowledge we all hold is completely inarticulate. That is to say, we know it, but we don't know how we know it. Riding a bicycle is a good example of this because even very small children can perform this complex act with no articulate knowledge of *how* they do it. Language is another worldwide example of inarticulate knowledge. All of us can make ourselves understood perfectly well in our native language without needing to have a clue about the complexities of the grammar that we are using.

TRUE KNOWLEDGE DEPENDS ON "WHOLES"

DRAWING FROM THE PHILOSOPHERS Whitehead, Hayek, and Ryle, Lavoie reminds us that all inarticulate knowledge, so important for the formation of decisions, thus relies on circular, or intuitive, "wholes," which form an ever-present, subtly shifting, inarticulate basis for our knowledge of the world. It's not that we don't need facts, but that knowledge of the facts alone does not help. Pushed hard enough, most philosophers and certainly most physicists today would argue that even what we normally refer to as "facts" are subjective bits of reality cut and quartered from our experience. And if this is so, and I think it is, then how can a bureaucrat in some central planning office, with no means of tapping this enormous national network of inarticulate knowledge, make the right decisions on our behalf? Bereft of such knowledge, he cannot. So he does what any one of us would do in the same situation. He makes not an economic but a political decision, and normally and naturally *one that will also advance his own career and the life of his bureaucracy.*

THE PRINCIPLE OF "MASS COMMUNICATION"

IF THE MOST IMPORTANT KNOWLEDGE is inarticulate, how, then, is it communicated? Here, Lavoie compares human mass communication to that of ants, termites, and bees, as there are striking similarities. Ants, after all, build complex communities and accomplish tasks no single ant could perform alone. Yet there is no master ant, smarter than all the rest, directing them. On the contrary, there is a "spontaneous order" of a kind quite common in the biological world, whereby we see an "ordered pattern that emerges without being the product of anyone's deliberate design but only as an unplanned outcome of the mutual adjustment of its parts."[26] This Lavoie terms "a higher level order that evolves out of a furious turmoil of lower level disorder."[27] (This apparent disorder is the equivalent of the free-market activity socialists dislike so much.) For such communication to work, insects use chemical substances called "pheromones" to send each other signals. To achieve the same spontaneous economic order, humans use prices, and "for either of these processes to work, information not only has to be sifted out of pheromone or price signals but must also be injected into them. These signals carry only as much knowledge as has been imparted to them as an outcome of the rivalrous multidirectional tugging taking place among competing individuals."[28]

The key point in this complex but common-sense argument is that "to make all material factors of production common property," which is what Marx and, after him, all democratic-socialist nations want to do, *"would be to deprive the economy of its main source of economic knowledge."* And that's the key reason, from economic theory, why socialism cannot work.

FAULTY EXECUTION: COST, EFFICIENCY, AND TRANSACTIONS OF DECLINE

SOCIALISM COSTS TWICE AS MUCH

IN A REFRESHING little pamphlet entitled *Friedman on Galbraith*, the Nobel laureate Milton Friedman maintains that "there is a sort of empirical generalization that *it costs the state twice as much to do anything as it costs private enterprise*, whatever it is."[29] He says that, in fact, the ratio *is* almost exactly 2:1 for everything examined, and cites the example of U.S. studies done "on the productivity in handling accounts of people in the governmental social security system and in the private insurance system and private commercial insurance agencies." As he puts it, "Lo and behold, the ratio of productivity was 2:1." The same ratio holds for private versus public fire departments, and schools: "In schools there is no doubt that there is at least a 2:1 difference." That is, if you divide total costs of schooling by total students in the public and private systems, you find that private schooling is approximately half as expensive.

Since Friedman made this point, much more detailed work has been done by economists to support his view. In a study done under contract for the Canadian federal government, the economists Douglas Auld and Harry Kitchen summarize a few of the more striking differences between the cost of goods and services provided publicly and privately, as analysed by a wide variety of economists. Of the fifty studies reviewed, about 90 percent supported Friedman's point. Here are a few of them: [30]

Author	Organizational Unit	Efficiency
Davies (1971/77)	Australian airlines	Private 12% to 100% more efficient
Oelett (1961)	Bus Services (West Germany)	Public buses 160% more costly per km
Bennett and Johnson (1980)	Debt collection (U.S.A.)	Government 200% more costly
Ahlbrandt (1973/74)	Fire protection (U.S.A.)	Municipal fire services 39% to 88% more costly
Bennett and Johnson (1980)	Ocean tanker repair (U.S. Navy vs. commercial tankers)	U.S. Navy 230% to 500% more costly than commercial
Crain and Zardkoohi (1978)	Water utilities (U.S.A.)	Public 40% less productive
Bennett and Johnson (1980)	Weather forecasting (U.S.A.)	Government service 50% more costly

Conversely, in *Minding the Public's Business* (table 10-1), the Economic Council of Canada showed the improved profit performance of nine newly privatized British companies: average improvement was about 250 percent! Thousands more such studies have been conducted by economists all over the world.

If we ask how socialism fares internationally as a practical system of political, economic, and cultural production, we find repeated examples of its inefficiency. Swedish economist Sven Rydenfelt's examples of agricultural costs and his productivity comparisons between socialist and private systems have staggering implications. In the view of many such economists, when push comes to shove, the best rule of thumb is how well each system can provide for its people materially and morally. Will they be full-bellied, secure, and free, or hungry, frightened, and half slaves? Listen to Rydenfelt's view:

• "In all poor countries, the peasants constitute up to 90 percent of the population."

• "With few exceptions the regimes in these poor countries pursue socialist policies."

• "The socialist countries of the world are, as a rule, unable to feed their own people. An economic-political system with such a fundamental deficiency must be inefficient and, in the long run, dangerous."[31]

In Chapter Nine's review of foreign aid, we will see just how much hard-earned Canadian money is thrown prodigally at such regimes by Canada's government. For now, here's what Rydenfeldt tells us about the efficiency of the world's largest socialist state, the U.S.S.R., and how well it feeds its own people.

In the United States and Sweden (the world's "model" socialist state, which we will put under the microscope shortly), a mere 3 to 4 percent of the population is involved in agricultural production, while 23 percent of the Soviet people are so involved. However, U.S. and Swedish farmers "produce substantial surpluses for export, while in the Soviet Union approximately one-third of the food supply must either be imported *or produced on private plots which are not included in the Soviet agricultural statistics*." The ostrich mentality implied in this horrendous Soviet inability to feed itself is simply inconceivable to us, but it illustrates how ideological fervour can be a mind-trap for a nation once a monolithic morality is built upon it and a complete infrastructure of lives and careers becomes dependent upon it. Everyone looks the other way.

The Soviet private garden plots are the best — and most embarrassing — example of this. Because of legal restrictions, the average size of such private gardens is only a third of an acre (.02 hectare), yet with 35 million of these, representing only 3 percent of total Soviet cropland (the rest is farmed communally by the State, in a form of wage-slavery), these tiny private peasant gardens turn out fully 27 percent of total Soviet agricultural production annually! It is fascinating but sad to see in operation what amounts to a duplication of the mediaeval feudal system of output whereby the serfs, now owing homage to the State instead of the feudal lord, are virtually paying him in slave labour on communal farms, then turning any leftover energies to private production. The face of oppression has not changed much in the U.S.S.R. Only the labels and the ideas have changed, to protect the oppressors. This is typical of all such regimes (Romania, Ethiopia, and the like follow suit), wherein the output of the peasants is milked dry to support the urban elite that feeds on their energies. Rydenfeldt quotes history's best authority, V.I. Lenin: "If the workers and peasants do not wish to accept socialism, our reply will be: Why waste words when we can apply force?" This is a blunt form of what I call the "coercive humanitarianism" of which we can see more well-meaning but no less immoral forms in all social-welfare states.

So how does this affect us in our cosy Canadian social-welfare state? It's a matter of degree only, for "in . . . the United States [and Canada] and Sweden, most entrepreneurs are still private entrepreneurs. But outside agriculture they are so hampered and burdened by government regulations [inside it they are artificially supported by taxpayers] that they no longer can be labelled free entrepreneurs." What Rydenfelt argues so simply is that the obvious conclusion to be drawn from the world's experience in trying to feed itself over the centuries is that *there is a direct positive correlation between the degree of freedom permitted to private entrepreneurs and the level of national agricultural output.* The direct result of this worldwide historical experiment in self-nourishment is that "the United States is the greatest exporter of food — in the early 1980's it exported 55 percent of all food sold on the world market — while the other, the Soviet Union, is the world's greatest importer of food."

EFFICIENCY AND "PUBLIC CHOICE"

THE PRIMARY REASONS for socialist inefficiency, in addition to the "knowledge problem," are two matters which arise from it — namely, the problem of "economic calculation" and the problem of "public choice."

There is a whole academic industry grinding out arguments and counter-arguments on both these matters. But it all boils down to common sense. If no basic unit of value, such as prices, is allowed in the political-economic system, then economic calculation will be near impossible. Since hard-core socialist theory repudiates the idea of commercial activity and actively attempts to steer an economy by using central political measures, it loses its basis of economic calculation. It substitutes a political basis for an economic one. The very First Principle of Canada's socialist party, the NDP, is:

That Production Shall Be for Use, Not Profit

Economic Activity will be directed to meeting the social and individual needs of the people. It is the aim of the New Democratic Party to modify and control the operations of great productive organizations . . . [to] ensure that economic production will be directed primarily to meeting the economic and social needs of the people and not to the profits of private enterprise . . . The powers and responsibilities of all levels of government, federal, provincial, and municipal, will be invoked to carry the plan to a successful conclusion.

Federal NDP Convention, 1963, T.1.2

Close study of this seemingly humane paragraph will produce a shudder of anxiety in anyone who has ever studied economics, the dreadful track record of socialism, or run even the smallest business. When the NDP says it will "direct" economic activity, it means it will force people to do its will. When it says the powers of all three levels of government will be "invoked," it means that it will create an army of bureaucrats, regulators, and inspectors who will have virtual police powers over private citizens and their enterprises (rent police, pay police, wage police, discrimination police). In Midland, Ontario, we now have even garbage police, as reported in the *Toronto Star* on September 1, 1988: "A garbage cop begins pounding the beat today in this Georgian Bay town." Apparently the town is now forcing residents to "recycle" their garbage or pay a summons for costs. Well, I really don't like using the word "police" to describe these people. But every other word just camouflages what in fact are their true powers. They are not merely "inspecting" or "reporting": they are actually enforcing and punishing. But what does "directing" an economy mean?

It means you lose your basis of economic calculation in direct proportion to your attempts to direct the economy by political means. For political and economic signals are mutually exclusive. The reason for this is that political decisions, even those made by the lowliest bureaucrats in the system, have a different "economy" from true economic decisions. Their economy is designed to make the directing agency itself work best, not what it directs. To expect otherwise would be to ask for a result contrary to human nature. As it turns out, the bureaucratic equivalent to the profit motive is *size*. For with growth in government come more power, bigger budgets and, of course, bigger salaries for those in control of this growth. How could we expect to set up a world in which people unanimously and coherently make decisions against the best interest of their own political organization? The world's most famous "public choice" theorist, the Canadian-born 1988 Nobel laureate, James Buchanan, says:

> *Even if the socialist state should somehow discover an oracle that would allow all calculations to be made perfectly, even if all preference functions are revealed, and even if all production functions are known with certainty, efficiency in allocation will merge only if the effective decision-makers are converted into economic eunuchs.*[32]

In other words, even if the fundamental difficulties implied by the "knowledge problem" are solved, a social-welfare state cannot generate efficiency unless "men can be trained to make choices that do *not* embody the opportunity costs that they, individually and personally, confront." Socialists would need to create an anti-world to succeed in their goals. Which is just what they have tried to do. For "the idealized manager of the socialist enterprise must be assumed to act solely on the basis of nonindividualistic criteria" — a tall order for anyone. The result of this conflict of principle inherent in the two systems? "Nonmarket choice cannot, by its very nature, be made to duplicate market choice until and unless the ownership-responsibility pattern in the former truly matches that in the latter, an achievement that would, of course, eliminate all institutional differences between the two."[33]

What Buchanan says basically reinforces what the entire democratic-capitalist system since Adam Smith has been implicitly saying over the centuries: that only "the natural system of liberty" will result in the greatest good for the greatest number, without the need to stoop to the immorality of coercive humanitarianism. Now, "the greatest good for the greatest number" is also the goal of all socialists. What divides the two camps so radically is the *means* used by each. Democratic capitalists want this social result to flower naturally. The socialists want to force the flower; but they kill it in the forcing, and the well-being of everyone declines as a result.

SOCIALISM GENERATES "TRANSACTIONS OF DECLINE"

SUCCESSFUL ECONOMIC ACTIVITY has its own tools and internal logic and will be a success or failure according to the use of those tools and compliance with that logic. It so happens that most of us have been taught to think of economic activity as a *national* phenomenon. But Toronto's own Jane Jacobs, in an absorbing book entitled *Cities and the Wealth of Nations*, convincingly argues that the process of wealth creation has little to do with the lines on the map that confine the nation, but a great deal to do with the economic and trading relationships within and between cities, the basic engines of wealth production. Of course, nations get involved in economic transactions in a major way, and can *accelerate* a process of growth, or decay, according to their style of government. But they do not *produce* the wealth. People do that. And people doing that live in cities of all shapes and sizes which have vital intercity trading relationships that can be growing or decaying according to the types of social, economic, and cultural policies promoted by the people and their governments. In Jacobs's convincing view,

> the very policies and transactions that are necessary to win, hold, and exploit an empire are destructive to an imperial power's own cities and cannot help but lead to their stagnation and decay. Imperial decline is built right into imperial success.[34]

In her most important chapter, "Transactions of Decline," we learn why successful empires "become too poor to sustain the very costs of empire." In a nutshell, it is because once cities become strong and wealthy, they enter into too many political, economic, and social policies that amount to transactions of decline in which the wealth created by a productive part of the empire, or nation, is siphoned off to support a weaker, unproductive part. If you like, this is how they cope with the regional strife generated by envy. This is the price such empires or nations pay to sustain their unity. Welcome to the modern empire of Ottawa. Behold, our national strategy to achieve unity by appeasing poor regions and, particularly, Quebec.

Until such a point in the history of a nation is reached, the major tool of economic expansion operating both between nations and between cities within nations is a phenomenon Jacobs calls "import replacement," whereby dependent economies progress to *creating* finished products, instead of *importing* them. Briefly put, this is a process with three "master characteristics" in which: (1) economic life becomes more urbanized and less rural; (2) former subsistence regions and supply regions are drawn into volatile city trading networks; and finally, (3) increased quantities of all goods and services are sucked into the great cities and subjected there to the upward spiralling process of import replacement (requiring more sophisticated supplies from the formerly backward regions, which in turn become sophisticated, now creating products they formerly imported, and so on).[35] In short, it is only when trading cities (towns, villages) begin to replace their imports with products and services created by themselves that true, stable wealth creation begins, leading, "in swiftly emerging logical chains" to an upward spiral which provides a myriad of positive economic after-effects. Economic life begins, she tells us, by innovating, but it expands by import replacement.

The most vivid example of this has occurred in modern times in Japan, which has not only replaced its own imports, but now floods us with exports. Canada's own level of import replacement is poor, and not likely to improve a lot because of the transactions of decline we wholeheartedly enter into, which have the effect of skimming off earned revenue from the strong areas of the country and pouring it into the bottomless and unproductive pit of "regional equality." That revenue could have been used by producers to manufacture goods to replace certain imports. The most prevalent transactions of decline in history, however, have been military spending to support far-flung empires; Canada has so far been spared this. But virtually all large nations have internal "empires," constituted by relations between their major cities and their "hinterlands," or supply regions. For these, the second-most prevalent transactions of decline are welfare and regional-support policies, and in our race to create the perfect social-welfare state we have become masters of this kind of transaction. In fact, we are "the only country in the history of the world that has enunciated regional economic equality as a national objective and constitutional purpose."[36] But, as Jacobs warns us,

> *welfare programs [that aim] to bring standards of living and services in poor regions into line with those of prospering city regions unfortunately also work out as transactions of decline. If*

*they are unremitting, they too drain city earnings unremittingly. If
they are at all generous, then if anything they are even more
voracious feeders on cities than military programs.*[37]

In countries like Canada, it is "the hundreds of varieties of national
insurance, welfare benefits, and special grants and subsidies that are
now distributed" that push us into decline. But even "agricultural price
supports and other agricultural subsidies are analogous to welfare
programs in drawing upon city regional economies to support poorer
regions." So how does this result in decline? Very simply,

*the discrepancy between what any individual city and its region
pay toward national or provincial welfare, agricultural and other
subsidy programs and what they receive back represents losses of
earnings diverted . . .* [38]

And it is not as if these transfer payments add to national wealth, for
the

*goods and services the subsidies buy turn up, just as military goods
and services do, at destinations which don't and can't replace
imports with local production. Nor does receiving subsidies —
unearned imports — help them become capable of doing so. Not
being earned, these do nothing to promote versatility at producing
in subsidized economies.*[39]

In short, such social-egalitarian manoeuvres are sumps of wasted
money that merely buy time for central governments and create
mounting debt which they are ever harder pressed to service, let alone
repay, as the claims of the nonproducers mount and the dollars from
producers dwindle relative to these claims. This is especially true if
there develops a demographic shift such as we are now experiencing,
in which the ratio of young producers who pay the taxes, to older people
who claim the benefits, alters swiftly. Such debt then must be serviced
by the inflationary governmental practice of increasing the money
supply faster than the productive capacity of the nation, by further
long-term borrowing, and often by currency adjustments — in general,
by asking future generations to pay for present excesses. All these
methods are what I have called the tools of wealth destruction, and they
are inherent in that slow, downward-spiralling process. In fact, if you
were asked to destroy a free-world economy, slowly and deliberately,
these are the very tools you would invent.

The reaction of the socialist to this revelation is usually disbelief, for, as Jacobs writes,

> it seems unfair that programs undertaken out of compassion or to combat the injustice of poverty in regions that remain obdurately poor should unwittingly work as instruments for spreading stagnation and deepening poverty. But one might as well say that it isn't fair for unfertilized soil to deplete itself when it is exploited to feed the hungry rather than for less defensible purposes. The soil doesn't know the difference; neither do city economies being drained of the nourishment they need to remain creative and productive.[40]

But many of us are more cynical about State compassion, and believe that "large nations plagued with active or latent separatist movements use subsidies to contain restiveness and discontents," and that "subsidies, precisely because they are transactions of decline, are economic time-bombs."[41]

The Western world has witnessed the destruction wrought by many such time-bombs in the decline of the Turkish, Spanish, Portuguese, French, British, and now, it seems, American and Soviet empires (including Canada's "internal" empire) — all bled of revenues to finance expansion, war, welfare, and regional equality; all by depressing "volatile intercity trade in favour of city trade with inert economies."[42]

Canada, we can see, is now constitutionally primed for a difficult trip into the future. Choosing my words carefully, I would say that rarely has a wealthy nation so cheerfully, so un-self-critically, with so little learned from the past and so scant a concern for the future and for the loss of personal freedom, so smugly launched itself on such a wide-ranging orgy of transactions of decline in the name of justice and equality.

SOCIALISM'S FAULTY MORALITY

SOCIALISTS WILL OBJECT most of all to this section of my critique. And for a reason. They have been unable to sweep the evidence under the carpet. There are three basic forms of immorality, or sin, under socialism. These are what I call the Sin of Coercive Humanitarianism, the Sin of Elitism, and the Sin of Repression. The first two are the stock in trade of all social-welfare states like Canada, or Sweden. The last sin gets thrown into the mixture with true totalitarian socialism of the kind that exists in much of the world.

COERCIVE HUMANITARIANISM

THIS IS A PHRASE I use to describe what happens when governments try to reconstitute human life by reshaping their legal and political institutions, giving them the power to secure equal social outcomes for the people, who, because they are different in infinite ways, would never arrive at this state of "equality" on their own. Since it is apparent that they would not and, furthermore, would not *want* to, *the State must coerce the people to create the humanitarian society* it envisages. All socialists, or social-welfare policy types, are therefore confronted with a moral dilemma: Can immoral methods be used to bring about moral results? My answer is a resounding "no." And why is this so? Because in order to give to one, you must take from another. Whether what is taken is money or individual rights and freedoms, there is always a debit and a credit side to egalitarian programs. Either one hard-working person is taxed to support an unproductive person or one person's freedoms are reduced to give another some right he has not earned. No government can win at this game, for it will always alienate some to please others, and will thus set in motion long-term social divisions created by political favouritism or the fashionable social-policy theory of the day. In such a game, no one is safe, and any innovative, productive, successful, or just plain different individual becomes a potential target for the legalized levelling process, which is normally brought to bear through taxation or social-policy legislation on millions of Canadians. When we realize, as mentioned earlier, that 76 percent of Canada's social spending is going to middle- and upper-income earners, we must ask what kind of social-policy game we are funding. *Is it good for society, or is it merely good for government?*

ELITISM

IN 1957 A YUGOSLAV diplomat named Milovan Djilas wrote a book called *The New Class*. It was about the way in which his supposedly egalitarian socialist country had quickly evolved, through coercion and terror, into a nation split into two distinct classes: the governed, who had always existed, and the new governors, who reaped considerable benefits from maintaining their hold over the people. Exactly as Buchanan theorizes in *Cost and Choice*, these people become hardened career bureaucrats who manipulate the system to aggrandize themselves and their colleagues at the expense of the people, and they maintain control through law and terror, eating up the nation's resources as they do so. In addition to the sin of coercion, such new bureaucratic classes are guilty of the sin of elitism, a fault common to all socialist regimes. Those who are structuring and controlling society have both a utopian idea that guides them and a large class of people whom they in turn are guiding by the light of this higher vision, a vision that eventually erodes into a cynical, opportunistic front for career-building financed by others.

Here's how Ontario Premier David Peterson reacted on the telephone when I called to criticize his "pay-equity" program on similar grounds: he became hopelessly intellectually snarled when I told him why the foundation for the whole program, the so-called "wage-gap," was a dishonest statistic. He concluded the call by saying, "It's a matter of social policy." What he meant was, a matter of "appeasement." Of course, all government is about the use of power. But what distinguishes all forms of socialism, from our own to the most totalitarian, is the widespread use of that power and its institutionalization as a tool of "social policy" without regard to the fundamental freedoms of the people.

I am not saying that Canada is the U.S.S.R. But I am saying that the traditional glory and strength of our nation has been its foundation in principles and values diametrically opposed to those of such hardened socialist nations, and that flirtation with the socialist abuses of fundamental freedoms such as we are now seeing in Canada is a fateful step in the wrong direction. This is the only context in which I am happy that we are an ideologically unsophisticated people, for hardened ideologists are far more dangerous than our appeasement-oriented leaders. Ideologists are like sophisticated engineers who know very well how to change a car into a boat. Our Canadian leaders, on the other hand, saunter in with a wrench and mess around with the car until it stops working.

REPRESSION

THERE IS NO NEED to dwell on this, except to say that the logical, historical, and actual end result of all socialism is the use of repression, in one form or another. For most thinking people, the real-world evidence is sufficient to damn socialism in all its forms for the rest of human time. But people enamoured of a utopian ideal find their critical faculties overshadowed by zeal, so that the means they use always justify the ends they seek. For all forms of totalitarian socialism, there have been the obligatory *gulags* created for dissenters and individualists. For the rest of the herd, there are walls. The vaunted "building of socialism" around the world has been mostly wall-building of one kind or another. Institutional walls, barbed-wire walls, guard-dog walls, passport walls, internal-security walls, poverty walls, and so on.

When an American organization called Freedom House classified the 160 nations of the world in terms of their "degree of freedom," not a single hard-core socialist country enters the top ranks (Canada does). Nevertheless, in "free" social-welfare states like our own, the same regulatory/bureaucratic/discriminatory/redistributionist barriers are in place, doing much the same job of generating dependence. But freedom and socialism are inherently incompatible, and the severer the socialism, the less the freedom. There is no point in going on about the death and destruction this has wrought in socialist countries, except to say that the carnage and cruelty of socialism — all from a political philosophy that promotes humanitarianism — overshadows that of any other form of human tyranny. If you wish to get a thorough picture of the workings of such tyranny in this century alone, Paul Johnson's magisterial book *Modern Times* will provide it in awesome and eloquent detail, and cure you forever of any flirtation with socialism or any other form of collectivism from left or right — one's as bad as another.

A lazy critic might say that these assertions about the sins of socialism are based on a personal dislike of the social-welfare state. They are nothing of the kind. I am not claiming that Canada is about to undergo a revolution that will turn it into a collectivist state like the Soviet Union. But in political affairs there is either revolution or evolution, and I am concerned about the direction of Canada's evolution. I see our elitist leaders toying with political, economic, and cultural tools of wealth destruction that are slowly eroding the traditional, strength-giving foundations of this nation. While I think it unlikely we will ever commit the ultimate sins of the totalitarian socialist nations, I never thought we'd see the thoroughgoing type of Canadian socialist programs we are now committed to, either. But they are here. A relative of my neighbour's who was visiting from the Latvian Soviet Socialist Republic underlined this when, after a few weeks here, she said with astonishment, "You are more socialist than we are!" I think Canadians should be conversant with the fact that all types of socialism are based on the same ideology, the same immorality masquerading as humanitarian "fairness," the same coercive strategies, the same elitist control of the electorate. The difference is one of degree only.

A Brief Look At Sweden

INEVITABLY, WHEN DEFENDING SOCIALISM, its proponents cite Sweden as a model socialist state. It is usually the only case anyone dares to cite, although, strictly speaking, it is not truly socialist. It is a social-welfare State in which close to one half of society administers the lives of the other half. For good measure, I am going to set out here a few insights from two very brief articles by Professor Eric Brodin describing this "model State." Brodin, now a naturalized American, is a native of Sweden and a professor of philosophy. Readers interested in the Swedish case are encouraged to acquaint themselves with his work, with the journalist Roland Huntford's chilling book, *The New Totalitarians*, and perhaps most rewardingly, with David Popenoe's *Disturbing the Nest*, which makes the point that such societies are perfectly capable of trudging along for a long time and that before real economic break-down occurs (often triggered by an exterior economic trauma), there is widespread internal breakdown of social mores and particularly of the family. Take careful note, for I believe that Canada is marching straight into the waiting Swedish straitjacket.

Brodin draws a useful distinction between true socialism, in which the state *owns* everything, and what he calls "the social-welfare State," in which it doesn't *own* everything but *controls* everything, primarily by means of legislation and taxation, which is the Swedish case. In other words, it might as well own everything. He tells us that even the architects of Swedish socialism, Gunnar Myrdal and his wife, Alva, felt as long ago as 1932 that if socialism did not succeed in Sweden "it would probably not work out anywhere else." This is because of Sweden's uniqueness in having an unbroken peace for over 150 years, being highly industrialized, racially homogeneous, rich in natural resources, and so on. Summarized below are the results of that experiment as reported by Brodin, first from an article published in 1980:[43]

• Swedes pay the highest taxes of any people on earth.

• More than 64 percent of Gross National Product (GNP) goes to financing the public sector.

• Sweden in 1980 had an additional Value Added Tax (VAT) of 22.5 percent (higher today) that basically taxes *all* stages of every transaction whenever value is "added" to a product or service. All social-welfare states eventually resort to these in their drive to feed themselves. (Finance Minister Michael Wilson has introduced a new "goods and services" tax for similar reasons.)

• The only expanding sector of the Swedish economy is the underground economy. As a result, "Sweden is becoming a barter society."

Myrdal himself feels that because of bad tax laws, Sweden is "becoming a nation of cheats."

• On any given day, 10 percent of Sweden's workforce is legally away from work on one or another kind of subsidized leave (up to 20 percent on Mondays and Fridays!) totalling four million days lost per year.

• One-third of the workforce is employed by government. (Canada is closing in fast.)

• Budget deficits grew from 649 million Swedish crowns in 1960 to 50.2 billion in 1980, over 40 percent of which are transfer payments from strong regions or classes to weak; from productive to unproductive (transactions of decline).

• Dr. Sven Rydenfelt has exposed the myth of "full employment" in Sweden (officially 2 percent unemployed). When he calculates the numerous "make-work" and subsidized job programs, he says that "if these items are added we find a total of 11 percent unemployed . . ." While private-sector employment went down by 100,000 jobs between 1975 and 1980, public-sector employment went *up* by 250,000 in the same period!

• Curt Nicolin, chairman of the Board of the Swedish Employers' Association, said in 1979: "It is high time we comprehend that we are under severe threat . . . we, like sleepwalkers, have moved straight into an economic crisis so serious that we must count on social unrest and the loss of freedom for most of us."

Here is my summary of some insights from an article Brodin wrote in 1987, entitled "Sweden's Empty Smorgasbord":

• The economic situation of Sweden today is desperate, a fact which is not associated with Sweden in international public opinion.

• He quotes from Professor Erik Dahmen's article, "The Swedish Economy: An Ignored Scandal," as follows: "The Swedish model for economic policies and the Welfare State has for much too long been spoken about on very loose foundations. We ought to be ashamed of 'the Swedish scandal' and allow this sense of shame to lead us to a reasonably intelligent conduct of our actions in the future."[44]

• Between 1976 and 1982 Sweden had major currency devaluations (totalling 45 percent!), and accumulated a large foreign debt at the same time, not to finance future development, but for current consumption!

• 33 percent of Sweden's population, in effect, provides productive work with its resultant wages and taxes to support the remaining 67 percent of the population.

• The public sector's proportion of total national income increased from 50 percent in 1975 to 67.4 percent in 1982. No nation which hopes for economic growth can exist under these conditions for very long. (In Canada, government already consumes about 50 percent.)

• Swedish "absenteeism" is a national scandal. The average Swede is off work "sick" for 23.4 days per year. (Canadians average 6.4 days.) Also, 500,000 Swedes — known as "early pensioners" — claim physical or psychological illness. A third of them are under 49. Major Swedish companies report 21 percent *daily* absenteeism — double for women! (*Financial Post*, Oct. 2, 1989.)

Although Sweden has been the dream model for socialists of the Western world, we can see that its condition is far from admirable and that this moribund condition has resulted from the surrender of a host of individual rights and freedoms, and a disastrous decline in social and family cohesion: " 'Freedom' in Swedish is a word that appears to be taboo. It does not exist in the political vocabulary, and it is rarely mentioned in everyday language, in spite of the advancing regimentation of the country."[45]

In his book *Disturbing the Nest*, David Popenoe shows the impact of the social-welfare State on society and particularly on the family. Sweden is highly atheistic — only 27 percent say they take strength from religion, compared with 79 percent of Americans (information not available for Canadians); it is the Western world's most apartment-oriented society; Swedish social policy has focused not on the family, but on the autonomous individual. Sometimes mistakenly called "individualism," this is really "autonomism." True individualism, self-reliance, responsibility, and so on is the bulwark of democratic capitalism, while a State-created autonomism, mostly interested in subsidized, equalized independence and self-satisfaction, is the ideal of the top-down collectivist State.

The State can always control single persons, but families, which are ever shifting and which create a private, nuclear loyalty, are harder to influence. Thus, Sweden has developed social and tax policies specifically designed to break down the family, and the State specifically intervenes in family life. In 1981, Finnish authorities took 552 children from their parents for reported "child abuse." In the same year, Swedish authorities, from a population only one-third greater, took 22,000, and were criticized internationally on the grounds this was not "child abuse," but State control of families. *Sweden is the first Western nation to have the majority of its voters dependent on public funds* — and thus beholden to the hand that feeds them. Sweden also has the lowest marriage rate in the industrialized world. Nearly half of all children born in Sweden today are to unmarried parents. About 36 percent of marriages end in divorce, and the dissolution rate for cohabiting couples with one child is three times that of married couples, giving it the highest "family dissolution" rate among advanced societies. Sweden also has the smallest average household size and the highest percentage of single-person households in the West. In 1980, 33 percent of households contained only one person — 63 percent in Stockholm. Along with the decline of family life, marriage, childbearing, and the generally alienating "age-stratification" of Swedish society has come a complete decline in volunteerism and private charity.

Such losses as the Swedes have surrendered for the security they love we would normally consider outrageous in Canada. But the Swedes don't. And tomorrow, our children won't, either.

CHAPTER

6

The Political Parties
Where They Stand And
What They Stand For

NOTHING QUITE EQUALS the naked confusion that dances in the eyes of an otherwise competent person when he is asked what he thinks his chosen political party *really* stands for. What were and are its underlying principles, beliefs, and standards (as distinct from its promises), and its plans for acting on these? Such conversation-openers are usually unproductive and lead to hostility. Embarrassment is followed by doubletalk, which is followed by a hasty change of subject or retreat to a comparison of political personalities. Political choice in Canada, especially since the advent of television, has become a media event, while public awareness of the underlying ideological motives of our political parties is sadly neglected. Through this neglect, we have left ourselves exposed to the emotional manipulation of political events by the parties and the media in a daily drama that hides the truth. The result of this neglect of principles is what I call "prostitution politics." The parties have got the electorate trained to relate to them in the way a customer relates to a prostitute. The story goes like this: A man arrives at an intersection, and there is an attractive prostitute on each of the other three corners — an NDP, a Liberal, and a Progressive Conservative prostitute. With his mind made up to have the best time he can for his fifty dollars, he quickly discovers that each will compete with the others to promise him the most for his money. The decision is not too difficult, because he has already decided to go with the one who persuades him that her list of benefits is best, regardless of any other virtues or vices present. This story changes considerably, however, if he has come to the corner seeking not only a good time, but also a good wife. Suddenly, in addition to his interest in sex, he wants to know about long-term conduct, morals, principles, character, and all such matters that distinguish the good from the bad, the temporary from the durable, the true from the false, and so on. In short, his questions, and the answers he expects, are now very different indeed. "You get what you ask for," as they say.

The parties have behaved like prostitutes, and we, the voters, have been acting like naive customers with short-tem self-interests, turning a blind eye to the fact that inevitably we will have to pay for everything. We recklessly vote for programs we are encouraged to believe are "free," without regard to the burden these place on our children's futures, to the kind of nation we ought to be building, to the freedoms we've surrendered without a struggle, and so on. So they've got us trained. Or to be fairer, we've got each other trained. We deserve each other! And I think it's high time we faced the fact that it's a rotten relationship that can only end up on the rocks.

But a political prostitute won't start behaving like a good spouse until we require it by asking different kinds of questions and making it known that we expect answers of a certain quality — or we're not interested. The only way this will be possible is if the electorate knows what *principles* the parties stand for and can then relate the wild *promises* they make to these principles. Are they just putting a wet finger to the wind of political expediency or are they steering a true course, regardless of the wind? Are we getting more Band-Aids, or a true cure, in keeping with the party's ideals? I hope anyone reading this chapter will afterward feel abler not only to distinguish between the parties, but also to place them in a political spectrum that is communicable — and judge behaviour accordingly.

WHAT DO THE PARTIES STAND FOR? — A GUIDE TO POLITICAL LITERACY

THIS IS A TOUGH ASSIGNMENT, but in the space of a few pages I will try to give an overview of what the political parties stood for in the past and stand for, or fail to stand for, today. Over the years there has been considerable shifting and changing of political *philosophy* in the interests of expediency, but very little change in political *labels*, so this guide will be structured into a "Classical" and a "Modern" section.

People who mourn the loss of principles in politics can often be heard describing themselves as a "classical" something or other, mostly because they've decided they do not fit into any of the available modern political moulds. I certainly feel this way, and perhaps you do, too. Here in a nutshell is a survey of the three classical options, none of which exists today in its pure form, although this does not prevent present-day politicians from characterizing themselves in this fashion or from citing these traditions when they want to impress voters, most of whom, they know too well, have long forgotten the values on which these traditions were based.

THE CLASSICAL LIBERAL

WHAT IS CALLED "CLASSICAL," or "true," liberalism emerged with force near the end of the eighteenth century, after a period now called the Enlightenment, which was characterized by a high enthusiasm for science and rationality and the possibility of finding an ultimate solution to the problems of organizing society. Like its cousin, classical conservatism, liberalism preceded Marxism and the social-welfare State by a good margin. It declared with confidence that mankind would prevail in establishing a just and free society. For the ideological foundation of classical liberalism was "the assertion that the fundamental value to be recognized and respected in all political arrangements is the exercise of individual liberty."[1]

The defence of individual liberty has venerable roots in the works of a host of political philosophers important to our tradition, such as John Locke, John Stuart Mill, Jean Jacques Rousseau, and recently John Rawls, Robert Nozick, and a large group of "libertarian" thinkers (considered below). It is further based on a number of "natural rights" and beliefs that form the basis for individual liberty, such as property rights, privacy, free association, secession, self-reliance, and responsibility, which were outlined in Chapter Four. In a nutshell, the classical liberal venerates *the morality of individual responsibility, under limited government with equal opportunity and just rules of conduct for all under the law.*

If you were to memorize that sentence, you would have a perfect capsule description of the central political ideal that has shaped Western civilization, and which is now so sadly under attack on all fronts. Used as a test of political freedom, this standard will relentlessly expose everything from petty to major tyranny.

It is fashionable today to argue that Canadians are different from Americans in this regard. Political philosophers here are unanimous in their belief that "Canadian liberalism is based in a historic and traditional sense of community that contrasts starkly with an almost religious stress on individualism in the United States."[2] Americans, we like to say, are guilty of "rampant individualism." I find extremely objectionable this assumption that Canadians are inherently superior in feeling and generosity. First of all, it is clear on the face of it that we are not. Even though both nations provide a vast range of social services for the disadvantaged, individual Canadians give, as a percentage of GNP, less than half as much to charity as Americans, as do our corporations. Further, it is clear that our vaunted sense of community can as easily be described as a wimpish lack of moral fibre that has resulted in a national surrender of personal as well as communal responsibility to the powerbrokers of the State. Clearly, Americans have resisted this encroachment of the State more vigorously than we, and rely more on personal, family, and community charity — a stance we should praise, rather than criticize. At the least, let us resist the smug promotion of our weaknesses as virtues — especially by philosophers on the government's payroll. Most importantly, philosophers should know the moral difference between state charity (a coercive humanitarianism made possible only because so much property — tax dollars — is first taken from the people) and true charity (which is voluntarily given to others). Could a harsh totalitarian State that confiscated everything from everyone only to redistribute it therefore argue that it was the most generous? A false conclusion, I should say. In short, it is illegitimate to compare forced, with voluntary, giving.

So much for the moral superiority of Canadians.

At any rate, below, under "Modern Liberalism," we shall see how deformed the original standard has become, unbeknownst even to most so-called liberals, who cheerily vote onward, imagining they are upholding those original standards. But they are not, for "one of the more extraordinary developments in the intellectual history of the twentieth century [has been] a profound change in the meaning of liberalism."[3]

Somehow, in the rational search for equal opportunity and justice for all, the laudable standards of the classical liberal were submerged by liberals all over the world as they eagerly joined hands with the State, not to ensure equal *opportunity* for all, but through "progressive" social engineering to *coerce* the productive members of society to provide everyone else with the equal *results* the liberals craved. In the name of justice, they succumbed to injustice by using the law to favour some and penalize others, and are still doing so. The true classical liberal would have declared such behaviour abhorrent.

THE CLASSICAL CONSERVATIVE

THE CLASSICAL, OR "TRUE," conservative is much less optimistic about human affairs than the classical liberal. Although he values individual freedom, private property, free enterprise, and related matters perhaps even more than the classical liberal, *he fundamentally objects to the liberal idea that human reason alone will enable us to achieve the good society.* Following the enormous influence of Edmund Burke, whose essay "Reflections on the Revolution in France" (1790) so powerfully moved the minds of half the world against radical excesses, the conservative argues forcefully that men will always forge tyranny from anarchy. To him, civilization cannot be dialled up on a planner's computer or outlined in a manifesto. Rather, it is like a tree of great age, with deep, invisible roots. Revolution, or for that matter any sudden, unwise change in social policy, will cut those roots, leaving dead leaf and branch but no civilization. History, of course, has proved him quite correct. The liberal view that humans are basically born good and are all the same at root, and that human reason will eventually produce a society of "material and cultural achievement," must be tempered by a deeper truth: that we are all a mixture of angel and devil, that perfection is never available to us (therefore watch out for the social engineers), and that over the centuries we have developed hundreds of imperfect but satisfactory political, economic, and cultural institutions and traditions that have served civilization tolerably well up until now.

A true classical conservative believes deeply that tradition in its best sense is just another word for virtue (manners and morals) made a habit. Societies that lose (or destroy) such fundamental habits are faced with a daily reinvention of morals and manners — of civilization — without benefit of custom. These are political and cultural customs so old and venerable that they speak to us as if with the voice of a deep and profound collective human wisdom that can never be fully understood by mere rational analysis or inspection. Almost a voice of the collective unconscious, which can be heard by those who listen for it (but not by others), a voice that speaks with the tongues of the ages, and therefore ought to be "conserved." It is because human knowledge is always imperfect and because human beings, especially governments, have a way of mucking up most things they try, that the conservative is skeptical of utopian schemes, social engineers, and theorists. He believes strongly that

*the business of politics is to keep things going on a fairly even keel
so that the individual may go about his business as far as possible
in his customary chosen manner. [Conservatism] eschews all vision-
ary dreams, from whatever source they may come; it suspects the
abstract theorist in politics because, to quote Burke once more, "in
the groves of their academy, at the end of their vista, you see nothing
but the gallows."*[4]

While the true conservative therefore supports many of the principles
of the classical liberal, he wants to put a *brake* on imprudent efforts to
change society for the better, in the absence of any evidence that it *can*
be changed for the better. For the conservative, civilization is not a
matter of politics or mere "social policy," as today's social engineers are
so fond of assuming, but a matter of *individual morals*. For "the Tory
has always insisted that, if men would cultivate the individual virtues,
social problems would take care of themselves."[5] And these virtues are
born and nourished in the oldest social institutions of marriage, family,
church, local community, private property, daily work, and so on. They
may be tempered by reason, *but cannot arise from it. Neither can they
be created by government nor conferred upon the people by a Constitution in a top-down fashion.* Therefore, the onus of proof is always on
those who want to change what already exists, and the conservative
finds their proofs for the most part sorely lacking in persuasiveness.

The conservative is not, however, against *prudent* change. Nor does
he wish simply to preserve the "status quo" at all costs. But he is
extremely wary of imprudent change. In the absence of a better system
he says, let's stick with what we have, which works tolerably well.
Above all, Burke felt, let us avoid and reject like the plague all abstract,
theoretical solutions to man's woes as insufficient reasons to restruc-
ture society. For such ideas spring not from experience or true sympathy, but from cold calculation of those who would use the force of the
State to make others do their will. Burke aimed his barbs especially at
"egalitarians" of the type so prevalent in our own society, whom he
considered to have hardened hearts "nearer to the cold malignity of a
wicked spirit than to the frailty and passion of a man." The word
"progressive" used in connection with conservatism he would have
found an abomination invented by intellectually impoverished politicians. Lest the reader believe this to mean conservatives are against
progress in the sense of basic political, material, or scientific advances,
this is not so. Their objection is to the use of the word "progressive" to
imply that our present arrangements are unsatisfactory, not as com-

pared with an existing better method, but as compared with an abstract idea in a politician's mind, in the name of which he is prepared to sacrifice living, breathing, workable relationships and institutions.

Above all, Burke upheld a belief in *the necessity of a moral order that transcends mere men and their ways*, without which they would eventually devour themselves like mad dogs. He wrote: "I allow that, if no supreme rulers exists . . . [to enforce] . . . the moral law, there is no sanction to any contract, virtual or even actual, against the will of the prevalent power."[6]

Sentiments such as his were later echoed through the works of Dostoevsky, one of the world's greatest and most profoundly moral writers, whose character Ivan Karamazov said, "If God is dead, everything is permitted." By this he meant that without a so-called "transcendent" common moral standard, either for ourselves or our governments, any sort of moral outrage whatsoever could be brought about as soon as a majority of the people were in favour of it. With no absolute, or common, moral standard against which to measure human action, what would prevent mob rule? What *could* possibly prevent it? Without any absolute moral constraints on man's excesses, then mob rule, disguised and packaged as morality and sanctified as "democracy," will prevail, and any group or government that gets its hands on power and tax wealth will force others to do its will. Welcome, not to morality, but to the power of the majority — right or wrong. How do we tell when the majority is right or wrong? Very simply, by measuring them against our concept of "rules of just conduct equal for all under the law." It is legitimate for government to tell us the limits beyond which we cannot go; but it is *not* legitimate for government to order our lives for us.

The clearest example of how this works is the rules of the road in our traffic system. We are all free to go anywhere we like in the system, provided that we do not break the rules, and the differences between us, or our cars, matters not at all. We are treated in the same way by the law. This is a perfect model of legislation in a free society. But if those who set the rules suddenly decide that different people ought to have different rules, well, imagine the chaos, the immediate sense of unfairness! Suddenly, at any street corner, out jumps a little policeman to say, "Volkswagens straight ahead, Chevrolets turn right, Mercedes turn left." Or, farther along, another jumps out to say, "Males turn back one mile, females speed up; all blacks pull over to receive a free car." Really. Would this work? Of course not. Which is why we apply the rule of just conduct, equal for all. If democracy exceeds this rule, it is exceeding the proper limits of government in a free society, for it doesn't stop at directing the traffic according to the whim of the day. It soon wants to control *how* each driver drives, *where* he goes, and ultimately *what* he thinks or says as he drives.

We can now say with certainty that it was largely the mind, the words, and the passion of Edmund Burke that prevented England from flirting with egalitarian government of the kind that swept France in the name of social justice. And it was the force of this same "conservatism" in British society that slowed the awful and regrettable — but in Burke's view inevitable — distortion of classical liberalism as it abandoned its heritage and philosophical underpinnings and rushed headlong as the State's new partner into its modern role as shaper of the social-welfare State. Nothing could have surprised Burke less than to see Pierre Trudeau, a "liberal," use his party for this purpose; nothing would have surprised him more than to see Mulroney, a "conservative," do the same. As for Broadbent . . . he was committed by the fundamental ideology of his party and that of the Socialist International to subvert the classical liberal as well as conservative traditions, in the name of his abstract "new society."

THE CLASSICAL SOCIALIST

CHAPTER FOUR CONSISTED ENTIRELY of a description of the origins, rationale, and development of socialism, broadly speaking, so little more will be mentioned here. Suffice it to say that these three "classical" political positions emerged more or less during the same historical period, and were relatively precise formulations of philosophical ideas having to do with the relationship that their proponents felt ought to obtain between the State and the individual. All three were and still are concerned with the limits of power — and with the end purposes of society. But most importantly, they were clearly different visions of how *freedom, virtue,* and *authority* ought to be managed in the modern world. Quite obviously, voters weighing these three alternatives were provided with a real choice.

Of all the views, classical socialism was obviously the most radical, for it set out to replace the existing social and political order with one based on entirely different values. Simply put, whether in its *revolutionary* Marxist form or in its *evolutionary* utopian form, classical socialism sought to create a new society in which the means of producing wealth were owned by the State and not by individuals; in which individuals would be subordinated to a social purpose greater than themselves; in which differences between individuals and classes would be eradicated through social engineering; and, most importantly, in which the production of goods and services would be managed not by free markets using financial success as their motive, but by a centrally controlled government, using the well-ordered society as its motive. Guidance as to society's goals and methods would be provided by a corps of elite bureaucrats and politicians.

Arising, as it did, substantially in reaction to the enormous increase in wealth and the consequent social dislocations caused by the Industrial Revolution, socialism was in the eyes of many observers merely a secular manifestation of the ideals of a weakened Christianity. As faith in God and churches weakened, this would simply be replaced by a new faith in man and government. The heavenly kingdom would be created by socialists here on earth. It was D.H. Lawrence who described this strange secularization of spirituality in his metaphor of the "earthly" and the "heavenly" bread. Man toils all the days of his life for real earthly bread. But because he craves miracle, mystery, and authority, he finds the earthly bread insufficient to satisfy his longings. What he really craves is heavenly bread. So in religious times, he gives his earthly bread to the Church, both materially by supporting it and spiritually by surrendering his moral life to its authority. In turn, the Church blesses his earthly bread (all his works), and he now thinks of them as heavenly bread. Then, and only then, is he happy.

But in secular times, with no church or transcendent moral order to worship, he gives his earthly bread to the State in taxes, which stamps them with its own moral seal and gives them back to him in the heavenly form of government-approved social services. Thus is socialism a reflection not of a practical, but of a theoretical and dangerously utopian urge.

All three of these classical positions can be thought of as conflicting answers to the question, What moral order is required to produce a good society? Classical liberalism rests its case on the individual's ability to decide for himself how best he ought to live, within the context of rules of just conduct equal for all. The classical conservative is wary that despite this laudable standard, the liberal will, in the absence of a profound respect for the institutions, traditions, and moral habits of a civilized order, be misled by the frail candle of reason which he takes to be a beacon. He will then succumb to mere rationality, social sciences, and the temptations to use State power in an effort to produce a good society. Finally, the classical socialist attacks the entire philosophical and moral basis of both these orders and wishes to ground the good society not in the moral choices of the individual, but in the deliberations of a future centralized state which has an abstract concept of the common good as its motive, one it insists is superior to any individual morality.

What, then, *restrains* the individual under each of these systems? Under classical liberalism, the individual is restrained by the rules of just conduct, which must be the same and enforced for all without exception (like the rules of the road), or the justice inherent in them is lost. Under classical conservatism, he has the further restraint of the weight of custom, tradition, and the venerable institutions of civilized life, all tempered by reference to a transcendent moral standard (most often a religious morality). Under classical socialism, all of these are rejected in favour of restraint by a unitary and — by virtue of this ideology — coercive, all-intrusive State that strives to fulfil its vision of a just and egalitarian society, *whether the people want it or not.* (Our Gallup Poll survey in Chapter Seven shows this gap between public policy and the wishes of Canadians.)

Once we are familiar with these classical positions, we can see that except for the watered-down socialism of the NDP, they bear only the faintest resemblance to the principles, even where discernible, of political parties bearing these names today. What has happened to these modern counterparts?

Against objections I can hear in advance, I will attempt to outline where the present choice among political parties lies with reference to the standards of the classical past, and also within the context of previous chapters of this book. In a general sense, it is important to know what kind of world our party of choice is creating for us and for our children. For example, which parties are pushing us toward more of the social-welfare State, and which are doing the opposite? Which will result in a better bonus system? in a more severe handicap system? in something in between?

THE MODERN LIBERAL

CANADA'S MODERN "LIBERAL" PARTY has nothing to do with classical liberalism and its defence of the individual. In fact, like U.S. Democrats, the modern Liberal in Canada is much more strongly associated with the promotion of the State and all its powers than with defending the freedoms of the individual. This wholesale switch in the ideological position of liberals took a mere century to bring about and in Canada was vastly accelerated by Pierre Trudeau and his "liberal" — especially

French Canadian — colleagues. The Supreme Court Justice Gérard LaForest, Serge Joyal, Jean Chrétien, Marc Lalonde, and many others are on the public record as striving to bring about a more highly centralized, and more thoroughly French, State in Canada. What we have referred to in this book as the French style of top-down government, which is highly centralized, elitist, and egalitarian in method and posture, has been a result deliberately engineered by Canada's federal Liberal party. Perhaps the best study of this shocking phenomenon is Peter Brimelow's *The Patriot Game*, which minutely documents the sell-out of English Canada to the French style of government and to the "liberal" dream of a centrally controlled, multicultural, regionally balanced, harmonious nation sustained by the financial and emotional nourishment of French-English relations, and enormous, constitutionally mandated interregional transfer payments. He shows how, with unmatched ambition, the Liberals under Trudeau embarked on their quest for total power in 1968 and were eventually to amass a "concentration of federal government employees in Ottawa [proportionately] three times as large as that in Washington, D.C.," to help them.[7] Unnoticed by most English-speaking "liberals," Canada's Liberal party drifted — no, it charged — toward socialism in all but name, dragging Canada after it. For,

> *quite suddenly, classical liberalism was abandoned by the parties and social groups originally espousing it. Instead, the same parties and social groups came to favour the more statist, interventionist, mixed-economy complex of attitudes describing itself in the U.S. as "liberalism," a.k.a. "social democracy" or (daringly) "socialism" in Europe and Canada.*[8]

In short, the six "isms" upon which the Liberal party has based its political life since 1968 are: centralism, elitism, official bilingualism, multiculturalism, egalitarianism, and nationalism. The first two take care of the Liberals' political, economic, and cultural vision of a socialist or (for the squeamish) a social-welfare governance (one directed nation under one group of directing governors); the other "isms," to which more could be added, are essentially like the marketing arm of this political philosophy, presented to the people as national unifying programs, dependent on all the normal fanfare, federal spending, transfer payments, and other control devices such programs must create to be successful. In speaking of nationalism as a form of radicalism, Brimelow once again reminds us that all such "isms" are "essentially a cover for a hidden agenda of unlimited social engineering, concerned not with the past but with the future, not with patriotism, but with power."[9] What this means is that in one of the most stunning and publicly unconfessed reversals in all political history, the classical liberal movement (not only in Canada, but also in Britain and the U.S.A.) from which so much of what is good in our Western civilization has grown — our most fundamental political, governmental, cultural, and legal institutions, our very lifeblood — has been unceremoniously shown the door, and may never be seen again.

THE MODERN CONSERVATIVE

THE MODERN CONSERVATIVE is embarrassed. So he hides his head. Unsure any longer of what he stands for, or against, he attaches the label "progressive" to his party in order to win approval from an electorate even more confused than he about his purposes. For those with classical conservative sympathies, this is a great disgrace, for a true conservative is far more concerned with civilization, its morality and institutions, than with "progress" for its own sake. At heart, he believes that nothing new under the sun has been invented in regard to basic human values, nor will it be. The fundamental things in human life, such as the need for honour, truth, decency, care for others, hard work, and so on, have been known for millennia. The problem, therefore, is, How should we properly order society around them? The linking of the terms "progressive" and "conservative" is an embarrassing contradiction because it implies that conservatives are mostly interested in changing what is. The day Canada's Conservative party changed its name to the *Progressive* Conservative party, it publicly acknowledged its philosophical weakness and its willingness to play prostitution politics. With that one stroke, it could abandon any true conservative vision of the world and do battle solely on the basis of out-promising the Liberals; two political parties hugging the centre to death from different sides. (This behaviour appears quite commonly in three-party States where each party vies for the central bloc of voters. In two-party states each attempts, conversely, to distance itself from the other, for fear of being thought the same.)

Refreshingly, Conservative Prime Minister Margaret Thatcher of England and President Ronald Reagan of the U.S.A. have not acted in this contradictory fashion. While some conservatives will want to quibble with the purity of their political stances, these two people alone have done more to rehabilitate practical conservatism than anyone else in the entire half-century past. (Needless to say, many had hoped for such a revival in Canada.) Thatcher's "Iron Lady" reputation has arisen most of all from her resolute drive to restore her society along classical conservative lines, mostly by dismantling the social-welfare State that had developed what the world's economists now refer to as "the British disease." Both she and Reagan have stressed individual responsibility, local control of policy, decentralization of government, privatization and deregulation of industry, entrepreneurship, and the need to reverse "the nanny state" brought about by those who are liberal in name only, of which both leaders, as conservatives, have been rightly suspicious. (Yes, Britain still has serious economic problems — the healing process is a long one.)

Although our own Prime Minister Brian Mulroney has been less than resolute and has all but ignored the true ideological foundations of the Conservative party, he, too, has taken some important steps to dismantle the social-welfare State in Canada — while taking others to ensure its longevity. Immediately after he came to power with the largest Progressive Conservative majority ever, he promptly proceeded to confuse every true conservative in the country. There is no simple answer why he did this. Mostly, I think, because he is a politician like all the others, who tests the winds and — not to be too unkind — because he appears to be ideologically naive. With no philosophical centre to guide him, he is driven more by the need to be popular than to offer a conservative vision of his country. In this respect, he is without any compass and has become a centre-hovering — in many cases a left-of-centre — politician, vying with the Liberals for much of the same turf.

Much as I dislike many of his programs, I defend him in so far as he has introduced a number of distinctly "conservative" measures. Once in power, he wisely and quickly dismantled the Liberal's disastrous National Energy Program, which was "one of the most far-reaching and revolutionary policies ever to have emerged from a Canadian Government."[10] It had driven half the nation's oil rigs south of the border in what the business columnist Peter Cook called "the biggest exodus of capital in Canadian history . . . In one year, following the National Energy Program, more than $11-billion in direct investment was lost, either through foreigners selling out or Canadians putting their money elsewhere" (the *Globe and Mail*, Nov. 5, 1987). In that first year of the NEP alone, Albertans contributed $6 billion more to Ottawa than they received. Needless to say, Trudeau had badly alienated western Canada, for the net effect was that the NEP "siphoned off an estimated $50 billion in oil industry revenues" from it (the *Financial Post*, Nov. 17,

1986). At bottom, of course, the NEP was about much more than money. It was about power. It was about a central, superior force exerting its dominion over a region. That the NEP was a symbol of the top-down, French style of collectivist, egalitarian government, was made manifestly clear by one of its most "French" powerbrokers, Marc Lalonde, in a speech given in Sherbrooke, Quebec, on October 22, 1981, in which he said that

> *a stronger threat to Canadian unity than Quebec nationalism could soon be the growing wealth of Alberta. The other nine provinces would soon be at the mercy of Alberta's every fancy and a wave of Alberta nationalism of unprecedented strength could rise up if the federal government held back from showing its teeth.*

So, ending the NEP was the outcome of a clash not of personalities, but of ideologies.

Mulroney also ended the damage caused by FIRA, the Trudeau Liberals' Foreign Investment Review Agency, which had resolutely discouraged international investment in Canada. In addition, he established the Meech Lake Accord, which, though badly flawed (see Chapter Sixteen), has the conservative effect of decentralizing power in favour of more local decision making. Most importantly, Mulroney pushed tenaciously for what could turn out to be the single greatest (modern) conservative measure in Canadian history: the Free Trade Agreement with the U.S.A., the world's largest and richest trading nation. While this will hurt some who have built businesses on tariffs or subsidies, it will in the long run enrich every Canadian, based, as it is, on the essential conservative (and classical liberal) ideal of voluntary exchange. For these measures alone, all of which have helped produce the longest-sustained economic growth period in our history, Mulroney deserved re-election. If these were his only measures, we could easily give him top ranking as a conservative. But he falls short for good reason.

First, he is primarily issue-oriented. He appears incapable of standing on his own two feet and conducting a coherent debate on conservative principles, substituting instead convenient homilies and emotionalism — at which he can be quite effective. But it is this tendency that leads to his pursuit of confusing welfare-state policies that run counter to his conservative thrust. For example, what can explain in a true conservative the energetic manner in which he has thrown himself into the creation of a national daycare program (now defunct, not for reasons of principle, but for lack of cash)? This program, which, if it ever comes into effect, I believe history will show to be a crucial factor in the breakdown of the Canadian family (primarily because it subsidizes the transfer of personal family childcare to impersonal State nannies), is an openly socialist measure. It relies on the extraction of billions of dollars from parents who often sacrifice to raise their own kids and doles it out to millions of others who would rather work at something else. For the "truly needy" (some widows, or single mothers who demonstrate need and who have been refused all family or community help) we don't object. But for all the others? Give me a break, as they say. You would never find Thatcher supporting such a program or, for that matter, any true conservative.

Again, would a true conservative appoint avowed NDP socialists like Stephen Lewis, Ian Deans, or Gerald Caplan, or big union bosses like Dennis McDermott, to senior government posts? Just imagine the effect on the rest of the world as it heard Stephen Lewis speak as our ambassador to the United Nations. Lewis launched into a flight of rhetorical fancy when he publicly attacked the famous Heritage Foundation of Washington, a conservative think-tank that has been instrumental in shaping America's recent and very successful economic boom. Lewis was not unaware that an attack on the Heritage Foundation was an attack on the core of American conservatism. Our own Michael Walker, head of Canada's conservative Fraser Institute, said Lewis's "assault on the Heritage Foundation was an assault on President Reagan himself . . . and an assault on the sensibilities and attitudes of a large number of individuals within the administration and the Congress and the Senate of the United States" (the *Globe and Mail*, Sept. 24, 1985). So when Canadian Press (Aug. 5, 1985) reported Lewis as saying that the Foundation had made "sleazy accusations" in its attacks on the U.N. and therefore the Foundation "had to be dealt with," we wonder to what ultimate power he was referring? Mostly, we wonder why a Canadian ambassador to the U.N., representing a Conservative government, would presume to speak for Canadians in attacking the most prestigious conservative think-tank in America? Is this how a "conservative" prime minister should want us typified? Of course not.

Further, how can a true conservative promote what he calls the "sacred trust" of universality? How can he keep and even enlarge a nationalized oil company like Petro-Canada (as of this writing, there is talk of privatizing it)? How can he dole out our tax dollars to feminist and anti-defence organizations? How can he publicly hug South Africa's Oliver Tambo, leader of the openly terrorist and Marxist-infiltrated

African National Congress? How can he push for disinvestment in
South Africa when even Gatsha Buthelezi, the hereditary leader of six
million Zulus living there (South Africa's largest black constituency),
tells us that "disinvestment is anti-black" and pleads with us not to do
it? For that matter, how can our hypocritical government say so much
against South Africa and so little against the far larger and more
devastating tyranny of Afghanistan — let alone the atrocities and
tribal/racial massacres in so many of Africa's one-party dictatorships?
How can a true conservative so strongly promote the Draconian Bill
C-72, imposing official bilingualism on all of Canada? And I'm not even
attacking his hundreds of patronage appointments or his ignoring of
the Nielsen task-force recommendations on cutting government
spending, and the Forget report on reforming our Unemployment
Insurance mess. And so on!

The point here is not to crucify Mulroney. It's to show that with
respect to true conservatism, he has vacillated and wandered and
seems philosophically irresolute. I would vote for him anyway — until
a better conservative comes along — because the other options are a
lot worse for Canada; and I'm speaking of our direction taken as a
nation, of political philosophy, and not of personalities.

THE MODERN SOCIALIST

CANADA'S NEW DEMOCRATIC PARTY is our national socialist party. Of
the three federal parties, the NDP, the furthest from the seat of power,
has had the least to lose by attempting to remain ideologically pure.
Nevertheless, it has cheated in the sense that it has resolutely disguised
the truly radical nature of its ideology and objectives by downplaying
its socialist roots. What are its objectives? We hardly need to ask. As
mentioned, the NDP is a registered member of the worldwide organization for socialists called the Socialist International and Ed Broadbent
has been a vice-president of that organization. Enough has been said
in Chapter Five about the objectives of socialism as a political philosophy. However, I strongly suggest that anyone who wishes to understand
the true heart of the NDP ought to read through the "resolutions" of
that party for the past two decades, which are predictably subtitled
"Taking the Future On."[11]

In those more than 265 pages can be found detailed party resolutions
of the most radical nature on every conceivable social, economic, and
cultural subject. Almost without exception, these resolutions seek to
resolve each and every national, community, or personal problem of

the Canadian people through the use of government power. Almost without exception, they call for more tax dollars, more redistribution of wealth, more agencies, commissions, inspectors, Crown corporations, and all the paraphernalia they drag along with them, to do this. The NDP has been resolute in its call for "planning" to achieve its "new society" (federal convention, 1977); its aim is "to modify and control the operations of the great productive organizations" (1963). It is "proud to be part of that great world-wide movement of democratic socialist parties" that has the goal of providing "an egalitarian society" (1983); NDP/socialists "believe in planning" and "reject the capitalist theory" regarding supply and demand, and they wish "the transfer of title of large enterprises to the State" (1983); they also want every "affirmative action" policy conceivable, unilateral disarmament of the West (including withdrawal from NATO), total "universality" of all conceivable social services, equality of incomes, and banishment of corporate competition (1977). In short, the NDP "will not rest content until we have achieved a democratic socialist Canada" (1983).

All this speaks for itself, and there is no need to elaborate on the rampant philosophical confusion, especially the contradictory coupling of "democracy" with "socialism," which ought to embarrass a man with Broadbent's education. For true democracy is a bottom-up form of government, while true socialism is top-down. They cannot be reconciled. In summary, one's jaw simply drops at the utopian yearning for perfection on earth in every NDP resolution and, not least, the constant recommendations to use State power to coerce some Canadians to produce this dream for others. Never mind that nowhere in the NDP strategy is there any mention of what I have called the "tools of freedom and wealth creation." The NDP simply assumes that freedom and wealth will always be here, just as children believe that money grows on trees or that Christmas is just around the corner.

This brief summary of the modern parties and their positions should serve to explain why so many Canadians are frustrated at the true lack of a choice in Canadian politics. What kind of choice is before us when the leaders of our two largest and ostensibly different parties are merely vying with each other to spend all our taxes and borrow almost a quarter as much again, while the third wants the government to run everything on wealth the people couldn't possibly produce under such a system — a conclusion driven home by a simple study of the miserable productive capacities of all socialist nations of the world? Hence, our frustration. Hence, our unheeded cry for a clearer choice.

WHERE HAS THE YEARNING FOR FREEDOM GONE?

HERE'S A PROPOSITION: our three modern parties have so trampled upon the classic individual freedoms and wise restraints on governmental power that made great nations possible, and have so tightly joined their coercive purposes to the powers of the State, that all three parties, lacking any truly principled ethical standard that could control the abuses of government itself, are now simply vying for a greater or lesser right to engineer society. The result of this lack of principles, in which the only race left is for power over our freedoms, is the reduction of political warfare to promises and personalities. Exactly what we see in the press every day. Prostitution politics. If someone were to ask me where our time-honoured concern for freedom has gone, I would say, underground for some fifty-odd years now, and showing its head today in much-misunderstood libertarian political theory.

A capsule summary of libertarian thought is presented here, not to suggest it is the answer to all our prayers (it definitely is not), but that it is the answer to our question, Where has the concern for freedom gone? The modern Liberal party no longer discusses the matter and certainly has not formed its policies on the principle of individual liberty vs. Statism (its classical starting point) for more than a hundred years. The modern Progressive Conservative party is hardly any better. Not only has it abandoned its traditional promotion of freedom vs. Statism, but its promotion of free enterprise and the familiar conservative values and institutions like the traditional family is halting and cowardly, to say the least. At any rate, if you enjoy the philosophy and writings of the classical liberals and the true conservatives, you will find much to enjoy in modern libertarian works.

THE LIBERTARIAN ALTERNATIVE

WHAT IS A LIBERTARIAN? He is someone who holds *that the only good reason for one person's interfering with the freedom of another is self-protection.* That's the bottom line. Anything that exceeds that standard is coercion and therefore inadmissible. For many of us that is a thrilling moral standard and one with the weight of a lot of heavy-duty thinkers like John Locke (*Second Treatise*, 1690), John Stuart Mill (*On Liberty*, 1859), Adam Smith, and Thomas Jefferson to help support it. But libert*arianism* should not be confused with libert*inism*. The latter has to do with adoring the sins of the flesh. The former has to do with adoring freedom and the personal responsibility that goes with it. Therefore, libertarians in general are against centralized, interventionist government in the political, economic, or moral-cultural lives of the people. They are in strong support of equality before the law but abhor any use of State power to coerce equal social outcomes. And they are in passionate support of individual freedom and responsibility, especially economic freedom.

The bulk of political writing today on the subject of freedom and State power is coming from the pens of writers with libertarian sympathies in works such as Robert Nozick's *Anarchy, State, and Utopia*; Richard Epstein's *Takings: Private Property and the Power of Eminent Domain*; and, of course, in the works of the great Austrian writers and sympathizers, like Hayek (*The Road to Serfdom*) and von Mises (*Socialism*), and in well-known works like Milton Friedman's *Capitalism and Freedom*, Sennholz's *Money and Freedom*, and Buchanan's *Limits of Liberty*. This is not a crowd of idle intellectuals, for Hayek, Friedman, and Buchanan have all won the Nobel Prize in Economics.[*]

My only point in detailing briefly the libertarian movement is that in the "push-down/pop-up" sense, the human quest for freedom in the face of Statism had to go somewhere, and where it is popping up today is in libertarian writing and politics. Libertarians even have a political party to express their views both in Canada (where it ran candidates in 80 ridings in 1988) and in the U.S.A. (since 1972), where there are a reported 200,000 registered members, with 200 candidates running in the fifteen states that allowed them to register; they received 2.9 million votes in the 1984 election.

If asked what is wrong with libertarian thought, I would say only one thing: it ignores "the small patriotisms" that the conservative Burke thought were so important as instruments of local authority, such as find expression in the relationships between parent and child, teacher and pupil, elder and junior, supervisor and employee, master and apprentice, priest and congregation, and so on. It ignores the "traditions are virtues become habits" theme. Not that libertarians refute these sources of local authority, it's just that they regard them as matters of personal choice and would find the world just as good without them or with other freely chosen institutions. Like the classical liberals before them, who went about their business pursuing individ-

---

[*]   Readers interested in such books should contact Laissez-Faire Books ("The World's Largest Selection of Books on Liberty"), 532 Broadway, New York, NY, U.S.A. 10012-3956; telephone (212) 925-8992, for information. Ask them to send you their catalogue. It's a feast of books on political philosophy, economics, and liberty. If you give them your credit-card number, the books will be shipped right to your door. End of advertisement.

ual freedom, this leaves libertarians exposed to the mob rule of the majority as it goes about its business of pursuing power. For in the sense that all that is necessary for evil to triumph is for the good to do nothing, libertarianism is weak. Doing nothing is enough for evil to triumph, but it is not enough for the good to triumph. For a true conservative, the good is not defined by temporal hopes and dreams; it is defined by a transcendent moral standard of timeless and enduring moral values, ones that we cannot hope to create on the spot, with each generation.

A libertarian would respond to this complaint by saying that the "good" is a matter for individual decision; it is not pre-established by the State (or by a church). Many agree with that. The difficulty is that unless you have some shared prior notion of the good, of high moral values, and put in place institutions, laws, and customs to protect them, individual actions are based on mere personal or sectarian desire. For if your definition of the good is only temporal, then the moment those who believe in it die off, wiped out by a real or moral plague, the good has no social progeny, no social or cultural artifact, no "infrastructure" that continues beyond individual believers, no enduring roots. That's the conservative's complaint about libertarianism, a philosophy that seems to work best in a world of educated individuals who have a strong personal sense of responsibility. The party tends to attract such as members and candidates. It falters in the imperfect world of ordinary humankind who will tend to drift toward irresponsibility if their community is not based on a set of established moral values.

In summary, this has been an overview, first, of where our current parties stand — not in terms of the "issues," which anyone can read about in dailies like the *Toronto Star* (see, for example, Sunday, Oct. 2, 1988, an article in which each party's "stand" on the issues was presented), but in terms of their commitment or aversion to their own founding principles; and second, of where they fit into the broader spectrum of collectivism/individualism, that is, into the scale of values either of democratic capitalism or the social-welfare State: the bonus system or the handicap system.

Everything that appeared before this chapter has been written in an effort to spell out a macroview of the two major political possibilities vying for dominance in the world at large and in our own society; namely, democratic capitalism, and socialism in its various forms. Schematically, both these opposing systems can be understood in the wider context of a simple line diagram running from left to right, with *extreme collectivism* on the left and *extreme individualism* on the right. Neither of these extremes is desirable, in my view, for both lead to unworkable societies. But having said that, I strongly favour individualism in the context of a limited government that is restricted to setting rules of just conduct equally applicable to all. I abhor collectivism or any political policy veering toward it, on the grounds that it is based on coercion and thrives on a government bureaucracy without limits that constantly strives to equalize outcomes by discriminating against inherently different people, and robs us of responsibility and independence. So for me, this "range of political possibilities" works very well as a measuring stick, allowing me to assess quickly any political motive or party. Let's see how the scale serves to illuminate our own parties in the context of the other political choices open to us.

The Range of Political Possibilities

extreme collectivism						extreme individualism	
1	2	3	4	5	6	7	8
X	-	-	-	X	-	-	X
100	70	60	50	40	30	20	0
%							%

(rough percentage allocation of GNP to government)

The following political philosophies and parties more or less correspond to the numbers on the line extending from extreme collectivism to extreme individualism:

1-2. *Totalitarian systems (Marxism, Fascism, etc.).* As presented in this scale, the "left" or "right" language is immaterial. The crucial fact is that however labelled, such systems take total totalitarian control of the nation. Thus, Nazi and Marxist parties alike share most of the same sins.

2-3. *Socialism and the social-welfare State.* Such established "mixed economy" nations try to purchase socialism with the proceeds of capitalism. They keep the latter alive enough to finance the former (Sweden and our NDP fit here).

3-4. *Canada's modern Liberal party and U.S. Democrats.* Both of these parties have been sliding leftward over the last half-century, and no

longer stand for the defence of classical liberal values. They have been
the chief architects of socialist policies in North America, and advocate
more State power in the effort to equalize outcomes for different
individuals and groups.

4. *Canada's "Progressive Conservative" party.* Let loose from its classical conservative underpinnings, this party has lurched leftward and
is trying to keep both sides of the equation happy. It hasn't yet
Thatcher's courage or the intelligence to delineate clearly a workable
philosophy, but happily, still prefers free enterprise to modern "liberal"
Statism.

5-6. *The U.S. Republican party under Ronald Reagan,* and *British
Columbia's Social Credit party.* In North America these two parties have
clearly enunciated, if not always followed, their principles, which are
resolutely individualist and conservative. Reagan has revivified an
entire population. Vander Zalm is losing the opportunity to do the same.

5-6. *Margaret Thatcher's British Conservative party.* Words cannot
express the staunch and clear-eyed focus of this party, perhaps the
closest to classical conservatism in the modern age. Thatcher set about
virtually to dismantle the social-welfare State in the name of individual
freedom and responsibility, under rules of just conduct, equal for all.

7. *Libertarianism.* This party is structurally cemented to its principles
of freedom, free enterprise, and anti-Statism, and could well serve the
West as a beacon of principled political philosophy into the next
century. Even if it never holds power, it is at least shaping policies. It
has especially powerful writers and philosophers of political economy.

8. *Anarchism.* The extreme of individualism is the anarchist, who
seeks to end all government on the grounds that government in its
essence is an evil presence based on the immorality of coercive power.
It is utopian in its lack of concrete solutions as to how such a society
can be operated.

So there you have it. This scale, which cannot be applied too rigidly,
is nevertheless like a slide rule and will help you determine toward
which extreme a political argument tends. Curiously, both of the
extreme positions are utopian, and propose social arrangements that
are unworkable in the long run. In extreme collectivism they are

unworkable because of the excessive use of force and financing required, and the subsequent suppression of the individual spirit and therefore of the general morality this naturally brings about. At the anarchist end, society is unworkable because of the impossibility of sustaining any community of values whatsoever and therefore of any coherent or continuous social action. It is the *degree* of movement toward either extreme that ought to concern Canadians. For reasons of history, tradition, and just the plain old success of trial and error, it would seem self-evident that we have done the best when we have positioned ourselves, in terms of our community of values, as a nation that stresses individual freedom and responsibility, under a limited government, that endorses just rules of conduct for everyone equally. Anything beyond that standard is a shift toward collectivism and the social-welfare State. To the extent that we allow the government to take our property, to the same extent it will naturally expand. It has asked, and we have given. This is not a mark of communitarian spirit but of individual cowardice in the face of State aggression, the lack of any will to resist. To the extent that the State expands, individual freedom and responsibility shrink. Just so does the second line in my diagram allocate the rough percentages of total GNP transferred to government for its work.

Clearly, once a people has decided what its core political, economic, and cultural values are to be, the only method that can be guaranteed to preserve them will be control of the pursestrings, for ideas alone are not sufficient. The lure to spend for power is too strong. So, combined with borrowing constraints, a constitutional limitation on taxation and spending is surely the most effective way to limit government and thus to protect the values we cherish. We must remember that a politician with limited money is a politician with limited power.

7

Canada At A Glance
Canadian Opinion
And Performance

ENOUGH OF THEORY. How does it work in practice?

The simple purpose of this chapter is to give readers an *objective* overview of The Trouble With Canada to complement the first six, more theoretical chapters, and at the same time serve as a basic reference point before heading into the more emotional "Issues" of Part Two.

First, readers can study the mood of Canadians as seen through a variety of Gallup polls over the years, and compare the *people's* vision of Canada with what the *government* has actually done. The difference between them is a measure of the distance between the governors and the governed, between representative democracy and true, popular democracy.

Next come the charts. Close study of and reflection on these charts will repay the reader handsomely by meshing the political, economic, and social arguments in the first six chapters with the real-world results of the ideological course Canada has followed over the past few decades.

After the effort of researching this Chapter, I can truly say it's awfully difficult for the average person to find out exactly where Canada *is*. It would frustrate anyone. One day, we get a presumably factual report on the national debt, or the poverty level, or the personal tax rates, from one "expert"; and the next, a variation or outright disagreement from another. After a while, there is an unwilling suspension of belief that

creates distrust in "the numbers." Once a populace develops a sufficient degree of distrust, both in the numbers and the people quoting
them, ripened skepticism is afoot. Other than political motivation —
which is rampant — there are lots of reasons for confusion. For example, even though governmental, academic, and think-tank organizations try to co-ordinate with each other, they often use different data
bases; some use calendar, some fiscal years; some publish in constant
dollars, some in current; they use different base years to calculate
trends; they have different definitions for their terms, and different
countries often include different items in their reports. Enough said.
There is a lot of quicksand out there. Some of these numbers (like the
total national debt) are changing so fast, you almost need a new chart
every week. (Our Auditor General, Kenneth Dye, has himself an-
nounced that he underestimated the total debt by some $20 billion!)
Even so, the government vs. the people profile, and the charts that
follow, will give readers a grasp of where Canada was, where it is now,
and where the people want it to be.

THE GOVERNMENT VS. THE PEOPLE

ONE WAY (NOT PERFECT, but a pretty good indicator) to tell how
divorced the government and its legislators are from the will of the
people is to ask the people serious questions about what they think, to
get an informal profile of their opinions. (See pages 164-65.) The
distance between what the people want and what the government does
then becomes a measure of the distance between the governing elite
and the will of the citizens governed. Judge for yourself how large the
gap is. Then consider the situation in a country like Switzerland, where
referenda are commonly used to legitimize policies that people living
under Swiss democracy require their governments to implement. Consider, that is, what Canada might be like today if we followed the Swiss
example and required government to provide us with policies that
match our vision of Canada. If we had true bottom-up government, so
to speak, with policy by jury, instead of policy by judge.

WHAT THE CHARTS TELL US

THIS IS A SUMMARY of some highlights of the charts that follow in this
chapter.

1. *We're spending beyond our means.*
Canada is spending beyond its means and has done so with persistent

regularity since the energetic launch of social-welfare policies under Pierre Trudeau and his "liberal" government.*

2. *We cannot reverse this without suffering.*
The current government is slowing this trend, but has not succeeded in stopping it, largely because the people have grown accustomed to considering their wants as claims against the State. Mulroney's "conservative" government has amassed huge public debt.

3. *We have been fiscally irresponsible.*
Although the smallest of the Group of Seven, Canada continues to spend relatively the most — but for Italy — unmindful of its status and real capacities. In 1984 it spent 53.5 percent more than it received in revenue — a formula, if not for bankruptcy, then for stagnation and tax oppression of the citizens.

4. *Our debt will eventually have to be paid.*
Trudeau and his colleagues were fiscally irresponsible, and suffered from the illusion that borrowing from ourselves was all right. If any of these politicians had ever "met a payroll," as the saying goes, we would not today be in such deep trouble. Today, over $240 billion of our public and private debt is owed to foreigners. (At least the private debt is for growth, whereas the public is primarily for consumption.) Such debt will have to be paid off through more taxes taken from us and from our children. Paying it off will reduce the living standards of all unless privatization cuts waste. At current rates of increase, the average Canadian family will owe $100,000 by 1992. Canadians have to understand that deficits are really "deferred taxes." A constitutional limit on spending is required.

5. *We hardly ever hear of the "total" debt.*
Most Canadians are unaware of Canada's *total* government debt — the sum of the debt of all *three* levels of government — now about $550 billion. For in addition to our federal debt — which is what most of us generally hear about — our country carries a lot of provincial and local debt to boot. (While the U.S. states, as a whole, are in surplus, our

* "Debt" and "deficit" are not the same. We use the word "debt" to refer to the total amount of money borrowed since 1867 (total government debt). The word "deficit" refers only to the amount of money spent in excess of revenue received in the year in question. Of course, each year's deficit gets added to the total debt, which is how the debt grows.

GOVERNMENT vs. THE PEOPLE

WHAT CANADIANS WANT

0% 10% 20% 30% 40% 50% 60% 70% 80% 90% 100%

WHAT THE GOVERNMENT DOES

#	What Canadians Want	%	What the Government Does
1.	Cut spending, don't raise taxes.	84%	The "Consumer Tax Index" compiled by The Fraser Institute every year has risen 1000% since 1961, and is still growing. Governments continue to spend more and tax more!
2.	End universality of Social programs.	59%	"Universality" is regarded by all three parties as inviolable, despite this general dislike.
3.	Government wasn't cut enough in the 1986 budget.	66%	Spending at all levels continues to rise. Half of all personal income taxes generated each year are used to pay interest on Canada's Federal debt.
4.	Taxes are too high.	79%	Taxes continue to rise. All three levels of government - Federal, Provincial, and Municipal - are running aggregate debt of $503 billion as of 1988.
5.	Eliminate UIC benefits to those who quit, or refuse to work.	63%	Forget Commision reforms were attacked by the unions, and shelved.
6.	Allow private insurance coverage for doctors' and hospital bills.	64%	Canada is the only Western country in which to buy or sell basic private medical and health insurance services is illegal.
7.	Canadians welcome foreign investment	62%	Two of the major political parties want strict control.
8.	Big government is the biggest threat to Canada's future.	42%	Government continues to expand. (Only 30% thought "big labour" was a problem. and a mere 15% said "big business" was a problem.)
	Big labour	30%	
	Big business	15%	
9.	Workers in essential services (like the Post Office) should not have the right to strike.	58%	They have, and do.
10	Unions should not use forced union dues for political causes.	78%	Up to 20% of union dues believed used for political causes. (Sources: Toronto Star, July 8, 1986)

SOURCES

1. *Gallup Poll, Mar. 16/86* & *The Fraser Institute*, Tax Facts Six, *1988*
2. *Gallup Poll Mar. 16/88*
3. *Gallup Poll Mar. 16/88*
4. *Gallup Poll Apr. 27/87*
5. *Galluip Poll Mar. 16/86*

6. *Gallup Poll Mar. 16/86*
7. *Gallup Poll Mar. 16/86*
8. *Gallup Poll Feb. 2/88*
9. *Gallup Poll Apr. 23/87*
10. *Gallup Poll Apr. 13/87*

GOVERNMENT vs. THE PEOPLE

WHAT CANADIANS WANT

WHAT THE GOVERNMENT DOES

0% 10% 20% 30% 40% 50% 60% 70% 80% 90% 100%

#	What Canadians Want	%	What the Government Does
11	Immigration policy should not change the ethnic balance of Canada.	78%	In 1987 70% of immigration came from non-traditional sources (from other than Anglo-European sources).
12	The death penalty should be reinstated.	61%	The death penalty was rejected by Parliament in 1988, despite the clear wish of Canadians to reinstate it.
13	More respect for authority	88%	The people want traditional values and authority - we get less of each.
14	Sex outside of marriage is "always" or "almost always" wrong.	73%	Our public agencies fail to support traditional morality.
15	Sex between two adults of the same sex is "always" or "almost always" wrong	67%	Our government promotes toleration of abnormal "sexual orientation," and promotes this anti-traditional, unpopular attitude.
16	It is very important (60%) and fairly important (26%) to balance the federal budget.	86%	The irresponsible borrowing at federal, provincial, and local levels continues.
17	All public schools should offer a course in religion.	52%	Religion is now a case of reverse discrimination in the separate vs. public school system. Ontario bans the Lord's Prayer from public schools (but not from Catholic schools.)
18	Government should increase family allowances, but pay them only to families in need.	78%	Government persists in its "universality" policies, paying allowances to the wealthy.
19	Fight an all-out war rather than live under Communist rule (Canada: 1962-65% USA: 1982-83%; UK: 1972-75%).	40%	Compared with other free nations, we appear to be submissive.
20	Welfare recipients should be made to work.	84%	This attitude is remarkably consistent, and yet government continues its free "hand-out" policy.
21	More emphasis on traditional family ties.	94%	The government continues to pursue anti-family policies.
22	Courts are too lenient with criminals (1968-43%).	78%	Our criminal justice system continues to favour the "rights" of criminals and ignores the victims.

SOURCES

11. Gallup Poll June 1987 and Annual Report on Immigration, 1986/7 Gallup Poll Nov. 14, 1979
12. Gallup Poll May 1987
13. Gallup Poll Feb. 4, 1989
14. Gallup Poll Oct. 1, 1977

16. Gallup Poll Feb. 19, 1977
17. Gallup Poll Nov. 14, 1979
18. Gallup Poll Oct. 24, 1988
19. Gallup Poll Jan. 26, 1982
20. Gallup Poll Nov. 30, 1989
21. Gallup Poll Feb. 4, 1989
22. Gallup Poll Jan. 19, 1987

provinces, except Alberta, are in debt.) And this is despite the fact that the provinces get, on average, transfer payments amounting to 20 percent of their annual revenues — and local governments get 50 percent. Most Canadians are also unaware that in terms of total national debt, we are twice as bad, per capita, as the U.S.A. We need an act of parliament or a referendum to control government spending, as in the U.S.A., where the Gramm-Rudman amendment is now in force.

6. *We are just passing most of the money around.*
Most of the money being "redistributed" by Ottawa in an effort to fulfil its self-imposed egalitarian mandate is taken from the well off, given back to them in the form of services deemed good for them, and paid for with what is left over after three levels of government take their considerable fees. We need to stop the whirlwind of "redistribution" and allow people to spend their own money responsibly on their own well-being.

7. *Meanwhile, our national real property is decaying.*
Canada is entering a phase of infrastructure decay for the repair of which it will not have enough funds, as indicated by the sinking levels of Gross Fixed Capital Formation. The trade-off here will be the competition between the need to deliver on promised social services and the need to fix potholes — all without further borrowing. The impossibility of doing both without the help of a magician will become increasingly obvious and create tensions as our society, borne ever higher on the sort of illusion suffered by all big spenders, learns to face the reality of having to get by with less.

8. *Taxation has become the heaviest drain on the average Canadian — the greatest liability he has to face.*
One ominous result of the State's game-plan to finance its phenomenal growth has been the unconscionable rise in the Consumer Tax Index — relative to the Consumer Price Index — of 1,005 percent since 1961! How long will we continue being led to the fiscal slaughter before bleating loud enough to be heard? "Tax Freedom Day," which came about the middle of February fifty years ago, arrived July 7 in 1988!

9. *A land of unions.*
Canada is a land of unions. Especially government unions. Our preference for things "public" — for ownership or management by the State — is manifest in the difference between ourselves and the U.S.A.

This is especially dangerous in Canada, where there is no "right to work" legislation, meaning that a person's right to associate or not to associate — considered a basic human right by the United Nations Charter — is nonexistent in Canada.

10. *A growing fear of government.*
Canadians are increasingly aware that big government is a threat to Canada. But they are not doing much about it, for the most part because they haven't the means, like referenda, as do the Swiss, who are basically able to veto all public spending directly. Worst of all, in Canada, it seems to be only the political Left, with its call for *more* government programs, that gets any media or political attention.

11. *A growing fear of taxation.*
Ever since the early seventies, Canadians have consistently said that taxes are too high. But as yet, no political party has dared run on this platform, primarily because vocal pressure groups make this platform extremely unattractive to any sensible politician. Also, via the free-lunch illusion, everyone wants more "free" services. Recent provincial and federal tax budgets require the consumer to tighten his belt, but government refuses to tighten its own (it's been frightened into modest cutting — but not from principle!).

12. *There is no end to government spending in sight.*
Total government spending as a percentage of GNP has risen more than 50 percent since 1965. Government is now the largest Canadian employer. More than 20 percent of the Canadian people work for government at some level. The average Canadian spends greater than 52 percent of his income on consumer taxes of all kinds.

13. *We have developed an adversarial society.*
One result of the increasing presence of government and the increased intervention this always brings is higher taxes, and lower honesty — a burgeoning "off-the-books" or black-market economy estimated to be about $42 billion, or 14 percent of the total GNP in 1980, probably more than $75 billion now (14 percent of $550 billion GNP in 1988). Simple honesty and a sense of national duty have been replaced with the tax-avoidance war. Higher taxation to fund government excesses drives honest work underground, creating a professional class of "tax experts" who profit from their parasitical, unproductive activity. Even worse, we now have an economy in which every important business

transaction is being structured according to its tax implications, rather than for good investment or development reasons, which ought to be the case.

14. *And we have developed a less caring society.*
Another dispiriting result of government's "we'll do it all for you" programs is the predictable crowding out of private charitable giving — down 25 percent individually, and more than 60 percent corporately in the last fifteen years. Besides the drop in actual funds, there is the incalculable loss of the charitable spirit required to sustain a sense of community — another casualty of the social-welfare State and the loss of the sense of responsibility it always engenders.

15. *We are a nation of small businesses.*
Although the media and the business community itself tend to focus on big business, Canada is a nation of shopkeepers, and it is this segment of the economy that has created all the jobs in the past decade. Each year, there are up to half as many business "deaths" as there are "births." As business is the only engine of wealth creation we have, legislators and politicians ought to think more carefully about how to protect it from their activities.

16. *The seeds of dissolution are present.*
Although the government tries to force uniformity upon us, and spends lavishly to create the impression we are one big, happy, bilingual, multicultural family, Gallup polls do not suggest this is the case. Attitudes toward such matters as bilingualism vary widely across the land, being most negative, of course, the farther away you get from Quebec (only 29 percent support it in B.C.). Our experience with Bill 178 in December of 1988, and the "notwithstanding" clause, in January of 1989, further demonstrates that the constitutional favouritism on which our leaders have tried to build this nation cannot work. Once English-speaking Canadians realize the inherent unfairness of this, the country's very being will be threatened, through separatism in the east with the Parti Québécois, or fresh challenges to the existing order, from new parties such as the Reform Party in the west.

17. *We have two classes: the governors and the governed.*
Finally, our chart of The Government vs. The People shows how far apart are the policies of the government from the wishes of the people of Canada. The consistency of these differences suggests that a New

Class of bureaucrats, academics, journalists, and politicians have driven a wedge between the people with their wishes and values, and the course chosen by a government that no longer represents them or cares to carry out those wishes.

20. *The transition from a bottom-up to a top-down society is nearly complete.*
Our burgeoning bureaucracy, results in an increasing number of regulations, agencies with special police powers, and social engineering at all levels. In short — less freedom for the people. Surrender of more tax dollars to government means more surrender of personal responsibility for our own well-being, and the transfer of more power to Ottawa.

Now come the charts, after which Part Two will focus on the impact of this all-important change on the many issues that concern all Canadians.

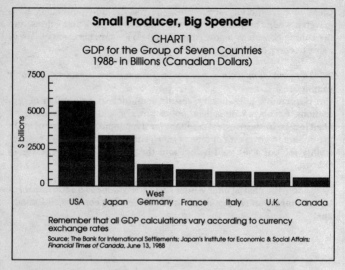

Small Producer, Big Spender

CHART 1
GDP for the Group of Seven Countries
1988- in Billions (Canadian Dollars)

Remember that all GDP calculations vary according to currency
exchange rates

Source: The Bank for International Settlements; Japan's Institute for Economic & Social Affairs;
Financial Times of Canada, June 13, 1988

Comment:
This chart gives us a good feel for Canada's productivity level relative to our
economic allies. It says nothing about annual spending or total debt of these
nations. Loosely speaking, you could think of each nation as a kind of national
economic unit that conserves, invests, or wastes its financial resources, just as
a business may do, except that its last creditor and owner is itself. GDP tells
how much volume of wealth the owner nation has to manage. Although
technically such owners can't go bankrupt and shut the doors, they can suffer
all the same symptoms, with the doors open.

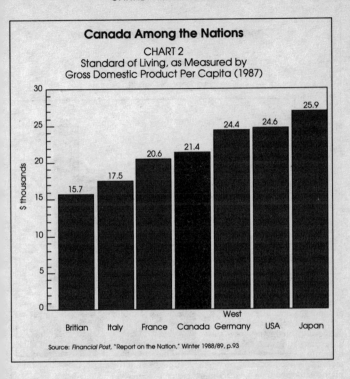

Canada Among the Nations

CHART 2

Standard of Living, as Measured by
Gross Domestic Product Per Capita (1987)

Britian	Italy	France	Canada	West Germany	USA	Japan
15.7	17.5	20.6	21.4	24.4	24.6	25.9

Source: *Financial Post*, "Report on the Nation," Winter 1988/89, p.93

Comment:

By any measure, our "standard of living" (SOL) is among the highest in the world. In itself, "standard of living" is hard to measure, and, if it only measures dollars, is misleading. For example, a high dollar SOL alone might not attract a physician who despises our socialized medical systems; nor will it attract entrepreneurial activity from risk-oriented people who deplore excess government controls and intervention, regulatory red-tape, high taxes, etc. While we must be happy about our mineral resources, and our spin-off economic benefits from the booming U.S. market, all of which keeps our SOL relatively high in dollar terms, we should not be too smug. Unlike *all* the other Group of Seven countries, we are still, overwhelmingly, a colonial, branch-plant economy. We still think that our success lies in attracting foreign operations to set up in Canada, as opposed to creating our own new enterprises. We are a bit like a dinghy in a race, pulled by a rope behind "Ship U.S.A.," comparing ourselves with the other dinghies that are sailing on their own.

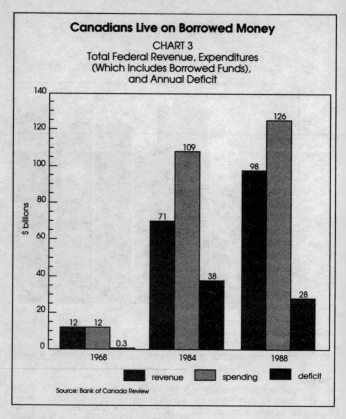

Canadians Live on Borrowed Money

CHART 3
Total Federal Revenue, Expenditures
(Which Includes Borrowed Funds),
and Annual Deficit

Source: Bank of Canada Review

Comment:
We have got used to living on borrowed money, increasing amounts of it from foreigners. In 1968, we had almost no deficit, and sixteen years later, in 1984, the deficit amounted to 35 percent of total government spending. But *revenue* that year was only $71 billion and $21 billion of that went to pay interest. What kind of shape would you, your family, or your business be in if you borrowed 53.5 percent more than you earned? Although this has improved recently by a good measure, as the chart shows, Canadians need to exert real pressure on their MPs and MPPs to balance budgets and pay down the total debt ($503 billion in 1988). Annual deficits, which are added to total debt, reduce proportionately the amount of money that the government can spend on government's legitimate functions, like roads, bridges, and so on. (See Chart 17.)

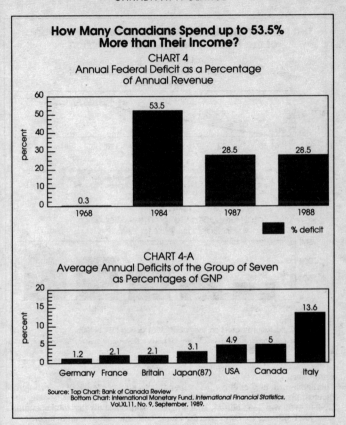

How Many Canadians Spend up to 53.5% More than Their Income?

CHART 4
Annual Federal Deficit as a Percentage
of Annual Revenue

- 1968: 0.3
- 1984: 53.5
- 1987: 28.5
- 1988: 28.5

■ % deficit

CHART 4-A
Average Annual Deficits of the Group of Seven
as Percentages of GNP

- Germany: 1.2
- France: 2.1
- Britain: 2.1
- Japan(87): 3.1
- USA: 4.9
- Canada: 5
- Italy: 13.6

Source: Top Chart: Bank of Canada Review
Bottom Chart: International Monetary Fund, *International Financial Statistics*,
Vol.XL11, No. 9, September, 1989.

Comment:
 Canada's long habit of "deficit financing" — borrowing more money each year to finance current spending (it's like going into debt to pay the interest on your debt) — has become the political norm. Trudeau wrote that "a country isn't ruined merely because it has lent itself a lot of money." Nonsense. Debt must eventually be paid and interest on it must be paid on time if credit ratings are to be preserved. As Michael Wilson pointed out (Nov., 1985), government borrowing pushes other borrowers offshore; and "even if the public debt is held by Canadians, its existence severely limits the fiscal room to manoeuvre of the federal government . . . [and] interest paid on the public debt represents a transfer of income away from production and risk-taking . . . "

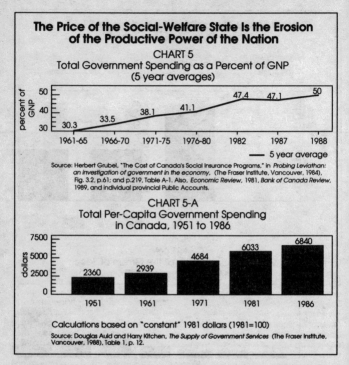

The Price of the Social-Welfare State Is the Erosion of the Productive Power of the Nation

CHART 5
Total Government Spending as a Percent of GNP
(5 year averages)

percent of GNP

30.3 — 1961-65
33.5 — 1966-70
38.1 — 1971-75
41.1 — 1976-80
47.4 — 1982
47.1 — 1987
50 — 1988

—— 5 year average

Source: Herbert Grubel, "The Cost of Canada's Social Insurance Programs," in *Probing Leviathan: an investigation of government in the economy*, (The Fraser Institute, Vancouver, 1984), Fig. 3.2, p.61; and p.219, Table A-1. Also, *Economic Review*, 1981, *Bank of Canada Review*, 1989, and individual provincial Public Accounts.

CHART 5-A
Total Per-Capita Government Spending
in Canada, 1951 to 1986

dollars

2360 — 1951
2939 — 1961
4684 — 1971
6033 — 1981
6840 — 1986

Calculations based on "constant" 1981 dollars (1981=100)

Source: Douglas Auld and Harry Kitchen, *The Supply of Government Services* (The Fraser Institute, Vancouver, 1988), Table 1, p. 12.

Comment:
Total government spending means spending by all three levels of government, federal, provincial, and local. According to the *Bank of Canada Review*, our GNP in 1988 was $583 billion. That and other sources show that total spending was $291 billion. In other words, about half the nation's total income — corporate and individual — is spent by governments! Money is taken from individuals and corporations who earn it — then more is borrowed — and spent by government on activities and services, some of which are seen as beneficial (though costly compared with the same service rendered privately), such as health care, pensions, and so on, and many of which are not (the myriad advocacy-interest groups, and other activities, institutions, jobs, and programs that spread the influence of the social-welfare State). Using a *"constant"* dollar (1981) method, we can see that per-capita government spending is climbing at a fearsome rate. The 1988 figure is $11,165 per-capita in *"current"* dollars.

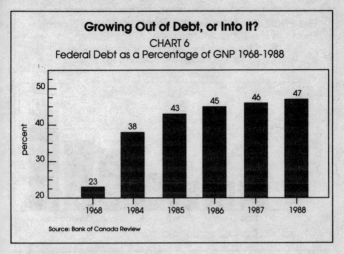

Growing Out of Debt, or Into It?

CHART 6
Federal Debt as a Percentage of GNP 1968-1988

Source: Bank of Canada Review

Comment:
Some commentators suggest that the trend we see here is not a problem, because we will "grow out of our debt" eventually, as the relative percentage drops to zero over time. But as a response to over-spending, this is inadequate. For example, what if there is a recession, combined with high interest rates? We could end up in serious trouble. Rather, Canada should at least *cut deficits*; *balance* its budgets; and find a way to *limit government* growth and spending. Then, we could indeed grow out of a fixed debt. But as long as we *add* to the debt each year this is close to impossible, and, regrettably, this means that an enormous number of our tax dollars (between 35 percent and 50 percent in recent years), representing the hard work of Canadians, must continue to be used to pay for debt and consumption.

This chart illustrates Ottawa's mischievous use of its borrowing power to subsidize provincial and local governments. Chart 7 shows the cumulative effect of this behaviour.

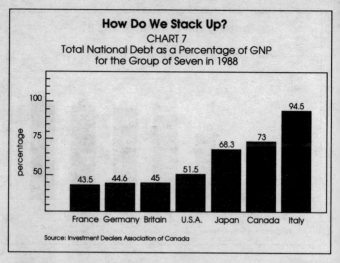

How Do We Stack Up?

CHART 7
Total National Debt as a Percentage of GNP
for the Group of Seven in 1988

Source: Investment Dealers Association of Canada

Comment:

How does Canada compare with the rest of the "big seven" democracies? This table gives a fair idea of the degree of indebtedness of a nation in relation to its ability to generate wealth. A lower percentage is desirable. While Italy is the hands-down winner for irresponsible borrowing, there is a compensating factor: Italy also has the highest rate of personal savings as a percentage of personal disposable income. Perhaps the Italians' long memory of Rome's decline inclines them to keep their money out of the government's hands! Canada, of all the great Western democracies, comes in a roaring second. Thirty years ago, a part of Canada's annual spending went to the retirement of debt. But today, Canada is borrowing money, in part *to pay interest on the money it borrows to pay interest*, and so on.

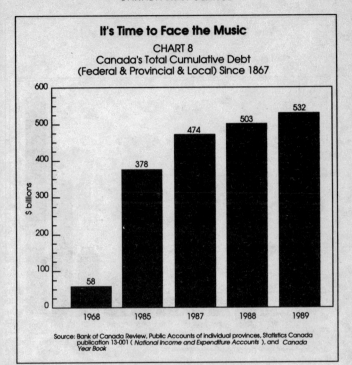

It's Time to Face the Music

CHART 8
Canada's Total Cumulative Debt
(Federal & Provincial & Local) Since 1867

	1968	1985	1987	1988	1989
$ billions	58	378	474	503	532

Source: Bank of Canada Review, Public Accounts of individual provinces, Statistics Canada publication 13-001 (*National Income and Expenditure Accounts*), and *Canada Year Book*

Comment:
Not only does the federal government run deficits each year, but so do most of the provinces. (Local governments must balance their budgets, but they also accumulate debt.) In fact, federal debt and annual deficits are inflated through transfers to other levels of government. (See Chart 11.) How many Canadians realize the magnitude of the debt run up by these three levels of government? The sad but powerful side-effect of our ignorance on this matter is that transfer payments to provinces and municipalities shield politicians from the taxpayer's wrath, *because they don't have to raise all the money they spend!* On average, 20 percent of provincial revenue comes from such transfers. (See Chart 23.) And 50 percent of all local expenditure comes from transfer payments from the other two levels of government (which, of course, means a lot of remote political control over local communities).

Regrettably, our government's plan is to reduce debt not by reducing expenditures, buy by raising taxes — thus giving the *appearance* of debt reduction and fiscal health.

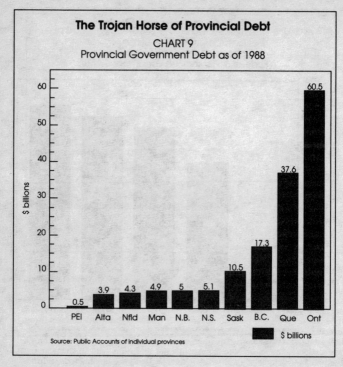

The Trojan Horse of Provincial Debt

CHART 9
Provincial Government Debt as of 1988

Source: Public Accounts of individual provinces

Comment:
Our provinces, too, are borrowing beyond their means to repay. Despite this accumulation of provincial debt totalling some $150 billion in 1988, the provinces are receiving, in addition to what they raise from taxes, and borrow, a further 20 percent, on average, in transfer payments from Ottawa. (See Chart 23.) A good part of Ottawa's debt, for which it (rightly) attracts the blame, is acquired on behalf of the provinces.

Notes: 1) We have included the debt of provincial Crown corporations, and of public utilities companies like Ontario Hydro and Hydro Quebec, in the provincial debt. Some argue that Hydro's debt is really not a true liability, because Hydro will pay off its debt by raising your rates (whereas the government would raise your taxes). We see no difference to the payer. If Hydro runs a bad shop, then raises your rates to pay for its inefficiencies, you are being indirectly taxed to pay its debt.
2) Two provinces, *Manitoba* and *British Columbia*, had surpluses in fiscal 1988. Both have Conservative premiers.

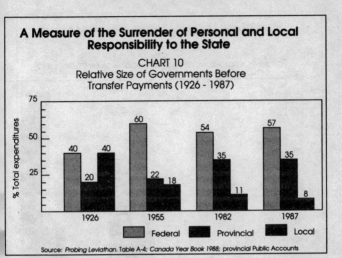

A Measure of the Surrender of Personal and Local Responsibility to the State

CHART 10
Relative Size of Governments Before
Transfer Payments (1926 - 1987)

Source: *Probing Leviathan,* Table A-4; *Canada Year Book 1988;* provincial Public Accounts

Comment:
If private individuals or corporations in Canada did what this chart suggests our governments are doing, they would be charged with operating fraudulently. Sixty years ago, federal spending (national concerns) and local spending (local concerns) were evenly balanced. Local communities ran their affairs responsibly, balanced their budgets, and controlled most of their own affairs. Now, however, federal spending has expanded far beyond national concerns into the shell game of redistributing incomes — now its chief activity — even though the relation between income groups has not altered a whit in thirty years. Meanwhile, provincial spending has grown partly by duplicating federal functions, and local spending has shrunk. (Half its spending comes from transfer payments.) But local politicians, who are closest to the taxpayers, and therefore have an interest in keeping taxes down, are actually spending double the amount they raise in taxes. By law, local governments are not allowed to have deficits. They must balance their budgets. *The transfer-payment system enables them to circumvent the law.* The same system enables provincial governments to spend beyond their constitutional powers to tax and borrow. (See Charts 11 and 23.)

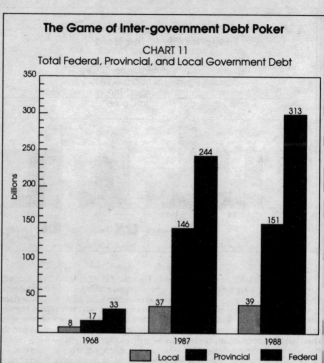

The Game of Inter-government Debt Poker

CHART 11
Total Federal, Provincial, and Local Government Debt

Source: *Bank of Canada Review*, Public Accounts of individual provinces, Statistics Canada publication 13-001 (National Income and Expenditure Accounts), and *Canada Year Book 1988*. Figures for local government for 1988 are the author's projections from the same sources.

Comment:
The federal share of total debt is growing fastest because, although its own share of total annual *spending* is just under half the total of all three ($126 billion out of $290 billion spent by the three levels in 1988), the federal government bears the chief cost of the interest required to satisfy the total debt. The provinces are required by the Constitution to borrow solely on their own credit, and local governments are required to balance their budgets. But the federal government borrows on the security of the whole of Canada as an economic entity. In effect, *the federal government acts as guarantor for what is in fact (though not in deed) borrowing by provincial and local governments beyond their ability to raise such funds themselves* (through borrowing or taxation).

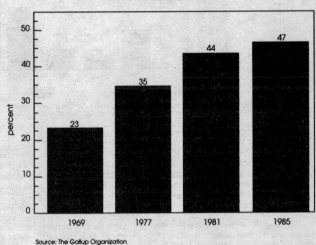

**A Government Big Enough to Give
You Everything You Want Is Big Enough to Take
Everything You Have**

CHART 12
Percentage of Canadians Who Say
"Big Government Is the Biggest Threat to Canada
in the Years to Come"

Source: The Gallup Organization

Comment:
Canadians have over the past twenty years increasingly recognized the danger of Big Government. Their recognition of this danger has paralleled the greatest concentration of centralized power in Canadian history — in fact, the most rapid and, relatively, the largest of any Western democracy! Yet "the free-lunch illusion" continues to operate. In his thorough examination of the governmental practices of the U.S.A., Britain, and Canada, entitled *Governments Under Stress*, Professor Colin Campbell states that "Among the three countries, Canada manifests the strongest tendency for creating central agencies or units within them" (p.77). Despite public recognition of the trend, however, Canadians seem to be unaware of the relationship between growth of government, and its spending. Annual deficits have declined since 1984; and yet, in 1988, the majority of the people voted for opposition parties that proposed still greater increases in government spending.

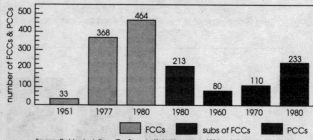

The State Out of Control

CHART 13

Increase in Number of Federal and Provincial
Crown Corporations and Subsidiaries (FCCs & PCCs)

Source: *Probing Leviathan* (The Fraser Institute: Vancouver, 1984, p.162, and facts below from
Minding The Public's Business (Economic Council of Canada: Ottawa, 1986)

Comment:

One objective measure of the degree to which the State has assumed control over the productive lives of the people is the number of State or "Crown" corporations that it creates, ostensibly in the "public interest." As public-choice theorists have warned us: the prime moving force for any government is *size*, the enlargement of its own purposes. When it alone decides what is in "the public interest," it has a powerful recipe for self-duplication at the taxpayer's expense.

The result? As the Economic Council of Canada has pointed out: "The federal government is the largest single investor in Canadian industry, and all provinces and many municipalities have major commercial holdings" (*Minding the Public's Business*, 1986, p.1).

Although since 1980 minor privatization efforts have been made (16 federal and 34 provincial Crown corporations had been sold, mostly to single buyers, by 1988), these were small scale. In fact, until Canadair was sold at the end of 1986, "the value of assets sold by the federal government was *less* than the $886 million purchase of Gulf Canada's assets by Petro-Canada in August, 1985" (Robert Bott, Report on Business, Sept., 1987, pp.56-64).

The Economic Council also reported that as of 1986 there were 259 corporations either *owned* or *controlled* by the federal government, and 268 subsidiaries. (Crown corporations do not require the permission of Parliament to create subsidiaries — some of which are larger than their parents.) When added to the more than 500 "local" public enterprises, this totals 1,027 public corporations in Canada. How effective are they?

Total debt for the federal public corporations was more than $37 billion as of 1986, and about $60 billion for all provincial public corporations. And (a scary fact if you stop to wonder who filters the news) the Council informs us that 50 percent of all employees in Canada's *communications* sector . . . work for the government!

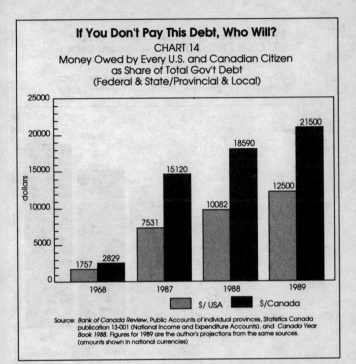

If You Don't Pay This Debt, Who Will?

CHART 14

Money Owed by Every U.S. and Canadian Citizen
as Share of Total Gov't Debt
(Federal & State/Provincial & Local)

Source: *Bank of Canada Review*, Public Accounts of individual provinces, Statistics Canada publication 13-001 (National Income and Expenditure Accounts), and *Canada Year Book 1988*. Figures for 1989 are the author's projections from the same sources. (amounts shown in national currencies)

Comment:

The three levels of government in Canada have taken on this debt in your name, and you have no effective check on their ability to take on a lot more. In order to stop this sort of irresponsible borrowing by the State on behalf of helpless debtor citizens, some brave jurisdictions, like California, have voted for restrictions on government taxation levels, on the grounds that the only way to halt government is to starve it. Milton Friedman has campaigned for years for both state and federal *constitutional limits* on spending. The American "National Tax Limitation Committee" by 1979 had more than 250,000 members and operated in about twenty states.

Canadians have yielded a large degree of local responsibility to the provinces and the federal government. The Americans have not gone so far. In the U.S.A., local governments carry a much larger share of the debt than do the states, $367 billion vs. $212 billion in 1985 — compared with Canada's $37 billion local vs. $146 billion provincial in 1987. (See Chart 11.) Furthermore, many of the U.S. states are in surplus, whereas in 1987, *every single Canadian province ran at a deficit!* (B.C. and Alberta had surpluses in 1988.)

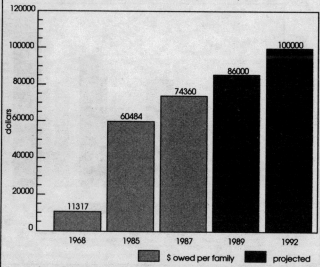

**By 1992 Every Canadian Family of Four
Will Owe $100,000 of Government Debt**

CHART 15

Amount Owed as Share of Total Government Debt
(Federal & Provincial & Local) by a Family of Four

Source: *Bank of Canada Review* Public Accounts of individual provinces, Statistics Canada
publication 13-001 (National Income and Expenditure Accounts), and *Canada Year
Books 1970/71, 1988.* Figure for 1989 is the author's projection from the same sources.
A continuation of the present trend would result in a $650-billion combined federal
and provincial debt by 1992.

Another title for this chart might have been: SO YOU'RE WONDERING WHERE
YOUR DOWN PAYMENT ON A FIRST HOUSE WENT? To the extent that our
three levels of government must necessarily tax you higher to pay their costs
and service their debts, they are taking money from you that otherwise would
have been used for your down payment, your mortgage, your car, credit-card
payments, a boat, you name it . . . they've got it. And what is not taken from you
will be taken from your children. And their children. It's not that we don't *get*
something from government. We do (e.g. Old Age Pensions, Unemployment
Insurance, roads, etc.). But we are purchasing more than we can pay for (much
of which we should provide for personally) and thus breaking our contract with
future generations.

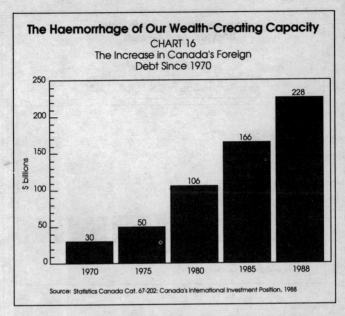

The Haemorrhage of Our Wealth-Creating Capacity

CHART 16
The Increase in Canada's Foreign
Debt Since 1970

Source: Statistics Canada Cat. 67-202: Canada's International Investment Position, 1988

Comment:
This chart vividly portrays our increasing dependence on borrowing from foreigners, and should serve to silence those who confidently assert, when advocating deficit financing, that it doesn't matter because "we owe it to ourselves." Once again, no matter to whom the money is owed, government debt is never good, because it crowds out private borrowing; it represents a transfer of income away from production and risk-taking; the greater the public debt, the greater the squeeze on real incomes; *this borrowing is being used, not for replacement of bridges and roads, but for consumption (payment of salaries, pensions, income redistribution, and other social programs)*; interest on foreign borrowing flows out of the country — virtually a loss of capital from our own wealth-creating processes (Chapter Four); such borrowing, even from our own people, establishes a competition for capital between government and business, and when from foreigners, between Canadians and other nationals. Finally, there is the obvious fact that the wealth we generate is being used to pay for government profligacy, instead of being left in the hands of its creators (the best solution), or at the least used for infrastructure refurbishment. In 1985, about 62 percent of the $166 billion borrowed was by governments, the balance by corporations. Alas, consumption spending, for which government's share is used, creates little new wealth; thus, borrowing abroad lowers standards at home.

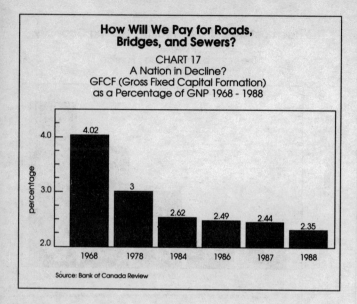

How Will We Pay for Roads, Bridges, and Sewers?

CHART 17
A Nation in Decline?
GFCF (Gross Fixed Capital Formation)
as a Percentage of GNP 1968 - 1988

Source: Bank of Canada Review

Comment:
This chart gives us another glimpse of the long-term effects of undermining the wealth-creating capacities of the people by government's spending beyond its means — or on the wrong things — and having little or nothing left to keep our house in order. This 39 percent drop in GFCF is very scary, and is going to have a lot of people running about looking for money very soon. In fact, it's already started. The *Globe and Mail* reported on December 5, 1988, that Deputy Prime Minister Donald Mazankowski was meeting with the Federation of Canadian Municipalities to discuss the need for $5-billion worth of serious "infrastructure repair" — which they collectively refer to as "a national issue." The group discussed decaying water mains, deterioration of roads, untreated sewage, bridges, and sidewalks. The federal government has repeatedly argued that this is not its jurisdiction, and that "chipping in for it would worsen the federal deficit." But the deficits continue. The transfer payments continue. We continue to pay, and the work doesn't get done.

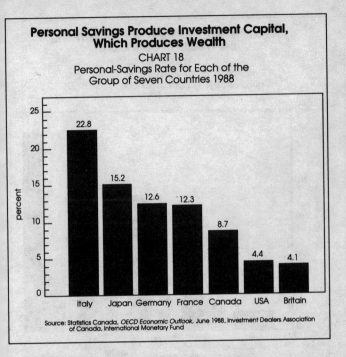

Personal Savings Produce Investment Capital, Which Produces Wealth

CHART 18
Personal-Savings Rate for Each of the
Group of Seven Countries 1988

Source: Statistics Canada, *OECD Economic Outlook*, June 1988, Investment Dealers Association of Canada, International Monetary Fund

Comment:

"Saving is the first step on the way toward improvement of material well-being and toward every further progress on along this way," wrote Ludwig von Mises in his magnum opus, *Human Action*.

"Private savings . . . *are* invested. Saving, in fact, signifies a commitment to the future, a psychology of production and growth. Since World War II the countries that have saved the most, preeminently Japan and other Asian capitalist lands, have grown the fastest" (George Gilder, *Wealth and Poverty*).

This chart gives an indication of the amount of savings as a percentage of personal disposable income taking place annually in each of our competitor countries. While Canada is not the worst, it is not the best, either. Canada's present agenda for increasing capital-gains taxation is going to have a further chilling effect on business transactions, capital accumulation, and therefore on savings.

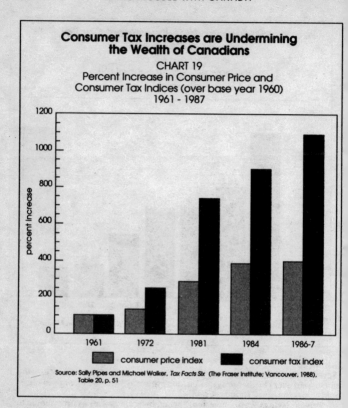

Consumer Tax Increases are Undermining the Wealth of Canadians

CHART 19
Percent Increase in Consumer Price and
Consumer Tax Indices (over base year 1960)
1961 - 1987

consumer price index   consumer tax index

Source: Sally Pipes and Michael Walker, *Tax Facts Six* (The Fraser Institute; Vancouver, 1988).
Table 20, p. 51

Comment:

The Fraser Institute, an internationally recognized Canadian think-tank, publishes every two years an in-depth study of Canadian consumer taxation levels. What is quite clear from this study is that the so-called CPI, or *consumer price index*, which concerns so many, is a bit of a red herring. In itself, it is inflated, because it includes a factor for the cost of new houses. However, most people do not buy a new house every year. But the real, hidden story is that all the while as we have focused on the CPI, the Institute's new index, called the *Consumer Tax Index* (CTI), has shot wildly upward and has escaped the attention of the public in its flight. The CTI is "an index of the total tax bill paid by the average Canadian family." This comprehensive index shows that "the tax bill of the average Canadian family has increased by 1005.1 percent over the period since 1960, and that the Index had a value of 1105.1 in 1987."

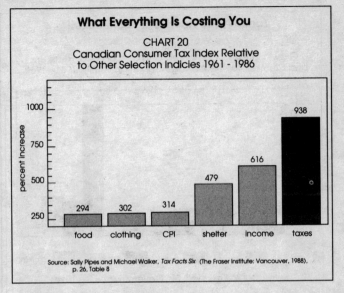

What Everything Is Costing You

CHART 20
Canadian Consumer Tax Index Relative
to Other Selection Indicies 1961 - 1986

Source: Sally Pipes and Michael Walker, *Tax Facts Six* (The Fraser Institute: Vancouver, 1988),
p. 26, Table 8

Comment:
Some of these increased taxes were spent on services nearly everybody uses;
some on paying interest on borrowed money (deficits and debt). But without
those tax increases, and with incomes outpacing prices, people could have kept
more of their own incomes to save, and invest, or to spend on their personal
preferences, which are not necessarily the same as those services government
supplies.

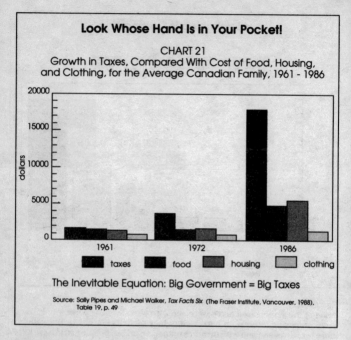

Look Whose Hand Is in Your Pocket!

CHART 21

Growth in Taxes, Compared With Cost of Food, Housing, and Clothing, for the Average Canadian Family, 1961 - 1986

The Inevitable Equation: Big Government = Big Taxes

Source: Sally Pipes and Michael Walker, *Tax Facts Six* (The Fraser Institute, Vancouver, 1988), Table 19, p. 49

Comment:

The average Canadian will surely ask what has been gained by this enormously increased output of tax dollars, compared with the ratio of taxes paid in 1961. The answer, I fear, is the subject of this book. Elsewhere, we comment on the effect of competition in keeping prices down. Despite this salutary effect, however, this chart illustrates hidden costs in the three leading components of family expense. Food contains the hidden cost of marketing boards (wheat, eggs, milk, etc.) and tariffs on imported food; clothing includes the cost of tariffs and quotas on imports; housing includes the same, as well as the cost of government-guaranteed "affordable" housing, subsidized rentals, rent controls, and so on.

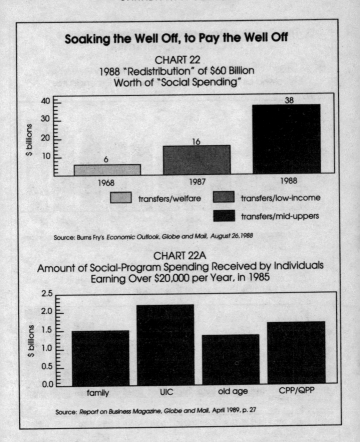

Soaking the Well Off, to Pay the Well Off

CHART 22
1988 "Redistribution" of $60 Billion
Worth of "Social Spending"

$ billions — 1968: 6, 1987: 16, 1988: 38

transfers/welfare   transfers/low-income   transfers/mid-uppers

Source: Burns Fry's *Economic Outlook, Globe and Mail, August 26, 1988*

CHART 22A
Amount of Social-Program Spending Received by Individuals
Earning Over $20,000 per Year, in 1985

$ billions — family, UIC, old age, CPP/QPP

Source: *Report on Business Magazine, Globe and Mail, April 1989, p. 27*

Comment:
In 1988, Canada's commitment to the various social programs of which "redistribution" consists cost almost $60 billion, or about 60 percent of the federal government's non-interest spending ($32 billion was spent to pay interest in 1988). *Less than $17 billion of that $60 billion went to the "poor." A full 70 percent of the social spending went to middle- and higher-income Canadians.*

As for individuals? Why do we tax ourselves, and allow our government to borrow more, in order to hand more than $7 billion annually to people making more than $20,000 income, less government's commission to pay for civil servants' salaries, offices, fully indexed pensions, and so on?

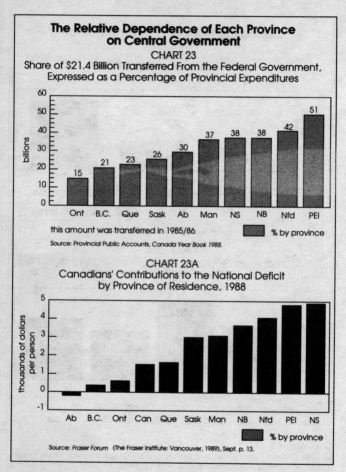

The Relative Dependence of Each Province on Central Government

CHART 23

Share of $21.4 Billion Transferred From the Federal Government, Expressed as a Percentage of Provincial Expenditures

this amount was transferred in 1985/86   ▨ % by province

Source: Provincial Public Accounts, *Canada Year Book 1988.*

CHART 23A

Canadians' Contributions to the National Deficit by Province of Residence, 1988

▨ % by province

Source: *Fraser Forum* (The Fraser Institute: Vancouver, 1989), Sept. p. 13.

Comment:
These charts provide an overview of the dependence of each province on transfers from the central government. The moral problem such transfers create, in addition to the blunt fact that the wealth was forcibly extracted from those who created it, is that the mere act of *giving* it to the unproductive does not make them productive. Rather, it subsidizes their unproductivity.

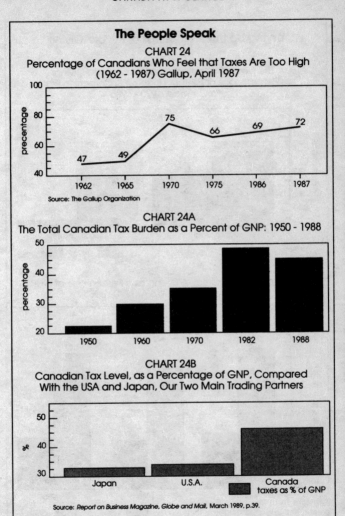

The People Speak

CHART 24
Percentage of Canadians Who Feel that Taxes Are Too High
(1962 - 1987) Gallup, April 1987

Source: The Gallup Organization

CHART 24A
The Total Canadian Tax Burden as a Percent of GNP: 1950 - 1988

CHART 24B
Canadian Tax Level, as a Percentage of GNP, Compared
With the USA and Japan, Our Two Main Trading Partners

Canada
taxes as % of GNP

Source: *Report on Business Magazine, Globe and Mail,* March 1989, p.39.

Comment:
These charts speak for themselves!

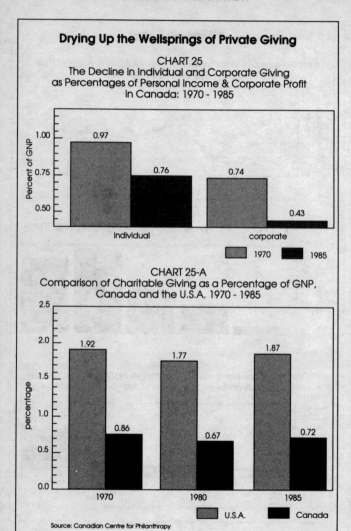

Drying Up the Wellsprings of Private Giving

CHART 25
The Decline in Individual and Corporate Giving
as Percentages of Personal Income & Corporate Profit
in Canada: 1970 - 1985

CHART 25-A
Comparison of Charitable Giving as a Percentage of GNP,
Canada and the U.S.A. 1970 - 1985

Source: Canadian Centre for Philanthropy

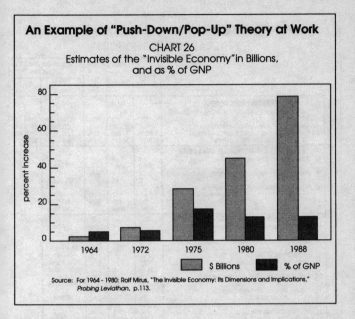

An Example of "Push-Down/Pop-Up" Theory at Work

CHART 26
Estimates of the "Invisible Economy" in Billions,
and as % of GNP

Source: For 1964 - 1980: Rolf Mirus, "The Invisible Economy: Its Dimensions and Implications,"
Probing Leviathan, p.113.

Comment:
This seems to be the natural result when government takes too much of the people's income in taxes. It's a classic example of "push-down/pop-up" theory at work — as the black market has always been. In self-defence, people avoid paying taxes by exchanging services ("contra" arrangements), or by taking cash without receipts. The unfortunate effect of this invisible-economy phenomenon is that whereas under levels of taxation deemed to be somewhere around 20-25 percent such activity is regarded as cheating, but when government exceeds such levels, it becomes the accepted norm. As a consequence, there is a thriving legion of tax lawyers and consultants in Canada to help people avoid taxes. Regrettably, most major business deals are structured not in ways that necessarily benefit the productive aspects of the arrangement, but in ways that reduce the tax impact on each party. At the extreme, in totalitarian countries, much of the real work of the economy is done privately through a "parallel," off-the-books economy. We are leaning increasingly in that direction.

CHART 27

OVER-REPRESENTATION OF FRANCOPHONES IN THE FEDERAL PUBLIC SERVICES*

	Total Public Servants	Francophones		Comparison to Population Ratio of 24%	
		Number	% of PS	Ratio in Excess	Job in Excess
OVER-ALL PUBLIC SERVICE					
1. Deputy Minister & equivalent (Governor-In-Council Appointments.)	532	168	32%	33% higher	40 jobs
2. Top Half of Public Service (Officer Categories)	109500	28700	26%	8% higher	2400 jobs
3. Bottom Half (Admin. Support & Ops. categories)	102500	31800	31%	29% higher	7200 jobs
4. Total Public Service	212000	60470	28.5%	19% higher	9600 jobs
KEY AGENCIES RE HIRING & LANGUAGE RULES					
5. Public Service Commission: Chairman	1		62%	.....	
Staff	2192	1356		21/2 times	
6. Official Language Branch (Treasury Board): Deputy Secretary	1	1	60%	.....	
Directors	5	3		21/2 times	
7. Office of Commissioner of Official Languages: Commissioner	1	1	71%	.....	
Staff	153	109	68%	triple	
8. Secretary of State: Staff	2860	1946		almost triple	
OTHER KEY AGENCIES OF GOVERNMENT					
9. Privy Council Office: Clerk of Council	1		47%	.....	
Staff	365	171	44%	double	
10. Supreme Court of Canada: Judges	9	4	61%	almost double	
Staff	71	43	52%	21/2 times	
11. Federal/Provincial Relations Office: Staff	48	25	41%	double	
12. Department of Supply and Services: Staff	9080	3756	57%	70% higher	
13. Canadian International Development Agency: Staff	1178	675		over double	
14. Governors General's Office: Governor General	1	1	68%	.....	
Staff	116	78		almost triple	
15. Elections Canada: Chief Commissioner	1	1	82%	.....	
Staff	66	54	48%	31/2 times	
16. Canadian Radio & Telecommunications Commission: Staff	385	186		double	
17. CBC: President/Chairman	1	1	41%	.....	
Staff	11151	4530	65%	70% higher	
18. House of Commons: Staff	1673	1092	55%	almost triple	
19. Senate of Canada: Staff	242	131	46%	over double	
20. National Capital Commission: Staff	703	323	60%	almost double	
21. Canada Council: Staff	234	140		21/2 times	
JUDICIAL & ADMINISTATIVE LAW AGENCIES			44%		
22. Supreme Court (already listed above)	9	4	62%	almost double	
23. Canada Labour Relations Board	85		54%	21/2 times	
24. Federal Court of Canada	210		50%	over double	
25. Civil Aviation Tribunal	5		41%	double	
26. Immigration Appeal Board	133		54%	70% higher	
27. National Farm Products Marketing Board	22		61%	over double	
28. Commissioner for federal Judicial Affairs	28		57%	21/2 times	
29. Patent Medicine Prices Review Board	7		53%	over double	
30. Public Service Staff Relations Board	140		70%	over double	
31. Cometition Tribunal (Registry)	10		62%	almost triple	
32. Tax Court of Canada	50			21/2 times	
33. Law Reform Commission	35		71%	almost triple	

* Position as of March 1988

Sources: Public Service Commission Annual Report. May 1989
Commissioner of Official Languages Annual Report. 1988, 1987, 1988, 1989 Official Languages Branch, Treasury Board, Orginization Chart, May 1988 Government of Canada, Telephone Book, May, 1989.

Comment: This statistical overview is alarming for two reasons. First, it shows a gross over-representation of "francophones" in too many key government departments. Secondly, by "francophone", it does not mean anyone who happens to speak French. It *means people whose mother tongue is French*. We are looking, not at *linguistic* ratios, but *racial/nationalist* ratios.
As barely 15% of Canadians are bilingual, the net effect of this is that fully 85% are effectively precluded from ever serving in top government posts or becoming prime ministers.

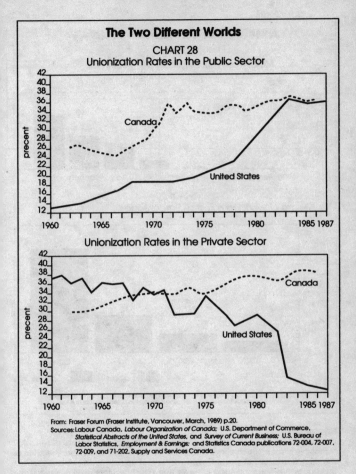

The Two Different Worlds

CHART 28
Unionization Rates in the Public Sector

Unionization Rates in the Private Sector

From: Fraser Forum (Fraser Institute, Vancouver, March, 1989) p.20.
Sources: Labour Canada, *Labour Organization of Canada;* U.S. Department of Commerce,
Statistical Abstracts of the United States, and *Survey of Current Business;* U.S. Bureau of
Labor Statistics, *Employment & Earnings;* and Statistics Canada publications 72-004, 72-007,
72-009, and 71-202, Supply and Services Canada.

Comment:
These two charts show that the difference in unionization trends between our
two nations derives mostly from the private sector. The Institute notes that
certain Canadian local public entities are included in the "private" sector
labour force. Although seemingly illogical, this is how the various sources
relied upon have always ordered their data. This quirk does not obscure the
magnitude of the trend of unionization difference between the two nations.

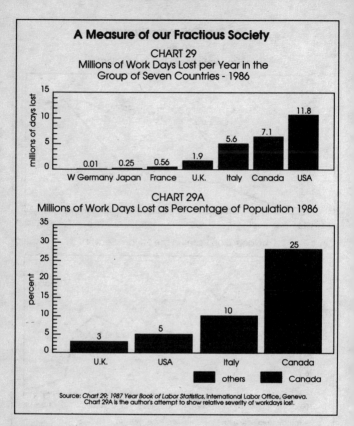

A Measure of our Fractious Society

CHART 29
Millions of Work Days Lost per Year in the
Group of Seven Countries - 1986

CHART 29A
Millions of Work Days Lost as Percentage of Population 1986

others

Canada

Source: Chart 29; 1987 Year Book of Labor Statistics, International Labor Office, Geneva.
Chart 29A is the author's attempt to show relative severity of workdays lost.

Comment:
For the past ten or fifteen years, Canada has had a very poor record of so-called "labour relations." Such social fractiousness can be seen as a manifestation of the "rights illusion" at work. Governments end up supporting claims that are lacking in fundamental justice. Laws that falsely protect unions against the normal risks of free association, or that require business owners to instigate meaningless quotas, or to pay wages they cannot afford, or that prevent owners from hiring non-union labour, and so on, are policy instruments of the State that drive a serious wedge between labour and the owners or managers of operations that pay the piper.

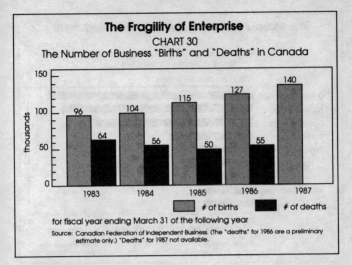

The Fragility of Enterprise

CHART 30

The Number of Business "Births" and "Deaths" in Canada

for fiscal year ending March 31 of the following year

Source: Canadian Federation of Independent Business. (The "deaths" for 1986 are a preliminary estimate only.) "Deaths" for 1987 not available.

Comment:

The small-business entrepreneur is the unsung hero of our society. Unfortunately, however, in an overly interventionist environment, the sort of courageous enterprising activity that built this nation is rarely honoured, and the magnitude of its results is unrecognized. The mortality figure above is more than 40 percent!

"Births" are businesses that actually succeed in beginning operations (as opposed to the 300,000 odd "registrations" — most of which remain only that). "Deaths" are businesses that cease to operate in the year quoted. The engine of wealth creation is obviously fragile, and needs a favourable environment (not grants) to run at full throttle.

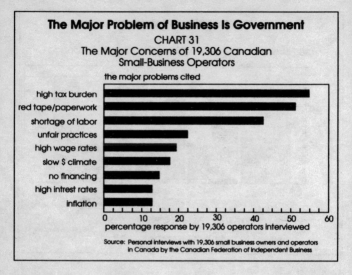

The Major Problem of Business is Government

CHART 31

The Major Concerns of 19,306 Canadian
Small-Business Operators

the major problems cited

Source: Personal interviews with 19,306 small business owners and operators
in Canada by the Canadian Federation of Independent Business

Comment:
We comment in other charts on the 1,005 percent increase in the Consumer
Tax Index since 1961. This chart is a measure of the material, daily frustration
and dissatisfaction felt by small-business operators all over Canada. These are
people who supplied *all* the new jobs in the private sector over the past five
years, who pay 43 percent of the nation's taxes, and are responsible for 25-30
percent of Canada's GNP annually.

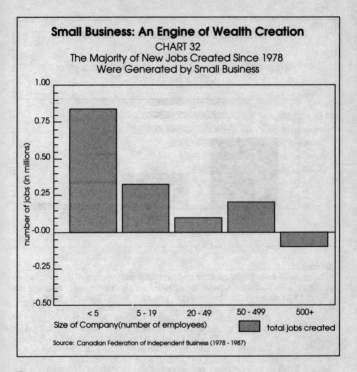

Small Business: An Engine of Wealth Creation

CHART 32

The Majority of New Jobs Created Since 1978
Were Generated by Small Business

number of jobs (in millions)

Size of Company(number of employees)

□ total jobs created

Source: Canadian Federation of Independent Business (1978 - 1987)

Comment:
It generally comes as a surprise that the bulk of new job creation in our country results from small-business activity. While it is the big businesses that attract the attention of the press, we are misled by their size. Our chart shows that big business, since 1978, has actually *lost* jobs, while small businesses — mostly very small businesses — have added hundreds of thousands of jobs to the economy. And yet it is these small businesses that can least afford the tax expense and red tape they say are their greatest burden. They are the people who can least afford to hire the lawyers and accountants that many larger firms consult routinely.

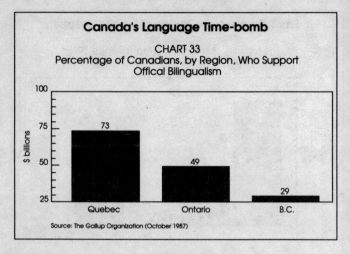

Canada's Language Time-bomb

CHART 33
Percentage of Canadians, by Region, Who Support
Offical Bilingualism

Source: The Gallup Organization (October 1987)

Comment:
Nothing could better illustrate the cynical social engineering of the egalitarian mentality than so-called official bilingualism. This chart vividly displays the difference in concern for this coercive program across Canada. Quebeckers have now won unilingual rights — rights they gave themselves in Bill 101 a decade ago — without a revolt from English Canada, which meekly submits itself to the illogical and unjust desire of government to force bilingualism on Canadians who don't want it. This chart foretells the potential break-up of Canada — not because of language, but because of the double standard of justice our central government has imposed on us in the name of language. The sad truth is that no party can govern Canada without first winning the Quebec vote. Quebec then exacts favours from government, one of which is the attempted francization of Canada. In thanks for Quebec's support, the federal government favours Quebec. On December 4, 1989 Prime Minister Mulroney declared, "We have delivered the goods" (to Quebec).

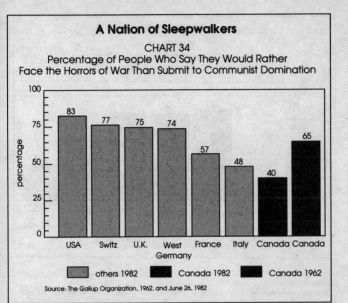

A Nation of Sleepwalkers

CHART 34

Percentage of People Who Say They Would Rather
Face the Horrors of War Than Submit to Communist Domination

others 1982   Canada 1982   Canada 1962

Source: The Gallup Organization, 1962, and June 26, 1982

Comment:
We will refrain from the many inferences that could be drawn from this Chart,
except for one: It suggests that Canadians by 1982 had dropped to a dangerously
low level of submissiveness as measured by their willingness to fight for what
they believe their nation stands for. We have referred throughout this book to
the fundamental danger of the social-welfare State, which is the gradual
diminution of the sense of individual responsibility, of community, of country,
this brings about in a "we'll do it all for you" world. This chart is also a measure
of our smugness, huddled as we are under the security blanket provided by our
neighbours to the south. It is likely also a measure of the effect of official
multiculturalism which our governments are all pushing down our throats so
hard. A "multicultural" policy reflects a willful ignorance of the fact that the
kinds of emotions that cause you to *want* to fight for your country arise, not
from a government-imposed "happy holidays" marketing program, but from a
long and profound tradition that permeates every aspect of daily life, and must
be defended.

Of the 25,309,330 people living in Canada in 1986, only 69,065 declared
themselves to be Canadians in the last census (*Saturday Night*, Dec., 1989)!

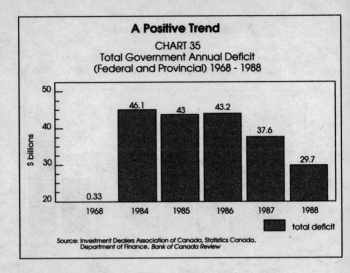

A Positive Trend

CHART 35
Total Government Annual Deficit
(Federal and Provincial) 1968 - 1988

$ billions

1968	1984	1985	1986	1987	1988
0.33	46.1	43	43.2	37.6	29.7

■ total deficit

Source: Investment Dealers Association of Canada, Statistics Canada,
Department of Finance, *Bank of Canada Review*

Comment:
We can only applaud the present trend of reducing government deficits, even
as we groan under them. For getting the annual deficit to zero is certainly a
major challenge in view of the many vested interests in borrowing and debt. In
1970, for example, wages and salaries accounted for close to 72 percent of
personal income, while last year, they counted for less than 64 percent. That
is, Canadians are ever more dependent on transfer payments — and on the debt
that now makes them possible. Canadians must let their MPs know that they
want government to control spending by balancing budgets — as we (almost)
did in 1968. Then, the debt would not increase, and the cost of servicing would
be reduced as a proportion of each successive annual budget. Then also,
governments could begin to set funds aside toward eventual repayment of the
debt. The present trend to reduce spending (it's going up!) is a cynical and
chilling reminder of the old French saying that "the art of taxation lies in
plucking the most feathers from the goose, while eliciting the least hissing."

Part Two

The Shape We're In

Introduction

THE WHOLE PURPOSE of Part One was to focus on the underlying causes of the trouble with Canada, constantly keeping in mind the intelligent, interested layman, who will likely never have the time to explore these matters in depth but who, intuitively dissatisfied with Canada's direction in the recent past, craves answers. I have tried to present as clearly as possible the background of the major ideological forces at work — often unperceived — in our country, and also to develop certain conceptual tools in the form of ideas and terms that help to communicate the subject.

Among those developed are concepts such as the "French" vs. "English" style of governance, captured in the "top-down"/"bottom-up" distinction; the "popular illusions" that arise when a whole society goes off its moral course, such as "the free-lunch illusion," "the rights illusion," "the equality illusion"; the underlying philosophy and virtue of democratic capitalism as a "bonus system"; the socialist reaction to it as a "handicap system," complete with its transactions of decline; and the differences between classical and modern liberals, conservatives, and socialists. Following this, a variety of charts and profiles of opinion and fact on Canada have been presented to illustrate the real political and economic effects of our misdirected policies. In short, it has throughout been my intention to provide a groundwork of concepts and language useful to the reader in his or her efforts to understand the forces at work in the evolution of our society.

Other than in books like this one, which are of necessity somewhat philosophical in tone, the way in which most people change policy — and the philosophy from which it arises (however incoherent) — is by taking concrete positions on "the issues." In the balance of this book, therefore, I will be discussing a number of these issues — all currently of great concern to Canadians (if column inches in our newspapers are any measure) and will try to show how the assumptions underlying these issues arise from and are directly linked to the clash of ideologies that historically have torn at, and currently are tearing at, the fabric of Canadian life.

To assist in analysing the issues, I have developed an imperfect but useful little metaphor — a set of mini-concepts, so to speak — that I hope will make understanding the forces at work in the issues a bit easier. It's a concept that you can apply creatively yourself to many social or political issues.

THE CONCEPT OF SOCIAL ENTROPY

IN THE PHYSICAL SCIENCES, the term "entropy" is used to describe the tendency of all things in the universe to come to a state of balance, or rest, through a loss of energy. For example, if two bottles are connected, one filled with hot water, the other with cold, heat energy will flow from hot to cold until both are the same temperature. Unless something intrudes to heat one of them up again, they will remain in balance. We are all instinctively familiar with this concept because we yield to it every day. Given a choice, most of us sit rather than stand, walk rather than run, and so on. We take the easiest way. So does energy in the whole universe (hot, faster-moving molecules seek to become cold, motionless ones). And so, I am postulating, do societies. They are created, like galaxies, by a certain creative force, and then they dissipate this energy over time by moving toward a state of random sameness. In physics this phenomenon, taken to its final conclusion, is referred to as the "heat death" of the universe; in communications theory the randomness that results from entropy, or lack of distinctiveness, is referred to as "noise." Thus do suns die out, planets cool, rivers eventually reduce to a trickle, randomized communication signals lose their ability to transmit information, mountains flatten out, and so on.

In fact, every physical thing seeks an entropic balance with its surroundings. Your hot bath will eventually cool to room temperature, the air in the bathroom will reach moisture saturation, and so on. Given enough time, the molecules of your evaporated bath water will disperse equally over the whole atmosphere.

I am suggesting, by analogy, that much of this holds true for human societies, as well. Leaving out disasters and wars, and if left to their own devices long enough, societies will move toward entropy, or dissipation of their many energies. They "cool" over time, and eventually stagnate, or die out in the sense that they lose their distinctive features. This has been the case for all great societies of the past, and appears to be the case for many of the present. We think of Greece, Rome, Arabia, Egypt, or, more recently, of the British Commonwealth and of the U.S.A. — which some half-heartedly insist is the first nation to go from barbarism to decadence without passing through civilization!

DISTINCTIVE FEATURES

TO A GREAT DEGREE, this book is about the entropic process at work in Canada, whereby egalitarian forces are gradually threatening the distinctive features that have made productive social life possible. This happens whenever predictable, useful, reliable, distinctive ideas, traditions, values, motives, or beliefs are slowly eroded and replaced with neutrality, or sameness, their force dissipated. When marriage is devalued and defined as a mere "union between two human beings"; when ordinary values lose their importance or get "relativized"; when work is replaced with social security paid for by others; when the freedoms so dependent on individuality and responsibility are everywhere diminished — entropy is at work. Our will to maintain the distinctive features of our society fails us, because "cooler" values, aligned with the general entropic force, supplant the hotter, distinctive values. What are the distinctive social, political, economic, and cultural forces in Canada? I have outlined them in Chapter Four. The whole of the welfare state/egalitarian "handicap" process described in Chapter Five — because it is aligned with entropy — is what is largely at work to dissipate them. It is possible to talk about this process in a loose, diagrammatic way with overlapping circles.

OVERLAPPING CIRCLES

ONE VERY FRUITFUL WAY to describe many of life's most difficult realities is in the form of "overlapping circles" — called Venn diagrams by mathematicians — that look like this:

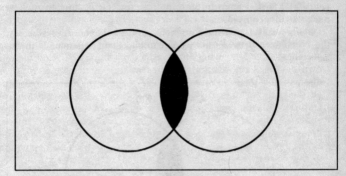

Such diagrams are useful to describe any flexible, relational "field" type of problem (the kind of problem that is easy to recognize, but has no easily definable boundaries), because the circles can be moved totally apart or may completely overlap each other, as desired. For example, if you wanted to describe a continuum from maleness to femaleness in human populations, you could do it like this:

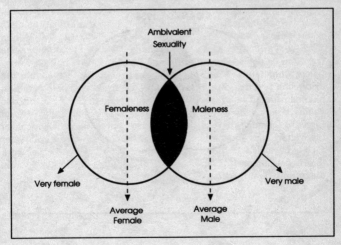

Such circles would move closer together in times of high sexual ambivalence such as we have experienced for the past twenty-five years, and farther apart in times of high sex-role distinction such as our ancestors enjoyed.

Another useful application might be political. We could describe, say, the continuum between individualism and State dependency in the same way:

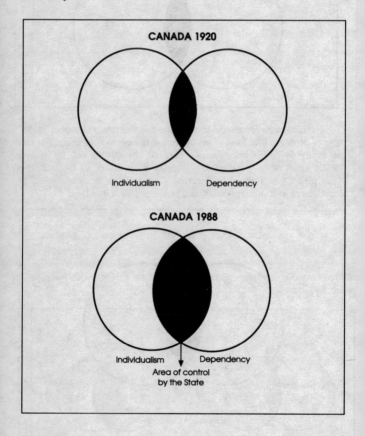

Overlapping circles can be creatively used to describe this dissipation process, with one circle for the positive distinctive feature, the other for the entropy-aligned force attacking, or undermining, it. For example, here's a view of the work ethic, so considered:

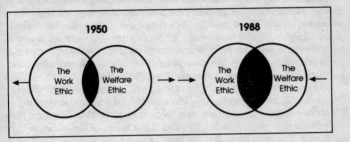

THE CULTURAL WEDGE

WITHOUT STRETCHING THIS METAPHOR too far, I want to make the following generalization. Unless a "cultural wedge" is constantly driven between any basic distinctive feature of society and the specific entropic force that tends to dissipate that feature, the feature will lose energy (value), and die out.

What is a cultural wedge? It is a strong idea, or attitude, or belief that constitutes *a resistance to entropy*, whether consciously or unconsciously, that is inserted between the distinctive feature and the entropic force, at every opportunity. It is the one element in the structure drawn that protects the feature from dissipation. We can now conceive of the complete metaphor, with feature, wedge, and entropic force in place, as follows.

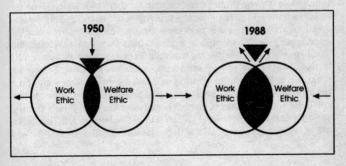

In a loose sense, then, the cultural wedge is the sum of a society's will to keep entropy at bay; it is the conscious or unconscious awareness of the *social utility* of that society's distinctive features. Such an awareness is primitive, in that we all share an intuitive knowledge that in same- ness there is no distinctiveness; no differences; and therefore no basis for action; therefore no basis for morality; therefore no basis for a society. When I used Jane Jacobs's concept of "transactions of decline" in Chapter Five, I was really discussing the entropic tendency in societies to dissipate their own distinctive features — the strengths that made them great in the first place — in an egalitarian sameness, through the war of all against all. Chart 23 (Chapter Seven) shows how the productive energies of some Canadians, as represented by their tax dollars, is taken from them — like heat from the bath — and scattered among others who absorb that money, or heat, thus bringing both entities into an even balance (which is the object of the social-welfare State). The problem is that the heat, or energy, or dollars, only flow in one direction, until a high degree of entropy is achieved. The energy is then gone, the temperature balanced, the money distributed. And productive life eventually declines.

This same metaphor can be used to describe the entropic process at work in our value system, our beliefs, whereby, over time, the cutural wedge we have kept in place gets virtually "squeezed out" by the entropic force. In short, we lose our will to fight strongly for the cultural wedge that kept entropy at bay. Examples are when, say, useful sexual distinctions become mere "orientations," or distinctions between the hard-working poor and the slovenly poor are lost by lumping them all together (all have equal universal claims on the energy [money] of others. Poverty is described as "systemic"); or when the importance of the traditional family is weakened, and replaced by mere "household- ers," and legal debates rage about what constitutes a "family"; or when individuals who ought to be responsible for their own actions lose this important moral sense under the protection of the controlling State.

Although not applicable to every situation, you may enjoy using this overlapping-circles metaphor yourself. Just focus on any important distinctive feature, analyse the entropic force attacking, or weakening, it (this always tends toward sameness, or loss of distinction), figure out what the cultural wedge is, and you'll have a dynamic description of the situation. In the end, each individual has to decide whether to help drive the wedge farther in (which requires energy) or, if only through yielding to the entropic force, allow it to get squeezed out. This fact of life is completely compatible with the familiar sentiment that the only thing necessary for the triumph of evil is for good people to do nothing. In other words, natural entropy will produce social decay if there is no will to resist.

The one arena in which everyone has an opportunity, large or small, to choose between resisting or yielding to the entropic force is that of the "issues." In what follows, these will be discussed in the light of all that has preceded.

8

The Great Welfare Rip-Off
Soaking Everyone,
To Pay Everyone

A decent society provides
A ladder up which all may climb,
And a net beneath which none may fall.

(Anon)

The waste is distressing, but it is the least of the evils
of the paternalistic programs that have grown to
such massive size. Their major evil is their effect on
the fabric of our society. They weaken the family;
reduce the incentive to work, save, and innovate;
reduce the accumulation of capital; and limit our
freedom. These are the fundamental standards by
which they should be judged.

Milton Friedman

IT IS CONSIDERED BAD form to debunk welfare. Taboo. You risk immediate classification as a cold and heartless person. Or, perversely — in
view of the fact that everyone is striving to be well off — your remarks
are disqualified if you *are* well off. How could you possibly understand?
So we wake up every morning to more news about how, despite
Canada's economic well-being, we are failing: "5 million in 1987 lived
in poverty, senator calculates," proclaims the *Globe and Mail* (Jan. 5,
1989).

Twenty percent of all Canadians? Very unlikely, we think. But who are we to say? So at best we mutter occasional disbelief to a close friend. But the chances of indulging in a full discussion on welfare or poverty in Canada are very slim for a very good reason: very few ordinary citizens *know* anything about welfare, poverty, or the needy, for the simple reason that very little is known, and what *is* known is in dispute even among experts. What the ordinary person learns about welfare comes from media journalists who usually support the growth of the welfare State and are by and large shockingly uncritical. Alas, entropy reigns, and the world we see or read about is the one the interested parties choose to show us.

To repeat, it is not fashionable to debunk poverty. Nevertheless, I am going to try. For nothing is quite so dangerous to an individual, a nation, or even to the poor themselves as the blind acceptance of a "condition" that many of us suspect has been largely defined by social policy experts, then used as a cudgel to beat us all into a sense of collective guilt, robbing most of us of money, and all the needy of self-reliance. How guilty, how responsible should we feel?

It depends. It depends how true all this is. And even if "true" — we have a right to ask — who says so? By whose definitions? And even if true by their definitions, we will want to ask ourselves a few questions. Are their definitions good ones? Do I agree with them? Are they reasonable? In short, are all the people I'm *told* are poor really *deserving* of all this free help — $60 billion in 1988, of which, we have learned (Chapter Seven, Chart 22), only $6 billion went to the *truly* needy? Policy experts ideologically sensitive to this field will already have had indigestion by the time they've read this far. And well they should. What is going on is a scandal.

But never mind the experts. Most of them are making a living out of the social-policy industry. Rather, how do the ordinary people who pay the shot decide what is right? I think it's reasonable to start by being honest with ourselves.

How do we feel about helping others?

My own answer is that I am probably like most people: nothing moves me to quite the same degree of pity as the sight of a helpless or seriously ill child; a helpless disabled person; a helpless elderly person; a helpless poor person. It would be very difficult for me to refuse assistance. I have never personally been in true need, but I have visited the slums of Mexico and the *favelas* of Rio de Janeiro, and brushed up against the poor of Hong Kong, the Caribbean, and Thailand, where can be seen what anyone would refer to as characteristics of "the truly needy": hunger without recourse, nutritional deformation, rotting teeth, mental illness, homelessness, death in the streets — true human horrors. For sure, there's nothing even remotely resembling this in Canada, in type or in scale, and it would be a gross exaggeration to suggest otherwise. From such experiences one draws a few conclusions.

Our definitions of the poor, the needy, and "the truly needy" and the whole moral envelope surrounding them are extremely relative and have changed radically in the past twenty-five years. Changed, I fear, to the great detriment of our society. Changed in ways that have created whole classes of "poor" and "needy" citizens who otherwise might have stood a chance of becoming self-reliant individuals. In what follows, I will try to show why. For this, the well-intentioned but shortsighted politicians and social engineers bear an enormous responsibility. For when we look through what they have done their charitable work begins to look more like a gross manipulation of society in the interests of their personal social convictions and careers.

THE WELFARE BOOM:
HOW A "HAND-UP" BECAME A "HAND-OUT"

THERE IS NOTHING MORE emblematic of the "handicap system," outlined in Chapter Five, than the social spending, welfare, and redistribution programs promoted by the social-welfare State. These programs strive to fulfil the socialist slogan: "From each according to his ability, to each according to his need." As we saw in Chart 23 (Chapter Seven), 32 percent on average of every province's expenditures — 51 percent of P.E.I.'s — is received from Ottawa. In other words, Canada has played the socialist's welfare-redistribution game vigorously.

How has this happened?

First of all, it wasn't always this way; neither in the United States nor in Canada, where the patterns have more or less followed those of our southern neighbour. In the U.S.A., for reasons peculiar to its development, social problems and the social-policy response to them all occurred more radically and earlier than here. In this sense, the American experience has served as a huge social policy experiment we would do well to watch more closely. America is like a patient with a more advanced form of the same disease from which we suffer. (In Europe this used to be called "the British disease.") We now have the opportunity, before it is too late, of returning to good health at a lesser cost by changing the course of treatment. But instead we behave as if our health is fine. We are still wallowing in justifications to support our "sacred trusts," "universality," and the like. But the Americans have passed this point. Major critiques of the social policy scandal, like Milton Friedman's *Free to Choose*, George Gilder's *Wealth and Poverty*, and especially Charles Murray's two major works, *Losing Ground* and *In Pursuit of Happiness and Good Government*, have shaken the welfare establishment to its core. These, and others like them, are very serious academic and, more importantly, moral examinations of what the Western democracies have wrought with their altered sense of charity. There are no comparable works published by Canadian authors — most of whom complain that we are not giving — or getting — enough. Few, if any, ever challenge the moral basis of the social-welfare State and its policies.

Both in the U.S.A. and in Canada, the story unfolds as follows. Throughout the nineteenth century, until the early part of the twentieth, the normal conception of welfare held by most people — including the poor themselves — was that welfare was a reward for indolence; that left to their own devices — given a free lunch, so to speak — most ordinary folk would choose to keep taking it and would prefer not to work; that, sustained long enough, this practice would lead to whole generations of indolent people. This attitude persisted through World War II until about 1950. The reigning philosophy then was that *the needy ought to have a temporary hand-up, but in no circumstances a long-term hand-out*. The hand-up soon lets go, forcing them to climb the rest of the way on their own. The hand-out creates financial rewards for not climbing. Murray tells us that even President Franklin Roosevelt, who is often blamed for creating the welfare State in America through his "New Deal" programs, only intended his Unemployment Insurance, Old Age Security, Workmen's Compensation, and the worst of these — "AFDC" (Aid To Families With Dependent Children) — to be *for the truly needy*.

In Canada it was the Marsh Report of 1943 that created the blueprint for the country's social-welfare State. Its first serious recommendation was the extension of welfare benefits paid to foster mothers for the care of orphans, to *all* mothers caring for their own children in their homes, well off or not. This was an example of social entropy at work as Canada moved toward sameness and loss of distinction (even though our reason for helping orphans is crucially *different* from any motive for helping the natural children of intact families).

In the early 1960s, when confronted with news of growing poverty in America (sensationalist news, based on very questionable assumptions, it now turns out), President John Kennedy, in the full flush of postwar economic success, changed the name of the game. He made impassioned speeches saying that it was not enough for the government to give temporary help to the needy. It now must take *an active continuing role* in helping them. Presto! With this attitude the paternalistic State assumed moral responsibility for the condition of the poor and needy — conditions previously assumed to be their own responsibility. The hand-up (and then you're on your own) had become the hand-out (we'll help as long as you ask us). Society was suddenly sliced up into two classes: no longer the responsible and the irresponsible, but the *responsible* and the *faultless*. Suddenly, poverty was *no one's* fault. Henceforth, it was declared "structural," the fault of "the system." In fact, Canada's National Council of Welfare calls it "system-induced" — a perfect example of what I have called "the Determinist Illusion" gone rampant.

In Canada, this very change was echoed in the 1960 policy conference of the federal Liberal party, held in Kingston, Ontario, in which "universality" policies were given broad support. In the U.S.A., under President Lyndon Johnson's "Great Society" programs, so much money was thrown at welfare and the needy that the Department of Health, Education and Welfare alone had a total budget greater than the GNP of most of the world's countries! During the 1970s in the U.S.A. — a trend followed obediently by Canada — "the forty-four major welfare programs grew two and a half times as fast as GNP and three times as fast as wages."[1] Concurrently in Canada, Prime Minister Pierre Trudeau and his Liberal party embarked on the most top-down, centralized social-welfare experiment ever seen in our history, moving the nation from a condition in which it was more or less balancing its budgets to one in which it was *spending a full 50 percent more than it took in annually*. He did this by creating a top-heavy elitist bureaucracy, raising taxes out of all proportion to other living costs to do it, and borrowing irresponsibly, thus committing future generations to pay for his internal empire.

No State can survive for long on such a basis. It turns out that, as in other socialist nations, much of this increase in social-welfare spending has resulted in the kinds of "shifting, diffusing, equalizing, concealing, shuffling, smoothing, evading, relegating and collectivizing the real risks and costs of economic change"[2] that desensitize the economy. Which is unfortunate, for just about the only thing on which poverty experts agree is that poverty does indeed change with GNP. The higher the GNP, the lower the poverty. And I mean *absolute* poverty, not *relative* poverty. Absolute poverty has to do with basic food, clothing, and shelter; relative poverty has to do with whether you have what someone decides is enough money or not. We can get rid of absolute poverty by raising GNP — this is the most compelling case for freedom and the bonus system. But we will *never* get rid of relative poverty. How could we, since we've defined it in such a way as to ensure that we don't? I believe that in Canada, through a combination of private charity, good neighbours, and some government programs, but especially through our economic success, we've all but banished absolute poverty. But it's impossible, both in principle and in theory to banish relative poverty, because it's "distributional" in nature (part of the normal curve discussed in Chapter Two). Canadians should not be taken in by this policy sleight of hand, the shocking ineptitude of which will be revealed more fully in the poverty calculation analysis to come shortly.

How Equal "Opportunity" Changed To Equal "Outcome"

THE FINANCIAL AND MORAL COST of this disastrous shift in moral responsibility and self-reliance, from our tradition of personal freedom and responsibility to the present morally contorted and constitutionally confused determinist ethic placing blame on a faceless "system," has been nothing short of catastrophic. It is designed to foster resentment and dependence at every turn because it specifically positions the State as an agency able to provide equal outcomes for all. Once this happens, the people become polarized. Like iron filings drawn to magnets, the country divides into those who produce and want to protect what they work for, and those who want to take what the former have produced. If I am not equal in some way, then I should run to the State and make a claim. In this respect, the shift from the idea of a State set up to provide and protect equal *opportunity* to one that is expected to provide equal *outcomes*, or results, has been decisive, and through reliance on "the rights illusion" has resulted in what the insurance industry calls a "moral hazard." George Gilder sums up this sad repertoire of misguided policy effects as follows:

> The moral hazards of current programs are clear. Unemployment compensation promotes unemployment. Aid for families with dependent children . . . makes more families dependent and fatherless. Disability insurance in all its multiple forms encourages the promotion of small ills into temporary disabilities and partial

disabilities into total and permanent ones. Social security payments may discourage concern for the aged and dissolve the links between generations. Programs of insurance against low farm prices and high energy costs create a glut of agricultural commodities and a dearth of fuels . . . All means-tested programs . . . promote the value of being "poor" (the credentials of poverty), and thus perpetuate poverty.[3]

And as Murray points out — just to illustrate the ingrained nature of this moral shift — members of the American "National Welfare Rights Organization" meeting in 1967 "were not demonstrating so much for jobs as for the right to long-term, unfettered, generous charity."[4] These are demands by the well-off to soak the well-off, using the legitimizing, reverse-discrimination provisions of constitutional law to do so. After this moral shift took place,

hardly anyone argued that it was fundamentally wrong to take tax dollars from one worker whose paycheck, the government had decided, was too large, and give them to another worker whose paycheck, the government had decided, was too small. Ten years earlier, hardly anyone would have argued that it was right.[5]

What were some of the most deleterious effects of this State-sponsored, elite-initiated program shift in the social and moral fabric of our society? The most harmful overall effect was the removal of the cultural wedge that had historically been driven between independence and dependence, between the moral, hard-working, honest poor and the lazy, shiftless, dishonest poor, resulting in what Murray aptly terms "the homogenization of the Poor." Once this wedge was loosened and the State moved in to equalize the poor, their distinctiveness was immediately lost — a victim of bureaucratic definition. But North America was built by poor people, or children of the poor, very few of whom ever *stayed* poor. And there had never been a distinct line between them and others that anyone could define. Most importantly, those at the bottom had their own status and clear distinctions within that status. In her authoritative study *The Idea of Poverty*, Gertrude Himmelfarb emphasizes the importance of such distinctions, telling us that "more recently, it has been recognized that such moral concepts were an important part of the social reality for people of all classes and persuasions." "Respectability" . . . [was] just as much a fact of life for the poor."[6]

In fact many of them — especially farmers — saw themselves as "the backbone of the nation and on a considerably higher moral plane than the effete rich."[7] Those of low income knew the differences between the good poor and the bad, the slovenly and the hard-working, the responsible and the irresponsible, the caring and the uncaring; in short, those who planned and worked hard for a better future for their families, and those that didn't. If they happened to fall into the net, they were aware of a complex, interrelating set of moral boundaries, sanctions, and spurs to success that inherently constituted "the ladder up which all may climb." In one short stroke, the State took away the ladder and started feeding and paying them for staying in the net. If you were poor, an alcoholic, uneducated, or pregnant, there would be a program for you. But if you were merely in a low-income category, disciplined, obeyed your parents, worked hard, struggled to get ahead, and stayed out of trouble and away from loose sex — you didn't qualify. From then onward, the logic of the whole business was predetermined. From now on, all would be victims. Social-policy thinking became like the snake that tries to eat its own tail. The experts everywhere began to argue that, since the condition of the poor wasn't their fault, the State had to set about "liberalizing" eligibility standards to get rid of the stigma of welfare and preserve the "dignity" of the poor (something of which our self-respecting immigrant poor had never been deprived). In the very same vein, our own National Council of Welfare deplores any effort to distinguish between the "deserving" and the "undeserving" poor.[8] Murray sums up this attitude tidily: "Because the system is to blame, all people on welfare are equally deserving of being given a hand . . . There was no longer a mechanism for stamping someone unworthy. On the contrary, many of the social-service programs required as a condition of eligibility that the participants be failures."[9]

In this object, the State has succeeded admirably. It has in the space of a few generations completely eliminated ordinary morality from the lives of millions of people whom it has classified as faultless. At the same time, it has taught them, through the rampant "rights illusion," that they can achieve equality not by sacrifice, hard work, and saving, but by making ever-increasing claims against the State for their "rights" — the list of which grows longer by the day. In this manner, the State and the New Class running the country fan the flames of resentment among the people. But the people are not stupid.

THE ELITE WISDOM AND THE POPULAR WISDOM

AGAIN AND AGAIN, IN *Losing Ground*, Murray shows how the elite wisdom of the social scientist, and policymakers is wrongheaded, and how "the popular wisdom" is right on the mark. In fact, the premise of the second half of his sobering book "is that social policy since 1964 has ignored these premises and that it has thereby created much of the mess we are in."[10] What are the premises of the popular wisdom, the *vox populi?*

> *Premise # 1   People respond to incentives and disincentives. Sticks and carrots work.*

> *Premise # 2   People are not inherently hard-working or moral. In the absence of countervailing influences, people will avoid work and be amoral.*

> *Premise #3   People must be held responsible for their actions. Whether they are responsible in some ultimate philosophical or biochemical sense cannot be the issue if society is to function.*

This is about the same conclusion we came to in Chapter Two in discussing "the Determinist Illusion": in order to create a moral and social order that *works*, we have to assume we are *all* responsible beings (not just some, sitting up in Ottawa), regardless of "fairness" or "luck of the draw," or any other merits or demerits of each person's case — or else we can never allocate consequences or rewards; the Bonus System cannot work; and the alternative, the Handicap System — in addition to the immorality of its coercive humanitarianism — always ends by robbing everyone of self-worth.

Now that we've swallowed the social-welfare State ideal hook, line, and sinker — what have we created with it? "Canada's social security system ensures that all Canadians have at least a minimum of resources available to meet their basic needs, and essential services to maintain their well-being." So says the *Canada Year Book, 1988.* Here's a very partial list of programs paid for with sixty billion taxpayers' dollars: Old Age Security, Guaranteed Income Supplement, Spousal Allowance, Canada Pension Plan, Unemployment Insurance, Family Allowances, Child Tax Credit, Veterans' Benefits, Indian and Northern Affairs Programs, Quebec Pension Plan, pensions for death and disability, Civilian War Allowance, Educational Assistance Fund, Bureau of Pensions Advocates, Veterans' Land Administration, Canada Assistance Plan, Workers' Compensation Programs, retirement pensions, survivors' pensions, disability pensions, children's benefits,

New Horizons program, National Welfare Grants program, fellowships, Vocational Rehabilitation of Disabled Persons program, tax-credit programs, provincial social-security programs, Guaranteed Annual Income Supplement (Ontario), Family Income Plan (Saskatchewan) — there are hundreds of other provincial plans — international welfare through UNICEF and the OECD . . . and on and on.

I am running out of steam. The *Canada Year Book* mentions hundreds of interlocking social-security programs, and alludes to the existence of thousands more, federal, provincial, and local. Worst of all, "the government has been pouring billions of dollars into social services without knowing how the needy are being helped" (*Toronto Star*, Oct. 25, 1989). In short, monitoring is minimal. Surely some of these programs are "necessary." But how many, and how much should they cost us, and most importantly, given their moral effect, should we have them at all? In the following chart, let's look at just a few of the larger commitments our government has made to present and future generations, keeping in mind that we have been borrowing heavily for twenty years to cover cost overruns and are still borrowing some $30 billion a year. Remember — total annual program costs for "social spending" are about $60 billion, of which only $6 billion, we are relatively sure, goes to the "truly needy" (yet to be defined); $16 billion goes to those of low-income, *and the rest — some $38 billion — goes to middle- and upper-income Canadians*. I think we should ask how, and why.

That's the big picture. That's what your federal government spends your money on. The programs marked with asterisks are all the "social spending" programs referred to previously, none of which, except the most paltry, even existed before the turn of the century (now, 57 percent of the government's non-interest spending) — that is, before anyone thought it was morally right to take money from some working citizens to pay other working or non-working citizens. In the balance of this chapter, we will put a few of these programs under the microscope.

Just before doing so, here are the increases in government's social-program spending since 1950, using *constant dollars* (one 1950 dollar = four 1980 dollars). Here's what has happened:

- Health and medical spending has increased 22.6 times.

- Social welfare spending has increased 11.3 times.

- Education spending has increased 18.4 times.

Of Canada's Total Spending Budget for 1988,
Here's Where the Money Went
(As published with the Government's
Fiscal Plan, Feb. 10, 1988)

Total Spent on Social Programs

1)	Unemployment Insurance	$10,150,000,000 *
2)	Old Age Security Benefits	14,465,000,000 *
3)	Family Allowances	2,565,000,000 *
4)	Canada Assistance Plan	4,310,000,000 *
5)	Established Program Financing (note 1)	8,925,000,000 *
6)	Fiscal Transfers (note 1)	7,340,000,000 *
7)	Other	7,955,000,000 *
	Subtotal:	55,710,000,000 *

Total Spent on Other Matters

8)	Defence	10,440,000,000
9)	Official Development Assistance	2,545,000,000
10)	Other (note 2)	27,385,000,000
	Subtotal:	40,370,000,000
	TOTAL, ALL PROGRAMS:	96,080,000,000
11)	Money borrowed to pay interest on government debt	29,220,000,000
	TOTAL, ALL GOVERNMENT EXPENDITURES:	$125,300,000,000

Comment: Social programs accounted for about 45 percent of the increase in spending from 1984 to 1990. The rest is largely public-debt charges. Government is now trying to control this through changes to indexation formulae, etc. However, at the same time as it does this, it extends other benefits, and takes on new programs like national daycare (now stalled). Increases are projected at 5 percent per year for the foreseeable future.

Note 1: These two items include *transfers* to other levels of government and *equalization* programs — key instruments of the egalitarian state as it strives to make its handicap system function everywhere — and key transactions of decline.

Note 2: "Other" includes the operational costs of government itself (salaries, rents, utilities, supplies), now about $18 billion per year. The balance is for grants, capital spending, and payments to Crown corporations. Also included here are about $9 billion in "subsidies to industry." Just like public transfers, these subsidies are ultimately ineffectual, and in the long run, damaging to industry. Why, after all, should our government give $6.8 million to Inco (assets $4.07 billion), or $6.6 million to Johnson & Johnson (assets $96.6 million)?

Comment: These latter are the areas where the present government has been successful in cutting its costs. Since November 1984, authorized personnel have been cut, and will total a 15,000-person-years reduction by 1991. In addition to other cuts, the government will achieve a 20 percent reduction in this category of expenses, comparing very favourably with the five years prior to 1984, during which they doubled.

THE "POVERTY" SCANDAL: WHO ARE THEY?

OUR LIVES ARE FILLED with a barrage of information on "the poor" which we are asked to accept at face value, most of it prepared by sympathetic journalists. And the story always seems to be the same: there are more "poor" than ever before; they are getting poorer as the rest of us get richer; Canada is increasingly populated by the poor and needy; our society is failing in its responsibility to make them not-poor. But is this all true?

Let's ask ourselves exactly whom, without question, you should be helping, failing which, any sane person would be justified in calling you heartless; and whom you should *not* be helping. In order to increase sensitivity to the whole subject, try answering the quiz opposite this page.

I am willing to bet that most people would feel a readiness to help the first four people listed here — with some qualifications, perhaps — and none of the remainder. And yet, provided the annual incomes of all these people were below "the low-income cut-off" point established by the National Council of Welfare — a government-funded committee in Ottawa — all of them would be included in the tally of this nation's poor; would form a part of the "five million" that the good senator calculated live in poverty in Canada.

Most hard-working Canadians find it extremely upsetting to hear this, because until they answer a quiz like the one to the right, they don't really think much about the *kinds* of poor, especially about the moral distinctions which they most definitely feel ought to be preserved (which is, of course, what the poverty establishment is trying to eliminate). I tell them that the National Council of Welfare's ostensible purpose is not to judge each case on its merits (this is done at the provincial level) but, according to a Steve Kerstetter with whom I spoke there in January of 1989, "to assess the level of poverty in Canada." No moral judgements here, just statistics. Unfortunately, it is these statistics that get all the alarmist press, shape the consciousness of the nation, and condemn us to a never-ending "poverty" problem. What Canadians really should know, therefore, is how the statistical calculations of poverty are arrived at by the Council.

THE DIFFERENCE BETWEEN ABSOLUTE AND RELATIVE POVERTY CALCULATIONS

HERE ARE A FEW KEY POINTS, with comments, from a paper on poverty

ARE YOU A KIND PERSON, OR HEARTLESS?

TO WHICH OF THE FOLLOWING PEOPLE WOULD YOU GIVE UN-
QUESTIONED ASSISTANCE IF YOU COULD?

1. A poor person, with four kids, suddenly struck with a terrible disease.

2. A poor, severely disabled person.

3. A poor person struck by natural disaster such as a house fire, no insurance.

4. A poor, elderly person with no income.

5. A poor person who refuses to work.

6. A poor person who cheats and does not declare all his income.

7. A poor person who continually commits petty crimes, is slovenly, etc.

8. A poor person who wins a substantial lottery.

9. A poor person who makes a lot of money selling his house or land.

10. A poor person who has low income but receives a large inheritance.

11. A poor man who has low income but lives on his own farm, grows his own food, and has no rent or mortgage.

12. A twenty-year-old working student with eligible low income.

13. A poor woman who continues to have children, qualifying for more welfare support with each.

entitled "The Mismeasurement of Poverty in Canada," delivered by Dr. Michael Walker of the Fraser Institute in Vancouver.[11] Walker's paper, delivered to the Ottawa Economic Society in March of 1986, specifically sets out to criticize the National Council of Welfare's "Poverty Lines," which are published each year. In 1986, the Council estimated the poor in Canada to number 4.35 million. This is a statistical illusion, says Walker, for the following reasons: Canada's method of calculating poverty is relative and "entirely arbitrary both in its origination and in its continuing revision," unlike that of the United States. There, poverty is based on a fixed formula accepted by much of the world, despite the problems with it outlined in "the Poverty Illusion" (Chapter Two). The basic formula is: *the cost of a minimum adequate nutritionally sound diet, multiplied by three.* The virtue of this measure is that it escalates only with prices according to the Consumer Price Index. But in Canada the poverty line is calculated quite differently. Every year, Statistics Canada establishes something it calls a "low-income cut-off" point and is quite careful to say that "the cut-offs are *not* poverty lines and should not be so interpreted." These cut-offs "do not take into acount a number of important factors, such as wealth, access to subsidized goods and services, age, future earnings potential, etc." Nevertheless, the National Council of Welfare tells us that these cut-offs are "the most widely used Canadian Poverty Lines."

The U.S.A., then, bases its poverty line on a minimum adequate *standard of living,* while Canada bases its poverty line on a relative *cash income* level. The American line goes up with prices, while the Canadian line goes up with average income growth. The U.S. standard is tied to actual cost-of-living increases, the Canadian line is tied to national wealth. Absurdly, if Canada suddenly produced a lot more wealthy people, even though the cost of living had not changed, we would suddenly have a lot more "poor" because of the new wealth. As Walker rightly points out,

> *this radical difference in the low income cut-offs or poverty lines has a dramatic effect on who will be regarded as poor and how many Canadians will be regarded as living below the poverty line. It will also have a dramatic effect on the perception of how we are doing over time in our war on poverty.*

Here is Walker's calculation of the difference between the two systems for Canada, assuming a city of 100,000-499,000 people:

	StatsCan cut-offs	Column A plus cost-of-living increases	National Council of Welfare's calculation
	A	B	C
	1961	1984	1984
1 person	$1,500	$ 5,791	$ 9,345
2 persons	2,500	9,652	12,321
3 persons	3,000	11,582	16,456
4 persons	3,500	13,512	19,017
5 persons	4,000	15,443	22,078
Percentage of families living in poverty:	25.9 %	10.28 %	17.8 %
Millions (in Canada) below poverty line:	N.A.	2,543,100	4,349,000

Frankly, this is quite shocking, for most of us have never once heard of this calculation difference, so staggering in its implications. As Walker says, "once we accept relative poverty measurements, then we must also recognize that it is meaningless to think of eliminating poverty in this sense. It is quite impossible to eliminate it and quite meaningless to speak of a policy designed to eradicate it."

What are some of the other very good reasons for dismissing Canada's method for assessing poverty? Here are a few:

1. *It excludes* "gambling wins and losses, capital gains or losses, lump-sum inheritances, receipts from the sale of property or personal belongings, income tax refunds, loans received or repaid, lump-sum settlements of insurance policies and income in kind."[12]

2. *It ignores* the extent to which individuals own their own homes (44.1 percent of those counted as low-income in 1980 also owned their own homes — 90 percent of unemployment insurance recipients in New-foundland own their own homes).

3. *It does not include* subsidized goods and services (much used by the elderly, who loom large in the ranks of the "poor" as defined).

4. *It ignores* the life-cycle aspect of people's income-earning experience (which is like a normal curve as we age). We earn less when we are young, and when we are old. And in 1986, 50.4 percent of all low-income families had heads who were either less than 34 years of age or beyond retirement years. And a full 65.7 percent of "unattached individuals" were in these portions of their lifetimes (old, young, students, etc.).

Walker says that the problem with our "snapshot" technique for assessing poverty is that it ignores the "explosion" of earnings normally experienced by the young as they continue working, and "the natural process of income decline associated with depletion of assets accumulated during the high earning years." Although of low *incomes*, the average *wealth* of those over 65 years of age, most of whom are counted as below the poverty line, is five and a half times their yearly income. In short, Canada's poverty calculation totally ignores the whole matter of social mobility into and out of "poverty."

Enough said. At the least, the foregoing should be enough to cause a great deal of skepticism the next time you encounter a statistic on Canadian poverty — especially from a government-funded agency. And just to put it all in perspective, here's a chart prepared from Statistics Canada information for 1961-1980, and extended by the Fraser Institute to 1987:

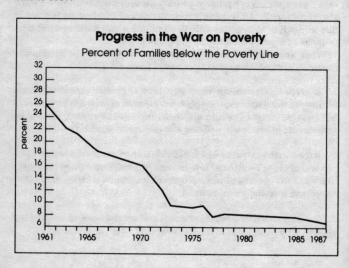

Progress in the War on Poverty

Percent of Families Below the Poverty Line

This chart is based on the "low-income cut-offs" produced by Statistics Canada which, the Institute reminds us, itself says that "the income cut-offs are not poverty lines and should not be so interpreted." In other words, the Institute concludes, "though the figures presented here demonstrate a consistent and steady progress in the fight against poverty, it is important to remember that they probably exaggerate very greatly the number of people for whom poverty is an ongoing reality."

THE PENSION SCANDAL

HERE'S ANOTHER PITIFUL RESULT of the "we'll do it all for you" ethic of the nanny State. This is particularly ironic in view of the fact that in the case of pensions, *you're* doing it all for the government. Canada's pension plan is a pyramid scheme that robs individuals of that most crucial responsibility to peer into their own futures, plan, and save accordingly. It is an arch case of the coercive humanitarianism of the social-welfare State. If you tried it yourself, you'd end up in jail.

Most Canadians are not aware that whereas any private pension plan is required by law to be "funded," the government's own is not. This means that if a private fund had to pay out all current benefits claimed, it could do so from its own financial holdings. Even private plans have their problems (which full disclosure would eventually eradicate), but at least they are solvent. But the government's plan is what is called, tongue-in-cheek, a "pay-as-you-go" system. In other words, even though you and your employer have been *forced* to make what are euphemistically called "contributions" to the Canada Pension "Plan" all your working life, the money isn't there. (Admirably, the Quebec Pension Plan has actual funds in the order of $32 billion set aside, but not the Canada Pension Plan.) The federal government couldn't pay the benefits, if demanded, from a fund. So where does it get the money to pay the benefits claimed? It gets it from general tax revenue, and borrowings from other Canadians or from foreigners. In other words, the money comes in the bottom — taken from the working population, and from borrowing — and goes out the top, to the retired. The government's CPP scheme is just that, a scheme. Actuarially, it is unsound. Demographically, it is in deep trouble because while there are now six of working age for every retiree, there will be as few as three in fifty years (*Financial Post*, April 5, 1988). The various governments of Canada that were supposed to act as trustees of your "contributions" (Friedman reminds us that Orwell, in his book *Nineteen Eighty-Four*, said "compulsory is voluntary") have colluded to take your pension money, and they use it to fund other social-welfare programs. In fact, the rules for the CPP were specifically written to permit just such a frittering away of trust funds. These headlines say it all: "Pensions Frittered Away" (*Globe and Mail*, Dec. 28, 1985), "Pension Plan Will Die Without Premium Hike" (*Toronto Star*, Sept. 28, 1985), "Pension Legerdemain" (*Financial Post*, Nov. 11, 1985), "Governments Worst Offenders in Pension Fund Abuse" (*Toronto Star*, Aug. 9, 1986). As this last article, by Diane Francis, points out, "Here's the pension game Ottawa plays . . . It merely makes a bookkeeping entry for the amounts . . . but the obligation is awesome. By March 1985, it was $15.5 billion and growing."

Worse, this pension liability does not get reported anywhere (the auditor general merely "notes it" in his annual report). And the provinces have smaller, but similar schemes in operation. By 1993, Ontario alone will have an "unfunded pension obligation" of more than $8 billion (*Toronto Star*, Sept. 2, 1986). A report published by the federal Department of Insurance in Ottawa tells us that Canada's total "unfunded actuarial liability" for its "pension plans" as of December 31, 1986, would be about $305 billion. That is the amount of money that would have to be set aside to produce sufficient interest to continue meeting obligations if the plan were a legitimate plan, and not, as economist John Goodman suggests in referring to social-security schemes — "a government-run chain letter," or an "accounting deception." As he points out, "For all practical purposes, every dollar that comes into Social Security is immediately spent — every hour of the day. No funds are being stashed away in bank vaults, or being invested in interest-bearing assets."[13] The upshot of this is that government pension plans rely not on sound investment, but on the government's power to tax younger generations to pay the older. The plans are moral deceptions, for they have broken the precious contract with future generations by forcing them to pay for this generation's indulgences. Goodman reminds us that they constitute what economist Paul Samuelson described as "a Ponzi scheme that works!" (because government is funding it). However, if there is one hitch in the system, or a depression, or a tax revolt — goodbye pension. Government can meet higher obligations only by higher taxation, or more borrowing, for which it will have to borrow still more to pay interest on the interest. Some pension plan!

OLD AGE SECURITY

IN 1988, CANADA WAS COMMITTED to spend $14.465 billion in payments
to all Canadians over 65 who met certain basic residence requirements.
There are more than 2.5 million such people, half of whom, because of
low income, also receive the Guaranteed Income Supplement, for
which there is an income test. There is also a whole series of interlocking provincial programs and services designed to help seniors. My first
reaction is — why not? My second is — why? Why has Canada decided
to take money from the working young and give it to other people just
because they are old? That is, why should the poor and the not-poor
alike receive money taken involuntarily from the working young?

If there is a scandal here, it is a moral, not a financial, one, since
there is no pretence at trusteeship of funds. The moral scandal lies in
the trade-off between self-reliance and dependence and the disastrous
moral effect this has on the public attitude to normal human and family
relations. Old Age Security payments to people who don't need them,
or who should otherwise have saved up for their own retirement,
weaken the moral bedrock of family, community, and nation. In this
sense, what I call the traditional verticality of society is transmuted into
a horizontality. That is, the State takes on a crucial role in changing the
social structure by subsidizing social entropy — making it easier for
the young to relinquish normal family effort and support of the old. Why
help Dad, since the State will look after him if I don't?

So where social relations used to flow from top to bottom and bottom
to top, old to young, then young to old, and so on, now they are stratified.
In Sweden, where the State crows about the need for each individual
to be "economically independent" (meaning dependent on the State at
every age), there is today almost no intergenerational financial support. Grandparents do not help the young, and the young banish
grandparents to institutions. What societies that take this course overlook is that with intergenerational financial transfers comes a lot of
crucial intergenerational value transmission, moral learning, and family bonding — which is now being lost. The State must assume the
fundamental responsibility for this damaging horizontal stratification:
children in State-subsidized daycare; students in State-subsidized
schools and universities; millions of "the poor" in State-subsidized
lives; millions of the old in state-subsidized "homes" for the aged. In
this way, the State has mounted a benevolent-seeming, vote-based
attack on the traditional family, through which its moral structure has

been dissipated and transferred to the professionals of "the client State."

Imagine one circle for government subsidies, and the other for the family, and you can see that if the cultural wedge keeping them apart is weakened the family is weakened, government becomes all things to all people; absorbs all; changes the morality of all. The very knowledge in the young that their taxes are paying for an impersonal group called "the old" — as distinct from their own parents — makes them wish the old in general out of their lives. Of course, some "independent" classes of people may be very happy with the arrangement — at least until the financial sham supporting it falls apart. For it is a considerable gamble to suppose that the State can continue to manage our private lives with impunity. The personal family bonds and responsibilities that normally sustain us have been replaced by social classifications blessed by the State. "The old" are now a fixed and impersonal class. The only way this can be changed is to insist that only the "truly needy" be so assisted, and only then if family and community fail them. Let us agree to drive the moral order back where it belongs. Charity must begin at home.

The UIC Scandal

According to Charles Murray, "The threshold condition for self-respect is accepting responsibility for one's own life, for which the inescapable behavioral manifestation is earning one's own way in the world."[14]

A revealing comment. In 1988, Canada was committed to paying out $10.150 billion in "Unemployment Insurance." This program was originally intended to truly "insure" workers against temporary and unforeseen job loss — it would allow them time to find a new job. But today it has grown into a massive welfare State program to subsidize almost *any* departure from normal work. It is available for workers who simply quit working, to those who simply retire, who take maternity or adoption leave, who work only seasonally, who are injured — in short, UIC has developed into a mechanism for redistributing income between income groups and regions and is therefore no insurance plan at all, but another of our welfare programs. In its effects, it is pernicious, and just about everyone knows it. The popular wisdom has always disrespected "the pogey." But now, under the "Rights Illusion," it has become another claim against the State. As was predictable, it exercises its greatest disincentive effect on the low-paid, because it represents a greater percentage of their earnings. Among these, single parents and married women loom large. In this respect, UIC can be justly charged with the label "paternalistic."

Further, UIC is even worse than ordinary welfare, because there is no true means test. It is intended to give time for job searching — and it does. It subsidizes this activity. In fact, it subsidizes it most where there are the fewest jobs to be found. Hasan and Gera, in a report for the Economic Council of Canada, state that "the duration of search for unemployment insurance beneficiaries is about two to three months longer than that for other jobseekers."[15] In 1971, when UIC benefits were "liberalized" — meaning larger, easier to qualify for, and easier to keep — the job-vacancy rate jumped from 5.5 to 11.3 percent in a mere two years. The average claim in Ontario in 1980 was $3,194, and in 1987 it had grown to $6,952 — and injured workers do not pay taxes on these earnings, with the result that many earn more net income by staying home "injured" than by returning to work.

No matter how you present it, it is clear that our UIC/welfare program lengthens job-search time, devalues work itself, competes with the private sector for labour, creates dependence, raises the "reservation" wage (the wage below which a worker will refuse a job), dampens the investment climate for Canada by diverting money from savings and business activity, and subsidizes the poor for remaining in unproductive regions of the country instead of moving where the work is.

Newfoundland's "out-migration" dropped from about 20 percent to about 4 percent shortly after the 1971 "liberalization" of benefits. In the mid-seventies there was a net in-migration to Newfoundland that kept pace with increased transfer payments to that province. Although most Newfoundlanders have the same amenities as other Canadians, household incomes are fairly high. As Michael Valpy of the *Globe and Mail* points out in a review of a Royal Commission study by the sociologist Douglas House, "they share jobs to enable as many members of the community as possible to qualify for unemployment insurance. Rural Newfoundlanders, with the collusion of government, use UI as a form of income supplement to boost incomes and bring them closer to the average Canadian . . . more than 80 percent of tax filers reported UI income . . . [although] 95 percent of residents owned their houses outright" (April 19, 1989). Most Newfoundlanders organize their working lives around the ten weeks of work needed to qualify for the pogey, to "get their flow for another 42 weeks. Ten weeks of work, UI benefits, a local cash economy (unreported for tax purposes), barter, and piecemeal labor amount to what the commission called a 'pluralistic economy.' " Economy? The locals laugh and say "Why do we need Lotto 6/49, when we've got the 10/42!" The effect of this has been to create a massive poverty trap for the poor: after liberalization, the voluntary "quits" rose from 90,000 to 255,000 in two years. Finally, take this example of a foolhardy policy: if a worker's weekly wage is, say, $300, and he has worked for ten weeks in an economically depressed area in Canada, he can be "laid off" and receive almost a year's benefits of $180 per week. He is also allowed to earn up to 25 percent of that without losing any benefits. That comes to $225, or 75 percent of his regular wage. With a bit of effort in the underground cash economy — estimated to be about $42 billion now (Chart 26, Chapter Seven) — he is back to $300 per week, *and* he has his free time. Basically, he is a semi-retired man, thanks to the taxpayer.

The Forget Report, Forgotten

In 1986 the federal government commissioned an Inquiry on Unemployment Insurance chaired by Claude Forget, which cost $5.2 million. Despite a host of solid recommendations, it was quickly shelved, never to be heard of again. It recommended cutting benefits from $8.97 billion per year to $2.87 billion; slashing the *28,000-member* UIC staff; returning UIC to more of an insurance and less of a social program, wherein benefits are financed by contributions, not from general tax revenues and borrowing; ending federal make-work projects that serve only to qualify workers for UIC for another year; and cutting benefits, especially for new workers. It especially recommended the ending of "seasonal" unemployment payments, which it called the most dysfunctional, uneconomic aspect of unemployment insurance, and said the whole scheme "fosters the social and labor market problems it purports to remedy" (*Toronto Star*, April 17, 1989).

But from the moment the report was released, there was such a howl from the nation's social-welfare and union crowd that it was never mentioned again. Too many votes would be lost. And since the middle classes were not complaining as loudly, the government thought — let's tax onward! In Finance Minister Michael Wilson's April 1989 budget, this is in effect what occurred. The government is getting out of supporting UIC, thus passing more of the burden to employers, in effect creating, as Diane Francis points out (*Maclean's*, July 10, 1989), an open-ended private welfare system paid for directly by private employers and indirectly through premiums passed along in the cost of goods and services. She quotes Claude Forget as saying, "The whole operation is merely a clever manoeuvre to increase payroll taxes. Canada will now have the dubious distinction of financing a program that is almost pure income redistribution through a flat-rate tax on wages and salaries."

For an indication of how this heavy taxation-UIC benefit-unemployment relationship works, here's a shocking chart from the OECD published in the Fraser Institute's 1986 pamphlet *Why Is Canada's Unemployment Rate So High?* (lower now, but still high in depressed regions), which compares benefits in Canada with those in the U.S.A. Again, this is another example of the top-down social-welfare State largesse to which we have treated ourselves — courtesy of our children and grandchildren — for so many years:

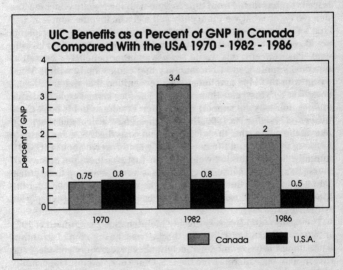

UIC Benefits as a Percent of GNP in Canada Compared With the USA 1970 - 1982 - 1986

Canada's auditor-general says that cheaters are rarely caught, and in 1989, "Ottawa paid out $135 million more in unemployment insurance than it should have" (*Toronto Star*, Oct. 25, 1989). And Statistics Canada figures show that more than half the families on UIC earn *above* the national average.

So we've got a big problem. How should UIC be reformed? Here's what the popular wisdom would suggest: don't pay quitters; don't pay anyone fired for cause; don't pay retirees; don't pay for pregnancy or adoption (these are personal choices); end extended benefits (as recommended by the Economic Council of Canada, among others); make it a true insurance plan, funded by contributions only; don't pay anyone under 21 years of age; tighten eligibility requirements; spot-check for cheaters; put teeth in the law for cheaters; outlaw job-sharing to qualify for benefits; privatize the job-placement functions of government; treat quits, fired for cause, pregnancy, and the like differently in the unemployment statistics; ensure that decent jobs are taken, whether or not beneficiaries "like" them — or withdraw UIC support.

THE COMING NIT IDEA — WATCH OUT!

CANADA, IN ITS DESPAIR OVER the moral hazard effects I've been describing, has flirted from time to time with the Negative Income Tax idea (NIT), or what we innocently call a "basic income supplement." That's a fancy expression for a graduated subsidy, by which recipients would receive a cash payment to bring them up to a specified income level. Theoretically, this would *replace* all other benefits — as well as the considerable load of bureaucracy that comes along with it. What toying with this idea amounts to is a recognition that welfare doesn't work — so let's just "give them money." The idea gained great credence when it suddenly got support from Milton Friedman in his book *Capitalism and Freedom*, in 1962. He, and others, have calculated that if you take all the money that the welfare system costs the U.S.A. and sprinkle it among the poor and the needy, each would receive about $40,000 annually! So, the thinking went, why not just *give* them the money? Of course, it's not that simple. But Canada is now cosying up to this idea. Before leaping into the abyss, it would be well advised to consider the famous SIME/DIME experiment conducted to try this out (as reported by Charles Murray).

The Seattle (and Denver) Income Maintenance Experiment of 1971 to 1978 — called SIME/DIME for short — was the creation of an enthusiastic union between modern social-policy researchers and idealistic government bureaucrats from the U.S. Office of Economic Opportunity (OEO) in the mid-1960s. Their sole and express purpose in creating the experiment was to *prove* that the only way to win the War on Poverty was to use some form of Guaranteed Income Supplement. "Somehow, *proof* must be established that a guaranteed income would not cause people to reduce their work effort, get married less often, divorce more quickly, or any of the other things that the popular wisdom said it would cause them to do."[16] The OEO's proof "took the form of the most ambitious social-science experiment in history. No other even comes close to its combination of size, expense, length, and detail of analysis." The study used 8,700 people as subjects, and lasted ten years. (A planned twenty-year sub-sample was cancelled in 1980.) One hundred titles were published from the data, and it cost millions of dollars. As Murray puts it, "The proponents of the NIT in the Johnson administration were out to slay the folk beliefs that welfare makes people shiftless. The NIT, properly redesigned, would provide work incentives and get people off the welfare rolls."[17]

The experiment took large low-income groups in these two cities and told half of each group that they would be guaranteed no less than the official poverty-level income if they couldn't earn it. The other half were on their own and would receive no benefits or guarantees whatsoever. What was the result? Here's a summary.

1. The NIT reduced the work effort "by 9 percent for husbands, and by 20 percent for wives." These reductions were caused by dropping out of the workforce altogether. Analysts said this was a particular disaster because it was often the wives that could push families out of poverty.

2. Even more disastrous: the hours of work per week put in by young males not yet heads of families was reduced by 43 percent! Just when they should be preparing for family life, they dropped out of the race. Even when these people married, their work effort was still down 33 percent.

3. Periods of unemployment for members of the experiment who lost their jobs were lengthened by 27 percent for husbands, 42 percent for wives, and 60 percent for single female heads of families.

4. The dissolution of marriage was far higher for all those receiving the NIT payments than for those who did not (36 percent for whites, 42 percent for blacks).

The economist Martin Anderson estimates, using elaborate and detailed analysis of the NIT experiment, that if the NIT were applied nationally, it would, on an average-case basis, result in a 50 percent reduction in national work effort. Further, the work reduction observed was *over and above* reductions already experienced as a result of existing welfare programs. In short, "the NIT experiment made a shambles of the expectations of its sponsors. But at the same time it was being conducted, the disincentives it would later demonstrate were being woven into the fabric of the welfare system."[18]

The mere idea that Canada's social engineers would even *consider* such a thing in the face of such a volume of conscientious proof that it won't work is a mark of gross incompetence.

REDISTRIBUTION

THERE IS PERHAPS NOTHING more illustrative of this top-down, collectivist, egalitarian mentality than its constant promotion of the idea of equality through economic "redistribution." This is the core instrument of the social-welfare State, its fondest dream. As a friend said, "They just won't be happy until we're all equally poor." On a scale of zero to ten for income equality, egalitarians would rather have everyone at four, than three-quarters at six, and the balance at eight. It is not possible to estimate accurately the amount of effort, money, and bureaucracy that has been devoted to this pursuit in modern times, all in the name of equality, just because social engineers have decided that "equal" is "fair." In the name of this myth, they construct an elaborate ideal of a fair and equal society, and then measure our reality in terms of this fanciful ideal. I am searching for a reason why they do this, since no such society has ever existed, and we, the people, do not need sociologists to tell us how money is made, kept, or squandered. More than that, *there is no particular relationship* between the virtue of a society and the wealth some in it may or may not have, or say they have, or don't have. Whole societies can be evil things, whether all are rich, poor, or much like ours — holding to a normal distribution. *No case has ever been satisfactorily made that our society would be morally, economically, or productively better if incomes were the same for everyone.* I suspect that it would be a good deal worse. For one of the keys to a good and productive society is not sameness — the victory of social entropy — but difference. The more differences, the better. Canada should welcome the widest possible variety of incomes, combined with the greatest possible range of opportunities to achieve them, and the most absolute freedom to strive for, or refuse them, as each pleases. Instead, it has swallowed the socialist's myth that we will all be happy if equal. Aside from the arrogance, the coercive humanitarianism, the constitutional distortions, and the plain old immorality required to bring this about, what has actually happened in Canada in the past thirty years? Study the Revenue Canada chart below and ask yourself whether the social contortions, the agonies, the soft-headed intellectual and legislative bungling, and the social brainwashing of the public have been worth it?

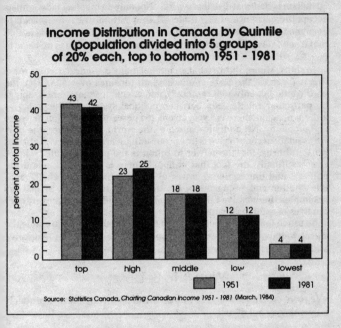

Income Distribution in Canada by Quintile (population divided into 5 groups of 20% each, top to bottom) 1951 - 1981

Source: Statistics Canada, *Charting Canadian Income 1951 - 1981* (March, 1984)

INTERNATIONAL REDISTRIBUTION

SO MUCH FOR THE EFFECT of income redistribution policies *within* Canada. Is there any evidence that democratic capitalist nations have income distributions "worse" than the hard-core socialist nations? None. So says Harvard University's Dr. Barrington Moore, Jr., in his now classic *Authority and Inequality Under Capitalism and Socialism*, "Though the determinants of the position on the ladder are different, mainly economic in the USA and mainly political in the USSR, the distance from the bottom rung to the top one turns out to be about the same in both cases."[19] As recent reviewers of this excellent little book have said of Moore's conclusion, "We should understand just how jarring it is. One of the great, generally unchallenged, 'laws' of social sciences is that centrally-planned economies trade freedom for equality, an exchange many American academics are willing to make ... The implication is that while Capitalism is better at producing wealth, Socialism is better at distributing it ... Not only do most social scientists accept the existence of this trade-off, they virtually never subject it to even moderately systematic examination."[20] But "the traditional notion that freedom is exchanged for equality under socialism has no basis in fact."[21]

In short, Moore shows what an intellectually dishonest, rickety mess this is ("even if the State confiscated all incomes over $25,000, the poor would get only $350 apiece"), and concludes that there simply is no particular relationship between political systems and equality — although, again, there is a very strong (84 percent) correlation between equality and GNP. Sadly for much of the world, says Moore, the only way socialism can survive is by encouraging scarcity. This is what gives it its authority, for "the power to ration is the power to rule." Moore stresses, finally, the fact that although there is much talk about the national and international power of corporations, this is chaff, mere idle chatter and propaganda, for the power they exert in no way resembles the massive authority that socialist officials can exert over the lives of millions of subjects.

So much for "redistribution" as an excuse for those who promote the social-welfare State — less bread, but more real as well as legislative and regulatory barbed wire seems to be the rule.

What Is To Be Done?

We have gotten ourselves into an awful mess, and there is probably only one way out of it:

1. As a society, we must recognize and promote hard the truth that the only sure escape from poverty comes through hard work, and the poor have to work harder than anyone else if they expect to escape — not less hard.

2. Scrap the whole, unwieldy, morally depressing mess of welfare programs and the bureaucracy that sustains them. Scrap them slowly, and humanely, but scrap them. "Leave the working-age person with no recourse whatsoever except the job market, family members, friends, and public or private locally funded services. It is the Alexandrian solution: cut the knot, for there is no way to untie it."[22]

3. Provide only emergency and in-kind assistance to the able-bodied of working-age.

4. As Murray insists, provide "billions for equal opportunity, not one cent for equal outcome, because government cannot identify the worthy, but it can protect a society in which the worthy can identify themselves."

5. Establish hard criteria to define the helpless and truly needy of society, and means tests to guarantee the public that their money is not wasted. Make them feel good about helping the "truly needy," but only after their own families, friends, and communities have failed them. This ensures that the moral pressure, the cultural wedge, stays in place, keeping the State and its egalitarian ideology out of the lives of the people.

6. Accept the fact of life that in a society built on individual freedom and responsibility there is no way to remove the "stigma" of welfare (the only way such a stigma can be removed is if those who take something free from society in some way repay it); rather, ensure that society vigorously promotes the sure-fire ways to avoid welfare: hard work, education, and a strong family. Ensure that welfare is the last thing for which anyone tries to "qualify." The *Economist* reports that anyone who keeps his first job for at least one year, gets a high-school education, and gets married, has a less than 1 percent chance of staying poor.

7. We must publicly reject the idea of the egalitarian State and its false confidence in economic equality as a panacea for society's ills. On the contrary, we must focus on freedom and the tools of wealth creation, thus forcing up GNP and real purchasing power for all. We do not want a society in which everyone is forced to be equal. We want a society in which everyone is free to be what he or she wishes in an environment of maximum opportunity. Once this formula is properly promoted, increases in real wealth automatically dissolve absolute poverty. Relative poverty will always be with us.

8. Use "workfare" for the able-bodied of working age who want help from the State. A full 84 percent of Canadians say that welfare recipients should be made to work (Gallup Poll, Nov. 30, 1988).

Should We Keep These?

1. *Canada Pension Plan?* No, unless contributions are voluntary, saved for, and fully funded. Premiums are inadequate now. The unfunded federal liability alone is $15.5 billion. Ontario's, another $8.5 billion. (Guess whose taxes are going to go up to pay all that off?)

2. *Veterans' pensions and allowances?* OK if fully funded and contrib-

utory; otherwise, no. Many peacetime ex-service retirees are now
receiving in fully indexed pensions, *double* the pay they were getting
on retirement.

3. *Medicare?* Only if funded by premiums, and if competition to provide consumers with such services is allowed. In Ontario, premiums
paid for OHIP covered only 15 percent of the costs of medical care; in
1989 they were abolished altogether for individuals, and passed on to
employers (for whom they will constitute a new consumer tax).

4. *Workers' Compensation, and Unemployment Insurance?* Only if
funded by premiums on a voluntary basis.

5. *Public education?* Should be retained only if a voucher system is put
in place to create competition for educational excellence in all schools.
(A parent receives one voucher for each child equal in value to the
per-student cost of a year's education, and can "spend" it at any school
he wishes — if he gets there quickly enough!) This makes the producers of education responsive to the consumers of it, instead of to the
government and its ministries.

6. *Aid for urban renewal?* Capital formation and infrastructure repair
is a legitimate function of the State.

7. *Family allowances, daycare, mother's allowances?* Only for the
"truly needy." Certainly not for anyone else. Any society must decide
and publicly declare its definition of "the truly needy" (which it is free
to change, if it wishes). But the definition must be in place, and enforced
stringently but humanely, always focusing on the better long-term
solution of work, community, saving, family, personal childcare, etc.

8. *Aid to the handicapped?* Yes, if they truly cannot work. But such aid
should be brought to bear only after local, family, and private efforts
have been exhausted.

9. *Public housing?* So-called "affordable" housing will be created at
the speed of light by the free market if communities will just change
zoning to allow such building. Scrapping rent controls and speeding up
bureaucratic delays will increase the speed to warp 7. Once government gets out of the way, the free world will create inexpensive housing
faster than ever thought possible.

9

Foreign Aid
Burning Canadian Money

Foreign aid is the source of the North-South
conflict, not its solution (and) . . . many donor
taxpayers are far poorer than many of the people
in recipient countries where much aid benefits the
powerful and well-off.

Peter Bauer, *Rhetoric and Reality*

THE MOMENT WE HEAR the words "Third World," a distinct image leaps
to mind — normally of an emaciated starving black child, with swollen
belly and haunting eyes — that evokes universal pity. This image
causes a moral wincing in most of us which, if we allow ourselves to
think about it a lot, makes daily life difficult. After all, what in the name
of Heaven can justify such pitiable anguish in the life of a small child?
And also, why can't the people who run those countries get it right?
Why can't they simply manage to feed themselves? Are they backward?
Stupid? Lazy? Exploited? What is *really* going on in these countries,
anyway?

This chapter is the result of my effort to find out. What I have
discovered is that over the past thirty years the Third World has
vigorously promoted a radical change in the moral relationship between the wealthy and the less wealthy nations of the world, and
Canada has been one of the willing dupes of this change. In this regard,
I will be discussing the matter of country-to-country foreign aid, not
the moral justification for humanitarian assistance by caring individu-

als or citizen groups. The latter has been more or less ongoing for generations, and much of it takes place privately between free organizations of the West, and individuals, families, or church groups in foreign nations. At the least, there is some hope that the private package you send personally will arrive in the intended recipient's hands. But "foreign aid" is another matter. This has to do with large sums of money transferred *between the governments* of nations, either directly or through a variety of subsidiary or international organizations. By its very nature, it is political.

There is a distressing scenario to explain why, even though we have an annual deficit of about $29 billion, hard-working Canadians are presently coughing up close to $3 billion annually for such transfers. Most probably believe that they are feeding starving little children. But this is far from the truth. The *Wall Street Journal* underlined this point in a 1981 article on food aid to Bangladesh in which it said, "It comes as a surprise to the layman, but not at all to the experts, that food aid arriving in Bangladesh and many other places isn't used to feed the poor. Governments *typically* sell the food on local markets and use the proceeds however they choose."[1] What is the reason for this immense international transfer of wealth to the Third World, and what *is* the Third World, anyway?

THE UNITED NATIONS: AN INSTRUMENT FOR THE REDISTRIBUTION OF WORLD WEALTH

Step One: When the United Nations was created in 1945, at the end of World War II, its ostensible purpose was to preserve world peace. It was set up specifically as a political organization, not an economic one. But through its voting structure — one nation, one vote — it became rapidly apparent who would be running the show — although not financing it. Of the close to ninety nations that quickly joined the UN, more than half were what we today call "Third World" nations. More have since joined, and such nations now form a large majority bloc of the 159 nations.

Step Two: By the time of the 1964 meeting of the United Nations Committee on Trade and Development (UNCTAD 1), such nations had already hit upon the idea of forming a kind of international union and calling themselves the "Third World." This was in distinction to the First, or free, world and the Second, or totalitarian, world of the Communists. In order to make this concept believable, this newly formed group had to develop a coherent ideology and use it to get what they wanted from the other two "Worlds." Basically, what they mostly wanted was money, and a few peculiar rights.

Step Three: Leaning heavily on arguments and ideas derived from Marxism-Leninism, and to some degree from the British Fabian socialists, here in essence is what they declared, through a variety of UN documents released in the 1960s and 1970s, initially by a group called the Group of 77. These nations were virtually the insiders at all the UNCTAD meetings. This is what the Third World claimed:

• When the rich get rich, the poor get poorer. (This is essentially the Fixed-Pie Illusion operating internationally.)

• The wealth of the rich is the result of exploitation of the poor nations. (This is the Determinist Illusion at work.)

• The rich world owes the Third World "restitution" — it must pay for its exploitation, past and present. The rich world is guilty as charged. (In this, we recognize the Soak-the-Rich Illusion.)

• A "New International Economic Order" is required (called the NIEO, for short). The role of the NIEO is to ensure that the world's wealth is equally distributed. (This is the Equality Illusion rearing its head.)

• Such restitution is not a matter of *charity*, it is a matter of *right*. The Third World has a legitimate claim on the wealth of the rest of the world. (Here, operating at the international level, is the Rights Illusion.)

Below is an excerpt from a speech by Julius Nyerere, ruler of Tanzania, and a master spokesman for international begging, which in one breath sums up this NIEO thinking. The cleverness in his remarks springs from the fact that no one would wish to argue with his motive — the eradication of poverty — but he uses it here to sell his egalitarian, redistributionist idea, an idea that permitted him personally to force his vision on the lives of millions of his own hapless peasants.

In one world, as in one state, as I am rich because you are poor and I am poor because you are rich, transfer of wealth from rich to poor is a matter of right; it is not an appropriate matter for charity. The objective must be the eradication of poverty and the establishment of a minimum standard of living for all people. This will involve its converse, a ceiling on wealth for individuals and nations, as well as deliberate action to transfer resources from the rich to the poor within and across national boundaries.[2]

In this vision, he fancies himself an international policeman in a world in which incomes are *extracted*, not *earned*; in which "everybody, everywhere is entitled to a substantial income regardless of economic performance."[3]

Such has been the evolution of the ideology of the so-called Third World. Study it carefully, for by now it is the entrenched game-plan designed to take many dollars out of your pocket and your children's pockets for a long time to come. Shortly we will ask how many dollars, to which countries, and for what purposes. Before doing so, we should consider how astounding is the Western blindness to the fact that although

the NIEO is the entrenched instrument of an ideological assault on the West . . . well designed to engender guilt feelings among Western intelligentsia, [it] has never really been answered by the West. No major political leader in a Western country has raised his voice to present a case for the free societies or to emphatically reject the barrage of accusations. Minor politicians daring a rejoinder suffer verbal abuse in the media for 'their insensitivity.'[4]

Professor Karl Brunner made this comment before the advent of Prime Minister Margaret Thatcher, President Ronald Reagan, and, importantly, Jeanne Kirkpatrick, U.S. Ambassador to the United Nations, who carried the critical torch to the Third World — unlike Canada's former Ambassador to the UN, Stephen Lewis, who quickly made one with them. Lewis is still on the international hustings, urging us to "write off African debt" (*Toronto Star*, April 2, 1988) and to give more in aid. He says that his aim "is to persuade Western governments to increase the amount of aid given to these nations." The same article mentions as an aside that Canada has already forgiven nearly $700 million in sub-Saharan debt to date. The current hot story running in the newspapers of the Western world is that Third World foreign debt is starving little children. The sly implication is that this is our fault. And what galls about this tactic is that our press are not angry at the leaders of these nations for their gross irresponsibility, their diversion of aid money, or their fancy lifestyles among their own starving. We hear none of this. They are angry at us for not being more generous still, and have the gall to blame these pitiful deaths on us. This is twisted thinking, and yellow journalism.

What is the ordinary Canadian to think of this Third World business? I am going to draw heavily from the internationally respected scholar P.T. Bauer of the London School of Economics for an answer. He supplies us with a well-researched, cool-headed analysis of the lamentable and weak-kneed posture adopted by the free Western democracies in the face of the Third World's unspeakable incompetence and rapacious greed. In a head-to-head debate, he would demolish international aid beggars like Stephen Lewis rather handsomely. Here's why.

THE "THIRD WORLD" IS A MYTH

FIRST OF ALL, THERE is no such thing as "the Third World." This term has been invented by a collection of nations that have only one thing in common — the receipt of large doses of free aid from the productive West. If all nations of the world are ranked by per-capita income from highest to lowest, there is no clear dividing line between the "rich" countries of the first world — also called the "North" — and those of the Third World — also called the "South." (In his latter days in power, Pierre Trudeau had a boutique intellectual interest in the so-called "North-South dialogue.") In fact, many groups and societies within what are called Third World nations are wealthier than large groups in the West. The incomes of middle- and upper-class citizens in many of these countries are quite high and growing fast, and far outstrip those of a humble taxpayer in, say, Kamloops, British Columbia, some of whose money is ending up in their hands. The Third World concept cannot be defended on economic grounds, for it is not an economic concept, but a political one brought about by the existence of foreign aid itself.

THE THIRD WORLD IS EXTREMELY HOSTILE TO THE WEST

SECOND, BAUER MAINTAINS THAT "the distinctive features of the official ideology of the Third World are: pronounced and often bitter hostility to the West, the market system, and the liberal economic order [expressed on platforms supported or even provided by the West — our own Prime Minister has provided such a platform]; virulent allegations of Western exploitation as the cause of Third World poverty; and an insistence on large-scale international redistribution of income and on the right to expropriate politically powerless groups."[5] And of course, this is often supported by Western media. For example, the *Globe and Mail* (April 27, 1987) printed an article labelled "West Assailed for Insatiable Appetite," the gist of the story being Western greed; but it failed to mention that the incredibly productive West is a huge net exporter of food to the rest of the world. Without our wheat, for example, even mighty Russia would twist in hunger.

The "powerless groups" Bauer mentions above are such as the thirteen million peasants Tanzania's noble-sounding Nyerere, socialist darling of Black Africa, forced to relocate into his failed experimental commune villages (called *ujaama*). Typical of socialist theorists, he despised the individualism of independent farmers, so he forced them to work communally; to prevent them from returning whence they came he burned millions of their ancestral homes, depriving the poor of their basic rights and property in the name of his unworkable vision. This was more coercive humanitarianism on an international scale. But because through the NIEO *he solicited support for this right at the UN*, the Western nations — almost all of which were giving him money — were silent on the immorality and cruelty of his measures. But such "large-scale maltreatment of many millions of politically ineffective or defenceless people is commonplace in the Third World. The maltreatment includes expropriations, expulsion, or even massacre and is tolerated, encouraged, or supported by governments prominent and articulate in the United Nations."[6]

Despite these evils, Canada and other Western nations continue to send capital. And the maltreatment continues as we turn our backs. That such things as forced relocation are pet socialist techniques is clear. Almost all the socialist nations have tried it, and are still trying it. "Romanian chief defends bid to raze 7,000 towns," reported the *Vancouver Sun* on December 30, 1988, indicating that the Romanian leader Nicolae Ceausescu would destroy seven thousand of his nation's thirteen thousand villages in order to "modernize" the Romanian economy. He forcibly evicts people from their own homes, burns them down, and drives the former owners into communes while you and I go about our business. This is top-down thinking with a vengeance. More than four hundred have already been killed resisting him. Of course, this arch-example of central planning in the interests of an egalitarian ideal has caused untold strife and grief already. According to the International Society for Human Rights, the border between Romania and Yugoslavia, where many were attempting to flee, is "the bloodiest in Europe." Border guards are shooting their own fleeing countrymen. Are not the actions of the likes of Nyerere and Ceausescu just more coercive humanitarianism, and the predictable result of their ideology?

THERE IS NO ECONOMIC ARGUMENT FOR FOREIGN AID

CAPITAL TRANSFERS TO THIRD WORLD NATIONS are largely wasted. Here's why. Any capital project either shows a good return on investment or it doesn't. Such a project either creates wealth or consumes it. It is always a net plus or a net minus to somebody. If it is a net plus, and this can be shown in financial pro-formas, it will have no trouble attracting capital from the private financial markets of the world. Aid is not needed. If it is a net minus, then it consumes capital on an ongoing basis — it is just another "show project," an economic sump draining productive dollars from the nation. Of course we could argue that without aid a particular dam might never be built. But in this case, the contribution of aid "cannot exceed the avoided cost of investible funds." In short, Third World nations benefit only from the avoided cost of borrowing — a minuscule advantage of "Aid" over privately raised capital. At worst — and most often — "official wealth transfers increase the resources and power of recipient governments compared with the rest of society . . . [and thus] enhance the hold of governments over their subjects, and promote the politicization of life."[7]

Foreign aid allows such governments to forestall turning to more productive measures; keeps unproductive ways going longer than normal; allows governments to continue to oppress productive minority segments of the population, to restrict the inflow of foreign capital, enterprise, and skills, and to continue with economic controls, price-fixing, and other policies that restrict any possible flowering of initiative. For Tanzania in 1980, aid was 18.1 percent of GNP, 106.8 percent of tax receipts, and 152.8 percent of its export earnings. Tanzania is therefore a non-country economically, dependent, disabled, and diabolical in its human rights policies, like many other Third World countries, complete with their fleets of Mercedes-Benz chauffeured cars for their big shots. And there's no end to this folly in sight. Honest, hard-working Canadians were taxed more to give Tanzania $26.8 million in foreign aid in 1987.

FOREIGN AID DOES NOT RELIEVE POVERTY

AS PETER BAUER POINTS out, "Foreign Aid does not in fact go to the pitiable figures we see on aid posters, in aid advertisements, and in other aid propaganda in the media. It goes to the governments, that is, to the rulers, and the policies of the rulers who receive aid are sometimes directly responsible for the conditions such as those depicted."[8] Unfortunately, Western aid money often aggravates the condition of the poor, not the reverse, for several reasons. It allows Third World leaders and despots to continue with fanciful socialization projects that amount to vast transactions of decline. It subsidizes such nations for remaining in their pitiable condition by creating a whole class of aid professionals, politicians, and bureaucrats whose vested interests lie not in ending poverty, but in ensuring their own continued well-being — *which can continue only as long as poverty remains*. It provides such people with huge show projects with which to impress and subjugate their people, but does not produce economic wealth. In short, the same phenomenon is brought about by international transfer payments to unproductive nations as is brought about by internal transfer payments to Canada's own unproductive regions: they reward people for remaining unproductive. But this is a fool's paradise. Nations that cannot feed their own children do not need fancy capital cities stuck in the jungle (Brasilia, Islamabad, etc.), they do not need fancy international airlines they cannot maintain or fly themselves, and which the locals certainly cannot afford to use, ever. Worst of all, virtually all these countries maintain very large and expensive armies and spend lavishly on arms — *about one-fifth or more of the world's annual armament expenditures are by Third World nations*. Is it not outrageous that the very same hungry nations that are begging for your money are spending it on arms? How do Canadian taxpayers feel to know that Tanzania received $67.85 million from Canada alone (1986), ostensibly to end poverty, and spent $128 million on arms the same year?

Finally, there are many rich people in Third World nations, the rulers of which, "while demanding external donations in the name of international redistribution, are not particularly interested in domestic policies to help the poor."[9] Aid, in fact, "enables governments to pursue even extremely damaging policies for years on end because the inflow of funds conceals from the population" the effect of such policies. For example, without our direct monetary assistance, President Nyerere would not as easily have been able to proceed with his large-scale forced collectivization of the peasants. Canadian tax dollars indirectly but undeniably assisted him in this inhumane project; in effect, we all bear a moral responsibility for this terribly sad and dislocating experience of the surviving poor of Tanzania that has been foisted upon us by our own leaders. This is foreign aid?

THE RIGHTS ILLUSION AT WORK

BAUER QUOTES FROM A West German school book on foreign aid that blares out, "Exactly the same for everybody — that's how it must be!" For many of the resentment-oriented in the world, this is a high sentiment. After all, it is much easier to coerce wealth from others than to earn it yourself; "they envisage aid as a natural extension of internal redistributive taxation from the national to the international plane, that is, the global application of egalitarianism."[10] Unfortunately, many donor taxpayers are far poorer than many of the wealthy that such aid assists. Why are we giving aid when a country spends the same or more on arms? When its people are starving but it refuses to kill animals (India, a recipient of huge Canadian aid payments, has the largest livestock holding in the world)? Why aid countries that refuse to allow women to do paid work (as in many Moslem nations)? Or governments whose policies are plainly just a handicap system? Or countries where there is no insistence on financially solvent projects?

In short, such "aid" in the ideal of international egalitarianism is really just a massive transfer of productive resources from the most to the least productive members of the world community; donor and recipient nations are both hurt by it. The galling reality is that the entire international aid fiasco is engineered by teams of professional bureaucrats and politicians from both donor and recipient nations, all of whom live a parasitical existence financed by tax dollars they have extracted from their populations. Although both donor and recipient nations are hurt by such transactions, the careers continue . . . and continue.

FOREIGN AID CANNOT HELP THE WEST

A FAVOURITE THEME OF Roy Megarry, publisher of the *Globe and Mail*, Canada's self-proclaimed "National Newspaper," and of many businessmen and unionists, is that foreign aid is helpful to the West (creates allies, markets for our products, etc.). But this is not so. We cannot say that by giving our dollars to others, to enable them to buy back our products, we are further ahead. Rather, foreign aid stifles entrepreneurship, creates unemployment in both donor and recipient nations, diminishes the volume of investible funds in the donor countries, and perpetuates anti-enterprise policies in both donor and recipient nations. If aid made these people themselves productive of wealth, that would be a different matter. But it doesn't. In fact, just like welfare at home, foreign aid subsidizes the condition for which it is given, is a reward for that condition. Foreign aid will "Newfoundlandize" the Third World. (Half Newfoundland's income is "aid" from Ottawa.)

FOREIGN AID DOES NOT PREVENT THE DRIFT
OF THIRD WORLD NATIONS INTO THE SOVIET CAMP

PREVENTING THE DRIFT of Third World countries into the Soviet camp is another poor excuse for aid. First, almost all foreign aid is channelled through international agencies that are restricted from earmarking funds according to the political interests of donor nations. In short, they attempt to neutralize the donor's political wishes, and most aid is given "regardless of the political conduct of the recipients" — although I can't imagine why. The leaders of many such nations have been actively hostile to the West — Nkrumah, Nyerere, Gadaffi, and Mengistu are Bauer's examples — and most get their political philosophies from the East. Most such nations are hostile to our way of life; demand money as reparation for fancied exploitation; institute top-down collectivist governments at the drop of a hat; divert aid into the lives and careers of their political elites, and away from the poor, without whom they would receive no aid. Further, these are extremely racist societies practising oppression and torture of a kind for which we quickly revile South Africa — of course while remaining silent when this occurs in our recipient nations. Tanzania, Zimbabwe, Peru, Jamaica, Zambia — in fact every country to which we give aid has a record of such evils (see the *Toronto Star*, July 26, 1987), and further, they all spend untold millions on armaments, mostly to fight each other and aggrandize their own New Class of aid professionals.

Here are some choice observations on the African debacle gleaned from an article in the *Globe and Mail* (Aug. 4, 1988) by Professor George B.N. Ayittey, a native Ghanaian economist now teaching at Bloomsburg University:

• Africa has received more than $70 billion since 1960.

• Africa has more than 3,200 State enterprises operating at only 40 percent of their production capacity.

• The World Bank estimates that as much as $60 million a year "leaks" from Liberian State enterprise into private hands. "Kleptocrats" (bureaucratic thieves) stole more than $50 million in 1983 alone.

• $10 billion in capital leaves Africa every year — far more than the amount that comes in as aid — because its own elites lack enough confidence to invest in Africa, even as they beseech us to do so.

• C-130 transport planes given by the U.S.A. are regularly used for smuggling and private transactions.

• According to Sammy Kum Buo, director of the United Nations Centre for Peace and Disarmament, Africa spends about $12 billion a year on arms and maintaining its armed forces, *an amount equal to what the continent has requested in financial aid over the next five years.*

• African leaders often use the imported arms to crush and butcher their own people — or their neighbours: senseless wars now rage in about fifteen African nations, despite famine and AIDS.

• More than eight million peasants have fled their villages to escape terror and violence in Ethiopia, Mozambique, Sudan, Uganda, and other African countries.

• Past aid underwrote oppression and foolish policies, which led to the need for more aid, and so on.

• In 1986 Ethiopia instituted a "famine tax" equal to the amount of food an Ethiopian received from foreign aid groups, and there was an additional "import fee" on food aid — to be paid in foreign currency. The same year, the president spent $100 million to celebrate the tenth year of Soviet imperialism in Ethiopia!

• Even Archbishop Tutu concedes that "there is less freedom in many African countries today than there was in the much-maligned colonial period."

AID IS NOT RESTITUTION FOR EXPLOITATION

HERE'S ANOTHER RED HERRING, for "the notion that Western prosperity has been achieved at the expense of the Third World is a variant of the familiar misconception that the incomes of prosperous people have been extracted from the less well-off." In other words, it's a variant of the Fixed-Pie Illusion. In Bauer's famous letter to *Commentary* rebuking U.S. Senator Moynihan for a few misconceptions, he rebuts this idea as follows:

> *Contacts established by the West have been the principal instruments of material progress throughout the Third World. For instance, all the foundations and ingredients of modern social and*

> *economic life were brought to sub-Saharan Africa by Westerners, mostly during the colonial period.*[11]

> *. . .far from the West having caused the poverty in the Third World, contact with the West has been the principal agent of progress there.*[12]

From sewers, to the telegraph, to shipping, to railroads, to electricity, to the computer, to the telephone, to all modern production technology, to agricultural methods, to ordinary construction, to medicine, to pesticide control of crop blight — you name it, the West took it there. Malaya had no rubber, nor India tea, until the British took them these things. Bauer shows convincingly that the wealth of Third World nations is directly related to their past or present contact with the West, not the reverse, as is so often claimed. Some will argue that the West took them rubber and tea all right, but then exploited labour there to grow these crops. But once again — and leaving slavery out of it on the grounds that just about everyone, black, brown, yellow, and white was involved in that nefarious practice — exploitation in the absence of force is philosophically a sloppy concept. Low wages? Perhaps. Hard work? For sure. But compared with no jobs at all, or destitution, or hard work for no pay, this is a boon. And the record shows that almost all nations that were colonized by the West are now better off (North America, Australia, Hong Kong, and many of the African and Asian colonies), whereas the countries that were never colonized, such as Tibet, Ethiopia, Afghanistan, Nepal, and Liberia, are still wallowing in developmental backwaters.

FOREIGN AID WILL NOT MAKE THE THIRD WORLD AMBITIOUS

MANY LABOUR UNDER THE IMPRESSION that material progress of the kind experienced by the West is merely a matter of resources, or hardware. But the truth is the opposite. It is the software of civilizations that creates material progress, with which any amount of hardware can be easily purchased. Ambition, willingness to work very hard, to sacrifice for family and children, to save for the future, and above all the desire to make progress in the sense of improving one's world, are the key factors. At the heart of such a cultural matrix there must always be present that most important ingredient — the entrepreneurial process. This is composed of a sufficient number of innovative, far-seeing, risk-oriented individuals who virtually utilize the capital saved by all the drones to create new capital ventures — and thereby employment, products, services, and so on, in a material upward spiral. Money thrown at any society without such tools of freedom and wealth creation in place is worse than wasted. At least if it were merely wasted, no harm would be done except the loss of capital pools for the donor. But instead, as we have seen, its insidious effect is to train whole societies to depend on it, and thus further handicap them. Bauer underlines this phenomenon:

> Economic achievement depends on people's attitudes, motivations, mores, and political arrangements. In many countries the prevailing personal, social and political determinants are uncongenial to material progress: witness the preference for a contemplative life, opposition to paid work by women and widespread torpor and fatalism in certain countries.[13]

Further, he adds:

> The poorest groups in the Third World tend to be materially unambitious. Official handouts to improve their economic conditions will have to be continued indefinitely if the beneficiaries are not to relapse into their original poverty. Poor people can therefore be turned into paupers. Whole societies can be pauperized in this way.[14]

Examples cited by Bauer closer to home are the Navaho Indians of the U.S.A. (Canada also keeps whole tribes of Indians dependent on handouts) and the people of Micronesia, who are so heavily aided that a U.S. government economist reports that "any kind of work here is very hard."[15] Bauer adds examples of Third World nations where soil and climate are suitable for multiple crops, but only one is bothered about. No one wants to do the extra work. If you wanted to set up a diabolically clever program to detrain people — make them unlearn whatever cultural habits and beliefs got them at least this far along, and prevent them from learning better — you couldn't do better than with a foreign-aid program.

HOW MUCH MONEY DOES CANADA SPEND IN FOREIGN AID, AND ON WHOM?

CANADA HAS AN ANNUAL DEFICIT of some $30 billion, the full impact of which can be seen in the charts in Chapter Seven. It is surely a great mystery to most that despite this enormous annual deficit, Canada continues to *borrow* money, which it then turns around and *gives* away to Third World nations, obviously in the confident assumption that we and our children will be happy to pay off such debts in the future. How much money goes out the window every year, and what are some typical recipient nations? Fasten your seat belts! Here's a brief summary of where some of your foreign-aid tax dollars are going every year, and why. You will be the judge of the logic of this whole matter.

Money earned by Canadians and taken from them in taxes is sent to other countries through a bewildering variety of organizations. The total for 1988 was about $2.7 billion from all sources. I will give figures below for the year 1987, a typical year reported by CIDA, the Canadian International Development Agency, which looks after all government-to-government aid directly and administers much of the rest that is filtered through a variety of non-governmental organizations (NGOs). In that period, the total "contributed" by all organizations (including NGOs, missions, industrial programs, etc.) was $2,521,241,OOO.

Country/Region	Total Given Away
Africa	$950.38 million
Americas	$330.02 million
Asia	$892.33 million
Europe	$ 0.41 million
Oceania	$ 14.83 million
Countries not specified	$191.96 million
Unallocated by country	$133.91 million
Total	$2,521.24 million

If, like many Canadians, you feel that Canada should at least get its own financial house in order before giving our money away to others; or if, like many, you think that even then, such charity is a private matter and government should not be giving away the money of citizens it has not consulted to countries with offensive political, economic, cultural, and human-rights practices; or if you believe that if we can't stop giving it away, then let's at least give it to countries in sympathy with our own values and dedicated to helping themselves — if you believe any one or all of these things, you are very much out of step with Canada's foreign-aid policy (which is also, of necessity, its foreign policy). Here are a few selected countries among hundreds that Canada helps with your money. You be the judge of the correctness of this strange notion of charity, and of the thinking of CIDA, which Bob MacDonald of the *Toronto Sun* called "about as leftist an outfit as you can find in the entire government," one that "thinks nothing of giving away money Canadians haven't earned yet."

COLLABORATIVE MORAL RESPONSIBILITY

CIDA BEARS A COLLABORATIVE moral responsibility for much of what is described below because it uses our tax dollars to support such activities directly and indirectly. In addition, it uses our tax dollars to lobby us to spend *more* such dollars. According to a Canadian watch-dog group called C-FAR, "Citizens for Foreign Aid Reform," CIDA, through its Public Participation Program, funds groups strongly supportive of more foreign aid and of foreign policies it likes. Examples are a magazine called *Villagers*, which both CIDA and the City of Toronto helped finance, which promotes heavy foreign-aid expenditures; and the *International Defence and Aid Fund for Southern Africa Newsletter*, which says its funding is "made possible through funding by CIDA's Public Participation Program." So CIDA funds groups that try to persuade us that CIDA needs more money. Who is safeguarding the public purse?

In 1987 a group of organizations including CIDA funded something called the "Theatre in the Rough" — a children's play designed to expose apartheid policies in South Africa. I don't like apartheid any more than anyone else. But what I like a lot less is the hypocrisy of Canada's selective indignation. For almost a decade, our government protested policies in South Africa, while turning a blind eye to the Soviet Union's occupation of Afghanistan during which such atrocities were committed as dropping "butterfly bombs" designed to look like toys, bombs that explode in the hands of the little children who pick them up. Who will ever know how many smiling little kids, plucking these toys off the ground with glee, were mutilated or met their end in this way? And where were the indignant faces of Brian Mulroney and Joe Clark when this news became common knowledge? They uttered not a whimper. Not a sigh. This is moral cowardice parading as statemanship. It makes a normal person feel sick. Never mind the three-million-odd refugees the Soviets caused to flee their Afghan homelands!

Just before giving you the run-down on some of our recipient nations, here's an extract from a *Time* magazine story (Feb. 2, 1987), entitled "Foreign Aid: Asking Some Hard Questions," that underlines some of the points made in this chapter.

A recent OECD study found "virtually no progress in per capita income over the past two decades" in countries south of the Sahara. Worse, Sub-Saharan Africa now produces less food per person than it did in 1960, despite the billions of aid dollars spent on rural development.

Further to this, Canada's own auditor general, Kenneth Dye, rapped the knuckles of the aid establishment in Ottawa ("Canada Throwing Away Millions in Foreign Aid," *Toronto Star*, Dec. 14, 1988), describing CIDA's sloppy operation, irresponsible business, buying, and record-keeping practices, and scandals such as:

• Providing 118 miles of steel rails at a cost of $2.2 million for a railway that needed only 18 miles of them.

• Spending $13 million to recruit and train workers for the farms (really collective communes) of Tanzania, with no idea of what they were to accomplish.

• Allocating $13 million for a Chinese hydro-electric "feasibility" study for a project the Chinese didn't know what to do with.

• Giving $17 million to fund a dam project in the Yangtze River that environmentalists say is a waste of money because the reservoir behind the dam will soon fill with silt.

AND WHAT ABOUT "FLIGHT CAPITAL"?

I HAVE BEEN UNABLE TO get a firm estimate on exactly how much unrecorded capital citizens of countries to which we send money, in turn send *out* of their own countries. Aid money in, investment capital out? Canadians are suckered into sending borrowed money to Third World countries that don't have enough confidence to keep their own capital at home. Here are a few snippets on the flight-capital situation, all in U.S. dollars.

• International bankers think flight capital totals "about $250 billion annually — about two-thirds of Latin America's debt." During its years of debt crisis, Mexico smuggled out an estimated $84 billion — a figure that rivals that country's $100 billion foreign debt. Venezuelans, with a foreign debt of $32 billion, shipped out $58 billion. (*Globe and Mail*, May 1, 1989)

• *Die Welt* said (Jan. 28, 1989) that Brazil and Mexico together sent out as much as $10 billion, as much as the two countries had to find to service their foreign debt. Former Mexican President José Lopez Portillo (1976-82) became a "dollar-billionaire" in this fashion (*Die Welt*, March 4, 1989).

• In a study of nine developing countries (to which Canada shipped about $92 million in aid in 1987), international economics expert Michael P. Dooley estimated these same countries shipped out about $100 billion in flight capital.

As if the illogical insanity of this revolving-door debt crisis were not enough, here's a peek at just a few of the countries we are helping:

INDIA

AMOUNT GIVEN IN 1986-87: $170.96 MILLION
AMOUNT INDIA SPENT ON
DEFENCE AND WEAPONS: $9.648 *BILLION* (1987)

While it is true that India has many poor (it also has many rich and many in between), anyone giving money to India would surely want to question its internal priorities. For one thing, in India, many starve in the streets — and yet India has the largest livestock holding in the world; India also has one of the world's best-equipped armies. Its armed forces total greater than 1.26 million combat-ready men, and their military equipment includes 2,500 tanks and 900 combat jet aircraft. Six of its air-force squadrons of strike fighters are armed with nuclear bombs. Couldn't India sell a few of these tanks and fighter aircraft, and feed its own poor, instead of coming to us for hand-outs?

Further, India employs a widespread form of slavery known as "tied," or "bonded," labour. This is labour — sometimes lifelong — supplied by extremely poor, low-caste Indians who have made the mistake of borrowing a few rupees from landowners or factory owners who then oblige them to repay it in work. The ignorant workers never really learn how much they owe, and the owners keep them in bondage by charging them back for all sorts of things (shovels, rent, water, interest, medicine) so that their debt can never be repaid. *Il Giornale* (Sept. 3, 1986) reports that there are more than five million such semi-slaves in India today. These debts can be transferred from one generation to another so that children are literally born into the debt-slavery of their parents. It's disgusting, and in my view at least as bad as any of the racial excesses attributed to South Africa. "Something like 105 million Indians remain untouchables and are regarded by the rest of society as inherently inferior. They are probably the largest oppressed minority in the world. Untouchable men are even forbidden from shaping their moustaches upwards — the act would signify an intolerable self-assertion."[16] Perhaps External Affairs Minister Joe Clark, and our prime minister, would care to raise this matter at the next Commonwealth meeting?

Further still, India is a major human rights violator, which should disqualify any country for aid. As for its "Third World" status, the *Globe and Mail*'s "Report on Business" (Jan., 1987) reported that "post-colonial India has moved beyond textile and steel mills and railways to climb to 10th place in the ranks of industrialized nations. Its engineering industries are world class. It has sent homemade satellites into orbit on Indian-designed rockets. And last year it commissioned its first fully indigenous nuclear reactor." India is also the tenth-largest producer and exporter of military arms in the world and openly supported the Soviet invasion of Afghanistan. In view of such expertise and obvious wealth, perhaps India should be giving Canada foreign aid?

All this is upsetting, to say the least, and Canada and its government ought to be ashamed. Indian poverty must be solved by changes in India's own attitudes and a re-allocation of its internal resources, and this shameless begging for funds from Canada and other Western nations must be stopped.

ETHIOPIA

AMOUNT GIVEN: $55.3 MILLION

AMOUNT SPENT BY
ETHIOPIA ON "DEFENCE": $447 MILLION (1986)

Like many Third World nations enchanted with socialist theory — usually picked up at Harvard or Yale or the London School of Economics by wealthy graduate students who then return home to solve their nations' problems — Ethiopia has indulged in extremely repressive forced collectivization of its poor peasants in the hope of resettling them in parts of the country it thought would cause economic activity to lift off. This top-down method of stimulating wealth has never worked, and cannot work for the simple reason that you cannot *will* people to produce. The result is the same as in the U.S.S.R.: "They pretend to pay us, and we pretend to work."

While the cameras were grinding away to persuade the rest of the world that Ethiopians were starving from drought, and begging for assistance, the truth is that Ethiopia itself was engaged in a genocidal war *against its own people*. The poor were uprooted, forcibly moved from their ancestral homes to new settlements, or left for dead if they refused. Civil war erupted. Productive life stopped. Food and monetary aid were massively diverted to government forces and never reached the starving. Much as the U.S.S.R. did in the Ukraine in the 1930s, the Ethiopian government set out to starve its own people, while our dollars flowed to help it do so. This may not have been our intent, but nevertheless . . . how many of the dead children of Ethiopia will lie upon our consciences? We'll never know. At its peak, Ethiopia's "reset-tlement" program (which we specifically helped fund) was eventually stopped because of world-wide outrage, and was estimated to be killing as many people as the famine itself. Priests and gravediggers at the resettlement sites alone estimated between fifty and a hundred thou-sand dead.

In addition to the sadness of all this, Ethiopia, like many of the most destitute African nations, is a Communist nation. Its leaders feed on Marxist-Leninist dogma, and because, as we saw in Chapter Four, Marxism has no theory of wealth production, Ethiopia, like all such nations, basically circumvents the true roots of wealth creation in favour of a central control of political, economic, and cultural life that amounts to a militarization of society and a rigidification of economic life. An article in the *Washington Monthly* (Sept., 1988) summarized this situation in its review of a book by Robert D. Kaplan entitled *Surrender or Starve: The Wars Behind the Ethiopian Famine:*

> It was war, as much as drought, that caused the famine in the first place . . . Since 1980 the number of blacks who died at the hands of security forces in South Africa has been historically insignificant compared to the number killed by the Ethiopian authorities by the force of collectivization — and this figure does not include the famine deaths.

Peter Worthington, columnist for the *Financial Post*, visited Ethiopia and took photographs of many Ethiopian army installations destroyed by the Eritrean rebels. In the abandoned army camps he saw and photographed the propaganda pamphlets, the disarray of the hammers and sickles, pamphlets, and slogans of the Marxist regime. *Stacked against the wall were a number of 50-kilogram sacks of flour marked "CIDA — Gift of Canada."* The refugees said it was normal for the Ethiopian army to use aid supplies. Other such foreign aid, such as scarce cooking oil, they said, were being sold by the government at $3.50 a gallon to help finance the army. By the end of 1987, Canada had given more than $65 million in aid to Ethiopia — $27 million of it in food. According to Worthington there is widespread unhappiness among the people of Ethiopia that Canada is helping the oppressor government. We naively believe that Ethiopia's problems are from drought. But Sudan, a non-socialist country right beside Ethiopia, has the very same weather, feeds its own people, and exports food, to boot.

BANGLADESH
AMOUNT GIVEN: $214.5 MILLION

AMOUNT SPENT BY
BANGLADESH ON MILITARY AND WEAPONS: $273
MILLION (1984)

The above amounts do not include an extra $14.5 million given in emergency flood aid. Overpopulation and the accompanying deforestation (for firewood fuel) and soil erosion have made crop life tenuous at best. Construction volunteer Kamar uz Zaman says, "Of course we have floods. The canals were four or five metres deep when we were kids. Now, they are maybe half a metre" (*Globe and Mail*, Sept. 14, 1988). But the biggest problem faced by Bangladesh is its own stubborn refusal to limit population growth, which is now around 2.5 per cent per year. The population is projected to be about 180 million by the year 2015, or 3,000 inhabitants per square mile. (In 1985 Bangladesh had about 1,800, Ethiopia 75, India 583, England 591, and Canada 8 inhabitants per square mile.) Bangladesh is about the size of our Maritime provinces, and its annual per-capita income is about $130. "Political insecurity, restrictive labour and commercial regulations and alleged corruption have retarded foreign investment. As for domestic investment, one senior diplomat said: 'There is a lack of faith by Bangladeshis in the future of their country. *Most of them send their money out of the country'*" (*Ottawa Citizen*, Sept. 17, 1988).

ZIMBABWE
AMOUNT GIVEN: $17.6 MILLION (1986-87)

AMOUNT SPENT ON MILITARY
AND WEAPONS: $390 MILLION (1986)

On January 29, 1987, in Harare, capital of Zimbabwe, Prime Minister Brian Mulroney gave $50 million of Canadians' money for an unnecessary power-line project that Zimbabwe and Zambia plan to build to Botswana (*Toronto Sun*, Jan. 30, 1987). The article also pointed out that our leaders "want to cut off the power now provided by South Africa." The article continues, "In the past seven years, since Marxist boss Mugabe took over Zimbabwe, more than $100 million of Canadian taxpayers' money has been given to it by our federal government. And that's a nation in which Mugabe has vowed to eliminate all opposition parties, including any representation by the remaining white population. Right now, the Mulroneyites are spending $120 million of our money on bilateral projects in the frontline states . . . The Mulroney government has committed itself to spending $220 million more of our money on future projects in the area."

Later in the same year, Mugabe's Information Minister Nathan Shamuyarira reported that coming legislation would strip the 250,000 whites in Zimbabwe even of the 20 seats of the 100-seat legislature promised to them at independence in 1980. If we have to keep giving them money, then why doesn't our prime minister refuse until the trampling of white minority rights in Zimbabwe is eliminated?

MOZAMBIQUE
AMOUNT GIVEN: $19.2 MILLION (1986-87)

MILITARY SPENDING: $276 MILLION (1986)

This is another Marxist nation that we support. Under Mozambique's "new order," there have been massive shipments of Mozambican youth to East Bloc nations where they provide cheap labour (twelve thousand in East Germany). The export of such cheap — some would say slave — labour, a fee for which is paid to Mozambique, helps to pay its military expenses. President Chissano does not believe in elections, and has never held one. It is virtually a one-party state ruled by a dictator. Why is it that we insist that South Africa institute a one-man, one-vote law, but not Mozambique? On the tenth anniversary of a "Friendship and Co-operation" pact with the Soviet Union, Chissano crowed, "Our ties of friendship and co-operation grow and consolidate on a basis of solid and common principles — Marxism-Leninism and proletarian internationalism." Mozambique has its own internal rebellion against Chissano's regime, and Canada, through CIDA, has been drawn into this by again providing "humanitarian aid" to Chissano's government. There is little doubt he uses as much of it as possible to fight his war against his own people and against South Africa — all under the guise of "famine." CIDA is even encouraging us as individuals to get involved in this sordid mess, as "the federal government, through CIDA, is matching individual donations by a factor of up to nine to one" (*Vancouver Sun*, March 13, 1987). Recently, and to the great regret of hard-line Marxists, Mozambique has been forced to allow market forces to play a role in agricultural production — which socialists see as a tactical retreat "dangerous to the long-term socialist objectives" of Mozambique (*South African Report*, Dec., 1986).

REPUBLIC OF SOUTH AFRICA

MONEY GIVEN: $3.4 MILLION ($7.83 million in 1988-89
budget. A lot goes to dissident groups)

MONEY SPENT ON MILITARY DEFENCE: $2.3 *BILLION*
(1986)

Canada has got itself embroiled in a foreign-policy war against South African Europeans, which it conducts with a fanatical and haughty self-righteousness. I have no problem with anyone disliking apartheid. It is nasty and brutish, and everyone wishes it were not so. But it pales in comparison with the human-rights infractions in just about every black African nation, most of which have always been and are this moment engaged in internal and trans-border racial warfare and persecution against other blacks, Chinese, Jews, "coloureds," you name it.

This is Africa's major sport, and I don't like any of it. But what I like a lot less is Canada's holier-than-thou attitude in giving financial "aid" support to all the frontline states, "aid" that even Mugabe told newsmen would take various forms, including "military training." Mugabe said that "he had received a commitment on military aid from Prime Minister Brian Mulroney during a private meeting between the two" in New York City in late September when Mulroney was to address the

U.N. (*Globe and Mail*, Oct. 4, 1988). Are we crazy? The journalist Eric Margolis wrote, "I met with a senior officer of the Zimbabwean Army. He told me that Zimbabwe's general staff considers the border with South Africa to be the nation's only safe border" (*Toronto Sun*, Oct. 6, 1988). In short, "Zimbabwe has troops poised on all its borders with its *black* neighbors — but not against South Africa, from which *there is absolutely no military threat.*"

Writing in *Commentary* magazine (Sept., 1985), the historian Paul Johnson told us that "all African states are racist. Almost without exception, and with varying degrees of animosity, they discriminate against someone: Jews, or whites, or Asians, or non-Muslim religious groups, or disfavored tribes. There is no such thing as a genuinely multi-racial society in the whole of Africa. There is no African country where tribal or racial origins, skin color or religious affiliation are not of prime importance in securing elementary rights."

So why the selective morality from Canadians?

What Is To Be Done?

OBVIOUSLY, THIS IS ANOTHER area of government activity rife with incompetence, waste, and hypocrisy. Canada has succumbed to the Third World myth marketed to it so heavily by proponents of the "North-South" dialogue, and by the NIEO. It has thus embarked on an official program of guilt-inspired (but very selective) socialist-style redistribution of wealth from producer to non-producer nations. In this, it has transported to the international arena the same misconceptions about the tools of freedom and wealth creation to which it is most often blinded at home. What we see out there is a huge international effort obedient to the stale collectivist jargon of self-styled gurus like Nyerere to install a world-wide handicap system designed to help the poor not by teaching them how to fish themselves, but by giving our fish away to them. But the despots who rule over many of these poor do not want them to help themselves; they have no particular desire to see their people progress. They either refuse, or, if such exist, resist using the medical and technical tools to limit their own population growth; they misuse humanitarian aid to make war on their their own populations or on their neighbours; their histories are blackened by unspeakable atrocities; their people are denied fundamental civil rights.

Interestingly, our own CIDA programs, perhaps in a belated effort to comply with the growing conservatism of the free world, have recently been preaching the idea that aid should be for "structural adjustment" (in a paper entitled "Sharing Our Future"). By this they mean funds for white elephant capital projects will slowly be dried up (they are embarassing "show" projects that recipient countries often don't need, can't operate, and allow to decay), and redirected to pressuring Third World countries to use free market techniques to vitalize their economies. But this is really just more top-down collectivism — donors with a social-welfare mentality imagining that democratic capitalism can be successfully imposed on an unwilling populace. But it can't. It has to percolate up from the bottom through a complete revolution in the political, economic, and cultural spheres of life, based on values much like those outlined in Chapter Four. Watch out for CIDA officials bearing gifts bought with your tax dollars. They will continue to redesign their failed philosophies just to keep the whole foreign aid scam going as long as possible.

Here's what can be done:

1. Stop giving all government-to-government aid.

2. Start balancing our national budget, and retire our own national debt.

3. Once our own problems are solved, encourage individuals to give true humanitarian aid but only when our government can prove that such aid is without question going to individuals and families in need. This can be encouraged by allowing the same tax deductions as for domestic charity.

4. Even then, Canadians must carefully distinguish between giving a hand-up, and a hand-out. Nations that refuse to help themselves, or persist in fatalism, or whose ideology is bent pell mell on burying ours (such as Marxist-Leninist or other socialist nations), must be encouraged to change before we will help them. If they want to learn, we can teach them how to fish.

5. Don't encourage aid to any country involved in war unless we want to fight that war, which is a decision for the nation, not for the minister of external affairs, or CIDA.

6. Don't encourage aid to any country that denies a minimum of civil and human rights to its citizens, while embracing policies, such as large

military budgets and inadequate health care and education, that impoverish the people.

7. If we are going to play conscience-of-the-world, then let us do so even-handedly. Let us ensure that our own minorities have equal protection of their rights — Quebec's English minority does not have such protection, and our treatment of native peoples is a national disgrace — before going abroad on a white charger. Then, if it makes us feel good to preach morals to others, let us be bold enough to do so evenly, to all concerned. Selective morality is reprehensible. For example, Soviet and Eastern Bloc repression, generations of Soviet repression, and the myriad oppressions occurring daily in black African, South American, and Asian states deserve at least as much attention as South Africa. The new wealth of freedom in the U.S.S.R. and Eastern Europe is refreshing, but it ought never to conceal their crimes against humanity.

The Real Shocker

On June 14, 1988, Doug Bandow of the *Wall Street Journal* reported that according to the Arms Control and Disarmament Agency, "between 1980 and 1985 developing nations spent $924.6 billion on their militaries. Many of these nations faced no serious security threat; instead, the arms were meant for foreign aggression and domestic repression." The article pointed out that if Third World states were to reduce their spending by one-third, "they would have had an extra $58 billion in capital in 1985 alone, slightly more than enough to cover the interest on all LDC loans [loans to Less Developed Countries]. In fact, *international aid largely serves to underwrite poor nations' prodigious appetites for weapons*." Bandow also points out, in reference solely to Third World nations, that in the same period they spent $213 billion on arms, and received $239 billion in aid. Ethiopia, for example, spent $1.6 billion repressing Eritreans between 1982 and 1985 and collected $1.8 billion in aid. Thus do foreign lenders "free up domestic capital for military use. Were the foreign aid — and commercial credit — not available, Third World governments would have to make far tougher choices before allocating so much of their limited resources to guns." Bandow concludes that Africa's debtor nations "are largely responsible for their own plight. They should start cleaning up the mess themselves instead of looking for a foreign bailout. And their first step should be to slash unproductive weapons expenditures" (C-FAR *Newsletter*, #119, July 14, 1988).

Below are the import shares for industrial market economies compared with the economies of the Third World, for 1985, excluding China. If, when you watch your tax bill climb, you are wondering how the Third World is using the money your government is so unthinkingly showering upon it, here's a clue:

	ALL IMPORTS %	MACHINERY %	ARMS %
TO THIRD WORLD:	26	28	67
TO INDUSTRIAL WORLD:	74	72	33
	-----	-----	-----
	100	100	100

(*Source*: Stockholm International Peace Research Institute *Year Book*, 1988)

A full 67 percent of the world's arms imports are going to Third World countries. In addition to the enormous stupidity of this reality, it is a huge insult to honest people and honest governments everywhere who have striven to transfer resources to such nations on the understanding these were helping to educate and feed starving children. Far from it. Those gaunt, emaciated eyes should be turned to their own leaders who, if there is any justice here on earth, must burn with shame.

10

Radical Feminism
The Destruction Of
Traditional Society

You see, we want a whole transformation of
society in the most revolutionary way . . .

Louise Dulude, former President, National Action Committee on the
Status of Women

It will be plain that the first condition for the
liberation of the wife is to bring the whole female
sex into public industry and that this in turn
demands the abolition of the monogamous
family as the economic unit of society.

Friedrich Engels, *The Origin of the Family*

THERE IS NOTHING MORE emblematic of the social-welfare State than
the ideas and programs of radical feminism. This is such an emotion-
ally heated subject that we must be sure to distinguish radical feminism
from the ordinary concern of reasonable people for fair-minded laws
to provide *everyone* with equal opportunities. Most women who think
of themselves as "feminists" today simply mean that fairness has not
always been evenly applied to women in our society, and that it ought
to be. (Of course in some cases they will argue it shouldn't be, because
women have advantages they don't want to lose. Paid maternity leave,
couches in women's washrooms, restraints on lifting heavy objects,
immunity from military conscription, special legal dispensations for

separated or divorced mothers, and so on; these they describe as "justified" discrimination.) But radical feminists go far beyond this. Theirs is a program for the radical restructuring of society through centralized social engineering of the most insidious kind. Radical feminists are not interested in equal *opportunities* for women; they want equal *outcomes*, or results, even if these have to be *forced* on people by the powers of the State; *even if men and women, left to their own free devices, would never choose such outcomes*. That is why, once dissected, every ill of socialism can be found in radical feminism: in its reliance on all the popular illusions; in its dependence on the coercive powers of the State; in its collectivist agenda; in its ignorance of the basics of economics; and in its psychology of resentment.

On its own, radical feminism would be a tempest in a teapot. But with the power of the State behind it ($13 million in 1987 for the "Women's Program," an estimated $60 million from all levels of government in Canada to bring "equality" to women), the radical feminist movement constitutes a fundamental attack on the whole idea of a free society as it has painfully evolved over the past five centuries, from principle to practice. In future our society will look back at its own crumbling walls and wonder how it so blithely allowed the Trojan horse of radical feminism within its gates. Of course, sometimes moderate feminism can be just as dangerous as the radical form, because it alters social structures without this expressed intention. After all, whether the trigger be pulled by a sleepwalker or a revolutionary, the same damage is done. Those of us who cherish the core values that made this nation strong — freedom, family, individual responsibility, reward for effort — must learn to recognize the very different values and tactics of those who are determined to destroy these core values, however unwittingly. In particular, we must learn not to be seduced by the gossamer language in which their aims are couched.

My intention in this chapter is to take the wraps off the feminists' ideology — the chain of arguments that makes them feel justified in coercing others — to expose feminism's intellectual and moral dishonesty. Then I will expose the political, moral, and social danger of just one of their noble-sounding programs — so-called "pay- equity" — to show the reader how a wolf in sheep's clothing is still a wolf. I would attack radical feminism whether proposed by men or by women — or by some third type of human being we cannot imagine — simply because it aims to destroy much that is good in our society, and replace it with something that is not.

Undoing The Past

IN RESPONSE TO THE widespread employment in factories of women and children that was threatening family life during the nineteenth century, social reformers fought hard to establish what was called a "family wage" sufficient to raise a family of five without the need to put mothers and children out to work.[1] The family wage would protect men with families from unemployment because they would always be given preference in the search for jobs, and it would get children out of the workplace and back into the home for care and schooling. Once it became established, the family wage, or "living wage" as it was sometimes called, was seen as a social contract fortifying the family, therefore all society, and therefore the nation. Single women vying for the jobs of men who had to support wives and children were seen as a direct threat to the welfare of society, and greedy to boot, since, with no children or spouse to support, they would be paid more than their life situation required. For this reason, women were regularly denied jobs, demoted, or dismissed in favour of a family-wage earner. Even recently, after World War II, women were let go in droves for the same reason — they held scarce jobs needed by men with children.

What an irony that just after more than a century spent consolidating and protecting the idea of the family and the importance of investing *personal* parental care in our children, we are now assiduously breaking all this apart, lobbying for both parents to work outside the home, and for universal and, by definition, *impersonal* paid daycare. Social entropy is at work. Then, society chose family and children over material wealth. Now, we are choosing material wealth over family and children. Then, reformers struggled to help women and children get off the streets, out of the factories, and into the home so that children could be properly raised and educated. Today's reformers are trying to drive them out again. The only thing common to the two sets of reformers is the use of State power.

Most then shared the deeply embedded notion that men are basically unruly scoundrels if left to their own devices. And women? Well, it was commonly understood they were the superior sex, because they controlled the high moral ground of society. For men, sex, family, and children were the Holy Trinity. And for most it was not money alone that brought moral stature, as we tend to think narrowly today, but a combination of common virtues for which rich and poor alike strove, the path to which was most often pointed out by the women of society.

But modern women, thanks to sexual "liberation," have yielded the high moral ground they once controlled. The good-better-best range of manners and morals that infused their world has been replaced by a general, feel-good, whatever-turns-you-on ethic. They may have wanted down from their pedestal, but that pedestal was also an altar at which men, however quixotically, worshipped. Having stepped down, however, they must now play on the same field as men. For this, alas, they are ill suited, owing to their generally lesser aggressiveness (which is not the same as *control*), and to the competitive handicap to which their biology leads — the care of children. Everyone knows, of course, that some women are just as aggressive as men, or more so, and that men *can* look after children; but men cannot carry them, bear them, or suckle them. Of course, any couple that wants to reverse traditional customs is utterly free to do so, and for some this may be preferable. And if heads and hearts were interchangeable, an absolutely equal sharing of outside work (at least the banal, repetitive kind) might make something like that possible. But they are not.

So the traditional familial division of labour has always had a purpose — simple efficiency. It is an arrangement that enables and always has enabled societies great and small to do the important work of ensuring their own continuation. What the important nineteenth-century social arrangement did so clearly was to consolidate the idea of marriage, the family, and *the importance of child-rearing by parents or relatives*. The inevitable result of this was to make men *dependent* on women for sex, family, and children — and women on men for sex, physical protection, and money. The implicit social contract specified that men would provide and protect, while women would process and nurture. Both sexes were seen to need each other equally, if differently. Women always knew they could bring men to heel by withholding what men wanted most. Men, in turn, could bring women to heel by withholding support and protection. In order to prevent the wanton occurrence of the latter — especially during a woman's child-rearing phase, when she was naturally handicapped in terms of competitive wage-earning power — there were always extremely strong social and legal sanctions upholding marital vows, responsibility, and child support.

A key element in this division of labour was a general acknowledgement of the obvious fact that men and women are different in many, many ways. In short, that "men are not better than women and women are not better than men; men and women differ."[2] It is these differences that rile feminists so, because they correctly see that *unless they can prove that men and women are the same*, they haven't got a case to prove social discrimination against women. Either men and women are naturally different, and these differences manifest themselves in different values and life choices; or they are exactly the same, and the different social outcomes are a result of oppression and discrimination against women. Let's look at the feminist case for sameness, keeping in mind that the main reason for exploring this in depth is to test the ideological grounds for the feminist attack on traditional society.

THE FEMINIST REACTION

THE FEMINIST REACTION to the cultural arrangement outlined above gathered steam throughout the early part of this century, and was accelerated by the experience of two world wars in which so many women worked in, as well as out of, the home. It was also reinforced by a growing egalitarianism in the world as expressed in various collectivist movements, themselves contributory causes of those wars. More specifically, the contemporary feminist movement was distinctly linked to the Marxist anti-capitalist movement through Simone de Beauvoir's book *The Second Sex* — basically a treatment of the condition of women much influenced by de Beauvoir's companion, Jean-Paul Sartre. In it, de Beauvoir was militantly anti-capitalist, anti-property, anti-marriage, and anti-family. She admired the Soviet model of society: "Marriage was to be based on a free agreement that the spouses could break at will; maternity was to be voluntary; pregnancy leaves were to be paid for by the State, which would assume charge of the children . . ."[3] Is she talking about Soviet society, or about Canada, 1989? De Beauvoir was succeeded by serious North American feminist writers like Millet, Friedan, and Steinem, most of whom shared her admiration for socialism under one name or another which, "together with hostility to 'capitalism,' can be considered virtually a further distinguishing mark of feminism."[4] When it comes to putting a finger on just what feminism's basic beliefs are, we can capsulize the philosopher Michael Levin's four points as follows. Feminists believe:

1. That "men and women are the same" — anatomical differences apart. (This is a version of the Equality Illusion at work.)

2. That "men unfairly occupy positions of dominance" because they have been raised in the myth that boys are more aggressive than girls, and have been taught mastery, while girls have been taught people skills instead (a version of the Determinist Illusion). Without this

stereotyping, all "leadership would be equally divided between the sexes."

3. "Traditional femininity is a suffocating and pathological response" to women's restricted lives and must be abandoned. Everyone must reject the idea that sex has any significant effect on one's nature.

4. All the above changes "will require the complete transformation of society." (The principal tool here will be the Rights Illusion.)

Do The Feminist Assumptions Hold Up?

HERE'S A REPORT ON the all-important assumption of male-female sameness, by Eleanor Maccoby and Carol Jacklin, two feminist psychologists from prestigious Stanford University, published in their exhaustive two-volume book, *The Psychology of Sex Differences*.[5] These two social scientists set out to survey the entire field of studies on psychological sex differences, under the assumption there were none. But what they learned was that clear and important differences exist between boys and girls *even before birth*. There are wide, and world-wide, differences across whole ranges of physical sensitivity, illness, perception, learning, tactility, language, spatial abilities, pain threshold, and on and on. Of course, there are great similarities, too. But significant differences are detected in all areas studied, through various stages of development. This would not surprise most parents, for as Levin humorously reminds us, "Any veteran of adolescence and parenthood still able to believe that boys and girls are born alike has already withstood more evidence than any laboratory can provide." The best known difference is the superior female ability with language, and superior male ability with mathematics and spatial relations — both noticed early and continuously throughout life. (My own case is quite the opposite.) But the most important difference, one I am sure Maccoby and Jenkins hoped they would not find, but certainly did, was in "aggression." In their chapter on "power relationships," here is what they report:

"It is time to consider whether the sex difference in aggression has a biological foundation. We contend that it does":

1. "Males are more aggressive than females in all human societies for which evidence is available."

2. The sex differences are found early in life, at a time when there is no evidence that differential socialization pressures have been brought to bear by adults to "shape" aggression differently in the two sexes.

3. Similar sex differences are found in man and subhuman primates.

4. Aggression is related to levels of sex hormones, and can be changed by experimental administrations of these hormones.

For anyone who seriously considers the whole subject of male-female sex differences, this sweeping survey must be conclusive, especially because these authors were working hard to *discount* male/female differences in the scientific literature. Quite clearly, *there are no grounds whatsoever for the pivotal feminist claim that males and females are fundamentally the same,* and "the accessibility of the immense volume of material on sex difference makes the continued respectability of feminism no less than a scandal."[6]

What this all means is that from birth, males tend to strive harder than females to reach the top of any power hierarchy they encounter. Furthermore, they "create hierarchies to reach the top if none exist." Now, you may want something very badly, but if you are surrounded by others who want it more, they are likely to wear you out eventually. Boys are usually more aggressive, more Machiavellian in their pursuit of power, and crueller and more willing to hurt than girls. Studies abound showing that men the world over despise victims — especially their own — whereas women tend to take pity on them. Nothing in this male attitude is particularly admirable, in my view, but that's the way it is. This was driven home to me by a television documentary on the entering of a concentration camp by Russian soldiers. The commentator remarked that many of the soldiers not only stole from the women prisoners, but raped them as well. Now these women prisoners were the most emaciated imaginable, some close to death. With sadness and disgust it hit home that no woman could possibly find a man in that condition sexually desirable, or wish to degrade him so. With that thought, my awareness of the chasm that exists between the physical and moral lives of males and females struck home even harder. And let us not forget that throughout history, it is the men who have been prone to abandon children, murder them, bayonet them in war, rape them, and take them into slavery — not women. The truly great crimes of history have been effected by men — I think of countless tyrants, especially the modern ones such as Stalin, Hitler, Lenin, Pol Pot, Mao, and their like, who wrought cruelties of a kind and scope that beggar the imagination. And anthropological studies the world over verify this reality of aggression and hardness, *which can be induced in any female, human or primate, by the simple administration of male hormones*. Athletes who have had occasion to mix with East German, Soviet, or Canadian female athletes on steroids have known this for years. Furthermore, both male and female athletes take only *male* hormones, for the very same reason — to enhance aggressiveness. Contrarily, *female* hormones administered to long-term violent criminals succeed in pacifying them. Naturally, as aggressiveness is highly valued in societies the world over, men are rewarded for such behaviour. In other words, learning plays an important secondary role, but not a primary one. Anthropological and biological studies the world over confirm that through hormones, men in general

> *are rendered more aggressive, exploratory, volatile, competitive and dominant, more visual, abstract, and impulsive, more muscular, appetitive, and tall . . . less nurturant, moral, domestic, stable, and peaceful, less auditory, verbal, and sympathetic, less durable, healthy, and dependable, less balanced . . . more compulsive sexually and less secure. Within his own sex, he is more inclined to affiliate upwards — toward authority — and less inclined to affiliate downwards — toward children and toward the weak and needy.*[7]

As a natural result of this, there is no society in the world in which matriarchy has ever existed, or is in any way emerging today.[8] Fascinatingly, the beginning of all these differences is right in the womb. For we all begin life as females, biologically.[9] We can become male only if the Y chromosome is present, and sufficient male hormones act upon our early development. Maleness *is* difference. Even genetic girls, accidentally exposed to male hormones, "consistently reject most of the attempts of the culture to feminize them."[10] Enough said. What are we to make of all this? Very simply,

> *that men monopolize leadership positions because they try harder to get them does not mean that men deserve these positions or that men do a better job in them than women would do if they became leaders. The only sense in which male dominance is "right" is that it expresses the free choices of individual men to strive for positions*

of power and the free choices of individual women to do other things.[11]

My addendum to this is that *aggressiveness* and *control* are two very different things. In external structures, like armies, or businesses, the former generally leads to the latter; but in interpersonal relationships, not necessarily so. Everyone can think of couples where the male is more aggressive, but the female controls the relationship and the family's tenor. Historically, a man's power usually comes from physical strength and money; a woman's, from sexual and emotional control of the relationship.

HOW DO THESE DIFFERENCES SHOW UP IN THE JOB MARKET?

HERE ARE A FEW SNIPPETS from a variety of sources:

• "Despite massive contrary incentives from government policy, women in this century have not increased their work effort or contributions to intact-family income."[12] Many more are working, but their contribution to family income has not changed (in fact, it has increased from 26 to 28 percent for two-earner families, but decreased for intact families.)

• In intact families, only "one-fifth of the wives worked full time all year" (1983), and they earned "only 16.5 percent of the total family incomes."[13]

• Eighty-three percent of American women say they would welcome more emphasis on traditional family ties; young women (between 18 and 24) confess to a greater longing for this than they think their parents had. One midwestern study examining the career aspirations of high-school girls shows that by far the majority (including the "brightest and the best") feel they will not be working more than five years after graduation.[14] This is as distinct from boys, who live with an early awareness that they will be bonded to the job market for life.

• "Women between the ages of 25 and 59 are eleven times more likely than men to leave work voluntarily, and the average woman spends only eight months at each job compared with almost three years for a man."[15]

• "Married men of working age use 87 percent of their earnings capacity, while comparable married women use only 33 percent."[16]

• A 1982 Harris Poll indicated that 53 percent of women "do not want to be on the job market at all."[17] I am sure this is true for most men, as well. If many women feel they are in bondage to home and children, many men certainly feel they are in lifetime bondage to their jobs and the job market.

• The 1982 U.S. Economic Census showed that 24 percent of all American businesses were owned by women. U.S. $98.3 billion in receipts divided by 2,884,450 businesses yielded an average *gross* revenue of some $34,000 per annum.[18] In 1980 the average *net* income of female-operated businesses was $2,200; retail establishments were the most common, and the average *net* income for these was $497.[19]

• In the U.S.A., female physicians "see 38 percent fewer patients per hour, and work 22 percent fewer hours than male physicians, female lawyers see fewer clients . . . and female professors write fewer books and research papers."[20] This has nothing to do with the quality of their work. Personally, I prefer a physician who spends more time with me. But in leaving their offices, I have often wondered how they ever make any money.

• Only 7 percent of top U.S. government jobs were held by women, whereas 75 percent of the bottom grades were. But the federal government is not discriminating against women — "women quite simply and commendably are discriminating in favor of their own families."[21]

• Despite the massive Israeli effort to communalize and socialize life in unisex, shared-work kibbutzim (communes), a forty-year study covering over more than 100,000 men and women "showed that each successive generation moved more decisively toward traditional roles. Today the kibbutzim show the most distinct sex roles in Israeli society."[22]

WHAT ARE THE EFFECTS OF SEX DIFFERENCES ON SOCIETY?

BRIEFLY PUT, THEY CAN be devastating — unless society sets itself to control them, as it did in the nineteenth century *simply by insisting on its values*. But we have sowed the wind of sexual egalitarianism in our time, and we are reaping the whirlwind. For, as Gilder poignantly shows in his *Men and Marriage*, the public philosophy of males the world over, to the great detriment of society, focuses on *immediate gratification.* Single young men are a distinct hazard to society and its procreative health for the following reasons. They vastly prefer hit-and-run sex. They are wildly more aggressive than females. Although single men number some 13 percent of the population over the age of 14, they commit nearly 90 percent of major and violent crimes.[23] They drink more, have more — and more serious — car accidents, than women, or than married men. Young bachelors are twenty-two times more likely to be committed for mental disease — and ten times more likely to go to hospital for chronic diseases than married men. Single men are convicted of rape five times more often than married men; they have almost double the mortality rate of married men, and three times that of single women, from all causes.

Because homosexuality is a "hit-and-run" phenomenon for males (distinctly not so for females), and suits their predilection for immediate gratification, male homosexuality is in accord with the sexual nature of males and thus thrives when male/female role distinctions are discouraged. Cultures that want to guard against the threat of homosexuality must therefore drive a cultural wedge down hard between maleness and femaleness, for it is no simple coincidence that homosexuality is flourishing in a time of feminism. They go together like the two sides of a coin. The attempt of the State to neutralize male and female differences is manifest in its effort to "normalize" homosexuality, marketing it to us in its agencies and schools as a "value-free" matter of sexual "orientation." In such matters, the State is promoting and financing social entropy — the elimination of meaningful and socially useful differences. Of course, homosexuality is much more than an "orientation." And today, there is a whole feminist school promoting homosexuality as liberation from men — and some of your tax money supports such causes through the Women's Program in Ottawa. (A project grant was given to the Calgary Lesbian Mothers Defence Fund in 1985, and again in 1986, to organize a lesbian conference. Tax dollars were doled out to workers at a rape crisis centre conference who described themselves as "radical lesbian feminists," August 24-26, 1985.)

But the truth is that this whole matter of sexual liberation has backfired. Men have benefitted in the short term, but certainly not in the long. Women have lost in both. For it has caused women to lose the one sure control they had over men, the one sure method that enabled women to have children, provide for them, protect them, and nurture them *personally* at the same time — all paid for by doting males — if they so desired. Now, in some despair, they are turning to the patriarchal State for this sustenance. Of course, this must eventually fail, because the State has no money. It can only be such a Father either by employing women in huge numbers (80 percent of public-service clerical staff earning under $15,000 per year are women: *Toronto Star*, Dec. 24, 1988) or by taking the money demanded by the increasing number of female-headed families from singles, and from fathers and mothers in intact families. Even worse, as Gilder explains, feminism, by default, has allowed men to create a system of polygamy — one in which the strong men can have many partners. A woman loses out in the sense that her child-bearing years and chances of locating a strong husband are biologically confined to a few fleeting years of her life. If she waits too long, the strong ones her own age are taken in a rapidly peaking, concave-sided pyramid of choices. Worse still, in societies that choose both to neutralize sex differences and to permit "liberated" sex, the homosexual underculture always vies for normality with the core culture, destroying core values and stealing otherwise procreative males from women. In other words, "polygyny produces homosexuality."[24] It does this both by liberalizing the choices of strong males (thus destroying the equal apportionment of mates) and by setting the female ethos against the male ethos, thus encouraging sexual resentment between men and women. This, in turn, leads to less marriage (after it enthusiastically embraced sexual liberalism, Sweden's marriage rate between 1966 and 1973 fell some 50 percent); more living alone (63 percent of the residents of Stockholm live alone); and more divorce — or "couple dissolution" as the Swedes call it.[25] Multiple wives? Easy sex? Mistresses? Homosexuality? Liberal ease of cohabitation and divorce? A booming pornography industry? All these inevitably undermine monogamy, which is unfortunate, because "monogamy is designed to minimize the effect of sexual inequalities — to prevent the powerful of either sex from disrupting the familial order . . . any sexual revolution, therefore, will tend to liberate more men than women."[26]

It is for this reason that "the crucial process of civilization is the subordination of male sexual impulses and biology to the long-term horizons of female sexuality."[27] Gilder convincingly argues that because of the male-female hormonal difference in biology, society basically must be set up to tame men and their barbaric proclivities. For without the long-range goals of women, men would be content to fight, enjoy their lust, wander, make war, compete, and strive for power, glory, and dominance. In his view, men are inherently inferior sexually to women, who because of their biology control the entirety of the sexual and procreative processes of life. In fact, males are neither sexually nor morally *equal* to females, and therefore "the man must be *made* equal by society." Thus is the contract struck between men and women whereby he provides and protects, she processes and nurtures. Again, a woman who wants to try all four of these things, or switch it all around, is free to try. But most, the world over, do not — because the system works. What this means is that men, lacking in the distinctiveness and biological determinateness of women, are "deeply dependent on the structure of society to define [their] role."[28]

In short, women channel and confine the generalized male sexual desire in such a way as to protect themselves and their children, and in so doing teach men to subordinate their impulses to the long-term cycles of female sexuality and biology on which society has always been based.[29] In order to avail himself of the intense and intimate sexual meaning a woman can give to his life, and the extension of himself into the future through children that only a woman can provide, a man must give something in return — and this must always be "the external realm of meaning, sustenance, and protection in which the child could be safely born."[30] And that's just the start. When you stop to consider deeply the complex, life-long physical, emotional, and financial requirements of the average family (I have five children), the seriousness of this undertaking sinks in. It requires what the anthropologist Margaret Mead called a "commitment of permanence" from each sex and a "deal" struck between the parties, the terms of which are supplied by the culture. We break the deal at our own — and our children's — peril.

While one can always quibble with details, or find exceptions, it will remain difficult to argue with Gilder's main thesis as outlined above, because it is so overwhelmingly supported by anthropological studies around the world, in every culture studied, past and present. In view of this, we must ask why, in our present society, the State-financed feminist influence is visible everywhere. Sex-education classes take fornication for granted, male/female differences are denied, homosexuality is presented as just another "orientation" (which stimulates the curiosity and fears of otherwise normal boys), "value-free" discussions and "feel-good" moral codes are promoted as primary, and the importance of marriage and the family is downplayed — why does the State finance only feminist advocacy groups, and not those that promote traditional family life? (The government's recent funding of REAL Women of Canada was provoked by its embarrassment, and not by any principle in support of the family.)

At a minimum, readers of this chapter should begin to suspect that the sort of programs the feminists are introducing in order to achieve their vision of equal outcomes is destructive of our social fabric, to say the least. Once again, I am taking aim at the ideology of radical feminism, not at the interests of ordinary women who have an understandable interest in the fair treatment of women — and of men, for that matter.

WHAT IS THE RADICAL FEMINIST REACTION TO THESE REALITIES?

As we have seen, natural male/female differences, and the free choices that spring from them, are reflected in the free marketplace. Even though many militant feminists have given up in their effort to prove that innate differences are the result of "socialization," they have developed a more sinister approach to getting what they want. In short, if you can't prove differences are learned, and you still want to end these differences, the way to do it is to make the market *unfree*, to militarize and rigidify it.

Let us now turn, for the sake of illustration, to just one of the key tools in the feminist effort to overturn our moral and economic order, to achieve the "whole transformation of society," as Louise Dulude, past President of NAC, cheerfully describes her government-funded social revolution (meaning you and I are paying for all this). I am referring to the radical feminists' program for so-called "pay-equity."

THE PAY-EQUITY SCANDAL

Almost everyone misunderstands so-called "pay-equity." They think it is a fair-sounding idea that basically says any two human beings should be paid the same if they do the same work. But "pay-equity" is not about that at all. The principle of paying people the same for the *same work* has long since been accepted as fair by almost everyone (although some economists still say that even this limits the freedom of individuals to offer their services for less, if they so desire, and is thus a form of minimum-wage legislation that discriminates against the very poor). But radical feminists are not satisfied with the rule that women and men must be paid the same for the same work. They want them to be paid the same for *different* work if they can show that the two different kinds of work have the same "value." For example, if a consultant can prove that a female computer operator's job has the same "value" as a male truck driver's job, then the government will order that the two must be paid the same. There's a twist, of course: this applies only to women. If he makes more than she does, she can complain to the government, and force her boss to pay her the same as the truck driver. But if she makes more than he does, he cannot use the same argument to force his boss to pay him the same as her! But I'm getting ahead of myself. Let's backtrack for a minute.

As it turns out, men and women don't very often *do* the same work. Since they don't do the same work but, feminists insist, are biologically the same — women ought to have the same earnings in the free market as men. But they don't. So radical feminists have decided that any difference between the pay of men and the pay of women must be due to "sex discrimination." Once having decided this, they quickly stigmatized the kinds of work women tend to prefer as "job ghettos," or "Pink Collar Ghettos." They conveniently ignore the fact that dental hygienists and legal secretaries are 99 percent female occupations, and have a starting wage around $40,000; these jobs do not qualify as ghettos. If you shoot for a high-paying job, you are assumed to be free; but if you take a low-paying job, or simply don't wish to earn any more than you now do, you are assumed to be exploited and discriminated against. Once the feminists succeeded in selling the government on this idea that any difference was really "discrimination," the course was clear. They then had to set about forcing the world to conform to their vision of fairness — whether free men and women wanted it that way or not. Despite the insult to the intelligence of free working women everywhere that this attitude suggests, the approach was very effective. Here's the radical feminist's formula so far: Men and Women are the same, but they are not paid the same when doing comparable work; therefore sex discrimination must be at fault: therefore *proof* of discrimination is required; then a *program* for correcting it; and finally, someone to *implement and finance* this vision. So . . . their *proof* was the so-called "wage-gap"; their *program* was so-called "pay-equity"; their *Sugar Daddy* was the State.

To tell the truth, one could marvel at the implacable and devious cleverness of the whole thing — if it weren't so dishonest and such an assault on our entire way of life. The result of all this, including the deception of the public required to bring it about (89 percent of Ontarians do not understand what "pay-equity" means — Gallup Poll, April, 1987), is that the province of Ontario, with its Employee Equity Act, now has the dubious distinction of having passed into law the most draconian pay-equity legislation in the free world, and has completely fooled the electorate in the process. Why?

BECAUSE THE "WAGE GAP" IS A RED HERRING

FEMINISTS SAY THAT THERE is a "wage gap" between the earnings of men and women in Canada, and that much of this difference is proof of wage discrimination based on sex. But this is an utterly misleading and dishonest thing to say. Here's why.

Never-married men and *never married* women in Canada (and the U.S.A.) make exactly the same money, and have for a very long time (see the chart below). The big difference in male/female earnings occurs because of marriage. Of course, if you average *all* women's earnings and compare them to *all* men's earnings you will indeed come up with a "wage gap" (women earn, on average, 60-64 percent the wages of men). Although there is nothing very surprising about this, politicians and the press have been inexplicably uncritical of the use being made of this natural statistical result.

IT'S MARRIAGE THAT MAKES THE DIFFERENCE

THE TRUTH IS THAT *marital status has an asymmetrical effect on earnings by sex*, as the economists say. In plain English: if a man and a woman working side by side *and earning the same wage* fall in love and decide to get married and raise a family, something absolutely normal happens. Visions of children dance in their heads, along with simultaneous worries. If both think even the best daycare is impersonal — "there's no way a stranger's going to raise our kids!" — then they worry immediately about how in the world they are going to give their children personal attention and both work full time as well. Will her boss still keep her on if she asks for part-time work? He worries about mortgages, university education, clothing, food, and ... Good Lord — I'm going to need a better job! The result of this totally predictable equation is that she reduces her work hours, or quits altogether, or quits and then takes a part-time job. And he? Well, the pressure is on. He arranges an appointment with his boss and lets him know in no uncertain terms that the promotion he wasn't so sure about last month ... well, he's had a serious change of heart. In fact, given a chance, he'd love to run the whole department. When this occurs millions of times over, and you average their respective earnings, you have the makings of a "wage gap." But the crucial factor is not sex discrimination; rather, it's laudable preferential choices made by both parties in favour of marriage and family. Here's a chart showing the ratios of earnings between *never*-married men and women, and *ever*-married men and women in Canada in 1971, based on a study compiled from Census data for Statistics Canada.[31]

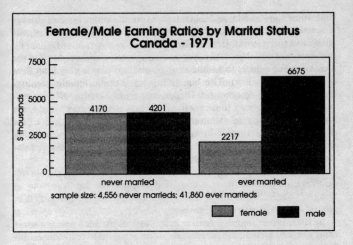

Female/Male Earning Ratios by Marital Status Canada - 1971

sample size: 4,556 never marrieds; 41,860 ever marrieds

The American economist Thomas Sowell tells us that the same picture is found in the U.S.A., for "as of 1971, single women in their thirties who had worked continuously since leaving school earned slightly *more* than single men of the same age, even though women as a group earned less than half as much as men as a group."[32] And a more recent study in the U.S.A. shows that "female academics who never married earned more than male academics who never married," even before "affirmative action" became mandatory in 1971. Sowell sums up this confusion by saying that most of the current income and occupational differences between males and females as gross categories turns out, on closer scrutiny, to be differences between married women and all other categories.[33]

And a 1987 Statistics Canada report called "Earnings of Men and Women" shows that never-married women made the following percentages of the earnings of never-married men:

never-married women	25-34 years of age:	96.8%
never-married women	35-44 years of age:	101.4%
never-married women	45-54 years of age:	107.2%
never-married women	55+ years of age:	102.4%

Astonishingly, the women made more than the men at *all* ages except the youngest studied.

Further, here's some economic logic to put the whole mess to shame: if women were truly supplying business with cheap labour, business owners would naturally hire as many women as possible and would let the overpaid men go. This has not happened. Further, one of the lowest-paying jobs around is that of an outdoor parking-lot attendant in winter — but you could count on one hand the number of females doing that in this country. Is this therefore a male ghetto? Not likely.

Firms that are said to be "exploiting" low-paid women would, according to the discrimination thesis, be making large profits. But they do not. Most, in fact, are fighting tooth and nail to maintain competitive margins in the face of world competition, especially in clothing, footwear, and food processing — all family staples.

Women who have been widowed, divorced, or separated should not be averaged into the figures and used as proof for the lower pay of "single" women. Obviously, after years out of the job market, they cannot expect to return at high pay.

In 1971, never-married female professors earned 9.8 percent *more* than never-married male professors — an impossible feat if discrimination were truly at work.

THE BACHELOR "WAGE GAP"

THERE'S FURTHER AND RATHER dramatic evidence to support the effect of marriage on earnings: it turns out that *bachelors*, in both the U.S.A. and Canada, show the same 60 percent "wage gap" with married men, as do all women as a group.[34] The reason for this is the same: bachelors don't need the money for family and children, so they don't engage in promotion-seeking behaviour. The result? They earn, on average, the same as married women. In fact, the Statistics Canada data referred to above show that bachelors as a whole made 42.8 percent of the wages of married men as a whole in 1987. Is this discrimination against bachelors? Obviously not. And yet the exact same arguments can be applied. Will "pay-equity" supervisors soon be forcing us to pay bachelors the same wages as married men?

So much for the "proof" of wage discrimination based on sex, and a "wage gap." How about the program?

If it weren't so sad and ridiculous, it would be funny.

I'll give you a sample of this shortly. Suffice it for now to say that the Commission's plan for "implementation" — on which millions of tax dollars have already been spent — has engendered a whole new class of paid bureaucrats, consultants, inspectors, and, let's face it, pay police. These ordinary folks are now empowered: to hear complaints from employees; to enter an establishment and seize records without warning; and to haul employers before their "pay-equity tribunal." The shining and enthusiastic faces of these tribunal members were flashed before corporate Ontario in the Commission's *Newsletter* in July of 1988. Clearly, this is a kangaroo court of the first order, empowered to "make final decisions of fact and law," made up mostly of unionists, feminists, and "experts" who make money at the social-policy trough. If the cook in your staff kitchen decides that she deserves the same pay for rustling up hamburgers as your maintenance man down in the basement fixing the boilers — watch out. The pay-equity system is "complaint based," which means she merely has to pick up the phone, and ask one of those friendly "inspectors" to drop in for a visit to your head office. These inspectors will evaluate her job — not her, but her job — in terms of four official categories: skill, effort, responsibility, and working conditions. They will then assign a "value" to each of these things, then run down to the basement, and do the same for the maintenance man's job. They will use either the Hay Scale or the Willis Scale (two of the best-known scales.) The fact that there are hundreds of aspects to every job and they consider only four is, of course, passed over elegantly by the Commission.

Here we have a case of the classic 80-20 rule. Eighty percent of the things they are measuring have only 20 percent to do with the job measured. How could it be otherwise? Even the witty Fabian socialist and elitist George Bernard Shaw, who criticized the market system because it paid so much to prizefighters, wrote, "To suppose that it could be changed by any possible calculation that an ounce of Archbishop or three ounces of judge is worth a pound of prizefighter, would be sillier still." Nevertheless, the Hay Study in San Jose determined through "an objective point system" that a puppeteer was worth 124 points — the same as an offset operator and a street-sweeper operator.[35] Of course no one can objectively defend, say, the pay of priests compared with the work of Michael Jackson. Is not the work of the Lord more important than the work of modern music?

The silliness of all this, of course, is that such evaluations are possible only by *reduction*, by reducing each job to aspects so common that you could walk an elephant through the subjective holes in the system. It's like saying that because a one-ounce diamond and a one-ounce piece of lead weigh the same they are worth the same. The Canadian economist Morley Gunderson says that "while comparisons across quite dissimilar jobs are possible in theory . . . the results of evaluation procedures become more tenuous the more dissimilar the jobs."[36] Charles Krauthammer ridicules the use of the Willis Scale in Washington State (a state where pay-equity legislation was thrown out as discriminatory and unconstitutional by three judges of the U.S. Court of Appeal), saying that the scale is

> *a mandate for arbitrariness: every subjective determination, no matter how whimsically arrived at, is first enshrined in a number to give it an entirely specious solidity, then added to another number no less insubstantial, to yield a total entirely meaningless ... everything is arbitrary: the categories, the rankings, even the choice of judges ... there remains one factor wholly unaccounted for which permits the system to be skewed in any direction one wishes: the weight assigned to each category ... Who is to say that a secretary's two years of college are equal in worth to and not half or double the worth of — the truck driver's risk of getting killed on the highway? Mr. Willis, that's who.*[37]

But ... we've left the inspectors in the basement. Suddenly, they dash breathless up the stairs and inform the president that he (or she!) is guilty of wage discrimination based on sex. He is ordered to pay the cook the same as the maintenance man. Flabbergasted, he cries out, "If I could find a maintenance man at her rate, I'd hire him!" ("Pay her!" he is told.) "I'll have to raise the price of hamburgers to twelve dollars each, no one will buy them!" ("Pay her!") "If no one buys them we'll have to shut down the kitchen. It's losing money already!" ("Pay her!") "There's a hundred others who would love her job!" ("Pay her!") "I'm going to shut down the damn kitchen, it's always been a pain in the neck to the whole organization. She'll be out of a job, for all your bungling." ("We're sorry, we can't help that. Thank you. Goodbye. We'll send your records back sometime next year.")

That's a little scenario to illustrate the arbitrariness and the failure in principle of the whole "pay-equity" *program*. The confusion, of course, arises from the fact that pay-equity is a socialist idea, as are most of the radical feminists' ideas. The National Action Committee on the Status of Women is overtly anti-capitalist. It actively campaigns for the nationalization of industry and banks, for a larger civil service, for "free" national daycare, pay-equity, and the like. But because pay-equity is a socialist idea, it cannot, as explained in Chapter Five, provide any basis for economic calculation. For there is no way to establish economic value outside of a market for goods and services. By its very nature, the value of anything can arise only from a cost/benefit transaction voluntarily entered into between two free parties. There is no such thing as *imposed* economic value. In fact, nothing has any economic value outside a free market. (Anything paid above the free price is really a kind of tax.) Why? Because the "value" of a job is strictly related to the demand for the goods or services that job creates. And what's called the "market-clearing" price for a good (or the wage for a job) is always a result of how willing people are to exchange a sum of money for that good or service, or job. You can pay the cook all you want, but if no one wants twelve-dollar hamburgers — goodbye, cook! If you keep the cook anyway, her cost to the economic unit, above what revenue she generates, will be a tax on the rest of the operation (or the industry, or the nation). After all, if the sale of hamburgers isn't paying for her keep, something else is, right? That's why I said the feminists were ignorant of the principles of economics, in the same way the socialists are. It hasn't worked for them, and it won't work for feminists, because it can't work.

Having no basis for economic calculation is like trying to play bridge with cards that change their value according to who the referee (or the inspector) is. You can *force* artificial values on people, but then the push-down/pop-up phenomenon sets in. If people don't want to pay for the higher-priced good or service, they won't. The job will disappear, or the person will be replaced by contract or part-time help; or the job will get mechanized; or — the person may get paid, but the higher wage will be reflected in the price of the good on the market, and this increase in price, which is not related to any improvement in the product, or the amount produced, will be strictly inflationary . . . more money will be paid to purchase the very same good. That's push-down/pop-up at work.

Here's a sample of the kind of political jargon to which the Commission must resort because its values are all subjective and bureaucratic. I'm leaving out the myriad qualifications, exceptions, and caveats the Pay Equity Act has had to include in order to get around the obvious injustices and unworkability of its shabby program to usher in "justified" pay discrimination to Ontarians. This is from the Commission's "Pay Equity Implementation Series # 11" — basically an expensive little flyer on official paper to say you are going to have to introduce official pay discrimination to your company. Although it's hard not to giggle when reading this offensive muddle, read on, and weep:

On definitions:

The Act permits differences in compensation resulting from the use of gender-neutral formal seniority or merit systems, and from gender-neutral red-circling, temporary skills shortages, and temporary training or development assignments (see Section 8(1)).

On job salaries:

The midpoint and the reference point [of a salary scale] are two different things, which sometimes coincide and sometimes do not. In some salary ranges, the reference point might be two-thirds of the way up the scale, for example. The reference point is the point that employees performing at the levels their jobs require may be expected to reach.

Isn't that an eye-opener for wishy-washy, circular thinking? Well, get used to it, because if you're an employer of sufficient size, they'll eventually knock on your door. Now here's a peek at how the government expects collective bargaining to take place:

Ontario's employers are going to be spending their time producing charts, arguments, and lawsuits, instead of goods and services.

At one stroke, the government of Ontario has introduced a program which is as complete a model of the socialist process at work in a free country as could ever be invented, politically, economically, or morally. In fact, it contains within itself an example of just about every evil outlined in this entire book. Here are a few: it is a collectivist, egalitarian, top-down scheme; it violates our fundamental freedom of contract and individual responsibility; it militarizes and rigidifies society and the economy; economically, it is a clear transaction of decline; it parades its concern for women (but not others) — a clear example of coercive humanitarianism; it is elitist, was never understood by the people in the first place, and was introduced as an issue only by radical feminist, government-financed lobby groups, who in no way represent the majority of Canadian women; further, it rides on the coattails of a whole series of Popular Illusions (see Chapter Two), among them: the Rights Illusion, the Determinist Illusion, the Discrimination Illusion, the Equality Illusion, and the Soak-the-Rich Illusion. Finally, it engages the State in serious reverse discrimination in the deepest tradition of social engineering, and uses constitutional powers (Section 15 of the Charter) to do so. There is no legal or moral reason why the same thinking the feminists have so far so deceptively and cleverly used cannot be invoked by *any* group of citizens that can make a specious case for "justified" discrimination of *any* kind in Canada. Colour, race, language, sex, obesity, nationality, religion — you name it. As the internationally respected economist Thomas Sowell, who, as a black, has had lots of experience with discrimination, says, "If we buy the key assumption of [pay-equity] — that third party observers can tell what jobs are 'really' worth — then our whole economic system should be scrapped . . . If somebody has this God-like ability, why restrict it to . . . 'pay-equity'? . . . why not rent equity, tuition equity, vacation equity, and all kinds of other equity?"

Of course, it's farcical, and unworkable. We know, for example, that as a group, non-Jews earn only 64 percent as much as Jews. Why can we not argue successfully, using the same fallacious tactics as the feminists, that this is discrimination against non-Jews? Either Jews earn more because they work harder to get it, or this is racial and religious discrimination against non-Jews, right? You see? There's no end in sight. There is no legal principle to prevent such an argument. But there are a lot of gullible politicians and legislators out there waiting to hear each case, who are not above eroding the high principles of our society and its most central traditions for a few votes.

THE BATTLE-LINES OF THE FEMINIST WAR ON SOCIETY

HERE FOLLOWS A BRIEF outline of the political values of the radical feminist movement in Canada.

WHAT DO THEY REALLY BELIEVE IN?

THE WOMEN'S GROUP, tucked under the Secretary of State in Ottawa, so to speak, alone spends about $13 million every year for various women's groups and projects around the nation. Estimates are that all such programs consume about $60 million per annum. Neither the citizens nor the women of Canada have ever been asked to authorize such expenditures on their behalf. The largest single operating grant is given to the National Action Committee on the Status of Women (NAC), more than $540,000 in 1987-88. NAC claims to represent the women of Canada, although the basis for its "membership" is spurious, to say the least, and includes hundreds of thousands of women who were never consulted on the matter. For example, NAC counts as members all Canadian women who use the YWCA, because the YWCA executive says it supports NAC. But individual women who use the Y, who may be violently opposed to NAC's agenda, know nothing of this relationship, nor that their names are cited as NAC members.

As for where your tax dollars are going, I have reviewed in detail the list of women's groups receiving the $13 million from the Secretary of State. What a sad legacy it is, and what an example of the way in which governments prostrate themselves for a few measly votes, despite the obvious compromise with decent principles. The list includes many hundreds of groups and projects ranging from the understandable to the ridiculous — there are too many to list. But suffice it to say that what began as a well-meaning (if misguided) effort to help women overcome perceived injustice has broken down into helping almost any women smart enough to form a group and complain about whatever is sticking in their craws: the National Association of Women and the Law ($245,640), the Canadian Congress for Learning Opportunities ($259,755), Canadian Daycare Advocacy Association ($213,000), National Council of Jewish Women of Canada [Downsview] ($18,580), National Farmers Union ($8,000), National Organization of Immigrant and Visible Minority Women of Canada ($7,798), National Watch on the Images of Women in the Media ($198,414). Well, it goes on, and on. Women's groups, Chinese women's groups, Indian women's groups, battered women's groups, women's Drama groups, French-language groups, birthing groups, magazine publishers, cultural groups, Christian groups, lesbian groups. Phew! And that's not the end. There is no obvious or rational end to the possibilities, which are being duplicated in every province, and in many municipalities, duplicated in French and English Canada, and springing up in all sorts of localities across our fair land.

To their great credit, two members of the House of Commons Standing Committee on Secretary of State Funding of Women's Programs, Jim Jepson and Ricardo Lopez, deputy chairman, issued a minority report in which they disagreed strongly with this whole process, saying: "In submitting our recommendations we would, first of all, like to unequivocally state that *we do not believe the government should be funding advocacy groups.*"

They complained that 85 to 90 percent of the women's groups the committee heard from were members of NAC, and that their presentations could not "be considered to represent a cross-section of the views of Canadian women." In submitting their report, they said, "We believe that due committee process has been circumvented."

NAC's political agenda is avowedly socialist, and virtually indistinguishable from that of the NDP — an agenda with which the great majority of Canadians patently disagree. In the last election, the women of Canada voted as follows (Gallup Poll: Dec. 3, 1988; the balance of those polled did not vote, were too young, etc.):

Progressive Conservative — 31%
Liberal — 23%
New Democratic Party — 18%

Despite the alliance of NAC with socialist values, the Progressive Conservative government continues to finance it lavishly. One wonders at the sagacity of a majority government that finances lobby groups committed to bringing it down. The June, 1987 issue of *World Marxist Review* carried an article by Nancy McDonald, a member of the Central Executive Committee of the Communist Party of Canada, in which she states, "The Communist Party participates actively in NAC . . . " Although the Women's Program was invented in 1973 to promote the status of all women, it has evolved into an organization run by a hard-core radical feminist group that uses government funds to crush other women's organizations when their values do not coincide. Even

Erik Nielsen's federal Task Force on government waste complained of this to Parliament (p.362).

Many of the leaders and public servants in the Women's Program were and are radical feminists. For example: Maureen O'Neil, former Co-ordinator of the Women's Program, is a well-known feminist activist (*Toronto Star*, Nov. 19, 1985); a recent past director, Lyse Blanchard, is also an activist feminist (*Toronto Star*, April 2, 1984); past president Louise Dulude is blinded by her radicalism; and current president Lynn Kaye is close to needing glasses. Why can't the government see this?

On February 6, 1985, in a letter from Tamara Levine, national projects officer of NAC, addressed to Louise Dulude, then vice-president of NAC, Levine wrote, "I have shared your letter with some of my colleagues in the Program, and your points should prove very helpful *in our continuing defence of the feminist orientation and direction of The Women's Program.*" (Signed, "in sisterhood, Tamara.")

Such an attitude would be perfectly acceptable and unobjectionable from a self-supporting group claiming to represent Canadian women. But from a department of government, funded by tax dollars, pushing an openly socialist, anti-government agenda so obviously out of step with the sentiments of the people of Canada — and more pointedly, of the women of Canada — it's nothing short of a scandal. Surely any thinking woman who does not share radical feminist views and who stops to consider how her country is being socially reshaped by radical feminists in her name, without her blessing, but with her money, must be outraged.

Another example of this lack of agreement between the Women's Program and the women of Canada is a Gallup Poll, August 28, 1986, showing that only 8 percent of Canadians support universal daycare.

An even more insidious example of NAC's opposition to the very principles and institutions of democratic capitalism is its 1984 resolution opposing the inclusion of private property rights in our Charter. Further, NAC frequently supports the nationalization of industry, wants us to withdraw from NATO, opposes free trade (Canadian women obviously didn't!), supports abortion on demand, and supports and funds lesbian and gay groups, and legalized prostitution. While some would argue that a number of these issues are personal, the point is that they do not reflect the mainstream views of Canadian women by any means, and yet despite this our government totally funds this organization. Without such funds, NAC would be a backwater collection of toothless radicals. With them, it is a dangerous force for social changes completely opposed to the values of most Canadian women. I say let them fight as hard as they like for their views, but don't give them my tax dollars to do it, nor the dollars of millions of men and women who often violently disagree with them.

WHAT IS TO BE DONE?

THE BEST, AND MOST just thing for the government to do, when it comes to advocacy groups, is nothing. There can be no justifiable reason, legal or moral, for taking money from those who can ill afford to part with it — most people — and give it to groups of citizens who lobby for their special interests. In doing so, the State is rewarding people for organizing ways to circumvent the democratic process.

By indulging in reverse discrimination — no matter how "justified" in the minds of some — through the provisions of section 15 of the Charter of Rights and Freedoms, the State politicizes society, setting one group against the other in a mad race for funding. As no supportable moral or logical reason can be found for supporting or "equalizing" one group and not another, the State, now a victim of its own appetite for votes as distinct from its search for justice, becomes embroiled in an expensive and divisive politicking game it cannot win, and is inevitably forced into the trampling of basic freedoms in the process.

As long as the State ensures that we have "just rules of conduct, equally applicable to all," and punishes the breaching of these rules in an even-handed manner, its job is done. To step beyond this and, through the power of the State, attempt to engineer society for the benefit of specific groups who have no mandate from the people, is illegitimate in a fair democracy. The democratic method is to change society through elected representatives, not by shelling out millions of tax dollars to citizens who make sufficient noise to scare the government.

As for radical feminists and programs like pay-equity? Any group in Canada should be free to organize itself and raise its own funds to make its vision known. But it has no legitimate claim on tax dollars for this purpose. And as long as all jobs are open to all people, and this principle is defended by law, the government of a free society has no right to force any free individual to pay more than he wishes for labour, or for any other goods or services he wishes to buy.

11

Medical Mediocrity
Canada's Sick Health-Care System

"Metro wait for surgery forces 100 heart victims to hit U.S."

"Patients wait in line for hospital bed"

"Public health-care system in danger, CMA warns"

"Second heart patient dies as surgery delayed nine times"

"U of T gene expert gives up on Canada"

"No one blameless in rise of health costs, study says"

ALL THE NEWSPAPER HEADLINES above have appeared in the past year, and there are thousands more like them in newspapers across the nation. Together they add up to a sad but predictable story: regular cost overruns, long line-ups for surgery, experts leaving the country, patients dying as they wait for service, lack of equipment, wage clashes between professional staff and hospitals, fee-schedule battles between physicians and the government, Charter challenges . . . it goes on and on.

Few Canadians pause to think about their health-care system, or how it got to be the way it is. Many are too young to remember, others too old to care (although they are the first shocked victims of cutbacks). But the predictable breakdown of our medicare system — yet another of our social-welfare schemes — will eventually confront us all, some in the most heartbreaking way, as we watch a loved one deteriorate at home, or die lined up in the corridor of some hospital, for lack of adequate service, facilities, or equipment. You or I may have to listen in anguish as a helpless doctor explains that the treatment for which we are quite willing to pay is reserved for certain patients because of a lack of government funding; and that should we offer to pay for it ourselves, *it is illegal for any doctor to provide this service privately in Canada.*

This breakdown is predictable. First, because as human nature and economic theory tell us, *the demand for an unlimited free commodity is infinite*; and second, because others who have tried to make socialized medicine work, whether in Eastern Bloc or Western nations, have failed miserably. In this chapter, I explain how our system got the way it is — how the State usurped an entire profession and the freedoms of millions of patients — and how it is doomed to fail. Finally, I question the basic idea of having "health-care systems" at all, which — most are shocked to learn — have no direct relationship to the status of the population's health, even though politicians present them as if they do.

How It Used To Be

UNTIL THE EARLY 1960S, "health care" in Canada was provided by freely practising doctors and other professionals who directly charged each patient a fee for their services. Such fees might have varied somewhat according to the experience and expertise of the physician, or the place where the service was given — in other words, for normal market reasons. After all, why, as is the case now, should a doctor fresh out of school be paid the same for a procedure as a doctor with established expertise? Or why should the fee be the same in Chilliwack as in Toronto? But generally, the cost for a doctor's services tended to be based on a Schedule of Fees, which served as a reference point for the physicians of each province. To lessen the burden of serious medical costs, 90 percent of the people also purchased some form of basic health insurance from private companies, or from non-profit, doctor-sponsored plans. As it happened, whether through personal neglect, irresponsibility, orneriness, or lack of funds, a very small number of Canadians got caught without insurance. Their remedy was usually the charity of the doctor or hospital, special community funds set aside for this purpose, mortgaging their assets, or assistance from family. But it doesn't matter how well or badly people then were looked after, because what the State could not abide was hearing of even one such incident. If medical disaster befell one individual, the State saw a role for itself as public protector. (Today, when disasters are *caused* by State medical policy, it looks the other way, or blames everyone but itself.)

Enter medicare. It was "successfully" introduced in Britain in 1948, and Canada began to flirt with the same idea under the Liberal government of Lester Pearson, who was powerfully attracted to the (vote-getting) image of the all-caring State he thought it would provide.

"We Will Stuff Their Mouths With Gold"

These were the words of the British minister of health, Aneurin Bevan, in response to the fear that British doctors would loudly object to State-run health care.

The British National Health Service (NHS) was conceived by Lord Beveridge and craftily implemented by Bevan, who first divided the doctors and then conquered them. He "stuffed their mouths with gold" by ensuring that they earned more under his plan than previously, which only illustrates the age-old maxim that every principle has a price. The NHS basically *runs* health care in Britain (our system only *insures* health care). Unlike the Canadian system, however, it allows physicians who wish to do so to practise and be paid privately outside the NHS, allows "pay beds" in public hospitals, and allows private companies to compete in the medical-insurance market. But to lure them, Bevan assured the British doctors they would be "freed from the money factor" at last, and need only concern themselves with being professionals. Thirty years later, as John Goodman wrote in his book *National Health Care in Britain: Lessons for the U.S.A.*, "doctors have discovered a great many reasons why the doctor-patient relationship should not be 'freed from the money factor.' "[1]

The Choirmaster Of Canada

In canada, the architects of a national health-insurance scheme were a British immigrant, Tom Kent, the socialist-minded adviser to Prime Minister Pearson, who was often characterized by Conservatives — quite rightly, it would appear — as "a dangerous radical"; and after him, Prime Minister Pierre Trudeau and successive health ministers, including one of the more recent, Monique Bégin, who has described her experience in her 1987 book, *Medicare: Canada's Right to Health*.

In a review of Kent's own book, *A Public Purpose*, Peter Desbarats, dean of the School of Journalism at the University of Western Ontario, writes, "Kent was one of the two or three most influential men in Canada in the mid-1960s . . . and *at times he came close to running Canada singlehandedly*" (*Globe and Mail*, March 5, 1988, italics added). Kent, he explains, was Pearson's "chief strategist-adviser-speech-writer," who often had to listen to Pearson break down sobbing over the telephone as he thanked Kent for yet another rescue from some political embarrassment. Kent was "the choirmaster who orchestrated much of [the government's] production."

How a single *unelected* individual can so change the course of a nation's history is a question that does not seem to bother Canadians. At any rate, Kent said he was "a fervent believer in Medicare. . . I saw it as the jewel in the record of achievement on which the government might go to the people in the following election" (*Toronto Star*, Feb. 20, 1988). Kent based the whole of his moral fervour for medicare on a single proposition: "I regarded it as morally wrong that money in the bank, rather than severity of need, should determine who got what health care services." This is a sentiment with which most of us would agree. But as a devoted collectivist, determined to shape Canada's own brand of utopian socialism, Kent was hitting a fly with a sledgehammer, for he totally ignored the ready availability of private insurance and the alternative of confining the State's role to insuring only the truly needy. Furthermore, like all the social-welfare thinkers who followed him, while insisting on "free" and "universal" medical care, he made the naive and, as we shall see, drastic mistake of failing to distinguish between *kinds* and *qualities* of medical service. It's one thing for a government to promise everyone a hamburger. It's another to give them all an unlimited credit card for gourmet dining as often as they wish. While any respectable businessman could have forecast a bad result from this free-lunch mentality, such perspicacity was too much to expect from ideologues and bureaucrats. In short, his was a simple-minded idea, an outgrowth of his ideological commitments, and a poor reason to quash the people's freedoms, virtually control and oppress a once proud profession, and politicize the medical framework of the entire nation.

Let us now examine the three players in the game of controlling medicine in Canada, and then ask how Kent and his associates brought all this about so easily, and what damage they have done. To begin, it is clear that the unfinished revolution in Canadian "health care" is the result of a clash between three ideologies or, if you prefer, "belief systems," outlined below.

The Physician's Belief
"... that into whatsoever house I shall enter it shall be for the good of the sick to the utmost of my power ... that I will exercise my art solely for the cure of my patients ... that whatsoever I shall hear or see of the lives of men which is not fitting to be spoken, I will keep inviolably secret."
(from the Hippocratic Oath)

The State's Belief
"The medicare plan, which was established by a Liberal government, is of course one which is basic and essential and it is founded on the principle of universality and accessibility."
(Prime Minister Pierre Trudeau, House of Commons Debates, March 9, 1979)

The Politician's Belief
Medicare "is the most popular government program ever created."
(Monique Bégin, former federal minister of health, in Medicare: Canada's Right to Health)

In the diverse assumptions behind these three quotations lie the seeds of the enduring conflict between the State and the individual practitioner of medicine. On the one hand, as descended from the time of Hippocrates (c. 460-377 B.C.), we have the solemn oath of the individual physician to hold as the highest value of his professional life the *direct* medical care and *confidentiality* of his patient (such care must not be mediated by anyone), and on the other, the oath of the State and its politicians to ensure that the care such physicians provide is "universally accessible" to all people (to ensure which, the State would have to control *all* health care).

From the beginning, the problems that would arise from such a clash of values were not unforeseen. The 1970 Report of the Government of Ontario's Commission on the Healing Arts warned that "society would not regard as sufficient, the amount of health goods and services that could be produced, even if all society's resources were devoted to the provision of health care." In short, the introduction of a universal, compulsory, tax-supported, government-controlled, and bureaucratically operated national health-insurance scheme would give rise to infinite demand. And thus the government's initially high-sounding ambition would prove to be the origin of our present woes and of the decline of medicine in Canada. Of course, our health "insurance" is no insurance at all. Like our pension schemes, it is a sort of pyramid, or Ponzi scheme by which those at the bottom pay for those at the top. (Half of lifetime health care is consumed in the last year of a person's life.) But *there is no pool of money* there generating interest to cover the cost of health care. Instead, the bills are just paid out of tax revenue. It's a utopian, cradle-to-grave giveaway intended to buy vote support for government and increase its power over the people. So Trudeau and his successive health ministers simply rammed into public policy what the health economists call an "open-ended scheme with closed-end funding." That's a fancy way of saying that it was a recipe for financial and — as it would turn out — moral bankruptcy.

The moral clash with the Hippocratic faith of physicians is direct in that, to make good on its belief, the State had to intercede between doctor and patient in order to control the nature of their relationship and all their rights vis-à-vis each other. Making it all possible, of course, we have the people themselves, sheltered from the realities of cost by the same benevolent-seeming government, eager to receive a "free" service, and blinded to the moral and economic distortions of everyday life that would be necessary to provide them with such a program. In any struggle for dominance of these two visions, the deck is loaded, directly against the physician and indirectly against the patient. For if a physician wants to object, say, by striking, he must revoke his solemn oath, thus losing moral integrity in his own eyes and in those of the public, while the State merely has to affirm its own oath, once it is confident it has the support of the people.

It is true that medicare is very popular with the people, at least thus far. But it may not be so popular when it has run its natural course and they run straight into its moral shortcomings — the advent of which is signalled to us daily in newspaper reports of rationing, long queues, and expensive trips to the U.S.A. to get what we thought we were paying for here.

ORGANIZING SCARCITY

THIS POLICY OF EQUALIZING misery and organizing scarcity instead of allowing diligence, self-interest and ingenuity to produce abundance, has only to be prolonged to kill this British island stone dead." So said Winston Churchill in 1945. There is no subject more poignantly illustrative of the conflict between the individual and the State than health care, for which the battleground is the human mind and body. The State knows that for many of its humdrum programs it can always withdraw legislation, cut budgets, or change policies, for many of these are manufactured issues designed to win the favour of the electorate of the day. But health is different. For people will continue to fear illness and death in the same way they always have and get sick at more or less the same rate. (We will discuss later how much of this is imagined and how much is "real" illness.) In other words, there is something of the primordial in sickness and health, and for this reason, in every free Western nation, health care has been a ready symbol for the paternalistic State, and an especially ready target for takeover. Why? Partly because "health care" serves up endless situations that evoke a disproportionate share of pity or sorrow, ripe for the front pages and thus ripe for control by politicians. But it is the physicians who have always been perceived to hold a certain power over life and death, and therefore a technical control over human justice. The title of the internationally renowned health economist Victor Fuchs's book *Who Shall Live?* poignantly addresses this power to dispense the very stuff of life itself, a power that the State lay waiting to assume.

I will argue that the blindness of the State in its grasp for such power has been to the very great detriment of all involved. For the State has really dug itself into a pit of financial and moral quicksand. Physicians have gained income, but lost their souls; and the patient is the biggest loser of all, for socialized medicine, no matter where or how introduced, must inevitably lead to deterioration of quality and availability (the very things Trudeau said it was trying to guarantee), an increase in cost (to be prepaid through taxes and debt, that is, borrowed from future generations who cannot speak for themselves), and a misallocation of human and financial resources.

Any medicare system will always amount to what I earlier called a "handicap system." It relies on a handicapping of excellence and productivity in the ostensible interests of equality. Unfortunately, it handsomely achieves the first, but never the second. It *cannot* achieve the second, for handicap systems always rely on central planning and thus lose any sound basis for economic calculation as they exert budgetary pressure on services and assign "values" to medical activity based on political ("rationalized") guidelines, instead of on real-life economic variables. The fate of millions of patients is thus determined not by themselves in concert with their personal physicians, but by a handful of bureaucrats. Further, a medical handicap system will always create a suppression of initiative; a parallel market in private services (ours is situated in the U.S.A.); a substitution of political values, methods, and privileges for market and personal ones; a deterioration of capital stock and investment; a flight of talent; and a cynical populace. Far from being the generous-seeming, "free," State-supplied program of benefits alleged by the politicians, it is the opposite. For medicare, like any other socialist program, *eliminates the fundamental connection between freedom and responsibility on which moral life depends*. It does so by eliminating any cost penalties for abuse of the system or for poor personal care. It also eliminates rewards by financially penalizing those who lead healthy lives: they pay the same as they would if they led dissolute, unhealthy lives. Of course, we cannot blame those who become ill through no fault of their own. Many diseases do not discriminate. But the fact is, medicare "rewards" personal irresponsibility and health-care abuse by transferring the cost of healing to others.The result of seventy years of socialized medicine in the Soviet Union and the Eastern Bloc should give us pause. In his book *The Poverty of Communism*, Nick Eberstadt reports that infant-mortality rates in Warsaw Pact nations are almost *twice* those of NATO nations (in the U.S.S.R., it's equivalent to the rate in Panama and Trinidad, and has increased by nearly a third since 1970). Since the 1960s, life expectancy has actually *fallen* in the Soviet Union and Eastern Europe — by as much as four years for males!

How The Doctors Were Softened Up For Takeover

To some extent it is true that physicians are "gatekeepers" by virtue of their training and authority and have some control over the public consumption of their services. It is said that they can "induce" demand for their services, thus putting at their disposal the purchasing power of their patients.[2] For the small minority of traumatized or seriously ill patients, this is undoubtedly true. But this argument doesn't hold up for the majority of those who consume the State's medical services. For it assumes that the average consumer is a dolt with no interest in his own health, incapable of saying "no" to more treatment, or that he can't distinguish between a hamburger and an unlimited credit card to eat whatever he likes as often as he likes. Of course he can, and he naturally wants the credit card. We all do. But as the historian Michael Bliss remarks,

> *everyone . . . knows that much of the demand for over-servicing is patient driven rather than doctor driven. When we are sick we want our doctors to do something. We are more discriminating than*

the ... model of the patient-as-ignoramus assumes. And the givers of service are much more professional than [is believed]. These days it is always the doctor who resists prescribing an antibiotic for a common cold, and always the patient, this reviewer included, who wants some pills, just in case. ("Bliss on Books," in the *Globe and Mail's Report on Business* magazine, July, 1989)

At any rate, the profession itself, and governments, have long been aware that doctors do have some economic power — one now afforded them by the State itself — and this has provoked an ongoing struggle between the profession to maintain this power, and the State to usurp it.

Let us review the sequence of events through which the profession prepared itself for the plucking whenever government was ready to dine. First, it resolutely resisted the idea that anyone but a doctor should be able to make a profit from medicine. It was "unprofessional" said the American Medical Association — followed by the Canadian — for a physician to permit a third party to profit from his work; it was "harmful alike to the profession of medicine, and the welfare of the people, and is against sound public policy."[3] This meant that *doctors could insist on remaining free entrepreneur-practitioners in a free market for their services.* They could make income, wages, fees, and the like from medicine, or group together for profit. But in not allowing a third party to profit from their work, doctors were vulnerable from the start, because without solid profit, capital formation and investment are impossible, and so, therefore, are the large organizations and technical infrastructures capital makes possible. Without established fixed assets, so to speak, the only card in the doctors' deck would be the ability to withdraw services — to strike. This proved to be a weak instrument in the absence of any other bond, and into this manufactured vacuum of "profitless" but vital activity marched the State. Perhaps the best way to sum up the profession's philosophical objection to profit-making on their services was the slogan — *"no third party."* In other words, the fundamental professional relationship was to be one to one, doctor to patient. This was entirely in keeping with the whole ethos of Western life, with English institutions, law, morality, freedom of contract, the Hippocratic Oath, and the individual freedom and responsibility of both patient and doctor. But because of such professional restrictions, doctors became dependent on public infrastructures like hospitals and medical schools to supply their capital needs.

Suddenly, the medical profession had all the actors, but the government owned the theatre. Essentially, through hospital privileges and the like, doctors could give private care at public cost. They were already in the snare. But costs rose dramatically, and as they did some "third party" was indeed needed to spread those costs around. Enter private insurance. The third party would be other free citizens, including doctors, who wanted to protect themselves against bankruptcy caused by illness. The State was still not in the game. By this time, however, the profession was already in bed with the State in two other ways, both of which had the effect of limiting competition and keeping incomes up, both of which ripened it for takeover. The first of these was the institution of a professional Schedule of Fees. Such schedules were established by the State itself centuries ago, to prevent price-gouging of hapless patients, but more recently by physicians and their professional societies as a "guide" to prevent price-cutting — in other words, to keep their incomes up, thus creating a kind of elite cartel. (This has always been informal, although many times in the last two centuries the profession has lobbied for enforcement of fees.)

Another way in which the doctors were in bed with the State was through control of the number of physicians allowed to practise, ostensibly to prevent what used to be called "overcrowding," and to ensure high-quality practitioners. A welcomed side-effect in keeping the supply of physicians down was to keep their incomes up. The State, in Canada, has always assisted them in this endeavour, however informally. In exchange for helping doctors avoid excess competition, to keep demand for their services high, and to ensure high-quality care, the State got to control their profession to some degree. (Today the State wants to keep the number of physicians down because under socialized medicine physicians are accused of "milking the system.") At any rate, the doctors and the State have been hand in glove for a long time. It was bound to lead to no good. Nevertheless, something fundamental had never been violated before: *a physician in Canada, until the mid-1960s, was always a free man.* In a free country, no one is owned by another. Voluntary exchange is the rule. But if you cannot negotiate a price for your own labour, you are not free. If as a patient you have no choice either of an alternative or of better services, you are not free. If you cannot change your employer without leaving the country, you are not free. How did thousands of Canadian doctors, and millions of their patients, who lost all choice to seek better care for themselves *inside* Canada if they could afford it, lose this fundamental freedom?

THE RIGHTS ILLUSION

BASICALLY, IT WAS EASY. Even though, through its "shared-cost" program, the federal government had nearly complete control over the provinces' health programs, it was aware that what it called "extra-billing" (what doctors called "balance-billing") was a spreading practice (though never more than 2.5 percent of total health billings). So-called "extra-billing," a government-created vice, occurred whenever the government refused to reimburse a patient as much as the doctor had charged for his services. In short, a doctor's freedom to charge what he felt his services were worth threatened the sanctity of the government's oath, for it implied that some could charge more, and some purchase more than others. Mr. Justice Hall was therefore asked to study the health situation in Canada, and he tabled his report on September 3, 1980. His report basically recommended the nation-wide banning of extra-billing in addition to doing away with health-insurance premiums in any provinces that charged them, and it set the stage for federal action. In essence, it had the legal effect of converting all medical services in Canada from a privilege to a right.

So, as for most aspects of the welfare State, medicine would be subjected to the "Wants > Needs > Rights > Claims" chain described in Chapter Two. That's why Monique Bégin, Trudeau's minister of health, entitled her book *Medicare: Canada's Right to Health.* But the *rights* of some imply *obligations* on the part of others. Once the State proclaimed that Canadians had a "right" to health, and that as Bégin proudly said, echoing Tom Kent's moral belief, "no financial barrier should hinder access to health care,"[4] the irreversible process of professional and moral corrosion had begun. The State was hooked. What the State *should* have said was that once the *truly needy* and the indigent were guaranteed *basic* as well as "catastrophic" health care by the State (hamburgers, not credit cards), any Canadian had a "right" to purchase as much additional care as his own resources would permit. But instead it opened up a moral can of worms. For all of a sudden it meant that *any citizen could claim as a right the most expensive and technologically advanced health care possible.*

Now there is no medical reason why every Canadian shouldn't have a CAT-Scan right away, because the likelihood of discovering some latent problem in a very small percentage, unobservable with any other present technology, is very high. This would seem to be a sound and basic preventive measure. But these machines cost millions to produce, and millions more for the highly skilled technicians to operate them. It turns out that *this one procedure could consume the entire budget of the government of Canada* — never mind the countless other procedures that would soon be considered "rights." It was ridiculous. Nevertheless, on April 9, 1984, the Canada Health Act received the support of all federal parties, effectively banning "extra-billing" throughout the realm, completing the socialization of medicine, and thoroughly extinguishing the fundamental freedom of all Canadians to offer or purchase medical services privately. To date, *Canada remains the only Western democracy to have made basic private health-care services illegal.* Ironically, we are more severe in this regard than either the U.S.S.R. or Sweden. In the end, the physicians ended up with the worst "third party" of all, and for this reason, unperceived by most, the moral authenticity of medical care came to an end in Canada. From this point forward, everything would necessarily unfold according to collectivist values. Here are a few of the consequences of these perverse values, which show that under collectivism the patient is always the loser.

IT COSTS EVERYONE MORE

THE GOVERNMENT HAS INDEED stuffed the mouths of physicians with gold. On the whole, they are doing much better under medicare than before. Directly following the onset of socialized medicine in Canada, between 1966 and 1970, physicians' incomes increased by 58 percent, while the CPI increased only 20 percent. This increase is a cost to everyone, whether we use health services or not, because overspending on health just creates more deficits, or deferred taxes. The result, according to the OECD's November 1985 report on health-care costs, is that Canada, as of 1982, *had the fourth-highest per capita health costs* in the Western world. (In \$US: U.S.A. — \$1,388; Sweden — \$1,168; Switzerland — \$1,158; Canada — \$989; and, for comparison, U.K. — \$506; Japan — \$602; Italy — \$401.) We will see later how many billions of these dollars are for trivial care.

THE PATIENT LOSES HIS CHOICE

THE MOST SERIOUS MORAL and philosophical loss introduced by State medicine is the loss of liberty. As Michael Bliss told me, "In a free society, citizens ought to be able to make up their own minds about how much of their own resources they wish to spend on their own health care."

But there is a practical loss of choice as the bureaucrats move in to "rationalize" the available medical care and resources. "Rationalization" is the bureaucrat's term for streamlining and budget-cutting. This is obviously a top-down process typical of the collectivist State, and is responsive not to patient need or physician preference, but to bureaucratic political theory and financing. It is as clear an example of socialist practice as we have seen in this book, and is equally clearly designed to undo every virtue of the democratic capitalist process as applied to the medical field. For each physician now answers to government, not to the patient, who no longer employs the physician, as he did for centuries; thus physicians are beyond the control of the consumers who pay them (although we may still choose among them).

Finally, the patient loses access to sufficient medical care — again under the guise of "rationalization" — as the bureaucrats move in to reduce services, empty or close entire hospitals, limit equipment purchases, set arbitrarily the number of patients a doctor may see in a day, and prohibit free doctor movement within the country, thus encouraging emigration. Why is it that we have a public cry for more beds, and patients stacked on cots in corridors, at the same time as the government is closing facilities? A physician friend explained this illogical fact to me. Available beds go empty despite the demand, because there are not the funds to hire staff to look after the patients who would otherwise be in the beds!

THE TRULY ILL PATIENT WILL NOW COMPETE WITH THE TRIVIALLY ILL

THE PATIENT LOSES because once medical care is set up as a free and unlimited "right," equal for all, the truly sick will have to compete for limited medical resources with the marginally ill, with hypochondriacs, and with the growing number of trivial demands now put upon the system by the millions of people enjoying their unlimited credit card for medical services whether they are truly ill or not. Such people are getting a wonderful sort of free pampering carried out by white-frocked specialists, eager to help. Of course, their trivial demands would be greatly reduced if an up-front user fee were present to discourage them, as it is in Sweden, and if patients who wanted trivial or nonessential treatments like medical counsel for minor aches and pains, or elective surgery, could get them privately without drawing on the resources of the State. For many ailments, such as most sports injuries, the simplest and cheapest remedy is — rest. But this is unattractive compared with the eager, "free" attentions of a specialist.

ALL OF US HAVE LOST OUR PRECIOUS PRIVACY

THE PATIENT LOSES his privacy because doctors are now required by law to feed the details of every visit, diagnosis, treatment, lab test, or operation into the voracious medical computers of the State. Previously the Hippocratic Oath protected the intimate details of our private lives from any prying eyes; now *these matters are public property*, courtesy of the audit provisions of the Health Insurance Act.

The computers that process this information in most provinces can send any physician to a Medical Review Committee. Thereupon, a physician inspector working for the government — that's right, medical police — will pore over hundreds of patient records, copying a significant portion of these and sending them to members of the committee. *The patient has no right to disallow such an inspection of his private life by total strangers*. His right to confidentiality has been legislated away. This process may continue even though the patient has never complained or been consulted and is not notified that his private life is being reviewed by all and sundry. In Ontario alone, about a hundred doctors per year are reviewed. At about three to four hundred charts each — that comes to between thirty and forty thousand invasions of patient privacy per year. In fact, Ontario's new Bill 147 will allow such medical police to inspect all health facilities and records, without a warrant. Mr. Justice Horace Krever, in his 1980 report, was "shocked . . . by the inadequate laws, the abuses of confidentiality, and the fact that so many people — except the patient — had access to medical records" (*Toronto Star*, April 29, 1989).

SOCIALIZED MEDICINE DEMORALIZES EVERYONE INVOLVED

THE PATIENT LOSES through the demoralization of the whole profession, specifically through the subtle moral transformation whereby the authentic doctor-patient relationship becomes a doctor-government-patient relationship and whereby the doctor becomes a scapegoat of government in its relentless search to trim costs as medical budgets compete with other public programs. The whole system thus becomes fractious. Doctors are set against bureaucrats, nurses against doctors, union staff against everyone, hospital administrators against patients, and patients against politicians.

This process of moral unravelling is a predictable result of any situation in which the freedom-responsibility chain is broken, for this collectivist process, so set against the personal responsibility on which Western morality is based, is designed to generalize everything, including the blame. So we get treated to endless newspaper stories searching for the culprit. Because the moral chain of command has been ruptured, this results in a rotating round of official scapegoats, followed by official denials of responsibility, broken up by endless spending on commissions and committees to study costs as the whole system deteriorates. The patient further loses because mandatory bureaucratic norms eventually become substituted for professional norms, leading to a government-directed, assembly-line type of practice. The average time spent with a patient under the British National Health Service is from three to five minutes. In Quebec, which is even more statist than Ontario (although Ontario Premier David Peterson is racing to catch up), medicine has so deteriorated over the years that Quebec patients have been flooding over the border for years to avail themselves of Ontario medical services — even though this means paying more out of *their* pockets, because the schedule of allowable fees for many procedures is higher in Ontario (*Globe and Mail*, Feb. 21, 1989). Three years ago, Quebec paid Ontario $90 million for the use of Ontario hospital beds, but is now moving to restrict this freedom of choice of Quebeckers. Typically, it is addressing the symptoms of the problem, not solving it.

THE GREAT BRAIN DRAIN

THE PATIENT LOSES because a lot of excellent doctors leave the country to go where they can again practise under the Hippocratic Oath, and be free. As early as 1974, our own Department of Health and Welfare predicted that 1,500 doctors — 4 percent of the total — would leave the country, mostly for the U.S.A. Increasing numbers of Canadian students write the U.S. medical board exams — preparing for future exodus; in 1977 alone, Canada lost 9.4 percent of all its medical biochemists and 4.5 percent of its specialists in nuclear medicine to the U.S. In a survey reported in the *Medical Post* in January 1979, almost half of all Canadian doctors admitted they had "given serious thought" to emigrating. *About the same number said they would not encourage their children to enter medicine.*

Eventually, of course, doctors in Canada will become unionized, as interns and residents now are — another inevitable result of collectivist polarization. Medicine will become a civil service, like the post office. Then, there will be time-and-a-half pay for over-time, strikes for 35-hour weeks, sick pay, disability pay, travel pay, dollar-parity pay with the U.S., legal services, estate-planning services — and so on, all at the taxpayers' expense. Ultimately, under such a union mentality, physicians will end up exactly where the social-welfare State pushes everyone: in a condition free of all moral and legal responsibility, but with tenure and salary guaranteed, with indexed government pensions no

one else can afford, no fear of competition or dismissal — and no
concern for excellence, either. We will have travelled in a mere generation from a condition in which we had an unequal distribution of
blessings to one in which we have an equal distribution of miseries.
Thus has the patient lost. On a scale of quality from zero to ten, our
government would prefer that everyone gets four, rather than most get
six, and some eight.

WHERE STATE MEDICINE LEADS

THE TRANSITION FROM HIPPOCRATIC TO VETERINARY MEDICINE

TO EXPLAIN THIS STRANGE terminology, I am going to quote Dr. Hans
Truffer, of Switzerland, long an opponent of socialized medicine:

> *The real danger of collectivized state medicine is that the patient
> becomes a tool in the hands of the holders of power, and is dispos-
> sessed of the protection afforded by Hippocratic principles. This
> amounts to a rejection of the medical Hippocratic ethic — which is
> to care for the patient according to the latter's specific require-
> ments — in favor of a veterinary ethic, which consists in caring for
> the sick animal, not in accordance with its specific needs, but
> acccording to the dictates of its master and owner, the person
> responsible for meeting any costs incurred.*

In other words, the government. This analogy is far from perfect, but,
with no slight intended to those who care for animals, it does highlight
something crucial. *The medical well-being of an animal is controlled by
others.* We consider this to be normal for animals, but not for humans,
who differ fundamentally in that they usually have a say in their own
well-being. At least, they did before the advent of the welfare State.

DO THE STATE'S POLICIES IMPOSE PREMATURE DEATH?

THIS IS A HARD ONE for most people to swallow — at least it was for me
when I first heard of it. But upon further thought, it seemed dead right,
so to speak. In a country where all medical relief and cures are
controlled by the State, and where individuals are forbidden by law to
purchase medical care beyond what the State is able to provide, we
indeed are able to trace the premature deaths of hundreds of individuals — at least those who cannot afford to travel outside the country —
directly to the State's restrictive medical policies. In other words, death
is often imposed (on the poor, not the rich) as a direct result of the

State's medical laws. We cannot escape the conclusion that this amounts to a form of bureaucratic execution, for the State forbids you to use your own resources to save your own life!

How could this be possible? Each hospital receives enough money in its budget for, say, a hundred serious operations annually. If you are the hundred and first — you will simply have to wait until the next budget allocation. Maybe a year or more. But, you complain, are there not eager surgeons, willing nurses, and available beds? The answer is "Yes" to all these queries. So because you are naturally afraid to suffer or die, you offer to pay for the service yourself! But in Canada, as already stated, it is illegal to accept money for private health care. Thus, if you are a poor Canadian, you will suffer or die. If wealthy, you will probably fly to the U.S.A. for treatment. (OHIP in Ontario will reimburse you 90 percent.) *However, if you are a foreigner and offer to pay for it yourself, you will be treated right away. No problem.* Canadians die, while foreigners live? It's a scandal! Never mind the argument that the policy of charging foreigners double helps fund our own hospital programs. If we are so inclined, why not charge Canadians who can afford it double, too, and thus subsidize the poor, and keep the business in Canada? But even this would not alter the fundamental injustice — the severe restriction of choice. The only way this can be corrected is by allowing Canadians to purchase private basic health services. But here's the rub: freedom of choice constitutes an affront to collectivist ideology, and will be resisted tooth and claw. Which once again illustrates how deeply wrong we have been to surrender control over our own well-being to the State.

Alas, as the Canadian population ages, we will surely see a great deal more of such imposed suffering and death. When performed openly, as in war, this practice is called "triage" — a French label derived from an old wartime habit of dividing the wounded into three groups and allocating available medical resources to them according to their chances of survival. I'm not sure it's possible to totally avoid this under any system, but it's unofficially at work in Canada right now. For no matter how wealthy a nation, there will always be scarcity — either real or imagined — to contend with. So the most serious question is: How well does the political-economic system relied upon to *produce* medical resources actually function? It seems clear that democratic capitalism is the clear winner when it comes to such medical productivity, for medical care in socialist, or socializing, nations is a disaster, or soon becomes one; and that there is a clear relationship emerging between the scarcity of such resources and the degree of government control of medicine.[5] Some will answer that in free nations there is a problem of equality. This may be the price of freedom, in the sense that we cannot *force* a person to insure or protect himself. In Canada, where a free market in medical care is forbidden, and spending on medical services is controlled by politicians, scarcity of medical excellence, research, capital, and labour will become the norm. Even now the system represses invention, innovation, and the development and acquisition of equipment to keep pace with the advances of science.

RATIONING BY THE QUEUE

BECAUSE THE LEVEL OF medical resources available will always be lower than the level of demand in a system that tells everyone they have a "right" to the best, scarcity is inherent in our delivery of medical services. This means that not everyone will be able to get what in a perfect world he might wish to have. There will always be a *brake* (formerly the brake of personal finances, self-help, and insurance; now, of government budgets) on the amount of money spent on health care. In a free country — and assuming for the moment that the State has the means to protect the truly needy from medical disaster — *the natural brake on spending is the patient's own resources, coping ability, and concern for personal health.* In other words, the patient makes a judgement and balances the cost/benefit to him and his family of purchasing increasing amounts of medical care. He chooses between two or more forms of service, and he imposes a form of rationing on himself which is controlled by his cash on hand or by the cost of his annual private medical-insurance premium. This is called "rationing by price." Again, in a free country, this works very well, because if, let's say, a million people suddenly decide they all want some special kind of non-vital medical treatment and are willing to pay for it, a market for this treatment will be created by entrepreneurs, drug companies, and so on, all financed and paid for by the buyers, without drawing on the resources of others who have no interest in the treatment.

In particular, nobody would be drawing on the resources of low-income people, who would far rather spend their resources on other goods, like food and shelter. For even though the very poor may pay no income tax, they are increasingly and indirectly taxed on everything they buy. At any rate, rationing by price creates a sort of value system in the medical field that is directly related to available resources, but without any need for the coercive-humanitarian policies of the State. It is a perfect bottom-up solution to a society's medical needs. Further, there are usually valuable entrepreneurial medical spin-offs from such investment that trickle down to the less well-off in the form of inexpensive drugs, technologies, and so on. The price system generates solutions for all, financed by the few. It fits in perfectly with the "bonus system" outlined in this book, for it rewards success, not failure.

But under a system based on egalitarian resentment that promotes and protects failure instead of rewarding success, there is a different, insidious form of rationing of which the State is always the arch-practitioner, called "rationing by the queue." This is very simply brought about by the State's budgetary restrictions. After all, it's easy to keep costs down in a State-controlled system: you simply refuse to provide the funds. But because the State tends to reward inefficiency and spend money on its own bureaucracy, its own needs grow within the available budget, crowding out true medical needs. A shocking example of this comes from Britain, where by 1978 there were five administrators for *each* hospital bed.[6] Rest assured there are great numbers of them, on high salaries or contracts, crawling all over Canadian hospitals right now, obsequious to their political bosses (who pay them), arrogant to medical professionals (the enemy), all the while searching desperately for ways to cut costs.

Thus does the State consume resources that might have gone to patients. Thus is the State forced, *largely because of costs it has itself created*, to limit budgets and force patients to line up for services. Sources inform me that in Toronto there is now up to a one-year wait for cardiac surgery, up to two years for hip replacements. Although there may be some weak evidence that the very poor, for whom waiting has a lower cost, are better served under our system, it discriminates against the great majority of productive people by creating a kind of "co-efficient of adversity" for all who want a timely medical service. Implicit in socialized medicine is the expectation that the waiting patient will eventually get better, stop asking for the service, or die. In short, after sufficient rationing by the queue, the slogan of "equal access to quality care" becomes "equal access to non-existent" or inadequate care, as the once-private professional doctor becomes a hand-servant to the State's campaign of shoddy quality and deception; the once private and free patient, a number on the State's computer. In Britain, the free market is already alleviating the defects of the NHS. There private health insurance was never legally prohibited, private hospitals are thriving, and more than five million people are covered by private insurance, including members of many of the trade unions, who insist that the NHS service is "just not good enough for our people."

STATE MEDICINE LEADS TO DECEPTION OF THE PEOPLE

PERHAPS THE WORST EFFECT of socialized medicine is its demoralization of everyone involved. The mechanics of this are predictable. First, the State promises everyone equal access to health care; once having promised this, it cannot afford to be honest about why some are receiving a service, and some are not, for this would cause political embarrassment, with patients suing doctors and institutions for their medical "rights." So here's the situation. The doctor knows that if a patient could get a certain kind of care, he would recommend it. But he knows the care is not available. So where formerly the doctor might have told the patient the truth and allowed him to decide whether or not to purchase the treatment, he now remains silent. For the truth would lead nowhere except to court, or to political troubles. The doctor must quash his instinct for integrity. Thus the morality of the system spirals downward, with everyone on the defensive.

A further cynical consequence of the new system's lack of integrity is the market it creates for social or political influence. Getting into a Canadian hospital quickly in future will have a lot to do with who you know. Here's a view of this from economist Pierre Lemieux:

> *In Quebec, you can be relatively sure not to wait six hours with your sick child in an emergency room if you know how to talk to the hospital director, or if one of your old classmates is a doctor, or if your children attend the same private school as your pediatrician's children. You may get good service if you deal with a medical clinic in the business district. And, of course, you will get excellent service if you fly to the Mayo clinic in Minnesota or to some private hospital in Europe. The point is that these ways to jump the queue are pretty expensive for the typical lower-middle-class housewife, not to talk of the poor.*[7]

Lemieux adds the insight that "we often forget that people who have difficulty making money in the market are not necessarily better at jumping queues in a socialized system."

DEFENSIVE MEDICINE

ONE OF THE RESULTS of this downward moral and professional spiral is the rise of litigation and malpractice insurance as a permanent feature of a doctor's life, one in which he must learn to see every patient as a potential adversary. In short, he must learn to practise what is called "defensive medicine." This phenomenon — widespread in the U.S.A. and now growing rapidly in Canada — is largely a reflection in both countries of generous judicial awards. Plaintiffs succeed with outrageous awards, so more sue. The result? When by all reasonable lights the physician knows that the patient needs only one or two lab tests, the doctor orders twenty — just in case, *for it costs the patient nothing more.* Thus is personal protection rather than experience and judgement becoming the new basis of professional decision. For the kingdom of rights always leads to the kingdom of claims, and these lead to defensive medical strategies under an open-ended system where "someone else" is picking up the tab. This surely explains, in part, the phenomenon of "over-serving." For example, in Saskatchewan, in 1964, there were on average 3,457 patient visits per 1,000 beneficiaries (people covered by the plan); by 1984, that number had grown to 5,991. In the same period, laboratory services went from 690 per 1,000 beneficiaries, to 2,347. The same number of people now demand or are prescribed twice the number of services. Short of reforming the system, there is no particular reason why this shouldn't triple, or quadruple, in future.[8]

How Does The Government Wriggle Out Of This Mess?

It doesn't, for there is no way to reorganize human nature by decree. To get out of the moral, professional, and financial mess it has created, government would have no choice but to undo the welfare State. This it will not do. Canada's political leaders simply lack the necessary understanding, vision, and courage; unlike Margaret Thatcher, for instance, who does not. In "the biggest shakeup in Britain's free health system" (*Toronto Star*, Feb. 1, 1989), she recently introduced proposals for user fees and for allowing large public hospitals to charge fees. But Canada's leaders, having led the electorate to clamour for "rights," are in no position to urge it to act "responsibly." So government resorts to the desperate promotion of new organizational strategies in its effort to evade the underlying truths. Two such strategies used in the U.S.A. (and here under a variety of names) are DRGs and HMOs.

"DRG" refers to a system of funding medical care in the U.S.A. (don't forget, their system is 50 percent socialized, too) on the basis of "Diagnosis Related Groups." This is an elaborate system designed to beat rising costs of medicare by forcing hospitals (coercive humanitarianism at work again) to become more efficient. Basically, the hospital gets funded according to the diagnostic grouping of your medical complaint. If healing you takes more time and effort than the *average cost* the government is willing to pay for a complaint in that group, the hospital loses. If less, it wins. You are an economic unit — a "winner" or a "loser" — assigned an average healing value, and the idea is that the staff will try to get you out of there quickly. The result? Hospitals are encouraged to "manage the case mix" of their hospitals — meaning to bring in more profitable patients and get the unprofitable ones out "sicker and quicker." Doctors, of course, have incentives to split procedures under this system, doing, say, a patient's double knee operation on two different days, instead of both knees at once. In effect, under such a system, the doctor gets paid for *not* being efficient.[9]

Health Maintenance Organizations (HMOs) or Health Service Organizations (Ontario is now introducing CHOs — "Community Health Organizations") are also meant to address the scarcity-queue-cost problem. Individuals pay monthly or annual fees to cover all their basic medical needs, and the onus is on the doctor to keep them healthy (discourage them from coming back). Both these methods squirm around the fact that the responsibility for health care has been taken out of the hands of patients and the doctors they would normally employ to help them. Once the control of medical services gets divorced from the payment mechanism, the provider gets more and more remote from the patient's true needs and preferences, at which point distorted incentives come into play, quickly followed by punitive methods to control costs, such as "utilization reviews," "medical review committees," "quality assurance" committees, "rationalization" standards, and other such management control systems. In short, *the patient becomes an integer in a cost-reduction strategy*; the physician answers not to the patient's needs, but to those of the systems manager. About a quarter of a typical hospital bill can be due to the cost of compliance with such constraints and regulations.[10]

What Lies Ahead?

Unlike great britain, which went a lot farther down the socialist road before struggling back to partial sanity under Thatcher, Canada will refuse to confront the crucial realization that it made a disastrous decision under Kent, Pearson, and Trudeau, when it opted for social-welfare programs like medicare. This fact is now obvious. But there is no one in a position of political leadership in Canada with sufficient determination and understanding of the underlying ideological forces to persuade the people that this nation has entered a cul-de-sac.

Furthermore, our media are so inclined to favor left-liberal policies, that there is no hope for a brave assault on them from that quarter. For not only do the media uncritically accept such policies, their affection for the social-welfare State effectively excludes free market alternatives from public discussion. So there is much worse to come.

CANADA'S HEALTH SYSTEM AT THE CROSSROADS

HEALTH-CARE EXPENDITURES as a percentage of GNP in Canada have risen from 2 percent in 1940 to about 9 percent in 1987, according to Malcolm Brown in *Caring for Profit*. Health expenditures have been rising in Canada in current as well as in constant dollars — meaning that even when you eliminate inflation Canadians are spending more on "health care." In 1985, Canadians spent close to $1,600 each on health care. (That's total spending divided by the whole population, including the many who didn't use health services that year.) Surely the cost for a family of four — $6,400 per year — is a shocking tally, and reflects a system gone predictably wrong? And let us not smugly compare our lower medical spending to the U.S.A. OECD figures for 1982 showed that while *public* spending on medicine in Canada was 6.2 percent, it was 4.5 percent for the U.S.A. The rest of their spending is *private*. If they wish to spend all their private resources on medicine, that's their own affair.

Here are a few highlights from Brown's study, done for the federal government under contract with the Fraser Institute.

• The number of health professionals per 100,000 population was 1,114 in 1970, but 1,706 in 1985. (This verifies the prediction that socialized systems tend to become self-justifying entities, generating more jobs for technocrats and professionals with little regard to economies of scale or delivery of high-quality service to the customer. The number of physicians per 100,000 population was 198 in 1984 — up 36 percent since 1970. And we are supposed to be a healthier society?)

• In 1961 Canada had 1.8 personnel for every public hospital bed. By 1983 that became 4 personnel for every 1.6 beds. More than 6.85 percent of Canada's workforce is employed in health care.

• Here's a summary of Brown's Table A-3, to show this trend of increasing costs of service personnel as capacity decreases. It is on a per-100,000 population basis. A private business that operated this way would have gone bust long ago.

	personnel	beds	nurses
1961	1,286	1,058	387
1971	1,793	983	693
1981	1,629	712	847
1984	1,702	703	868

• Between 1956 and 1971, measured in 1971 dollars per capita, hospital expenditures and medical services increased from $1,141 to $4,403 (averaging 9.42 percent per year!).

• In Saskatchewan, between 1963 and 1983, the number of services per doctor, measured per capita, increased 4.19 percent annually (from 6,577 to 9,849 services per doctor).

• Brown suggests that in addition to the costly effects of medicare on increased patient demand for "free" services, doctors themselves, in an attempt to increase their incomes under medicare's fixed rates, might resort to: "time shuffling" (treating patients after hours to increase fees); "upgrading" (the paying agency is billed for a service that pays more than the one actually performed); "injury enlargement" (overstating the nature of the problem); "ping-ponging" (referring to other physicians or professionals without sufficient reason); "service splitting" (splitting the treatment into many smaller fee-paying parts); "phantom treatment" (billing for services not performed); and "assembly line" treatment (patients treated at too high a speed). While no one can be sure this is going on, suffice it to say that the incentives built into any medicare system create a perfect environment for such activities.

EXPLODING A MYTH

MUCH IS OFTEN MADE in the media about the superiority of the Canadian medicare system to that of the U.S.A., where only half of health care is State-subsidized. I lived there for almost eight years and always found the American health-care system to be first-rate. It certainly delivers most of the high-class medical research in the world, and about 75 percent of the best articles published in international medical journals are by American medical scientists. There are also more Nobel laureates for medicine there than in all other countries combined. This I knew. But I hadn't seen much on comparative health coverage. In a recent speech in Toronto, John Goodman exploded the "ten myths" about U.S. medicine by pointing out that the poorest in the U.S. are covered by Medicaid; the elderly, rich or poor, are covered by Medicare; by law, the uninsured *do* get treated; government-mandated insurance laws have priced "no-frills" insurance out of the market — otherwise it would be available to all; 90 percent of all hospital bills are paid for by insurance and 70 percent of all medical care by third-party insurance; one-twentieth of 1 percent of U.S. families suffer medical bankruptcy; U.S. high infant mortality is due to ethnic heterogeneity, drug and alcohol abuse, and poor nutrition — it's a cultural problem; U.S. life expectancy at birth is the same as Britain's, because at age 65+, U.S. citizens get the best care in the world; U.S. health care did not explode in cost until 1965, when the federal government got involved: it went from 5.2 percent of GNP to the current 12 percent; the U.S. system is not a free-market one; it is a "cost plus" system that rewards cost increases. The reader may find the proof for Goodman's contentions by reading his essay "Rationing Health Care."[11]

THE HUGE MORAL QUESTION

IN CLOSING THIS CHAPTER, it is time to pop the moral question. The whole reason for the State's coercive humanitarianism in introducing compulsory national health-care insurance, taking over the medical profession, eliminating fundamental freedoms of the patient and the physician, and so on, was expressed earlier by Tom Kent. The moral platform of the liberals was that "no one should be without health care because of his bank account." We now have some inkling of what hitting this fly with a socialist sledgehammer has done to one of the most honoured professions in our country — let alone to our national budgets. But I have a more fundamental moral question that the socialist will now have to answer, as follows. Most of our health-care dollars are spent on people who suffer from lifestyle diseases (not infectious diseases, or trauma). In other words, much of their ill-health is self-inflicted. So is it morally acceptable to take money from those who take responsibility for their own health, and give it to those who do not?

Well, you may ask, what percentage of health-care problems fall into that category? Here are some eye-opener facts from a few famous health economists, first from Victor Fuchs's book *Who Shall Live?*

Positive health can be achieved only through intelligent effort on the part of each individual . . . the notion that we can spend our way to

*better health is a vast oversimplification. At present there is very
little that medical care can do for a lung that has been overinflated
by smoking, or a liver that has been scarred by too much alcohol,
or a skull that has been crushed in a motor accident.*[12]

Fuchs has a fascinating section called "A Tale of Two States," which
basically shows the results of comparing the health of citizens of
Nevada with that of those of Utah, two neighbouring states with similar
climates, incomes, demography, and so on. While "the inhabitants of
Utah are among the healthiest individuals in the United States, the
residents of Nevada are at the opposite end of the spectrum." Until old
age Nevadans have a death rate some 40-50 percent greater than that
of those from Utah for all age groups! Fuchs asks what explains this
and shows that the answer lies in the different lifestyles of the residents
of the two states. Utah is inhabited primarily by Mormons, whose
influence is strong throughout the state. "Devout Mormons do not use
tobacco or alcohol, and in general lead stable, quiet lives. Nevada, on
the other hand, is a state with high rates of tobacco and alcohol
consumption and very high indexes of marital and geographical instability . . . The populations of these two states are, to a considerable
extent, self-selected extremes from the continuum of lifestyles found
in the United States." Fuchs shows the shockingly higher percentage
of diseases caused just by tobacco and alcohol in Nevada compared
with Utah. This does *not* include self-inflicted illness arising from
obesity, inactivity, drug use, consumption of fatty foods, and so on —
only alcohol and tobacco-related illness (Utah = 100%):

age	males	females
30-39	590%	443%
40-49	111%	296%
50-59	206%	205%
60-69	117%	227%

A recent University of California study says middle-aged Utah residents have only 34 percent the normal cancer death rate, and 14
percent the normal death rate from heart and blood vessel disease
(*Toronto Star*, Dec. 6, 1989). This study examined only *one* aspect of
lifestyle. But consider the enormous reduction in health expenditures
if everyone were to manage his health responsibly. Such a voluntary
reduction of all lifestyle habits known to cause self-inflicted "diseases

•

of choice" by the total population would cut "health" costs by at least half. The argument that cost would nevertheless equal out because healthy people live longer (thus they use the system longer) doesn't hold weight simply because healthy people don't always live longer, they live *better*, see doctors less, recover faster, and when they do see doctors, it's for less serious complaints, like strains or knee surgery, not terminal cancer from smoking. In addition, incalculable losses in human capital and social distress are prevented when premature disease, death, or disability are avoided by people in their prime productive years.

In the same vein, Belloc and Breslow studied American health habits and determined that those at seventy-five years of age who had followed their "seven rules" had the same health status as forty-year-olds.[13] Here are the rules: Don't smoke cigarettes; get seven hours sleep each night; eat breakfast each morning; keep your weight down; drink in moderation; exercise daily; don't eat between meals. And Cotton Lindsay insists that "access to health care resources has little impact on the aggregate measures of health of a population" — which is more a function of lifestyle than of resources. For example, Canada spends twice as much on "health care" per capita as Japan, for the same result. He concludes that if we study the cancer death rate, the heart death rate, the infant mortality rate, the maternal mortality rate, the death rate itself, and male and female life expectancy, "no [health] plan has even a ripple of an effect on either male or female life expectancy. If government medicine is preferred on the grounds of better employing our health resources, there is scant evidence for these effects in statistical measures of health of our population."[14]

This is reinforced by the fact that "the vast proportion of the G.P.'s work is concerned with the routine, the non-urgent, and often the non-medical."[15] A 1966 study found that 25 percent of doctors felt their consultations were for "trivial, unnecessary, or inappropriate reasons ... Fully 53% of these 'trivial' consultations were for such conditions as coughs, colds, morning sickness, dandruff, indigestion and the like ..."[16] A 1974 study "found that 28 percent of consultations were for non-medical services. Of the remaining 72 percent who actually sought treatment, in 43 percent of the cases, the doctor was unable to diagnose any definite illness ..." Various other studies have estimated that from 30 to 75 percent of consultations "are with patients displaying no objective evidence (either psychological or physical) for their attendance."[17] Striking testimony to the fact that most health care in Britain is determined more by *demand* than by *need* is a study covering a period of ten years that compared two groups: a group that *never* saw their doctors, and a group with an *average* number of attendances. The rather shocking conclusion of the study was that *there was little obvious medical difference in the health of the two groups*. These observations have to do with the triviality of complaints. When the self-inflicted nature of many illnesses is also considered, the picture is dramatically worse.

By now the gist of my argument is clear. Most of the great advances in basic "health care" (as opposed to care for rare diseases) have come from the control of infectious diseases, and lifestyle modification. For the most part, these were and are still not expensive interventions, and they *preceded* the technological revolution in scientific medicine (the vast proportion of which addresses increasingly rare diseases). In short, we know today that most of our health problems come from "diseases of choice"; that is, from diseases that people could prevent by an act of will (stop smoking, stop drinking alcohol and caffeine, reduce fatty food and total calorie intake, eliminate salt and most added sugar from the diet, and exercise regularly). We know now that up to 50 percent of all premature cardiovascular diseases and cancers could be avoided by such an act of the will on the part of individuals. In a recent Harvard survey, Dr. Rose Frisch says non-exercising women face twice the risk of cancer of the breast and reproductive organs as those who exercise regularly; also, that inactive women over forty have a 3.4 times greater incidence of diabetes. This is but one of thousands of solid studies that show a dramatic positive health effect on every single bodily system through exercise and wise lifestyle management.

Is it moral, then, for the State heavily to tax those who take personal responsibility for their own health care, to benefit those who do not?

I believe it is not, and furthermore, that such a policy is far more immoral than any condition that Kent, Pearson, and Trudeau imagined themselves to be curing when they introduced socialized medicine to Canada. There are millions of individuals too lazy, self-indulgent, or careless to look after their own health, who account for a very large percentage of our national health expenditures. I have not been able to find a reliable statistic on this, but I would estimate that at least 40 percent of our annual medical expenditures of $49 billion could be safely attributed to self-inflicted illness, broadly considered. Millions of people with such illnesses are beneficiaries of our medical handicap system, while those who manage their lives wisely unjustly pay the imposed cost of the unwise. Such is the moral distortion brought about by the welfare, or "client, State." But the result is that if *all* were as responsible as *some*, we could save $20 billion a year — two-thirds of the annual deficit. Wouldn't we be wiser to put the responsibility back where it belongs? Here's a little scenario to illustrate the moral and financial point of what I am arguing.

HOW MEDICARE CHEATS THE HEALTHY

LET US IMAGINE A 40-year-old woman who takes pride in the management of her own health. She weighs only five pounds more than when she was twenty, eats a balanced, nutritious, low-fat diet, enjoys moderate exercise almost daily, practises relaxation techniques, sleeps well, stays out of the hot sun, doesn't smoke, and although she enjoys drinking, restricts herself to an occasional glass of wine with a meal. Even when she gets sick with an unavoidable flu, she never stays in bed. She hardly ever visits a doctor because she feels vibrant most of the time. But more to the point, she decided long ago that life's occasional physical discomforts and suffering — headaches, menstrual discomfort, mild allergies, occasional back pain, sore muscles, a twisted ankle, stomach upset, and so on — were a normal part of living that simply had to be cared for by oneself, or endured until they passed. One's body had an amazing way of healing itself. What she could not abide, for herself or her family, was complaining and running to professionals for pills and soothing every time such situations arose.

Her neighbour is also 40. However, she has smoked a pack a day since she was 16 years old, likes to party a lot, and complains over the back fence of frequent hangovers. She is also thirty-five pounds overweight. In her house are lots of snack foods and soft-drink bottles. Fast-food services are always driving up to her door. She has no interest in exercise, and even draws a good laugh when she mocks others for doing it. Her husband and three kids are all lazy and overweight, too. It is no secret — she herself lets everyone know — that over the past twenty years she has made innumerable visits to her G.P. for everything under the sun (she blames her frequent discomforts on everything but herself); she has had a tummy-tuck (too fat), a gall bladder removed, surgery for varicose veins in her calves (too heavy and lack of exercise, her G.P. said), and one stern warning that she might be contracting liver problems associated with her drinking. She is on medication for high blood pressure (usually controllable with exercise and diet), has a chronic sore back (most back pain is also manageable with exercise and weight loss), and uses a cough suppressant to sleep at night (constant irritation from tobacco). Her medicine cabinet is overflowing with prescription drugs. Last week, after an extensive series of cardio-vascular tests, her doctor informed her that she had dangerously narrowed coronary arteries and that if she didn't stop smoking, didn't exercise, and didn't change her diet, she might need a by-pass soon. She told him that was a ridiculous suggestion — she was known to be a character, and her life wasn't worth living without a bit of fun.

Last week, the tax collectors came to inform everyone on the block that more money was needed to cover "health" costs. Because so many like the neighbour above were unwilling to change their ways, a further twenty years of heavy expenses had been projected by government analysts. Peering into the future they could see a high probability for the neighbour's by-pass, perhaps also lung cancer or emphysema, and ever more frequent visits to doctors both for her and for the rest of her family, who were already following in her footsteps. By their calcula-tion, every family in the neighbourhood would have to deliver an additional $1,500 per year for the next twenty years, indexed for inflation. The taxman remained silent when told that all those who looked after themselves properly were *saving* the government money. The complaint that these were *her* health problems, not theirs, and that if she had changed her ways they wouldn't have been brought on her, fell on deaf ears. The taxman said, "I don't make the policy, I just collect the money."

It is surely a wonder, and a sign of the moral flabbiness of our times, that after provision for emergency care and unavoidable illness — a minimal expense for the system — no single Canadian politician of any party has publicly argued this point: *that any socialized system designed to pay for the consequences of carelessness and irresponsibility is inher-ently unfair to those who are careful and responsible, and thus under-mines the moral fabric of society.*

What Is To Be Done?

Government must recognize it has made a mistake, that the demand for an unlimited free commodity is infinite, that, as the health econo-mist John Goodman says, "Most of the dramatic increase in life expec-tancy . . . has been primarily due to an improvement in the way people are living," and not to the level of "medical resources" available to a nation's people. Nor is there any relationship between the health of various nations and the amount they spend on "health care."

Government must pull out of medicare and the moral mess it has created before it is too late. It can protect the truly needy from medical disaster, restore the medical profession to its former status, and free medicine from the bureaucracy, as follows:

1. Require all Canadians to carry what the Americans call "major medical and catastrophic insurance," which is relatively cheap. This must be provided on the free competitive insurance market, and can be provided by the State for the truly needy.

2. Eliminate first-dollar insurance. In other words, bring in a "user-fee" for all but the truly needy, to discourage the draining of medical resources for trivial reasons, and to reduce the immoral taxing of those who manage their own health.

3. Continue a government service for basic care if that's what the people want, but:

4. Make private patients, private hospitals, and private, competing basic medical insurance legal again, thus restoring the lost entrepreneurial aspect of medicine.

5. Support only the truly needy with "free" health care — probably about 10 percent of the population.

6. Put the freedom and responsibility back where they belong by using patients as their own best caretakers, and cost controllers. Patients should pay physicians directly, as in the past, and claim from their own public or private insurer.

7. Once the above is in place, the State must stop telling free citizens how much of their own resources they are allowed to spend on their own health, and must also stop blocking their access to better care as it has done by making private basic medical alternatives illegal.

8. In a pinch, we could try a modified "Singapore Plan" in which citizens are urged to open their own special "medicare account" and place 6 percent of their income in it annually, thus spending their *own* funds on their *own* medical care. In Singapore, such plans are mandatory, and if a sick person uses more than is in his account, the State continues to withdraw after he is well, to cover the cost.

In Canada, consistent with a free country, such a plan could be set up voluntarily, but citizens who refused and then got sick and used State medical services would be told that their accounts would be garnisheed at the 6 percent rate until their medical debt was settled, on the grounds that they owed the State a debt. As a further creative twist, contributions to such medicare accounts could be a deduction from income, and interest sheltered from tax like an RRSP. Amounts contributed of more than 6 percent of income per annum could be loaned to a true medical pool of funds to help the medically needy, and so on.

In these ways, we could begin to heal Canada's sick health-care system.

12

The Criminal-Justice System
Public Safety or Public Danger?

There is only one thing crazier than me, and that's
the system that allows me to do what I do.

Statement by Allen George Foster after sentencing for the murder
of three women while on full parole

He's a highly sensitive and intelligent person —
one of the sanest people I have ever met.

Statement by Vasha Starrie, Foster's case-management officer at
Aggasiz Mountain prison, B.C.,
just before he was granted full parole

CANADIANS ARE INCREASINGLY FRIGHTENED of violent crime, and for good reason. Increasingly, we read of frail senior citizens being raped, beaten, or robbed by brazen thugs who show no fear of the law. Parents clutch the hands of their youngsters with an abnormal tightness, fearful that behind a mall pillar, or in a garage or washroom, lurks a sex maniac on day parole. Women are increasingly wary in ordinary parking lots and subway stations. Daily newspapers describe terrible crimes by violent criminals, many of whom have records as long as your arm. The living victims of these crimes and their families live with broken hearts, smashed lives, and the haunting fear that the powers that be — without informing them — will soon send their nemesis back into society, to smash again.

Daily life in Canada has lost its civility. Today, we think twice before we smile at passing strangers, pat a young child on the head, or leave a door unlocked. In 1963 there was one company in Toronto selling residential security systems. Now there are about three hundred!

There are more than 81,000 criminals on probation or parole in Canada each year, many of them violent, or on their way to violence. Violent crime has risen in Canada for the tenth year in a row (up 7 percent nationally last year, up 19.4 percent in Toronto). In 1987, according to the Canadian Centre for Justice Statistics, there were 219,381 violent crimes committed (about 10 percent of the total number of crimes). Between 1962 and 1986, violent crime in Canada increased from 221 crimes per 100,000 population, to 801 — a 264 percent increase (Statistics Canada, Catalogue 85-205). Gangs of aimless, fearless young thugs "rob, maim, and kill — often just for sport," says *Maclean's* magazine, May 22, 1989). Many of our schools are plagued with drugs, sex, and illiteracy. Inner-city teachers need karate more than teaching skills, and they confiscate a lot more knives than cigarettes.

About 20 percent of murderers on parole in Canada are returned to prison because they committed new crimes (often murder). *Of all prisoners admitted to federal and provincial prisons in 1988, more than 60 percent were repeat offenders.* The figure in Ontario is 63.2 percent. Believe it or not, our federal authorities cannot tell me what percentage of *all* those admitted to federal prison in the last twelve months had ever been to a prison *of any kind* before! But we can assume the federal percentage is higher because the crimes are more serious — perhaps 80 percent. In the U.S.A., 40 percent of those admitted to state prisons even in 1979 were on probation or parole for previous offences. In 1988, 116 Canadian prisoners escaped (down from a 188-per-year average, thanks to new electronic monitoring systems).

But what can we do? The criminal-justice system in Canada, as a police chief once said, is "great . . . great for the criminal!" Like so much else here, it is being managed by a small, nearly invisible group of specialists, often, as I shall argue, against the best interests of a moral society. In this chapter, I will try to show how the values embedded in official thinking about criminality are philosophically naive and morally confused. From Ole Ingstrup, former head of the National Parole Board and now head of Correctional Services Canada (CSC), down to the ordinary staff that manage hundreds of community facilities for criminals, there are intellectual, scientific, and moral misconceptions about human behaviour that in practice constitute terrible risks to all

Canadians. Below are just three examples of such risks. There are many, many more such cases, all products of the same assumptions. The work of Canada's excellent police forces is made all the more difficult by latent misconceptions (not among police) about human nature, criminal behaviour, rehabilitation, and the proper function of punishment in a civilized society — misconceptions that control the system they have to work within.

Just before looking at the kinds of risk we face, here are a few sobering insights on crime in Canada and the U.S.A. drawn from Robert Bidinotto's article "Crime and Consequences" (*The Freeman*, July 1989), which I combine with figures obtained from Canadian sources like Statistics Canada, the Centre for Justice Statistics, and the Centre for Criminology. It was Bidinotto who blew the whistle on the U.S. crime situation during President George Bush's campaign, in his *Reader's Digest* article on the repeat killer Willie Horton. Horton became a symbol of the "liberal" left's soft, pro-criminal agenda. Canada has a lot less crime than the U.S.A., but our rate profiles are becoming quite "American." We are increasingly urban and more densely populated, with older inner cities and more ethnic tensions. Our criminal environment and our "system," as explained to me by a convicted offender who has served time in both countries, will increasingly approximate theirs. Consider:

- Statistics Canada reports that 1 in 4 Canadian households reported criminal victimization in 1987 (*The Daily*, Statistics Canada, Apr. 15, 1989). In 1986, about 1 in 4 U.S. households was touched by some kind of crime.

- The number of U.S. crimes reported in 1987 was 12 percent higher than in 1983 and 21 percent higher than in 1978. (Figures are for serious FBI "index" crimes only.) Canada's increase was 7 percent nationally, 19.4 percent for Toronto.

- But even this is a rosy picture. Why? Because statistical reports on crime are based only on *reported* crimes. The American Bar Association estimates that the number of *actual* serious crimes committed is usually about 2.5 times as great as the number reported. And Statistics Canada says that of all criminal incidents in Canada only 40 percent "become known to the police." (The same 2.5 times ratio of actual to reported crime as in the U.S.A.) And only 31 percent of violent crimes in Canada are ever reported! In other words, official data do not even begin to convey the seriousness of crime in Canada or the U.S.A. where "only 8 serious crimes in 100 even result in an arrest." Many of these, as in Canada, are then released on technicalities, or acquitted after trial, or receive dramatically reduced sentences, or go on probation.

• In many current release programs, even dangerous killers (such as Willie Horton in the U.S.A. or Clifford Olson in Canada) are simply turned loose without any prison escort — presumably in the "custody" of a family member or friend (often called an "escort"). According to one of our best known criminal lawyers, whose name I cannot give here, it is "a fragmented system that would horrify me if I weren't using it to get my clients off!"

Here are three stories of a few such "clients." There are many more like them.

CLIFFORD OLSON

CLIFFORD OLSON WAS FIRST arrested in 1957 at the age of 17 for breaking and entering. When 42, he was "imprisoned for life" for the brutal rape and murder of 11 children. In the 24 years between he was in jail for 21 years. *But he escaped 7 times.* By the time he was caught for the murders, he had had 94 convictions. *He was convicted of 20 crimes while on parole,* including armed robbery, theft, breaking and entering, buggery, indecent assault, forgery, fraud, escape, possession of firearms, drunk driving, etc. Although breaking and entering a private residence carries a penalty of life imprisonment under the Criminal Code, he never received more than a three-year sentence for this repeated crime. At no time was he ever labelled a habitual or dangerous offender. Four of his murders were committed while under police surveillance! *He was given full parole twice, and supervised parole seven times.* He will be eligible for parole again in 2007, and by law may appeal for earlier release.

MELVIN STANTON

AT THE AGE OF 14, Melvin Stanton escaped from a juvenile detention centre and raped a 62-year-old woman. That same year (how did he get out?) he killed his own girlfriend. A few years later he raped another woman while he was on day parole. That same spring he escaped and raped a woman five months pregnant. Sentenced to a total of 24 years, he was on parole at a "halfway house" in January 1988, when he walked out and eight hours later raped and brutally murdered Tema Conter, a total stranger, in her own apartment by stabbing her eleven times and smashing full pop bottles over her head. Officials at the halfway house did not know Stanton's full name, date of birth, or convict number. His parole record did not mention that he had previously brutally raped three women *while on parole*.

JOHN FINLAYSON

ON WEDNESDAY, JANUARY 18, 1989, the *Toronto Star* reported that John Finlayson, labelled "dangerously insane" in 1973 for the sexual-abuse and mutilation killing of 9-year-old Kirkland Deasley and acquitted of murder on the grounds of insanity, stabbed a Brockville, Ontario, woman. He had been committed to a mental institution with no time limit. But at the time of the stabbing Finlayson had been living full time away from the medium security prison for some six months on a "loosened warrant." In 1974 *three psychiatrists had labelled him "insane and extremely dangerous."* The prosecutor in the original case was shocked and said, "I never wanted to see him out again. It was without doubt the most grisly murder that I've had the misfortune to prosecute." But after the recent incident, the hospital handling him said "they could not have prevented the stabbing." (They failed to mention that if he had still been locked up he would not have had the opportunity.)

WARRING CONCEPTS OF HUMAN NATURE

IT IS DIFFICULT TO understand the present climate of criminal justice in Canada without first understanding the warring concepts about human nature, personality, and punishment that created that climate. As with so many social issues in Canada, there is a radical polarization of views — few of which ever surface for public inspection — beneath a seemingly calm surface. The people who consciously or unconsciously hold these opposing views fight for control of the bureaucratic and political turf that constitutes the criminal justice system in Canada. Unfortunately, the laboratory for the experiments these people undertake is us: our families, our children, and the civility of our society. We are guinea pigs for social scientists, penologists, wardens, case-management officers, parole board members, and the politicians who legislate criminal justice.

In their important book *Crime and Human Nature*, Harvard professors James Wilson and Richard Herrnstein provide an overview of the two principal, and radically conflicting, views of human nature that have always divided criminologists.[1]

MAN THE CALCULATOR

THOMAS HOBBES MADE FAMOUS in *Leviathan* (1651) the idea that our minds work somewhat like little cost-benefit calculators that help us decide what we want. To avoid the state of continuous social upheaval that would result from our conflicting desires, we implicitly agree to submit our daily conduct to the authority of the law. In short, according to this view — one further developed by Jeremy Bentham and called "utilitarianism" — each of us is seen as quite capable of weighing the likely pain and pleasure to be obtained from our actions. The object of the law, therefore, is to ensure that the few do not take advantage of the many; to ensure that the community as a whole experiences the greatest pleasure and the least pain possible from the totality of social action. The justification for punishment is "to outweigh the profit from crime" gotten when some wish to gain by hurting others. Punishment prevents greater pain to the community and is meant not for vengeance, but to incapacitate, to deter, and to provide society with its "just deserts" — to make it morally whole again.

After their exhaustive survey of criminology, Wilson and Herrnstein say that "the view of human nature developed by Hobbes [and Bentham] accords with much of what we have learned about the causes of crime."[2] Of course, they allow that for truly insane individuals this theory cannot hold, and that we are governed by more than mere calculation (for example, by conscience, moral sanctions, and the like). Nevertheless, the Hobbesian-type view places responsibility squarely in the hands of the knowing, calculating offender. In this respect, it is harmonious with the political, economic, and cultural institutions of a free society surveyed in Part One of this book.

MAN THE NATURALLY GOOD

THE OPPOSITE VIEW WAS sparked by the Swiss philosopher Jean-Jacques Rousseau (1712-1778), who supplied the Romantic movement in literature and the arts with much momentum by declaring that man started as a "noble savage." It was his view that we are born naturally innocent, and that it is the existence of private property, laws, acquisitiveness, war, social conventions, inequality, and so on that sets one man against another, thus causing crime. He argued that only a healing education could return man to himself, to his natural goodness; that "through self-discovery, man will rediscover nature and his natural sentiments."[3] Hardly a good example himself, Rousseau gave all five of his own newborn children away to state orphanages because he feared they might get in his way. Despite the lie given by his personal life to his own ideas (many tried, unsuccessfully, to expose him), his writing had an enormous impact. In fact,

> *much of modern criminology, directly or indirectly, draws on Rousseau. It is indebted to him when it favors preventing crime through proper education and constructive social programs as well as when it prefers helping offenders by rehabilitation instead of preventing offenses by deterrence. This view . . . is sympathetic to the insanity defense, [and] to excuses based on human need and social stress . . . [But] there is less support today for the feasibility of rehabilitation . . . And for almost all of modern criminology, there is less optimism than there used to be about the perfectibility of human nature. But the view that crime is caused by social forces . . . and that the individual is not fully to blame for his behavior is still widespread.*[4]

In this respect, there is a policy lag in our society between professional psychiatrists, who have all but abandoned the idea of human perfectibility, and the politicians, the criminology establishment, and the parole and case-workers, who have not. After all, why should they? A bureaucratic mini-empire has been created to support the philosophy that sustains their departments and their careers. It is in their natural self-interest to defend Rousseauistic ideas. In the thorough, 300-page "Daubney Committee Report" to Parliament on sentencing, parole, and related matters (1988), committee members heard much evidence to the effect that rehabilitation and parole do not work, including evidence from the *1981 Solicitor General's Report*, which said that

> *a large body of empirical research which has been extensively assessed . . . has shown a lack of evidence of positive effects on recidivism [repeat crime] from any correctional program, either in prison, or in the community.*

Nevertheless, even after hearing evidence that some programs can actually do harm, we read: "The committee believes that people can and do change; it rejects the notion that 'nothing works.'"[5] This is a stunning statement, because — presto! — the committee *believes*. Nothing more. It has no evidence, and no expertise. In fact, it has contrary evidence.

So we are not dealing with hard facts here, but with emotions and belief systems. I will argue throughout that Canada's parole and correctional establishment is sustained by wishful thinking (except for the guards and the prisoners themselves, who know better), and that society has been turned into an unwitting laboratory for its experiments in human nature. To attack such experiments is like attacking religion; for the Rousseau-inspired, the it-was-caused-by-the-environment idea is deeply embedded in our egalitarian society, from Charter precepts, through affirmative-action laws, down to the way we treat criminals. Here's just one example: responding to the charge that five young murderers sentenced to nine years in penitentiary in 1985 but already out on parole were recommended for release too soon, the psychologist Stanley Newman, who authorized their parole, said, "The chief issue is how five apparently ordinary youths could end up with such vile thoughts. Average kids, average grades, involved in sports. They were very well liked. That's what makes it all the more chilling. It's not innate, it's the environment. I really believe that" (*Globe and Mail*, July 12, 1988).

There you have it. What he's really saying, echoing Rousseau, is that people are naturally good; that society (the environment) *causes* crime. The fact that these five criminals had a model environment deeply threatens his whole theory of crime, his belief system, and his sense of professional worthiness — so he rejects the facts. But the contrary view is expressed in Hobbes's belief that sane people innately know right from wrong and choose accordingly. After all, people from very good or very bad environments can commit equally atrocious crimes. And some people love the thrill of danger, a fugitive life, notoriety, quick rewards, easy cash, sadistic pleasures, or slavishly frightened sexual partners, and choose these goals by preference to the more demanding, less immediately exciting goals of an honest life.

To this point, I have outlined the two warring concepts of human nature that underlie all conflicts over how we ought to deal with criminal behaviour. But we must go deeper still, for underneath each of these concepts are even more fundamental assumptions about how the human mind works. You won't find this discussed in official statistics or justifications for parole, but serious debate on the causes of crime must eventually lead to the watershed difference I am about to explain.

WARRING CONCEPTS OF MIND

AN ANECDOTE ABOUT TWO genetically identical twin sons of a violent, drunken father, with the same family upbringing, poignantly sums up this whole matter.

QUESTION TO FIRST TWIN: "Why are you a drunken criminal?"
ANSWER: "With a father like mine, who wouldn't be?"

QUESTION TO SECOND TWIN: "Why are you *not* a drunken criminal?"
ANSWER: "With a father like mine, who would be?"

THE DETERMINIST VIEW OF MIND

IN THE ANECDOTE ABOVE, the first twin has a determinist view of the mind, the second twin, the opposite. Let us examine the first.

Inevitably, the Rousseauistic view of human nature leads directly to a determinist view of the mind, as follows: If it is true that we are born naturally good, and it is society that creates evil in us, then there must be some direct causal link between the events of daily life and our behaviour. The model for this notion is a combination of the Garden of Eden story (we were all good before Adam ate the apple) and Newtonian physics (for the first time a scientist had provided workable laws for the physical world): for every known action, there will always be a known reaction. Physics, of course, gives relatively clean results compared with social life (where we are forced to use such phrases as "is likely to produce"). Nevertheless, behaviourists, as they are called, will always strive to establish a direct link between some physical or social event in our lives, and our behaviour; between some stimulus, and our response to it. (Freudian psychiatrists do the same, but with inner, psychic "stimuli.") When challenged, they will stretch prior events to fit this model. When behaviourists speak of "socialization," they mean that social life works on us just like a physical event, and that we will all have predictable reactions to it according to our particular circumstances. When Karl Marx said that mind "is the highest product of matter," he meant the same thing. That's why in newspaper acounts of violent crime, you will often read about early events of the criminal's life, implying that a rotten childhood environment (society in microcosm) *caused* the criminal to do violence.

At a recent coroner's inquiry, social worker Dr. Khanna, in a file letter on the violent rapist-murderer Melvin Stanton, pleaded that Stanton told her of "abuse and neglect by his family" (the assumption is that he would otherwise have been normal); she recommended that "his attempts at pro-social behaviour need to be rewarded so that such behaviour will be strengthened" (the assumption is that the right physical stimuli — candy for good behavior — will cause a predictable change); and his psychologist, Maurice Klein, deplored how Stanton deteriorates "when community stimuli are encountered." There you have it: the patient as a physical entity, ruined by prior physical events, corrupted by the wrong "stimuli."

This is just another example of how, wherever encountered, determinist thinkers try to explain all behaviour as a result of prior physical-social stimuli. They are like materialists. They try to establish an unbreakable chain of events (no matter how complicated) between the earliest past of each person, and his current behaviour. Many of their theories are very clever. Nevertheless, what it boils down to is that this influential but simplistic view of the mind *more or less eliminates the conscious, choosing, knowing-right-from-wrong subject from the formula*. The subject is theoretically superfluous because all life unfolds in a determined way. This theory was dealt with in Chapter Two as "the Determinist Illusion," one of eight popular illusions that currently serve as explanatory models for social policy.

It is no accident that there is an intense compatibility between this social theory and the ideology of the social-welfare State, or what I have called "the handicap system." Each is built upon the same egalitarian belief that differences between people who are assumed to be born equal can be explained by environment, and that the way to equalize a society of unequal people is to handicap the advantaged and reward (or cure) the disadvantaged, until all are equal. Thus, the determinist theory of mind eliminates man-as-moral-being entirely from its analyses and tries to teach us that crime is not a matter of right and wrong, but of social disease and cure. This emphasis has been a moral disaster for our society.

What Canadians must now face is this question: Why have we accepted the creation of a vast academic, political, and social bureaucracy for the determination of criminal justice based on such a theory — one manifestly at odds with the moral values by which we and our families attempt to live? Why have they accepted an invasion by criminal lawyers eager to prove that bad parenting, sleepwalking, Twinkie cookies, or steroids deprive people of responsibility for crime? After all, what consistent connection could possibly exist between a mood, or a feeling, and a moral decision to act one way or the other? Moods and emotions, in themselves, have no *intent*. (If anger "causes" murder, then half the world would be murdered.) Rather, the intent to satisfy a mood is always shaped by a thought . . . which leads to another, more telling, and far more moral view of the mind, one which I believe

Canadians inherently support but which has been subdued through a morally misguided, therapy-oriented criminal-justice system.

THE FREE CHOICE VIEW OF MIND

ALTHOUGH THE DETERMINIST VIEW permeates everything in our society and is in keeping with its social-welfare impetus, there has always been another, very serious view of how the mind works. This view, essentially theological, but more recently developed by philosophers like Kierkegaard, Heidegger, and the early Sartre, claims that the crucial difference between man and the thing-world around him, is this: Man has an innate capacity to negate, or to refuse, whatever he *is* at any moment, and thus to constantly re-create himself through free choice. This is a humanistic view that rejects materialism and determinism by declaring that regardless of our circumstances, we can always say "no"; that the glory of human existence is based on this power, and theories that remove it remove also our essential humanity. Man is always free to negate whatever he is, to choose a new beginning, however humble, to escape past forces by an act of free will.

It is this ability alone that defines man as much more than a mere thing. There could be no humanity whatsoever without this distinction, since otherwise everything would be determined, and there would be no escape. It would even be useless to talk about changing behaviour by changing the environment, since such talk would itself be determined, or preordained. So the free-choice model of the mind is radically different from the determinist model, *and cannot be reconciled with it*: societies that choose one view or the other therefore embark on a particular course. Where there is a grey area between them, they must decide in favour of their particular course, and the individual will sometimes be sacrificed to that course. In fact, I would argue that societies that opt for freedom and responsibility end up sacrificing criminals to the moral urgency of the system, while those that opt for determinism end up sacrificing their victims, and society at large. Socialist and Communist states officially take the determinist view. But it is the free-choice model that underlies Christianity, democratic capitalism, and the legal systems of the Western world.

When the judges at Nuremberg said that following orders (environmental stimuli) was no excuse for war crimes, this is what they meant. When James Wilson in *Crime and Human Nature* said " . . . the very process by which we learn to avoid crime requires that the courts act as if crime were wholly the result of free choice,"[6] this is what he meant. Most importantly, it is *only* this model that makes morality possible, that frees mankind to distinguish between right and wrong. For if man is trapped within determined events, he cannot so distinguish — how could he, since he himself would be a mere product of those events, unable to help what he thinks or does? But freed from them by virtue of his essential humanity, he can choose between them. He can yield to, or refuse, a desire, a thought, an emotion.

Fundamentally, this view of mind is upheld by popular wisdom all over the world (even in totalitarian states that publicly espouse the opposite) and could be called, simply, the "moral" view. Nevertheless, academic determinism has so invaded the social sciences, including criminology, that the moral view has all but disappeared. Because it is an unmitigated threat to the theories of determinists, they have simply got rid of it! After reading about twenty-five pounds of documents to prepare for writing this chapter, I can assure the reader that they have done so in a thorough fashion. Our criminal-justice system is determinist in its understanding of the mind, statistical and sociological in its prescriptions for cure, and largely ignores the common moral basis for human behaviour.

Such thinking inevitably evolves into a materialistic idea of "personality" (which further permits determinists to sidestep the notion of moral behaviour). This view holds that we have a "self" (like a thing) that we can "get in touch with," or search for. The therapeutic types want to "rebuild" this self. But the confusion in this materialist view must be exposed. For how can I say I am searching for myself? Are there two selves inside each of us — the searcher and the searched? No, the self is not a thing, but a construct of free will, and is sustained or altered by free choice. The fact that people may choose to act as if they are determined beings gives us the illusion of their changeless character. But even this is a choice.

Such a view was commonly accepted until very recent times. The vast majority of articles in popular magazines of the last century dealt with the moral formation of "character" in the bosom of the family and society. But by the first half of this century such articles had all but disappeared, replaced by articles on how spanking, breast-feeding, and the unconscious would *determine* our "personality." In short, the moral-responsibility view of character so threatens determinists that they avoid it. The committees for the 1981 *Solicitor General's Study of Conditional Release* — and the 1988 Daubney Report that reviewed the same issues — failed to pursue the inescapable consequences of a society's holding of the moral view. No one in an official capacity is fighting for the moral view. In short, our present criminal justice system, which regulates the flow of dangerous criminals back into society, despite its flirtation with the idea of responsibility, is opposed to the popular wisdom on how society works. Instead, it promotes a form of determinist amorality alien to our traditional way of life. Inevitably, this produces a conflict between the popular view of right punishment, and that of the criminal justice establishment.

WARRING CONCEPTS OF PUNISHMENT

WILSON AND HERRNSTEIN, whom I will draw from here, basically summarize the traditional reasons for punishment as follows:

INCAPACITATION

BOTH PRISON AND EXECUTION protect the public by separating the offender from possible victims, thus reducing the opportunities for crime. The question to what extent such punishment ought to be used is at the heart of the conflict between the judiciary and the parole powers in our society: a wise judge may decide on a certain sentence, only to see it cut to ribbons by social workers and parole officers. In fact, a judge in this country today has no means of telling how much of the sentence he or she sweated over will in fact be served. This casts into disrepute the whole structure of the law, and especially the authority of judges who agonize over appropriate sentences. This also reflects on Canada as a community, because standards of justice should always be set by the people. Justice is a moral, not a professional matter, and every man and woman has an equally valid opinion on the subject of the right punishment. That's why juries work, and that's how the community's sense of *equity* is arrived at in the first place. But once the *therapeutic* idea takes hold (based on the man-is-naturally-good determinist model), the people's right to determine justice is taken from them by "experts" who want to cure, not in *addition* to punishment, but *instead* of it.

As the experts proceed (through the use of parole and "earned remission") to reduce sentences held appropriate by the community, they further undermine public respect for the law. This conflict has arisen because the determinists who have so influenced our system take the view that "if an act is not a choice but merely the inevitable product of a series of past experiences, a man can be no more guilty of a crime than he is guilty of an abscess."[7] The result is that the parole-probation system has the effect of eroding the moral authority of all those who favour the free-choice-and-responsibility view of crime.

Ironically, it often does so even while appearing to promote the idea of personal responsibility: the Daubney Report has on its cover the promotional phrase, "Taking Responsibility," when it really means that "society" is taking it, not the criminal.

DETERRENCE AND MORAL EDUCATION

ANOTHER TRADITIONAL REASON FOR punishment is that it deters crime while giving moral education to prospective criminals. Wrongdoers are punished and the example of their fate provides a punishment rehearsal for others contemplating the same acts. Even though interference with sentencing waters down the effect of punishment, it does deter: "If a connection has been established between action and aversive consequences, and if the aversive consequence is adequately intense . . . the action will be prevented or reduced in frequency."[8] In Wilson's view, *all crime*, for that matter all human action, is *controlled by its consequences* (not by prior stimuli); the reason punishment works is that it makes non-crime more attractive. Punishment also creates social sanctions, which are then incorporated in each individual as conscience, transferred from generation to generation through the family and incorporated in religious and civil law.

Lectures from parents, parking tickets, and reminders of the Ten Commandments do have an effect. Swift, sure punishment helps a society to internalize and thus clearly express its prohibitions. But a "punishment" that causes no psychic pain in offenders (the likely result of converting punishments to cures) will not have the desired effect of creating social conscience. Society is thus weakened; crime advances. What I have called cultural entropy gains ground, for "a community which is too ready to forgive the wrongdoer may end by condoning the crime."[9]

RETRIBUTIVE VS. HUMANITARIAN THEORIES

IN A FAMOUS ESSAY entitled "The Humanitarian Theory of Punishment," C.S. Lewis complained that those who took the determinist view of punishment — that it should be replaced by therapy, or what we today call "rehabilitation" — missed the point of punishment.[10] The "humanitarian" theory, he argues, removes from punishment the concept of "just deserts": the idea of legal retaliation according to the ancient *lex talionis* of the Bible (Exodus 21, 23). For, as he put it, "the concept of [Just] Desert is the only connecting link between punishment and justice."[11] To remove the idea of just deserts from punishment, is to remove justice itself, and thus to debase society as a whole. And Wilson, agreeing, reminds us that "an offender has violated an implicit social contract that ties the members of a community together. . . . Punishment as retribution balances the books."[12]

Such retributive equity, or fairness, can never be called vengeance. For vengeance results when vigilantes take the law into their own hands. But punishment as equity is a restorative concept that makes society whole again by exacting what the community as a whole (not any one individual) thinks is fair. When retributive equity is debased by parole programs proffered on the therapy-not-punishment model, society is cheated. Justice is neither done, nor seen to be done. Crime increases. This is not to say that we cannot seek justice and deter, as well as educate and cure, but that from an equity point of view therapy cannot be a *subsitute* for punishment. For as the criminologist Jeffrie Murphy writes, "A retributive theory of punishment . . . is the only morally acceptable theory of punishment . . . [and] the twentieth century's faddish movement toward a 'scientific' or therapeutic response to crime runs grave risks of undermining the foundations of justice."[13] In Canada, the foundations are already badly cracked.

Is Imprisonment Too Expensive?

A PROTEST OFTEN HEARD from the anti-punishment forces is that even if arguments such as those presented here are correct, it's just too expensive to keep criminals in jail. Parole, probation, rehabilitation, and supervision are much cheaper. The average annual cost of keeping one convict in a Canadian jail in 1986-87 was $42,695. The U.S. figure was about U.S.$20,000: $15,000 for soft costs, $5,000 for the amortized cost of the cell. (Americans bunk more prisoners per cell, and I suspect we have more administrators per convict.) This high annual cost — far more than the cost of two full years in medical school at a world-class private university — is persuasive. On this purely financial argument, the pro-criminal lobby argues that we ought to jail fewer criminals, parole more — and spend the money "helping" the poor. (The annual cost of supervising the average parolee in the same year was $6,580.) But wait! So far, the Canadian public has never been told the *true net costs of crime.* That is, not just the costs of the cell, food, guards, and so on, but the difference between this and the total costs arising from all the damage to all property and persons associated with each crime committed by criminals who are *not* incarcerated. And we may never be told. But there are some clues. Last year, in an important new study conducted by the Rand Corporation for the U.S. Justice

Department's National Institute of Justice, entitled "Making Confinement Decisions," Edwin Zedlewski reported the *net cost* of crime to society. The study surveyed 2,190 prison inmates in California, Michigan, and Texas, and showed that *the average felon out of prison commits 187 crimes a year.* (Ten percent of the group committed an average of 600 crimes per year — exclusive of drug deals.) This echoes a Metropolitan Toronto study that showed only 12 charges brought for every 100 offences reported. Peter McMurtry, a Toronto probation officer of thirty years' experience, said of his "clients" that many have committed numerous crimes, "maybe even thousands," before they got caught (*Toronto Star*, June 25, 1989). Even leaving out the psychological costs of crime to the victims, Zedlewski's study found *that the average criminal on the street costs society US $430,000 per year.* This means that every criminal locked up saved the nation a net US $410,000 per year. It would appear that *not* locking up criminals costs ten times as much as doing so!

THE CRIMINAL PROFILE

HERE ARE A NUMBER of sobering observations from established criminologists that run counter to the concept of a Rousseauistic, determinist, rehabilitation-oriented criminal-justice system. First, from *Crime and Human Nature*, comes a picture of the typical criminal: overwhelmingly, the typical criminal is a male. Males are from 5 to 50 times more likely to go to jail than females, and their offence rates reach more than 90 percent in many crime categories. (Canada had 12,049 prisoners in federal institutions in the year ended March 31, 1988, and only 142 of these were female.) The typical criminal is also quite young (crime declines rapidly with age); he is also of somewhat below-average intelligence, generally has a muscular body, is inarticulate (verbal ability is highly correlated with intelligence), and most telling of all, is extremely impulsive and given to heavy "time-discounting." In other words, criminals have a very short time-horizon. Also, most criminals show signs of trouble very early in life and do not form strong emotional attachments. Because they are very "present-oriented," they generally refuse to postpone gratification. (McMurtry describes this trait memorably as "I see it, I want it, I get it" — whether it is a woman, a car, or an item in a store.) We should note, however, that this is a calculated impulsiveness, for a criminal who knows he is being watched easily controls his criminal desires. Part of this syndrome is an extreme reluctance to plan for the future, and a buck-passing "it-wasn't-my-fault" mentality (reinforced by our therapy orientation). Criminals show a lack of anxiety over the things that would create anxiety in others, and a complete lack of dependability. Of course crime suits such individuals very well, because it provides a means to short-circuit the normal reward pathways of society, which require effort and time, while punishment always seems remote to them (because it is). Herrnstein concludes that it is the homogeneity of the criminal-personality profile that is so striking, not the variation.

WHY WE CAN'T BLAME SOCIETY

ONE OF THE MOST striking revelations in *Crime and Human Nature* deals with "Crime Across Cultures" (Chapter Seventeen). We learn here that international cross-cultural assessments of the heinousness of various crimes are uncannily similar, but that crime *rates* are quite different between nations; that societies have a lot to do, not so much with shaping criminals, as with shaping the morality that permits the easy expression of criminality.

This is especially so for Japan. (Tellingly, Americans of Japanese and Chinese origin have far lower crime rates than other Americans.) For the Japanese "have somehow managed to swim against the tide" of modern crime.[14] Between 1962 and 1972, crime actually *fell* in Japan, and by a whopping 40 percent. Meanwhile, crime in major cities of the rest of the world doubled, even tripled. In 1974, the U.S.A had *four* times as much *serious* crime as Japan had of *all* crime (including petty crime). Japan experienced a national crisis in 1982 when the number of street murders there rose to thirteen in one year (as many as in New York City on an average weekend). Japan is even more densely populated than America (with which it is mostly compared), poorer, and 70 percent urban, with fewer police per capita. But once indicted and prosecuted, a Japanese faces a 90 percent chance of conviction. Court cases are less adversarial. Japan has one-twentieth the number of lawyers per capita that we do. Herrnstein suggests the reasons for low crime in Japan have partly to do with racial, ethnic, and cultural uniformity (racially mixed countries have far more crime — a lesson that our government's emphasis on "multiculturalism" is now painfully teaching us); they have somehow preserved the village communal spirit, even in their large cities.

I lived in Japan for six months, and suggest that its cities feel communal because they have been largely unplanned. Once the sociologists and the planners get their hands on a community, the plastic culture begins. In Japan, the streets have an organic, meandering flow, most houses still do not have addresses; the most unlikely land uses spring up like mushrooms, naturally, beside each other, little food and vegetable stores and five-seat eateries can be found stuck everywhere. Japanese construction wouldn't pass inspection by our fire and safety marshals, but Japanese communities have a human shape. Further, the Japanese have a by now well-known sense of communal values and an inherent interest in national achievement; finally, they are far more concerned than we are about obligations, less so about rights. The suggestion in all of this is that the cultural internalization of sanctions against crime (just deserts and equity) leads to a stronger conscience in the people, who then self-limit crime.

PUTTING THE BIGOTRY AND POVERTY MYTHS TO BED

SOCIAL SCIENTISTS ARE FOND of saying that crime is primarily caused by social separation, racial discrimination, and poverty, but

> *during the 1960's, one neighborhood in San Francisco had the lowest income, the highest unemployment rate, the highest proportion of families with incomes under $4,000 per year, the least educational attainment, the highest tuberculosis rate, and the highest proportion of substandard housing of any area of the city. That neighborhood was called Chinatown. Yet in 1965 there were only five persons of Chinese ancestry committed to prison in the entire state of California...*

> *The experience of the Chinese and Japanese suggests that social isolation, substandard living conditions, and general poverty are not invariably associated with high rates of crime among racially distinct groups.*[15]

This should be a benchmark against which our own society's rush to blame isolation, poverty, discrimination, and housing for crime ought to be always compared. Despite everything going against them, these people made their own moral decisions.

PLACING RESPONSIBILITY WHERE IT BELONGS

ANOTHER CRIMINOLOGIST WHO REJECTS the modern pro-criminal ethos and clearly establishes a link between crime and psychopathy, is

Stanton Samenow, who with Samuel Yochelson conducted a fifteen-year study of criminals at St. Elizabeths Hospital, a psychiatric institution in Washington, D.C. The portrait they draw, summarized in his sobering book *Inside the Criminal Mind*, is strikingly similar to that of many other modern criminologists (including Sutherland, Lewis, Cleckley, Silberman, and Konner). His close work with hundreds of criminals over many years bears more weight than the assumptions or beliefs of theorists. Samenow tells us that as most criminals will one day be out of jail, rehabilitation efforts must continue. But if we are looking to the environment for causes, we've got it all wrong. The focus must be on moral responsibility.

> *Criminals cause crime — not bad neighborhoods, inadequate parents, television, schools, drugs, or unemployment. Crime resides within the minds of human beings and is not caused by social conditions. Once we as a society recognize this simple fact, we shall take measures radically different from current ones...*

> *Too long have the social sciences promulgated the view that a human organism comes into the world like a lump of clay to be shaped by external forces. This view renders us all victims!... Far from being a formless lump of clay, the criminal shapes others more than they do him ... [and] criminals are remarkable in their capacity to size up their environment in order to pursue objectives important to them.*[16]

It would be gratifying to see more evidence of such views surfacing into public awareness in Canada's criminal justice system. But instead, we seem to be moving the other way. "Correctional Services Canada has charted a future course that rejects the public's get tough attitude in favor of treatment programs and the integration of convicts into the community," reports the *Globe and Mail* (March 31, 1989). The same article introduces the reader to Ole Ingstrup, a "reform-minded veteran of the Danish correctional system," fresh from two years of running our National Parole Board and now the head of Correctional Services Canada (CSC). Ingstrup says, "The image of a group of people who are running in and out of prison is a myth. *The majority go in and out but once.*"

But is this really so? To test this cheerful claim, I asked the Correctional Services Branch of the Ontario government to answer this question: "Of all those admitted to Ontario prisons in 1988, how many had ever been in prison before?" Here's what they told me: 44,692 were admitted; 31,242 had been in prison before. (About 8,000 of these were double or triple-dippers — they go in and out of prison more than once in the same year.) That means *a whopping 70 percent of admissions to prison in Ontario were repeaters.* There are about 7,800 first-timers in our federal prisons (you go there if convicted for two years or more), but no one in Ingstrup's organization knows what percentage of them have ever been in prison before — so CSC handily just leaves this out of its published calculation.

Ingstrup's comment is misleading, and Canadians had better beware, because he has every intention of loosing *more* criminals into society, not fewer. He is an arch-determinist reformer whose "mission" is full of philosophical confusion, commonly known as doubletalk. Here are a few conundrums from his "mission" statements for CSC and the National Parole Board. Both documents read like a behaviourist's version of *In Search of Excellence,* couched in human-potential-movement lingo. I'm all for cheerleading, but we're not talking about psyching up managers in hope of gaining a greater market share. We're talking about a man who's supposed to be protecting the public — and he wants to do it by going softer on criminals. At the CSC Administrators Conference (Banff, Oct. 24-25, 1988), his speech was filled with talk of "excellence," the need for "vision," "positive human potential," the "potential for growth in our offender population" (I hope he doesn't mean it literally!), and "partnership" between staff and offenders. In the *Globe* article above, he speaks of the need for more money *to hire more psychiatrists.* Yet, in another *Globe* article (Aug. 20, 1988), an Ontario program for the treatment of anti-social criminals, billed as "one of the most ambitious in the world," was a dismal failure. Doctors reported that overall "the study sample fared worse than offenders who had been sent to prison without any treatment." The research head, Marnie Rice, said, "There's almost no room to do any worse." These researchers also said that unlike other criminals, anti-social ones do not appear to get less violent with age, and that lifelong incarceration was the alternative to treatment. Here's more: I have just been handed a new article, "Treatment Failing Sex Offenders, Conference Told" (*Toronto Star,* June 20, 1989):

> *A widely acclaimed treatment program for sex offenders at the Penetanguishene Mental Health Centre has produced dismal results. . . The study of 137 sex offenders . . . showed 29 per cent were convicted of another sex offence within a six-year period and more*

than 40 per cent committed a subsequent violent offence . . . [re-search director] Marnie Rice said if a less conservative definition of failure had been used . . . nearly 100 per cent of the patients would . . . have failed. . . The 50 men who took part in a treatment program that was started in 1972 fared worse than the 87 who didn't. Rice said : "It may be in fact that the treatment isn't helpful, but harmful." Lana Stermac, speaking at the same conference, said even programs like the one at the Clarke Institute, which admits only the most highly motivated offenders, have yet to be proved successful.

A University of Toronto law professor, Bernard Dickens, said, "Today's system is allowing an unsuspecting society to be 'guinea pigs.'" Nevertheless, Ingstrup suggests that we need to move parole decisions down the ladder to the more local level (meaning speed-up the process, get more of them out to establish "partnerships" with the public). This man is a dyed-in-the-wool Rousseauist. His brochures are filled with "protection of society" talk as a cover for his determinism-therapy notions, which he tries to sell to us as "opportunities" to protect ourselves. This is offensive salesmanship, since obviously the best way to protect us is to keep criminals away from us as long as legally possible. Further, he wants us to respect "the dignity of individuals" — a call to our humanity that is hard to resist. But the whole point of incarcerating a heinous murderer like Clifford Olson is that he forfeited any right to ordinary respect with each child he raped, murdered, and buried. Do we really believe he can ever earn it back, or that respect ought to be conferred upon him by government decree? Most would say that basic dignity in our society is conferred on all equally by birth. But after that it's earned, or lost, according to our behaviour. Sadly, in all of this we read very little of concern for the dignity of society, the victims, and the families that these dignified criminals decimated.

As for the additional psychiatrists Ingstrup is eager to hire? This is more of the same old stuff, and it won't work, for the determinist reasons I've explained. In a recent report in *Science* magazine, two researchers, David Faust and Jay Ziskin (both psychologists), showed that social workers, psychologists, and psychiatrists are batting zero when it comes to assessing the human mind and forecasting behaviour (exactly what these folks will be doing when Ingstrup's fresh new recruits, having fooled all his psychiatrists, eagerly apply for the right — citing our new Charter in their defence — to rampage through our communities once again). In screening for brain damage, "professional psychologists performed no better than office secretaries"; in predicting violence, the experts "are wrong at least twice as often as they are correct," and "the amount of clinical training and experience are unrelated to judgemental accuracy." But never mind, the therapeutic spirit is indomitable — as long as others bear the costs. So although we will get no better at assessing violent criminals, more of them are going to get out. Does that make any sense?

What, if anything, have various inquiries had to tell us about this matter? The *1981 Solicitor General's Study of Conditional Release* tells us that punishment is clearly *not* a National Parole Board objective (p.13); that about 27 percent of the decisions to parole turn out to be "errors"; that flipping a coin would result in the same number of errors regardless of the case factors involved (p.19); and, further, that "a large body of empirical research . . . has shown a lack of evidence . . . of positive effects on recidivism from *any* correctional program, either in . . . prison, or in the community" (p.21). Even worse for concerned judges who try hard to be fair, "parole necessarily changes the conditions of sentence." In other words, although we, the people, through our legislators set the legal limits of penalties, and judges sweat over the fairness and equity of them, *the social workers and parole experts then huddle behind closed doors and reduce them.* The reaction to this, of course, is "sentencing compensation," whereby judges over-sentence, in the knowledge that parole will probably be granted. Such judicial juggling is an insult to due legal process in this country, for parole has become "a less visible, administrative means of reducing punishment."

Even more damning, the research says that parole has "little measurable effect" on recidivism (p.75). What percentage of criminals on parole are convicted of new crimes? About 20 percent. That might not bother anyone too much if the criminals are, say, petty thieves, but it's a lot different if they're violent criminals. About 12 percent are re-imprisoned for violent crimes. (Canada imprisons 108 people per 100,000 population per year for *all* crime categories, which is 0.1 percent.) This committee also turned up truckloads of evidence of incompetence, poor esprit de corps in the Correctional and Parole services, miscommunication, and overlooked violence. Of 49 cases studied, all 49 had violence overlooked on file (p.102). This may be what we have come to expect of a government organization like the post office. But this is not mail we're dealing with, it's life and death.

From a practical point of view, there is an inherent fault in the administration of any parole system run by government. Namely, it is a system that camouflages incompetence. There are thirty-nine members of the National Parole Board, who meet in secret. Victims have no right to attend. Victims who wish to submit their side of the story seldom do because the criminal has the (Charter-supported) right to see everything in his file — so victims are understandably afraid they will be attacked again when the criminal is paroled (without any warning to the victim). Strange justice, this. Such a system naturally lends itself to buck-passing, because there's a whole sequence of opportunities for error, and no accountability. It is set up to encourage an uncontrolled display of humane feelings within a context that protects everyone from the direct costs of those feelings. The consequences of playing God are passed on to others.

But let us try a mind experiment here. What if those directly responsible for parole decisions knew that they would personally suffer some meaningful penalty if they made poor decisions? If their parolee steals again, they lose a month's pay? If he murders again, they serve a year in jail themselves? Harsh, you say? Perhaps. But I doubt the new victims of these repeat-offenders-on-parole would think so. At any rate, if some penalty were in place to correct the cost-benefit imbalance of this decision-making process there would be a lot fewer criminals on the street before the ends of their sentences. Which leads us to a conclusion: violent criminals should be released even though we know many will offend against someone else — but not if I will personally suffer from this decision. At present, Parole Board members need no special training for their jobs, and other than conscience there is no punishment for mistakes that lead to more victims. This is a situation typical of governments whereby everyone is praised for good work, but no one blamed for bad. There is no accountability, and no repercussion for direct personal decisions that often lead to death. In fact, relying on a good offence and a passive public, *Parole Board members often insist that even their mistakes were "correct"!* In a recent article, Parole Board Chairman Fred Gibson, in defending himself against charges that Melvin Stanton and Daniel Gingras should never have been released (both murdered again while on parole), said, "I'm not prepared to characterize those two particular decisions as bad decisions" (*Toronto Star*, June 21, 1989).

I submit that, when a paroled killer murders again, then by definition his early release was a tragic mistake. But here we have a situation in which a public officer is *defending* murder. As I said, such a system is inherently structured to weaken public protection. The result would be quite different if parole hearings were open to the public, decisions were made by jury, victims were allowed to submit confidential evidence, and hearings were held in the community where the crime originally took place, as they should be. Instead, violent criminals are released without warning to the victims or the community in which they offended, by an anonymous bureaucratic elite that bases its decisions not on community standards of justice, but on a therapeutic model of cure. It's just a microcosm of the determinist illusion, and the top-down, egalitarian State.

But perhaps there is a quick way to solve some of these problems with one stroke? In 1987 the Canadian Sentencing Commission recommended that parole be abolished, so that "truth in sentencing" could be restored. (Because of similar problems, about 25 percent of the states in the U.S.A. have abolished parole.) But the Commission's price was too high — it wanted to eliminate parole, but set maximum sentencing at twelve years. Alas, parole continues in Canada even though, in 1988, the Daubney Committee tabled yet another analysis of the faults of the system, found many of the same ones as the 1981 report, and underlined the latter report's finding that "there is no very accurate system for predicting violence," and that with present criteria, predictions would "more often be wrong." This committee studied 52,484 releases between 1975 and 1986 and found that fully 130 had resulted in convictions for murder or manslaughter, 5 of them by paroled murderers. (These 130 homicides, we are told, were "only" 2 percent of the more than 7,000 in the eleven-year period. But this latter figure results in 1 killing per 3,500 citizens, whereas among the parolees, the rate works out to 1 per 400 parolees. *As a group, parolees are ten times as likely to kill.*) The committee then had the temerity to say, "Even if we were prepared and could afford to [keep all such violent offenders in jail], *these homicides might only have been delayed.*" This is an astonishing statement, as if 130 irreplaceable human lives were like disposable inventory, or grist for the great parole experiment; that we might as well expose your son or daughter, or mine, to a bit more violence now, while they're children, because they have the same chances of getting nailed later anyway.

This is extremely offensive logic. First of all, we have seen that we *save* money in society at large by keeping such offenders in prison; secondly, perhaps the most powerful predictor of violence is age. As most criminals age, they get less violent. That's an argument for keeping them in until the end of their sentences. Then, if society is unhappy with the result, it can always lengthen or shorten sentences. But postponement of an evil act is always a good, and the committee has no right to play statistical executioner and decide on our behalf that 130 more murdered today is the same as 130 murdered ten years from now. It is not. For society is obligated to use any legal means at its disposal to spare its members a present life-threatening danger. Thus any *postponement* of crime by incarceration has a definite, measurable social value.

But despite such human tragedy, and the imperfections of psychology, Ingstrup argued before the committee that he *believed in parole* (no evidence given, and in utter contradiction to the committee's findings), and that society was "*better protected*" by parole (again, no evidence given). Besides his lack of professional evidence, his moral logic, as noted above, does not follow, for a danger kept apart from society now is always better than a danger released into it now, even if we could prove that the same danger might occur years later (less likely if the culprit is twenty years older).

How The Charter Endangers Us All

We have been led to think of our Charter of Rights and Freedoms as our friend and protector. But in the case of criminal justice, it is being used to protect the criminal — often endangering society ("Charter Bolsters Rise in Prison Litigation," *Globe and Mail*, June 24, 1989). Here's why. Before the Charter came along, evidence in a criminal trial, *even if illegally procured*, was admitted *if relevant to the case* (*Regina vs. Wray*). Suppose a police officer stopped someone for drunk driving and when the driver aroused suspicion searched the trunk of the car without a warrant, finding a severed limb and a bloodied knife. Before the Charter came along, that knife, and the limb, even though obtained without a warrant, could be admitted as evidence in the subsequent trial for murder, because they were relevant. But no more. Today, the Charter (section 24.2) says that such evidence "shall be excluded" *if* admission of it "would bring the administration of justice into disrepute." There is no talk of *relevance* any longer, and the judge alone decides on the "if." So, if the judge is a pro-criminal determinist, he just ignores the knife and the limb, and the murderer goes free or gets off with a lesser charge. Thus are obviously guilty murderers and other violent criminals being acquitted under the Charter, not because they are innocent, nor because their trial was unfair, but because some technical detail in procuring evidence was overlooked. It's fine to discipline the police severely for abridgement of procedures. It is not acceptable to release violent criminals we know are guilty into society when all the evidence clearly convicts them, on the grounds that some of the procedures used to obtain the evidence were technically improper. After all, *evidence may sometimes be unfairly procured. But this does not mean that the trial in which it is used is unfair.* Our present Charter does not make this distinction, and section 24.2 is now being used to free guilty criminals, and to endanger society.

WHAT IS TO BE DONE?

1. *Restorative justice.* Many Committees and Commissions on crime have said that Canada incarcerates too many people for petty crimes. If so, most Canadians would probably support a "restorative justice" ethic for petty, non-violent crimes against property, whereby first-time offenders were able to see the error of their ways, meet their victims (if reconciliation was mutually desired), understand their crime, and suffer both a penalty *and* repayment in full, instead of a jail term. However, restorative justice alone (what the determinists prefer) is not good enough, because it fails the test of restoring equity. So if used, it must be in combination with punishment. For it is not morally sufficient simply to restore a television set stolen from a house. A society that believes in individual freedom and responsibility must get the TV set back, and *also* exact fair punishment for the crime. For minor crimes against property, this can be accomplished by a combination of repayment and community work to help the needy, ordinary public works like public construction, or by work for the victims themselves. Most of us would be happy to know that first-time minor offenders were making restitution and "working it off," so to speak. But if they become repeaters — then it's off to prison.

2. *Sentencing.* The deplorable situation must end whereby judges — experts in jurisprudence — are forced to second-guess parole boards and social workers, thereby handing down longer than normal sentences in some tortured estimate of what the real time served might eventually be. Judges are thus emasculated. Equity and justice are not served. The community is weakened morally. We must move to a system of minimum determinate sentencing, so that everyone — especially prospective criminals — becomes aware of the minimum jail term carried by each crime. In this way, society's prohibitions will be inculcated and the proper moral climate restored. Then, if society feels that public danger is increasing, or decreasing, it can with confidence legislate sentences up or down. But it will no longer legislate its

penalties only to have them overturned in secret by social workers with an ideological or therapeutic axe to grind. If society wants to "rehabilitate" criminals it can do so within the sentence period. (Rather, we should say "habilitate" them: as Stanton Samenow says, "You can rehabilitate an old house. You can rehabilitate a stroke victim. But there is nothing to rehabilitate in a criminal because he never acquired moral values or concepts of responsible living." In a phrase acquiring increasing currency among criminologists, many criminals are "moral imbeciles.") Or a judge could always *add* rehabilitation time to the basic sentence. Such sentencing would be a "cost plus" system, whereby rehabilitation programs would be part of, or in addition to, incarceration, not substitutes for it.

3. *Parole.* This should be eliminated for many of the above reasons. It undermines justice, demoralizes and endangers society, undermines sentencing, is based on extremely tenuous assessment procedures no better than fortune-telling, and creates inequities between the sentences of different criminals, thus heaping more scorn on the system from criminals themselves and accentuating one of their problems — disrespect for the fairness of society.

So-called "earned remission" whereby criminals' sentences are reduced for good behaviour (critics call this "reward punishment"), should also be eliminated. Indeed, James Kelleher, solicitor general of Canada, has recommended this. For any criminal can fake good behaviour. Our papers are filled with stories of social workers who gasp in surprise that criminals who had smoothly conned them into believing they were rehabilitated, suddenly turned bad again. ("He was like Jekyll and Hyde" is a favorite expression.) Also, punishment is punishment. Good behaviour is *expected.* Society must have equity restored. Ending earned remission would also end the ridiculous situation whereby violent criminals are released by law when they shouldn't be, *even against the best judgement of their case-workers,* just because they now have a statutory right to release for "good time" while in jail. Prisons must also end day parole for so-called "humanitarian" reasons, originally meant for family funerals or emergency medical treatment. Thousands of violent criminals today are getting out to see friends, celebrate their own birthdays (Daniel Gingras escaped, and murdered, while on a "birthday pass"), go drinking, visit museums, do shopping trips, lectures, sports, you name it. Enough, we say.

At the least, if we don't have the courage to do this, then let us restore the idea of parole to the people. The top-down, elitist parole model in

existence is damaging. Parole, if used, should not be decided by some
secret cabal in Ottawa, or Kingston. It should be open to the public, and
decided by a jury of ordinary citizens from the same community where
the crime was committed (the place to which most released criminals
are likely to return), and the victims must know that the offender is
being released. Thus, even if we make the mistake of keeping parole,
it should at least be a bottom-up, local system, freed from the top-down
"experts" of the social-welfare State. Let justice come democratically,
from the people, not from the bureaucrats.

4. *The moral life of society.* Most of all, there must be a return to the
basic moral values of freedom and responsibility, values that have
always sustained our society. We must refuse to succumb to the determinist illusion, and the egalitarian, handicap society this promotes.
Principles of justice and equity must be restored to the system. Politicians and legislators, from top to bottom, must understand that moral
life and decisions are utterly independent of how good or bad someone
is feeling, or how poor or rich their family was; that one man in the
vilest of circumstances may feel disgusted with society and decide to
become a priest, while another equally disgusted may decide to murder
a total stranger. Nothing in their equally deprived situations dictates
which choice they will make. In short, emotions may be similar for us
all, but using our feelings to justify a poor moral decision creates a false
connection between feelings and action. For moral choice is unrelated
to the emotions that accompany or precede an act, except in the
thinking of the person choosing to act.

Frustration in life can be converted by anyone into a resolve to
change one's expectations and overcome adversity, or into a desire to
get even with society by hurting another. In the sense that all behaviour
takes place in a social context, society can play a disastrous role by
suggesting that we are not responsible for our actions — or, conversely,
a positive role by insisting that we are indeed responsible, and will be
dealt with accordingly. Unfortunately, we have allowed our entire
society to be permeated with a kind of slave psychology; it can be
undone only through promotion of the proper moral view, and an
insistence on justice being done in accordance with it.

For no matter what moral system a society chooses to operate
under, there will always be those who must suffer in order for society
to stay the moral course it has chosen. They are its sacrifices, so to
speak. Under free societies (where each individual is responsible) the
criminals are sacrificed; under the egalitarian state (where the envi-

ronment is blamed, where "society," or "the system," is responsible), their victims are sacrificed.

5. *The Young Offender's Act.* The mere idea that a person under eighteen can violently murder an innocent person and suffer only three years in prison is a moral scandal and a severe public danger. As an experienced criminal court judge has told me, "People think young offenders are rosy-cheeked innocents. But most of them are strong, aggressive, pumped-up males in their physical prime. They're violent, and scary, and they know the score. They know they can't get hurt much by the law. So crime pays handsomely for them. In fact, older criminals are using them to do crime for them. Having a record doesn't mean anything to them. They're proud of it."

This Act, brought in unopposed by the Liberal party, must be altered to properly protect society.

6. *How about capital punishment?* The Canadian public has long expressed its wish to restore capital punishment for capital offences. But Parliament voted (in a secret ballot!) against the wishes of the people — a strange but not uncommon practice in Canada. I think what matters is not so much that criminals do or do not get executed (for justice is imperfect, and some innocent persons have been wrongly executed), even though execution is a certain deterrent to the person executed — but that retribution and public safety can be equally well served by keeping them away from society for life. Just deserts and public safety are the issues, not an all-or-nothing position on execution. Thus, all can be satisfied and the public protected by a system of "capital imprisonment." In other words, life imprisonment would mean life imprisonment. Societies wealthy enough to be squeamish about execution for heinous crimes are wealthy enough to afford this moral luxury.

13

Pulpit Socialism
The Church Against
Democratic Capitalism

Socialism . . . is the economic realization of the
Christian Gospel.

William Temple, Archbishop of Canterbury

As bishops, we do not claim to be technical
experts in economic matters. Our primary role is to
be moral teachers in society.

From *Ethical Reflections on the Future of Canada's
Socio-Economic Order*, prepared by the Canadian Conference of
Catholic Bishops, Dec. 1983

THE ORGANIZED RELIGIONS of the world have always exercised a
certain authority over economic life. From mediaeval church regulations on the "just price" to be paid for an article, to penalties on the
charging of interest, to the kind of theocracy now entrenched in Iran —
religions as social arbiters of moral life wield a great, but not always
beneficial, influence on material well-being. In the free Western democracies, it was the formal *separation* of the political, economic, and
moral-cultural realms, combined with legal checks and balances to
prevent their re-unification under a tyrannical ruler or regime, that
spurred previously undreamed-of wealth. Chapter Four explored how
this separation unleashes phenomenally creative commercial instincts
everywhere the tools of freedom and wealth creation have been truly

and well used. It was precisely this threefold separation that allowed Western society to escape the rigidification, stagnation, and class confinement common to all older societies, much of which had been church inspired. (The difference can be seen in the stark contrast between North and South America today.) For the first time in history, the old top-down hierarchies had given way to a new, bottom-up "system" called democratic capitalism, which relied upon *the free expression of the humanity of each individual, under rules of the game common to all.* Much of the morality and industriousness of this system derived from the legacy of the Judeo-Christian tradition of individual freedom and responsibility against the background of human imperfection, or sin (hence, the need for checks and balances). Since the dawn of the Industrial Revolution, the Church has more or less accepted, and sometimes defended, this system (if not always openly admiring its results), because it is in accord with Christian views on morality: just rewards for hard work, personal responsibility, and God's command that man should "be fruitful and multiply, and fill the earth and subdue it" (Genesis 1:28). Today, however, the Church has shifted from not openly admiring the results of democratic capitalism, to openly attacking the results, and the system itself, on moral grounds.

DOES GOD LOVE SOCIALISM?

WHILE MOST OF US are aware that Christianity has never openly advocated the pursuit of riches for their own sake ("For the love of money is the root of all evil," Timothy 6:10), and has always been anti-materialistic in this limited sense, it nevertheless comes as a bit of a shock to learn that many of today's organized churches — especially the Roman Catholic Church — are campaigning from the pulpit and elsewhere for what amounts to a utopian collectivism that aims to subordinate all economic life to the Church's view of morality. For the Roman Catholic Church "has consistently maintained that there is an ethical order to be followed in the organization of an economy." This attitude is especially evident in Latin America, where, against the Pope's wishes, a Catholic-sponsored, pseudo-Marxist version of theology — "liberation theology" — has taken hold.[1]

This subject is so vast and far-reaching that we are confined to a brief overview here of what bothers the Church, and what it proposes be done. I will try to show that these proposals are politically, economically, and even morally confused and constitute a fundamental attack on our way of life that cannot be good for our economy and our moral life, or for the Church. For this limited purpose I will draw on only a few documents, namely, Pope John Paul II's encyclical "Laborem Exercens" (Sept. 15, 1981); the U.S. Bishops' Pastoral Letter (third draft, June 5, 1986); and "Ethical Reflections on the Future of Canada's Socio-Economic Order," by the Canadian Conference of Catholic Bishops (December, 1983). These will be referred to as LE, PL, and CB respectively. Other mainstream Christian churches regularly publish on many of the same themes, but usually in a more fragmented form. So when, below, a view is referred to as put forth by "the Church," it will be based primarily on the three documents cited.

There are two basic problems concerning economic life smouldering at the heart of Christianity. These have to do with the unique subjective nature of man, and with the nature of private property. Ironically, the Church is using these two most important building blocks of democratic capitalism against it.

THE CHURCH SAYS WE MUST TREAT EACH OTHER AS PERSONAL SUBJECTS

THE FIRST VOLLEY IN the Church's offensive is the idea that "man is made to be in the visible universe an image and likeness of God himself, and he is placed in it in order to subdue the earth" (LE: Intro.). In other words, because we are made in God's image, we must always act as subjects in that world and never allow ourselves to be treated as objects, or treat others as objects (to use a current favourite term, we must not exploit, or be exploited). Human relations must always be personal, never impersonal.

We will see how this is a common recurring theme used to justify the "reforming" of democratic capitalism. Even the secular philosopher Immanuel Kant relied on this principle when he insisted that we must all treat each other as ends, and never as means to our ends. And Karl Marx was elaborating the same theme (see Chapter Five) when he promoted the distinction between *usage* value and *exchange* value in condemning capitalism as "alienating."

What all these moral dicta have in common is a nostalgia for a primitive, communitarian way of life in which each human relationship is direct, personal, and fully consummated by the relationship itself. In authentic relationships, in other words, there should be no ulterior, or excess motive. Personal human relations shall be always at the centre of our actions. I-Thou, never I-It. This view fails to consider, however, that in a complex, populous, and therefore hierarchical world, in which hundreds of socio-economic "relationships" must be entered into, this is not only impossible, but counterproductive. For we interact daily with others electronically through financial or communications services in ways that affect total strangers, and often we must control people many layers beneath us, or answer to others many layers above, with maximum efficiency and minimum delay. While purely personal relations might be the norm in a hypothetical primitive community that had no problems of production and no real economy to deal with (the Garden of Eden), in a modern technocratic world they are wisely reserved for friendship, love, marriage, and family. Otherwise, they simply get in the way.

I will argue, contrary to the bishops, that a key factor in the moral and economic success of democratic capitalism is in fact its very *impersonality*, and that this impersonality is not cruel, but humane, for it exacts a high standard of objective performance from all without regard to favouritism, family, money, race, or personality. It is precisely the vast network of impersonal, economic actors, each serving the whole in a self-interested, but necessarily other-regarding way, that breeds success, and greater wealth for all:

> *Our basic mistake may be the belief that we must choose between personal, face-to-face societies and impersonal societies. If we accept as fully legitimate the impersonal, rule-coordinated societies in which we participate, we are not repudiating or depreciating in any way marriage, the family, intimacy, I-Thou relationships, the unique value of the individual, or the power and significance of personal caring and sacrifice.*[2]

The personal life the bishops naively wish to inject into necessarily impersonal economic relationships can only cause "noise" in the system. Communication confusion. Misinterpreted signals. In the many cultures where such noise is the norm, it inevitably leads to graft, politicization of the economic sphere, and economic and social rigidification. The Catholic societies of Latin America are typical of this. Because they have not stressed impersonality in economic life, under common rules for all, they end up with moral, political, or bureaucratic tyranny. The Peruvian Hernando de Soto's book *The Other Path* is a painfully elegant examination of the consequences: unimaginable bureaucratic stagnation, a sprawl of illegal businesses, a huge underground economy. Paradoxically, the most humane way to treat another *economic* person is impersonally — *provided* that this way is institutionalized and protected in law, with the same rules for all. Otherwise, graft and bribery become the easiest way to "win."

In Chapter Four we discussed the importance of individualism and personhood for morality and productivity. Although the Church formerly accepted and even supported this foundation of democratic capitalism and abstained from comment on social outcomes, it is now using these same foundations as arguments to "reform" democratic capitalism, hoping to eliminate what it sees as inequalities and social conflicts. In short, from its former position of supporting "negative rights" (the right of each person *not to be interfered with*, to exercise his freedom under common rules equal for all), it has now swung around to campaigning for "positive rights," for *claims against the State for equal social and material outcomes for all* (the Church promotes the Rights Illusion). In other words, the Church has rapidly become a secularized institution, adopting the fashionable political agenda of the day. It now asserts that as subjects of creation, heirs, you might say, to the fruits of the earth, "all persons have certain inalienable rights," which include "all that makes for a more fully human life such as adequate food, clothing, shelter, employment, health care, education, and effective participation in decisions affecting their lives" (CB: p.6).

This statement, which reads like a paragraph issued by the United Nations, sounds desirable, until we think about it hard. For unless God is going to provide all these things free of charge to everyone on earth, it means they will have to be forcibly taken from those who have them, and given to those who don't. In this respect, the Church today falls in line with the social-welfare State in seeing these commonly desirable things not as *goals* to be freely striven for by all, while private (especially Church) charity protects the truly needy, but as *claims* by some, against other honest, hard-working people, via the State (the agent that for a sizeable commission will look after the forcible extraction and redistribution). The Church no longer sees life's amenities as a reward for hard work, as security derived from wise financial care, or as benefits accruing from personal effort and foresight, but as plain and simple rights, *without regard to merit*. Thus the Church, which might once have been accused by the political left of being conservative, or right wing, because of its inaction in economic matters, is now distinctly socialist, or left wing, and in some quarters — mostly through liberation theology in Latin America — is openly Marxist.

Curiously, the Church utterly ignores the inspiring example of millions upon millions of destitute immigrants who came to North America before our benevolent welfare State existed. These people worked very hard and succeeded by their own efforts, to a great extent *because* they were too proud to ask for hand-outs, and too ashamed to claim that others should provide them with things they had not earned. And the Church supported the morality of that ethic. But today the Church has developed artful arguments to excuse dependence, and to spread the psychology of excuse and resentment among millions of people, especially in poor countries. Tragically, the Church relies for its reasoning on all the Popular Illusions. (See Chapter Two.) Paradoxically, it is now actively promoting a lust for unearned material wealth, as distinct from its traditional appeals for genuine charity, thus contributing not to the uplifting of individuals, but to their increasing dependence and moral confusion.

THE CHURCH SAYS THE FRUITS OF THE EARTH BELONG TO ALL

THE SECOND CORNERSTONE OF the bishops' attack has to do with private property, and stems from the argument that God's creation is originally given to all equally, and thus "all persons in a given society should have the right of common access to, and use of, the goods produced by the economy" (CB: p.5). In the Church's view, "the primary purpose of a socio-economic order should be to develop its resources to serve the common good" (CB: p.6). Notice that the Church is not plugging for wider access to public parks, but for common access to the *goods* produced by the owners of productive establishments, to things *created* by owners. The conflict with democratic capitalism is blatant. For the right to common access implies that unless someone *buys* these goods to distribute them to those who have less than others, they will have to be *taken* by force and redistributed by the State.

The Church says that "the right to private property is subordinated to the right to common use" (LE: p. 14). This is not a surprising claim in itself, for democratic societies usually delegate to government a power to expropriate for the common good, *provided just compensation is paid to the owner*. But taking a piece of your private land to put a highway through, and paying you for it, is quite different from taking a few thousand gallons of milk from your farm, or shirts you have just made from your linen shop, and giving them to the poor without your leave and without compensation. Naturally, the State will camouflage the theft-like nature of this act by extracting such goods in the form of taxes. For the Church's view, once again, is that of communitarian socialism, for it is de-emphasizing its own role as provider and promoter of voluntary charity and is promoting instead what I have described as the coercive humanitarianism of the social-welfare State. With an extremely dubious moral authority, the Church would replace what it claims are the impersonal, therefore unauthentic, economic relationships between free parties, with the decidedly more deeply unauthentic, and impersonal relationships of coercive humanitarianism. The U.S. bishops, but not the Canadian, are careful to distance themselves from collectivist and totalitarian methods, even while they fail to see that this is where their thinking must lead (PL: p.113).

In order to secure all property for God, the Pope talks of a "social mortgage" that requires all owners to use their property for the common good (PL: p.113). Ownership, under this view, is a legal, but not an absolute right. This is not so surprising either, since "you can't take it with you," as the saying goes. Hence, owners are said to be mere "stewards" of property put to the common good. By this, the Church does not mean the common good of their customers (the democratic capitalist view), but of society as a whole, and of employees (the Church campaigns for common share ownership, to be provided through profit sharing), and for "social control" of the means of production. We can once again see the conflict this creates between the "common good" as arrived at by millions, rather billions, of the world's consumers freely deciding what they want to do with their own hard-earned resources (good companies are totally beholden to them, and rewarded by them for supplying such goods), and the "common good" as a theological idea of equity superimposed on this free activity. The Church wants the supply of goods to be "produced" by taking resources from those who create them, and giving them those who do not, all dictated by the social policy of the State with the backing of the Church.

Alas, the Church's misguided search for material equality through a handicap system is in vain. Not only will it fail to provide for the disadvantaged, but it also will hasten the demise of our whole system of freedom and wealth creation — the only system that has ever successfully fed, clothed, and sheltered the poor. (One of the few things that economists agree on, regardless of their political stripe, is that the disappearance of true poverty and a high GNP are very highly correlated — at about the 84 percent level.)

But The Church Is Anti-Profit

Not surprisingly, the Church is against the so-called profit motive, referring to "economic strategies aimed at maximizing private profits and consumption . . . [as] *distorted models of development*" (CB: p.7).

Such sophomoric economic pronouncements ought to embarrass the Church. For profits are never the sole reason for a business. But they are essential to it, for re-investment, growth, long-term planning, creation of new and better products, and so on. That is, a business is no more in business to make profits than a ship is in the sea to float. It is in the sea to get to its destination, to meet its many objectives, and how well or poorly it stays afloat along the way is a sign of its buoyancy, or health. Profits are like a waterline to the business, or a grade for a term paper. High profits are an A+, losses are an F. But most crucially, profits are a sign of competitive and productive efficiency. They are a reward for high-quality performance bestowed upon the business by its satisfied customers. As a key element in double-entry bookeeping, profitability is one of the tools of freedom and wealth creation — part of the financial "language" that has made democratic capitalism so successful. For a consistent, objective, internationally understood def-inition of profitability tells everyone involved — customers, sharehold-ers, investors, bankers, buyers, economists — that the entity is efficient and gaining strength for new growth. Even though in the parable of the talents (Matthew 25: 14-30) it was "the unprofitable servant" (who failed to put the Lord's money to good use) who was cast into outer darkness — the Church apparently condemns such activity.

ARE THERE "GOOD" PROFITS, AND "BAD" PROFITS?

LET US IMAGINE A benevolent entrepreneur who wants to supply the poor of the whole world with loaves of bread and fishes at the lowest imaginable price. He borrows money and creates a factory for this purpose. But soon he discovers that as a profitless operation, he cannot expand, buy new equipment, and produce more loaves and fishes. In fact, unless he continues to contribute his own limited resources, he will soon go bankrupt, for more money is needed for upkeep, modernization, replacement of worn-out equipment, realty taxes, staff benefits, utilities, and debt service. He is locked in. What will increase his capacity to produce loaves and fishes? Only profits. If he tries to operate on a fixed flow of revenue, the factory must eventu-ally be shut down. On the other hand, steady profits will enable him to re-invest, grow, and build more fish and bread factories. The more the better. Only an "economic strategy aimed at maximizing private prof-its" enables him to fulfil his business objective of feeding the poor of the world.

Would the Church counsel him to cut profits and produce less? Or to give away his profits to the poor, thus forestalling new growth? Of course not. And so it goes, more indirectly, with every business. It is the productive, profitable businesses of democratic capitalism that produce bread and fish of innumerable kinds, and wherever these businesses are encouraged to thrive under the same rules for all, they directly or indirectly feed the poor of the world. Is it irreverent to suggest that a modern Jesus would approve of the "miracle" of the free market whereby loaves and fishes are made available in abundance to the multitudes? (Perhaps not as fast or as much as the Bishops would like — but by far much better than any other system has even approached.)

An example of this is available south of our border, where "even the 28 million blacks in the U.S., arguably the worst-off of the U.S. population, have a cumulative income ($200 billion in 1985) larger than the gross domestic product of all but nine other nations of the world."[3] Meanwhile, as those living under socialism become progressively worse off — 40 million Soviets earn less than $140 a *month* ("Soviets grappling with issue of poverty," *Toronto Star*, July 9, 1989) — democratic capitalism continues to turn out loaves and fishes for the world. Why would the Church want to make this cornucopia machine *less* productive, and *less* efficient, by dampening the profit motive? What my own parable suggests is that the Church is making an implicit distinction between good and bad profits. Economically, it cannot truly be against profits themselves, but only against what it must regard as misdirected profits. Which boils down to saying that the Church wants to decide for society — for millions of individuals — what profits should be used for what purposes.

A Clash Of Values

WHAT THE CHURCH REALLY WANTS, I suggest, is to transform the great wealth of some into its notion of sufficiency for all. Instead of a few eating steak, and others bread, it wishes to guarantee that everyone gets bread — and never mind the steak. But this is the Equality Illusion at work. For by taking away the steak from all those who produce the bread, the bread will disappear, too. The Soviet Union is our best example of this, where millions stand in queues all day long for a loaf of bread, even though the U.S.A. and Canada send their government nearly *all* their excess wheat! By outlawing the steak for some (always excepting the privileged governing elite), the Soviets have eliminated the bread for all. The resentment-oriented handicappers of the world refuse to admit that a free, democratic capitalist nation under the same laws for all will eventually create enough bread for all — and steak for a good number as it does so.

How strange it is that the Church today should cast its lot with the handicappers, telling us that "the needs of the poor take priority over the wants of the rich" and calling for "an equitable re-distribution of wealth and power among peoples and regions" (CB: p.8). You don't have to be super-bright to understand that wealth and power do not exist in the world as fixed commodities to be divvied up by churchmen or politicians. They are *produced* by the few, but benefit many. If they are not produced, they simply will not exist. Under our system, it is those who make the most important contribution or take the biggest risks that end up with the biggest share. (Sure, some undeserving fallen souls benefit, but these exist under any system.) In short, you may redistribute all the golden eggs we now have, but if you kill the goose, there will be no more eggs at all.

There is no socio-economic system that has ever succeeded in creating general wealth by stifling those who produce wealth and take high risks, and the Church will certainly not succeed in such a goal. The egalitarianism it strives for will be that of the equally wretched. This is something with which the Roman Catholic Church in particular is familiar, as a large number of poor nations are Catholic, collectivist, and authoritarian — and Communism seems disproportionately to have found a home in them. Such nations end up with neither food nor freedom.

THE CHURCH WOULD DEPRIVE WORKERS OF THEIR FREEDOM

As PART OF ITS misplaced concern for personal relationships, the Church has decided that there are two key "instruments of production": capital and technology. It promotes "the principle of the priority of labour over capital" (LE: p.12) and the participation and self-determination of employees, so that they can become "subjects of their own history." This makes about as much sense as the farmer who argues vehemently that the cart ought to pull the horse.

In short, "Laborem Exercens," the basis for most of these reflections, is about as close as one could get to a pseudo-Marxist economic analysis by the Church. It has the same faults as Marxism in that it falsely divides the world into capital, technology, and labour, totally ignores the entrepreneurial, wealth-creating, risk-based process of business formation, and outlaws the free contracting of labour which, it says, "should not be treated as a commodity, to be bought and sold in the market place" (CB: p.7). It complains that although in Genesis we learned that man is to be the *subject* of creation, this has become reversed under capitalism, where man's labour is bought and sold as a commodity *object* — now one of the unattractive marks of the capitalist system (LE: p.7). Alas, the Church fails to distinguish between man himself (the subject) and his labour (the object bought and sold). For only a fool or a slave has ever confused these two things, and some of our greatest literature — such as *One Day in the Life of Ivan Denisovich* — shows that even under conditions of unspeakable deprivation, man's distinctive feature is his enduring subjectivity. Contrary to the bishops, and to Marx, one of the great advances of human life is that subjects in the democratic capitalist system are free to sell their labour as a commodity, without sacrificing any of their individuality, and without engaging themselves in the risk of the enterprise to which it is sold. Further, because their labour is a freely traded commodity (not controlled by any authority), they can bargain, hold out for more pay, go on strike, or pool their labour and start their own businesses. Commodity labour, along with the use of money, has given working people a freedom they never had before in human history, through which they can forge their own destinies, beholden neither to king, politician, nor employer, trapped neither by fealty, political system, nor by the man who pays them for their work. It is for this reason that labour *must* be treated as a commodity. For otherwise it is constrained by some *political* notion of its value, as in the collectivist nations.

Where labour is not a freely bought and sold commodity, workers are told what their work is worth, told where to work, and told what to produce, regardless of their personal talents or ambitions. We had a recent example of this in Canada, where physicians were told where to practise in British Columbia. In Ontario, they are being told what they may or may not earn, and may soon be put on a fixed salary. And employers are now being told what to pay low-earning women (but not men). I'm sure that ordinary labourers will not be happy if their subjective right to sell their own services objectively is determined by the State. Alas, the Church's principle of "the priority of labour" is leading in this direction and will render no kindness unto labour. Once again, we see that, like the modified Marxism it regurgitates, the Church has no economics of wealth creation — only an economics of wealth distribution. The Holy Handicapper has arrived.

THE CHURCH WANTS COMMUNITY PLANNING

THE CHURCH WOULD ALSO like to see "local communities identify their basic needs . . . and acquire communal control over the necessary means of production" (CB: p.9). It seems to have in mind a warm, communal world in which the citizens of the nation sit around the campfire each night to decide what it is they want for breakfast, who will cook, clean up, gather wood for the fire, and so on. It is searching for a "sustainable model of development" (a phrase borrowed from the human-potential groupies), as if innovation, productive break-throughs, and marketing genius came from fixed "models." But they don't. They arise from the millions of striving, competitive commercial interactions (all bound by the same laws) that constitute the incomprehensibly complex but stunningly efficient economic sorting process at work under the Church's very nose. The creation and control of a "model" for national economic planning cannot work without first expropriating all the wealth in the nation and then controlling the daily choices of every individual (see Chapter Five). Even then, it will fail, as it has in all socialist nations so far. Central planning, whether on an atheistic model like Marx's, or on the theological basis of the Church, is doomed to failure simply because no central intelligence or moral being can ever know what would be required for success. For one thing, the "common good" is always debatable, as is the nature of "social justice."

Setting standards for such elusive concepts through coercive social policy can easily ruin a society simply because in the absence of any objective definitions, political goals are always set in their place. Societies then become thoroughly fractious as warring groups raid the public purse ostensibly in the name of these goals — but really at the expense of the politically weak. To envisage the result of national moral or economic planning we need only ask ourselves what would happen if a national chess coach were suddenly to order all chess players in the country to move their Queens two spaces to the right. The mere thought is ridiculous. Yet, in effect, that has been the moral and economic rule for more than seventy years in the U.S.S.R. where chess is the national sport. Today, we are witnesses to the chaotic, if stirring, result.

Typically, the churchmen's "model" is what the top-down collectivists are always searching for. It starts in the minds of planners instead of in the hearts and hands of ordinary people and their families. This is a great danger to us all: unity of control expressed through a model for development, directed by a Church ethic of what is good socio-economic policy. In short, it wants top-down, collectivist government making every important human decision, instead of what we have historically preferred, which is *every individual human being making his own important decisions*. The Church wants a social revolution, whereby the community "acquires communal control" (meaning, expropriates private property and businesses) and "empowers" the people to direct their own lives (meaning, subjects them to policy direction from above).

My suggestion to the workers of the free world is that they reject this innocent-seeming pastoral advice as quickly as they can, because it is designed to take their freedoms away. Oh, the very few might have more bread on the table for a little while (if there are resources left over after the Holy Bureaucracy finishes administering its social justice), but they will eat in sorrow, as new objects of the great social "model," for the Church says "the State has the responsibility to intervene in the operations of an economy to ensure that basic human rights and moral principles are realized" (CB: p.10). It's not a great leap from this to a situation in which the peasants, once they have finished their piece of dry bread, are ordered to relocate to a new industrial village where, the government has decided, a morally correct industry will produce for the common good. Not to worry that the house the peasant has toiled all his life to acquire must now be sold — again for the common good. President Ceausescu of Romania was relocating hundreds of thousands of workers and destroying their ancestral homes on precisely this moral concept, as did Nyerere of Tanzania before him, and Stalin before him.

THE CHURCH'S "ONE WORLD" THINKING

As IF IT WERE not enough for a theological body to secularize its teachings and insist on national social revolution, the Church now preaches the collectivist, one-world arguments of the New International Economic Order (NIEO), which we reviewed in Chapter Nine, telling us that "the structural causes of poverty and oppression in the Third World, for example, are linked to the international economic order dominated by affluent and powerful nation states of the First World" (CB: p.10).

Intellectual model-builders love the word "structural," because it enables them to blame what irks them on a seemingly autonomous, objective system that produces the evil results they wish to change. The

Church has really fallen for the Third World sham and ought to spend a few hours with Peter Bauer to get itself straightened out. If it did, it would learn that there is a continuously fluctuating range of wealth among nations from top to bottom, and no distinct group is identifiable as "Third World"; that all the former colonies, especially of Britain, have thrived compared with less developed countries that were never colonized, all their modern amenities having been brought to them by nations of the so-called "First World"; that multinational companies bring employment and wealth to otherwise destitute nations and are very much appreciated, in fact lavishly courted by them, for this; and that Third World nations *without* former colonial experience and *without* a multinational presence are the poorest of all. Just contrast them with the stunning success of Taiwan, Korea, Hong Kong, Singapore, and Japan — all once "Third World" nations that welcomed Western influence and multinational corporate relations.

The Church has got it backwards, to the detriment of its flock. The *last* thing the so-called Third World needs is more top-down collectivist government, more subsidies, more planning, and more redistribution of already scarce wealth. These are all "transactions of decline," in Jane Jacobs's words. Rather, it needs basic freedom from these very things and the tyrants who impose them (including Church tyrants) so that the people themselves can express their own economic being, and benefit directly.

How The Church Errs In Temporal Judgements

IN DECEMBER 1983, when the "Canadian Conference of Catholic Bishops" brief was published, Canada was enduring a recession the bishops said was "symptomatic of a deeper structural crisis that is taking place in the international system of industrial capitalism itself" (CB: p.11). The bishops echoed Pope John Paul II's view that "industrial societies are moving from a relatively benevolent to a more rigid stage of capitalism that holds forth the prospect of a grim future" (CB: p.11; LE: p.1). This predicted grimness is part of the catastrophism of the Church's thinking: masssive unemployment, replacement of workers by machines and technology, pollution, lower standards of living, higher energy costs and food costs, and so on. But what has really happened?

Since 1983, unemployment in Canada has gone steadily down, and in July 1989 was at its lowest in decades. In Toronto, the most entrepreneurial part of Canada, it is virtually nil, labour is in demand everywhere, and the so-called "unemployment" rate of 3 or 4 percent is mostly accounted for by those who are changing jobs, who prefer welfare to work, or think they are too good for a lesser job, or who are so shiftless, uneducated, and unconcerned they are unemployable, or (worst of all) otherwise employable people who have persuaded themselves that the pogey is a "right." You'd think the Church — so concerned about unemployment — would study why Toronto and its environs have created so many jobs and coax the rest of Canada to imitate this startling entrepreneurial explosion, instead of planning to sap Toronto's wealth and send it around the country in little equalization parcels, thus stifling the entrepreneurs and subsidizing the dependence of the recipients.

As for technology? Our fortunate commercial proximity to the U.S.A. has enabled us to benefit from the most exciting technological revolution ever known. The silicon chip, high-speed communications, and computers have changed the world since 1983, and there have been millions of jobs created in their wake. But while technology doesn't necessarily displace workers (the Church's fear), it may force them to relocate. In a free society, that's just fine, for the smart ones can see it coming and prepare themselves, their businesses, or their skills. And the faster the change in the economy, the greater the need for flexibility. (The not-so-smart ones still benefit by the general increase in wealth.) But in a rigidly bureaucratized society, where values are increasingly controlled by government, lethargy is the rule; people — in fact, whole nations — get caught napping (paralysed by government wage rates, government pricing, and government "training" programs, developed not by market forces for those who need the labour, but by bureaucrats who need to rationalize their programs).

As for the environment? Pollution control of industry has much improved. For the first time in thirty years, Lake Ontario water is life-supporting — thirty-pound salmon are being caught daily off the shores of Toronto (there are still too many chemicals in them, but at least they're swimming). And for a city its size, Toronto's air is better than most such cities in the world. As for dirty, bacteria-infested beaches? We should point the finger at local governments who persist in dumping sewage and road salt into our lakes and rivers. In Quebec, especially from Montreal, sewage flows into the St. Lawrence River untreated. Why is the environmentalists' campaign almost always directed at industry, and rarely at government? British Columbia is very fond of tourists and doesn't dare forbid them to dump raw sewage from boats straight into the ocean. No, the cure for pollution is not the destruction of industry but the restoration of common tort law so that ordinary citizens can stop anyone else from polluting their property.

As for our standard of living? It's never been higher. The democratic capitalism the Church wants to "reform" has given Canada about the fourth highest standard of living in the world, with GDP growth in these years averaging around 3.0 percent. And how about energy and food costs? Notwithstanding rapacious monopolizing by the OPEC nations, and our own past government's efforts to destroy our oil and gas industry through the National Energy Program, fuel is plentiful. There has been a fuel glut for a decade now, and energy prices have been relatively low and stable for years as a result.

In terms of food costs as a percentage of average weekly income, North Americans in general pay the least of any people in the world for food. And perhaps the only revolution worth the name to have truly succeeded in human history is the American, democratic-capitalist-inspired "green," or agricultural revolution that has resulted in continuous bumper crops wherever it has been introduced.

Embarrassingly, the Church has mired itself in economic and environmental catastrophism and made foolish predictions accordingly. It should stick to counselling us on personal morality, where there may well be grounds for a bit of catastrophism. (Chapter Twelve, on our criminal-justice system, suggests there is ample room for the Church to help society morally, whereas it can only hurt us with its unsolicited economic counsel.) As the classical conservative never tires of telling us: if we were all to conduct our personal lives properly and extend basic charity to any suffering neighbours, there would be no problem. This should be the Church's constant concern.

Everyone Must Share

But not the church. Throughout the three documents studied here we read of the need for more common and widespread share ownership and a call for "new forms of worker-controlled industries" (CB: p.22). The naive assumption throughout is that companies ought gladly to give away their assets to workers who have not invested funds in them. There is no reason why workers shouldn't own part of the action, so to speak. And many do. In fact, the world's democracies are distinguished by a broad share ownership of industry, and nothing prevents a worker from purchasing shares in public companies instead of other consumer goods. But what prevents the kind of general ownership so important to the bishops is not the greed of owners — many of whom are often searching for inexpensive capital — but the reluctance of workers to accept the risks of ownership, of losing their investments. For what if the share values go down? I came perilously close to such an event this past year when the shares of a company in which I was tempted to invest a substantial sum went from more than $12 to 76 cents per share in the space of twelve months. The bishops do not appreciate the fact that the average worker would rather have the security of a reliable wage, and gradual modest savings, than run the risks of investment in shares. After all, the "death" rate of small operating businesses in Canada in recent years has often hit 40 percent of "births," and no one protects these owners against losses. Well then, the thinking goes, could companies not guarantee the values of the shares the workers purchase? No, for such guarantees would then be a liability of the company and drag its share value down. It's a fiduciary circle. How about profit-sharing plans, then? I've had experience with these, too. First of all, they're really production tools, not ownership tools, for the employees share only in the profits and not in the losses of the corporation. Such profit shares are soon seen as rights, like regular pay, and the mood quickly backfires when the company suffers losses and no bonuses are available for a time, or are lost for good.

But general ownership by all employees doesn't even work in theory, simply because democracy in a corporation converts the latter into a government-like, political organization.

"Democratic" business decisions are automatically and inherently political because they are arrived at to please the strongest party's interests. They are addressed to concerns internal to the organization, not to external production and market matters, where the real business competition is taking place. And secondly, what might be good for the business in the long term may not be good for the strongest employee voting bloc in the short term. So there is always an inherent conflict between good business management and democratic decision-making, for the long-term purposes of a business and of the labour that serves it are rarely one and the same. The horse has to pull the cart, not the other way around. Millions of business people know this instinctively and have already settled the dilemma as to who should call the shots: the owners, those who are taking the biggest risks. It's common sense. The Church's "reforms" can only undo this highly functional and productive order, not improve it.

But perhaps the most ironical aspect of the Church's insistence on broad ownership, especially in the Pastoral Letter of the U.S. bishops (PL: p.347), is this. The bishops call upon the Church to set its own house in order first, by recognizing discrimination, poor pay, and the like. Then it calls upon its flock to give more money to the Church for this purpose. This seems innocent enough (not to miss an opportunity!). But here's the rub: although by any estimate the Roman Catholic Church is the owner of world-wide assets worth billions of dollars, there is not a whisper in its many documents about distributing share ownership in the Church's properties, and other assets, to its own employees, or to the poor of the world. What is good for the goose is apparently not so good for the gander.

WHY ISN'T THE CHURCH ATTACKING GOVERNMENT?

THE GREATER MYSTERY, though, is not that the Church attacks democratic capitalism — a perennial target — but that it does *not* attack the actions of government, which is responsible for a goodly number of social ills. For example, the Church calls for full employment, but defends the minimum wage. (It actually calls for the imposition of a controlled "just wage," just as the medieval Church controlled the "just price" of commodities.) However, one of the few things the world's economists agree upon is that the minimum wage causes unemployment, especially among the poor and the young.

The Church also wants to provide better social services but fails to see that the money for this must be taken first in taxes from productive citizens, and that if too much is taken they will cease to be productive. Furthermore, it fails entirely to address the immorality of paying for such services with borrowed money, as we have done in Canada ever since the late 1960s, and consequently of breaking the moral contract with tomorrow's children by obliging them to pay for social services consumed by us, while saddling them with our debt. Further, the Church fails utterly to attack the government's swollen and costly bureaucracies that are administering this glut of credit-financed goods and services. It never once insists that our huge debt burden could be solved and inflation ended by cutting government itself. By this omission, it supports increased taxation.

Thoroughly undaunted by such government-created fiscal and moral scandal, the Church now wants the basics of life guaranteed for all as "rights," but fails to ask who will be required by law to provide them. Of course, more will have to be borrowed, while the Church passes neatly over the greater immorality of encouraging whole segments of society to claim as "rights" from others material wealth that they had no hand in creating themselves, and often show no intention of creating. (Subsidies generate the behavior that attracted them.) It wants to find new ways to redistribute this claimed wealth and power among people and regions, without regard to the effort and sacrifice of those who create that wealth or the merit of those to whom it is given. (All are assumed to be equally meritorious.)

Worst of all, while ostensibly defending the traditional family, it fails to attack the State for drawing up State daycare plans that would provide incentives for parents to transfer their children to the impersonal care of State nannies while financially penalizing sacrificing parents who decide that anything less than personal care of children is inadequate. Consider the case of two couples with three children each that need $60,000 per year to live. The couple that bring home $30,000 each and opt to put the kids in state daycare will pay fully $7,000 less tax per annum than the couple of which one parent stays home to raise the kids, while the other earns $60,000 alone. This is ruinous for the preservation and nurturing of families. A simple proposal by the Church to allow all families to "split" their income on a pre-tax basis would correct this matter instantly, but on this the Church is strangely silent. Although all this dependence-creating redistribution is to be carried out by means of coercive humanitarianism under the social-welfare State, in the very same breath the Church wants to "break the bonds of dependency and develop new economic strategies based on self-reliance" (CB: p.21). How, after all, can we deal with a Church that fails to perceive the moral conflict between these two basic aims, a conflict spelled out in the very first chapter of this book?

Worst of all, the Church is silent on the extent to which government policies dampen the productive capacities of democratic capitalism, destroy the entrepreneurial spirit, overburden small businesses with paperwork and regulations, and interfere with the cost reduction effects of competitive pricing through marketing boards of all kinds. Further, the Church is deaf and dumb on the matter of how government fiscal policy contributes to inflation — perhaps the greatest killer of the hopes of the poor ever invented. And finally, it says nothing about the fact that an ever-increasing share of the assets of the poor is being taxed away by government in return for services many of them never see, or don't want. If our government today were proportionately the same size it was in 1961, everyone would pay on average about 50 percent less tax than they do now!

Why, then, is the Church so silent on the government, the one institution that most obviously consumes the wealth of the poor and erodes the productive capacities of the nation? If the Church really wants to contribute to economic life, why doesn't it hold seminars on the process of wealth creation, successful investment, skills training, and the like; why not focus on the *process* of creating goods and services, instead of the *politics* of distributing them? Cynicism would suggest that the Church does not criticize government simply because it needs government to implement its own collectivist moral vision. The Roman Catholic Church in particular has been experiencing an exodus of worshippers and clergy over the past two decades; is it too cynical to suggest it has decided that by defending collectivist principles of resentment and redistribution it can appeal to the wider market of dependent souls who favour the social-welfare State? If you rob Peter to pay Paul, you can be sure that Paul will never complain.

CHAPTER

14

Government Jocks
The State And The
Corruption Of Sport

IT SEEMS THAT NOTHING escapes the long arm of the State in its quest for power. In the U.S.A., sport is 90 percent private; in Canada, it's 90 percent public. There are bound to be serious political, economic, moral, and cultural consequences of any wholesale State program to control "amateur" sport. For amateur sport as it existed a mere two decades ago is gone forever. No longer is there any sporting realm where even the illusion of pursuing the thing-in-itself remains. Athletes, just like doctors, teachers, and so many others, have become pawns of the State; in fact amateur sport has virtually leapt into its arms for money, which is the State's moral anaesthetic, so useful in its inexorable drive to control Canadian life, from top to bottom.

For twenty years I have been asked what's wrong with amateur sport, and my answer, always in sadness, has not changed: the three facts of life that have utterly and irredeemably changed amateur sport for the worse in the space of one generation, are politics, money, and drugs.

Sport of any kind is political because of its symbolic and moral dimensions. We will never forget that last-minute heart-stopping goal in 1972 as scrappy little Canada beat the awesome Soviet hockey machine. Neither will we forget the sadness of our recent national experience. We rose and fell thunderously as a nation with our hero Ben Johnson in a re-enactment of ancient Greek tragedy. Such emotional swings serve as a purgative ritual in a play, because you can walk away, all the wiser to face the world. But our play got ruined because we had to go backstage and get into the messy lives of all the actors, managers, coaches, physicians, financiers, and the rest of the incompetent lot that brought us such joy and pain. How dare they ruin our play? How dare they undermine the moral and emotional basis of our collective experience? If we cannot have our play, then let us have the truth.

OUR TOP AMATEUR ATHLETES HAVE BECOME WARDS OF THE STATE

THE TRUTH IS THAT over the past twenty years amateur sport in Canada has become hopelessly political in the very simple sense that our athletes are now wards of the State. Welfare athletes. State jocks and jockettes. As for so many things in our lives, State involvement is the beginning of the end. When I competed for Canada in the Decathlon in the 1964 Olympic Games in Tokyo, the State had barely raised its sporting head. Athletes then paid their own way to track meets, assisted by their clubs, communities, parents, relatives, and part-time jobs. At the outside, they may have received a free travel ticket from a meet organizer.

Our track and field team in Tokyo was only fifteen strong, was responsible for one-third of all the points collected by Canadians in those Games, and brought back a *silver* (Bill Crothers, 800 metres), a *bronze* (Harry Jerome, 100 metres), and several respectable international placings by other athletes, at almost no cost to the taxpayer. Not one of us was employed by the State. Today, like every other country, and a mere twenty-five years and countless millions of dollars later, we send mega-teams of career athletes around the world in jumbo jets — and we are not doing as well. What has happened? There is no simple answer. But the bottom line is that, subtly, the minds and morals of the sporting youth of this nation have been altered for the worse.

Despite my great love and respect for amateur sport's unforgettable moments of challenge and grandeur, for its capacity to mature and embolden, this is not a legion into which I will send any of my five children. For truly amateur sport is sport for the love of it. It is a consuming passion in the context of one's daily life and receives its meaning from the sacrifice and dedication that most people are not prepared to give. The moment athletes are supported by the State, the moral essence of amateurism is gone. At that point they become employees who quickly rely on the Rights Illusion to claim against the State, just as the taxpayer suddenly has claims and expectations against them. Next, we can expect to see an athletes' union and strikes against the State for more support. Why? Because Canadians have unwittingly permitted the total transformation of amateur sport. In the place of free and private individuals performing in the context of self-development, we have a top-heavy sports bureaucracy with an army of subsidized single-purpose athletes who are now an instrument of government policy.

At an Olympic athletes' meeting I attended in 1982, a serious suggestion was put forth that hundreds of these athletes had been "deprived" of education because they were competing for Canada. They were demanding "compensation for lost education." In a recent newspaper article, University of Toronto physical-education professor Bruce Kidd (who was on that 1964 team with me) lobbied for a minimum salary for international athletes at $32,000 per annum. Next we will have pay-equity demands (does a female high jumper deserve the same as a male shot putter?), demands for wage parity with U.S. athletes, and so on. Very fuzzy thinking indeed.

MOST AMATEUR ATHLETES ARE PROFESSIONALS

THE MOMENT ATHLETES are paid by anyone to compete, they are professionals in every sense of the word. Suddenly we view their exploits differently. Is anyone really moved by the long hours of training, the pain, or the "sacrifices" of athletes who are paid to train, who can make very big money from sponsorships, or who complain of the difficulties of free world-wide travel to exotic countries to experience the thrill of international sport? Of course not. Because these are no longer just athletes, they are gladiators on the dole; instruments of foreign policy that are costing us an arm and a leg in a war we can't possibly win, because we won't — and should never — go to the totalitarian extremes common in Eastern Bloc nations. Nevertheless, ten minutes after the lights went out at the most recent Olympics in Seoul, the sports bureaucrats started crying for more money to solve their problems — just as do the medical and teaching professions.

Once a nation decides to politicize and subsidize sport there can never be enough money, for the intervention of the State and its easy access to tax dollars has bypassed the only natural economic limitation on the growth of such State programs — the individual producer of wealth. So the money just goes down the hole we began to dig the moment we started paying athletes and sport bureaucrats. For once amateur sport is performed for money, the whole undertaking changes its meaning from heroic to pragmatic. The sense of pure pursuit is lost.

The idea of a lofty challenge taken up for its own sake is driven out. The athletes miss it. The bureaucrats miss it. Everyone misses it.

But we never stop to ask: If people like Bill Crothers, Harry Jerome, Bruce Kidd, and so many others could work full time, or get college degrees, and also make Olympic teams, set world and Commonwealth records, and win Olympic silver and bronze medals at the same time, why can't today's athletes? We are told that training is a full-time occupation today. But this is nonsense. First of all, no one has ever trained harder than these earlier athletes did. And besides, no one is physically capable of real training more than four hours a day — and of this, very little, at most half, can be all-out training. Beyond this, there is only high-class athletic pampering, or time-wasting. What are they doing with the other twenty hours each day? I suspect that Parkinson's Law sets in, and the job fills the time allotted.

Admittedly, there are special problems of travel to international competitions. But if you're good enough, there are always ways to work these out. And if you aren't good enough, you haven't earned it. But the real tragedy of the politicization and professionalization of our amateur athletes, in addition to the horrendous cost of this folly, is that through such incentives we reward athletes for staying dependent and foregoing the more important aspects of their self-development, in the same way that welfare rewards a worker for staying on the dole. The result is that many of these young people for whom sport ought to be a passion, never a vocation, will end up stunted individuals, spending more of their precious youth than they should chasing elusive medals that tarnish quickly with time.

A Lot Of Athletes Are Cheating

As LONG AGO AS the Olympic Games of 1968 I personally saw American gold-medal athletes take steroids. The problem is not new — just more widespread. In addition to the possible medical hazards, this last problem with "amateur" sport is really another moral crisis. Drugs can benefit an athlete's career only as long as their use is *secret*. For the natural moral effect of the news of drug use, on the market that consumes sport, is the discounting of performances — just what an athlete fears the most. It's one thing to win. It's another to live the rest of your life worrying that people think you cheated, that someone else should have gotten your medal, that without the drugs you couldn't have done it. This ethical problem, in combination with those brought about by politics and money, will drive all sport further down in the estimation of the sporting world, and of the athletes themselves. The dynamics of this inexorable chain of events is the same in whatever area of life in which the State becomes involved. State medicine, or education, drives the quality of care and the spirit of selflessness out of medicine, or teaching, in the same way that it drives the morality out of sport. For it converts these pursuits from ones in which the moral agent is responsible for his own costs and benefits into ones in which he is merely a player in a larger bureaucratic game, the costs of which are borne by anonymous others. Such games always grow larger, as "rent-seekers" (people coming to the public trough for careers and grants) grow ever more numerous, the justifications for each activity ever more urgent, the source of funds ever more anonymous. This, sport literally cannot afford.

As for keeping up with the totalitarian countries? We can't. They are obsessed with the political and symbolic value of sporting victory and will go to almost any extreme to win. If the U.S.A. can't beat them, how can little Canada? As for their use of steroids and other ergogenic tricks, why don't we turn our backs on the whole mess and get on with the real thing? Let's redefine the game, so that if they want to play with us, they'll have to do it by different rules.

What Is To Be Done?

THERE IS A NEED for radical surgery, which I suspect will never be performed because there are too many people with their noses in the trough. But if I had a magic wand to wave, here's what I would say and do.

First, Canada should declare that it refuses to play the big-time game of international State-sponsored sport any longer, because it is too expensive and brings with it the moral distortions outlined above.

Second, we should decide that the only role for the State is the provision of sport facilities, accessible to all people, and financed not through taxes but through special sport lotteries. These would amount to a wonderful capital legacy for present and future generations. How do we really expect to turn out great athletes when Ontario, our richest province, hasn't one facility good enough for hosting an international track meet? Neither have we a velodrome for cycling, nor, despite the fact we are a winter nation, a single oval for speedskating. So let's get the facilities, first. International excellence can then be encouraged through local club and community organizations and the dedication of individuals, their coaches, and their families, as it always used to be. This would have the effect of transforming the top-down French style of developing sport back to the bottom-up English style we ought never to have left behind. Once such local facilities were in place, nothing could then stop a dedicated athlete from doing his or her best in Canada. Good, dedicated coaches, paid and unpaid, will always appear to help.

Third, we must stop subsidizing athletes, all of whom should be encouraged to pursue their sport with utmost dedication so they don't become "sport cripples." This way Canada will refuse to crank out sport cripples, or tired, injured, thirty-five-year-old jocks with their hands out. It will recognize the deadening hand of the State on its own youth and opt for another way. Our idea will be to fit sport into your life, not life into your sport. Go to school, or get a job while you train, and give your life and your sporting victory some meaning!

Finally, how do we solve the problem of sport purity and drugs? The policing approach will not work in the long run, because the scientific establishment works for both sides. And ironically, both sides draw their funding from the government. But the cheaters will always be one step ahead, driving the problem deeper underground in the race to elude. For even when the authorities nab someone like Ben Johnson, the procedure causes highly undesirable public-relations damage. By its drug-policing efforts, sport shoots itself in the foot. So, since drugs aren't going to go away, and we don't want to enter an endless and expensive spiral chasing them down, here's a radical solution: Why not simply provide *two competitive categories* in sport? Category One would be for those who refuse money and drugs and hold a normal job. Category Two would have no limitations.

I realize that some will find this hard to imagine, messy to administer, or expensive. But it would be a lot less messy and expensive than the situation we have now, and at least it would have the enormous merit of restoring some of sport to the purity of purpose for which many of us long. Under such a system, most athletes would gladly give up all drugs to compete against each other in Category One, for a win there would *mean* so much more. I can assure you they would police each other, because the stress now would be on honesty, not secrecy, and I know which medal they would rather win. Come to think of it, we tried this idea about a hundred years ago — it was called "the Olympic Games" !

But the most important step is to withdraw State funding from sport other than for the provision of good facilities, which can be considered a legitimate function of the State. Without free access to the money of others, the athletic establishment and athletes themselves would be thrown back on personal, community, club, and other local resources. Then the moral relationship would be where it has always belonged in a free society — between athlete and family, athlete and community, athlete and friends offering support. There are many athletes who will think nothing of cheating the bureaucracy by taking money or drugs; but very few will risk cheating those close to their hearts. Thus do freedom and responsibility repel at every turn the State and its inimical morality. Thus are freedom and responsibility repelled if we lose our grip on them.

15

The Silent Destruction
Of English Canada
Multiculturalism, Bilingualism,
And Immigration

It is idiotic to think that immigrants will help us save
our language . . . and multiculturalism is a further
stupidity, because one must start by being
someone before one can be everyone.

Gilles Vigneault, Quebec singer

OPINION POLLS IN CANADA, the U.S.A., and Australia consistently
show strong to overwhelming majorities opposed to multiculturalism
policies that erode the core culture, to official bilingualism that pressures people to use languages in which they have no interest, and to
immigration policies that change their country's traditional ethnic
balance. Any reasonable person might therefore ask how it is possible
that the governments of these democratic nations nevertheless persist,
and succeed, in forcing such policies on the electorate.

In the space of two decades, all three of these countries — all largely
colonized from the British Isles — have become deeply mired in "multicultural" social policies. This has not at all been the case in the older,
more homogeneous cultures like Japan, China, Finland, and Norway,
which have had historical experience with policies destined to cause
social dislocation. Switzerland, which already hosts many nationalities,
is especially wary.

I must be clear at the outset that a dislike for government-imposed "multicultural" policies has nothing to do with disliking other cultures; such a response does not imply a racist or chauvinistic attitude. Most of us enjoy travelling to experience the differences between cultures — their histories, religions, values, arts, and languages. We all have roots in common, but very few of us have common roots. Unfortunately, there are vocal groups out there that seek to quash any discussion of this subject by deliberately equating criticism of multiculturalism with discrimination against the people the policy affects.

It is in the interest of the collectivist State to deceive us — to make us think it is merely teaching us to enjoy other cultures. After all, what could be more reasonable, or benign? But cynically, the State *promotes* what I have called the Discrimination Illusion through its multi-culturalism, bilingualism, and immigration policies — all calculated expressions of a specific, definable State ideology designed for the manipulation of popular opinion. That ideology, now dutifully and uncritically echoed by the media, is the ideology of egalitarianism, which got a real push in Canada under Tom Kent. Like many socialists, Kent saw the Toronto-Ontario WASP power axis as inimical to his egalitarian ideals, an expression of the democratic-capitalist ideology that socialists the world over seek to change. The way to dilute this power axis, he saw clearly, was to flood the cities with immigrants who were not white, Anglo-Saxon, or Protestant.

The purpose of his brand of one-world socialism was and remains the eventual achievement of a world-wide equality of social outcomes; a forced equalization of wealth, regardless of merit; and the neutral-ization of all value-preferences between different peoples and cultures. The goal of this policy is to replace all *natural* cultures with the idealistic, *artificial*, bureaucratic culture of the State itself; to replace moral values with political ones; natural differences with quotas; reli-gious beliefs with secular ones. In effect, the political leadership of this nation hit upon the idea that with such a tripartite thrust, it could overcome the difficulties inherent in governing people who are socially and culturally different. By dividing them (in the guise of uniting them under an abstract ideal), giving them money, and thus acquiring their vote, it could rule. Readers may want to ask themselves how it is that a mere handful of individuals like Mr. Kent can so change the face of this nation. Alas, he may yet live to see his policies rend Canada asunder, for each of them is self-contradictory (and therefore ulti-mately self-defeating), socially divisive, and destructive of the best interests of all the people of Canada.

Let us look at the multiculturalism policy — the first of three major steps in the State's struggle to homogenize the people. (Cost between 1986-88? $53 million.)

MULTICULTURALISM

IN 1971, CANADA BECAME officially "multicultural," following the recommendations of the Royal Commission on Bilingualism and Biculturalism. In 1988, through widespread advertising, the government of Canada proudly invited the people of Canada to "Celebrate the World's First Multiculturalism Act." In 1988 alone, it would spend more than $25 million on multicultural activities, narrowly defined. And that's just at the federal level.

The Standing Committee on Multiculturalism recommended eight *principles*, many of which inherently promote the junking of traditional values and require for their realization the coercion of the State. Not surprisingly, in one way or another, every principle conflicts with each of the others:

- Multiculturalism for all Canadians.

- Advancement of multiculturalism within a bilingual framework.

- Equality of opportunity.

- Preservation and enhancement of cultural diversity.

- Elimination of discrimination.

- Establishment of affirmative measures.

- Enhancement of heritage languages.

- Support for immigrant integration.

Leaving aside for the moment the most serious question as to what right the State has to take money from the citizens and use it to shape their cultural attitudes (a chilling reminder: Lenin said, "We must be engineers of souls"), here are some others. How can "immigrant integration" be achieved at the same time as promotion of "diversity"? Integration implies some compulsion, an unnatural forcing together of different parts; assimilation implies a voluntary act. But into what are immigrants to be integrated, and who will do the integrating? With what values, beliefs, and cultural bonds will they integrate? Their own? Those of the disappearing core culture? The State's imposed values? Through "affirmative" measures, will government force immigrants to "advance" by using French? Will it "promote" (read: spend more tax dollars on) every one of the United Nations' 159 official national languages (never mind the 5,000-odd language sub-groups)? How about the core beliefs, values, religions, and ethics of each different culture? How about when they conflict with English- or French-Canadian culture? After all, "equality of opportunity," which rightly means immigrants will be able to play by the same rules as everyone else, conflicts with the "establishment of affirmative measures" and the use of State coercion to achieve social outcomes. Evidently, the committee is confused. Ethnic groups, including the English, I assume, can arrange their lives as they wish, without impediment. But if in so doing they freely form ethnic cliques or otherwise choose not to involve other ethnic groups in their lives, then "affirmative action measures," with quotas, will be used to force them to do so. The committee is trying to suck and blow at the same time in its frenetic and expensive effort to fit us into its Coca-Cola image of one big happy Canadian family, all singing the same song. Superficially, of course, it all sounds quite attractive. So, ignoring for the moment the cost and the coercion required — enough in themselves to reveal the fraud involved — why can't it work?

THE CONTRADICTION AT THE HEART OF MULTICULTURALISM

SURELY, EVERYONE WANTS a happy family, whether one's own, or that of the nation. But there's a contradiction at the heart of any egalitarian multiculturalism policy. For the essence of the family, whether nuclear or national, is *natural* similarity. Similarity in appearances, values, beliefs, goals, religion, language, food, or whatever. In other words, *the essence of affiliation is the presence of natural common denominators*. The greater the number of common denominators, the stronger the family or cultural bonds. A national *unicultural* policy can work, as in Japan, because it promotes natural similarities that existed before the policy. It is reinforcing natural roots, history, tradition, language, food, ideas, beliefs, religion, and so on. In his article "Asia: Nobody Wants a Melting Pot" for *U.S. News and World Report* (June 22, 1987), veteran columnist James Fallows wrote of Asian societies that

*most share the belief that a society is strongest when its members
all come from the same race or ethnic group... [The Japanese] seem
wholly convinced that their homogeneity is essential to their political stability and economic success.*

If you think about it, this is a formula for precisely the policy Quebec
is vigorously and quite successfully pursuing at this very moment. The
French are fighting desperately to preserve their culture, while the
English throw theirs into the multicultural stew. For any multiculturalism policy, as charitable and hopeful as it may sound, is grievously
flawed. The essence of its justification is not similarity, but *difference.*
It encourages and promotes the *equal* acceptance of natural *differences*
and then tries to force us to *subordinate* these very differences to the
artificial policy ideal of the bureaucratic culture itself, which is an
abstraction. Such subordination requires supine acceptance of the
state's cultural dictates so utterly alien to any traditional idea of family — which affiliates downward, to roots and history — that it is bound
eventually to breed fear and hostility, as the Canadian experience is
proving. Human-rights commissions are besieged with cases; our
newspapers, which until recent years rarely carried stories on racial
conflict, now let hardly a day pass without such items, often the subject
of banner headlines. A few politicians are finally beginning to complain
that the entire multiculturalism program is "insulting" to Canadians,
"stigmatizes" them, and "ghettoizes" people (*Globe and Mail*, Sept. 21,
1989).

THE FEAR AT THE HEART OF IT ALL

THE REALITY OF THE natural common denominator always lies at the
heart of cultural security. To the extent that such denominators are
dissipated by government policy, a void is created, then filled with fear,
a fear that the vanilla culture of the bureaucracy cannot quell. Most
important are passionate matters like language, religion, and nationality. Then, less emotional things like food, or dress. But people will
always affiliate quickly whenever they share a sufficient number of
these elements, regardless of whatever other differences may surround
them. A French Canadian and an English Canadian may avoid each
other at home. But if they stumble on each other in a strange and
threatening land, they will band together. The rule is always the same:
the greatest affiliation occurs with the greatest number of natural
common denominators, the greatest fear and anxiety when the least

number is present. This phenomenon can be observed by each of us daily in our own lives.

The greatest problem for English Canada — and I mean not only for its language, but also for its every tradition — is that this extremely unnatural policy of multiculturalism, which will have — has already had — the effect of reducing the country's core culture to parity with a hundred alien ones, is that it has been imposed from the top down, by politicians. As Peter Brimelow writes in *The Patriot Game*, "Multiculturalism was invented by politicians, not by the people."[1] Of course, some of the people (like Canada's Ukrainian community) were instrumental in persuading government to change from its *bi*cultural to a *multi*cultural position. But government saw this as its opportunity to segment the electorate, and buy votes. Brimelow reminds us that Raymond Sesito, in his fine study *The Politics of Multiculturalism*, discovered that the opinion polls always showed that this policy was decidedly unpopular with the host communities. Not because they were necessarily racially motivated, but because they feared the loss of their own culture. He tells us that *even the immigrants* had not expected, or wanted, multiculturalism. They *expected* to be expected to assimilate! But as Brimelow points out, leaning on Tulloch's now famous "public choice" theory, "individuals tend to act rationally to maximize their self-interest," and "when political parties are in competition with each other, *the politicians themselves will seek to segment the undifferentiated electorate*. They will appeal to it on the basis of whatever salient characteristics they can identify, offering programs with benefits concentrated on the special interest group, and costs dispersed across all taxpayers."[2] Brimelow acutely desribes the result of this: "A frantic *auction* develops between the political parties on the one hand, and the ethnic groups with their newly subsidized professional leaders," fundraisers and grant-seekers, on the other.

Alas, Canadians have had foisted upon them, by an intellectual and political elite, a State policy that is destined to destroy the very group of natural common denominators that held the nation together for three centuries. This policy is grounded in the Rights Illusion, the Equality Illusion, and the Free-Lunch Illusion, and all these are inherent in the Standing Committee's recommendations. It is also linked, by affinity, with the international egalitarian aims of the NIEO, as explored in Chapter Nine, because its one-world philosophy aims at a homogeneous population of very different world citizens sharing in an artificial bureaucratic ideal. In short, it is a proposal for a kind of utopian socialism, internationalized and invented by politicians and bureaucrats, all of whom are paid to engineer social outcomes.

But in its eagerness to acquire the ethnic vote, the government conveniently forgets that many of these cultures have been in conflict with each other from time immemorial: Jews with Arabs, Greeks with Turks, French with English, Spaniards with Basques and Moors, African tribes with other African tribes, Iranians with Iraqis, Chinese with Vietnamese, Sikhs with Hindus, Japanese with Koreans, and so on. How has the Canadian government deluded itself into believing that by preserving and promoting the national *differences* of these people here in Canada, these hostilities will disappear? For they will not. Even now, Canada has been easily entered by extremists who plot against their historical enemies, both those now living here and those in the land they left behind. Sikh extremists are only one such example. The government, long a supporter of Israel, has been lobbied hard by Arab and Moslem groups and is now recognizing the terrorist Palestine Liberation Organization. According to a February 21, 1989, report, the federal Department of Immigration has granted asylum to a Mexican, Zacarias Cruz, who admitted that while serving in a Mexican army death squad he murdered at least sixty political prisoners.[3] In our arrogance, do we really believe the mantle of multiculturalism will muffle such strife?

The only successful way to end such fractiousness is first to find a *natural* cultural system that works; then to encourage everyone to assimilate to it, thus gradually losing their prior differences. The English culture and system of government have been just such a solution, as Canada's peaceful development until very recently attests. For it was only *assimilation* to the high moral standards of freedom and responsibility under our English governing institutions that had *any* hope of dissolving these fractious and bloody differences. The philosophy of multiculturalism is destined for the same end as Esperanto. As an artificial language, Esperanto was designed to be spoken by all peoples. But it is a miserable failure for the same reasons that multiculturalism is a failure. It is a policy initiative designed for top-down imposition on the people and has no inherent roots in the life of anyone. It cannot succeed. With Esperanto, you don't even have enough in common to tell a joke. With multiculturalism you can't share any language, beliefs, or customs, just as in a literature class where students have not read any of the same basic books, there is nothing to discuss. This simple fact is now becoming obvious even to some of the intended beneficiaries of multiculturalism. Professor Shelby Steele, of San Jose State University in California, a black and a product of the

civil-rights movement of the 1960s, has considered the reasons for the
recent outbreak of overt racism in the U.S.A. One of his conclusions, in
commenting on "black identity" programs, is that "this elevation of
differences undermines the communal impulse by making each group
foreign and inaccessible to others" (*Globe and Mail*, Feb. 6, 1989). And
in a similar vein, in 1987, Dr. Bhausaheb Ubale, a commissioner on the
Canadian Human Rights Commission, said:

> *The political parties are ghettoizing ethnic groups . . . This is fright-*
> *ening . . . Each ethnic group is fighting with other ethnic groups to*
> *attain the position of power within a given political party . . . I see*
> *today more intracommunal and intercommunal fights than I wit-*
> *nessed 10 years ago when I first started as human rights commis-*
> *sioner . . . Personally, I wanted to make my own contribution to this*
> *country as any other Canadian, but I cannot do that unless I enjoy*
> *the support of the ethnic group I come from. This is what politicians*
> *expect of me in the current system. Because of these facts . . . today*
> *I feel less Canadian than I felt 10 years ago. This is not the Canada*
> *I dreamed of. Political considerations have made a mockery of*
> *multiculturalism.* (*Globe and Mail*, Dec. 17, 1987)

Regrettably, it is not the Canada *any* of us dreamed of, and *all* of us feel
less Canadian. Is this a policy on which to build a nation?

OFFICIAL BILINGUALISM: HOW ENGLISH CANADA FELL ASLEEP AT THE SWITCH

HERE ARE STARTINGLY HONEST WORDS in a letter to *Alberta Report* (Aug.
1, 1980) by Robert S. Matheson, Q.C., describing his meeting with the
Dean of Law at the University of Alberta, Gérard LaForest, principal
draftsman of the Liberal proposals for constitutional change: "I was
dismayed to learn how bitterly anti-British LaForest was and how
clearly he stated his position that he would do everything possible to
advance the position of French-speaking Canadians over English-
speaking Canadians."[4] Here are equally startling words from Prime
Minister Brian Mulroney: "It is the French dimension of our national
personality that constitutes the soul of Canada" (interview with *Le
Figaro*, France, 1989).

It should come as no surprise to anyone that a normal person asked
to choose between option A, which will strengthen his own language,
and option B, which will weaken it, will choose A. For the fact is that

there is no neutrality in linguistic or cultural matters. A language advances or retreats in the measure that it is used, or replaced with another. Every additional speaker, every additional adjective, or sign, or book published, is a step forward, or backward. A person naturally fears and mourns any reduction of his linguistic environment in the same way that a person going blind fears and mourns the dying of the light. For those of us surrounded only by English, this may seem a bit extreme. But it is far from it. The loss of language is like the concept of attempted murder — it doesn't mean much until you, or people you love are the intended victims. From then on, it's pure outrage. It must have been mourning and something close to outrage in 1982 that caused then secretary of state Serge Joyal to say,

> *Everything we undertake and everything we are doing to make Canada a French state is part of a venture I have shared for many years with a number of people . . . The idea, the challenge, of making Canada a French country both inside and outside Quebec — an idea some people consider a bit crazy — is something a little beyond the ordinary imagination.*[5]

MASTER PLAN FOR THE FRANCIZATION OF CANADA

As we stand on the brink of history and watch Quebec struggling toward nationhood, we must surely wonder what we will tell our children when they ask "how did it happen?"

Here, briefly, is how it happened.

After the English victory on the Plains of Abraham, the two linguistic communities lived in relative harmony until after World War II. Each side created a number of its own distinctive institutions. There was relatively flexible interaction among them, and the federal government was coping with people in the language of their choice long before this became an official requirement. But everyone took it for granted that this was meant to be one English nation, with English institutions; that "historically, legally, and factually, Canada was and is a nation with one language, within which there is a region which is bilingual."[6] But in response to nationalist stirrings in Quebec, Liberal Prime Minister Lester Pearson appointed a Royal Commission on Bilingualism and Biculturalism in 1963 to study the matter, and many of its recommendations subsequently became part of Pierre Trudeau's Official Languages Act of 1969. The crucial factor now was that Pearson's sanguine overtures to the French became, in the hands of the master politician and centralist Pierre Trudeau, *a fundamental tool for the francization of Canada.* In fact — which is to say the same thing — it was a fundamental tool in the creation of his dream of a collectivist nation, just as his dream was itself an extension of Saint-Simon's dream (Chapter Five). What the Charter of Rights and Freedoms would later achieve legally, his 1969 act achieved administratively and culturally. But unperceived by most English Canadians, who still see the learning of French as a fine cultural achievement (I enjoy being fluent in French myself), "Official Bilingualism" *is not about language!* As Peter Brimelow again stresses so forcefully in *The Patriot Game,* official bilingualism is about political power. For what Trudeau wanted most, distrusting as he did the English mode in general, and democratic capitalism in particular, was a strong socialist nation governed by the same institutions coast to coast.

In order to make this possible, *he had to suppress the desire of Quebeckers to become a separate nation.* For otherwise his dream would fail. His solution to the problem was to force the rest of Canada to accept official bilingualism, thus neutralizing any French complaint that they were second-class. *He would simply confer upon the minority the same status as that of the majority.* Because no party can win without Quebec's support, this policy amounted to both *appeasement* and *control* of the French fact in Canada. It was simple. And it was also a recipe for a very successful State-imposed program to discriminate against English Canadians, nationwide. While English Canada slept, Trudeau did something insidiously clever that was — and still is — invisible to parents trundling their children off to French-immersion classes (English-immersion classes for francophones are illegal in Quebec): *he made the minority and the majority equal in law.* But as the constitutional expert Eugene Forsey made quite clear in his 1966 lecture entitled "Seven Devils of Pseudo-History," the idea of Canada as a Confederation of *two founding peoples,* with two linguistic groups relatively evenly balanced, is a fairy tale: "It was certainly not intended to be two political nations. This is unmistakably plain. Over and over again the 'Canadian' Fathers of Confederation, French, English, Irish and Scots, declared emphatically that they were creating a *new* nation."

In short, the experience of the French and the English in Canada is an illustration of my argument on multiculturalism, above: once you give official status to cultural differences, you are then forced to give them "rights," *which each different group will then use to dismember the common social fabric through lobbying to protect its own interests.* How, otherwise, could a minority French population in a vast land like Canada have succeeded in dominating the linguistic, cultural, and constitutional framework of our nation? They have been very, very clever, and we, very careless. (Part of the answer is that we have shelled out, between 1985-88, about $730 million to promote official bilingualism.)

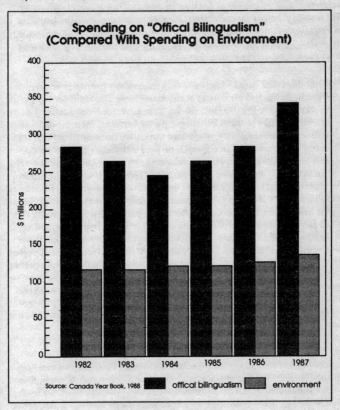

THE LOPSIDED EQUATION

BRIMELOW EXPLAINS THEIR SUCCESS in terms of public choice theory, to which I have referred before. This school argues that it's not enough merely to look at the alleged *rationale* for a policy. You have to study the *effects* of its implementation. Never mind what its inventors *say* is their reason for the policy — which is often a smoke-screen — what does the policy really *do?*

> *What are the Public Choice consequences of Official Bilingualism in Canada? The answer is stark. Relatively few Canadians are bilingual — it's about 15%, lopsidedly distributed, and shows no particular sign of expanding. So the imposition of institutional bilingualism has radical effects on the distribution of power and perquisites in the society. Bilinguals win, unilinguals lose.*[7]

What does this mean? It means that more than twenty years ago, the French, through their master statesman Pierre Trudeau, decided to go to war against the English social and governmental model I have described. They wanted to achieve parity between their minority population and the majority, to change the entire constitutional and legal status of Canada, and to control a disproportionate share of the power positions of the nation. They have done so by leveraging their powerful block vote — for spoils. It works. On December 4, 1989, Mulroney reminded Quebec that his tories had "delivered the goods": billions of dollars worth of favours. It is astounding they've got as far as they have. For unlike, say, Belgium, a troubled bilingual nation where more than 50 percent are bilingual, Canada has *never* had a truly bilingual basis for the legal imposition of official bilingualism. None. The highest percentage of bilingual Canadians, based on the flimsy self-reported census evidence — is 15 percent. When someone tells a census-taker that he can "conduct a conversation in both languages" — does he mean at the level of "Bonjour," or "Que faites-vous pour le weekend," or does he mean full conversational fluency? I suspect the 15 percent figure is inflated by half. Just getting by in a second language does not qualify as fluency in any important sense of that word.

THE EFFECT OF OFFICIAL BILINGUALISM ON POWER

FOR EVERY FRANCOPHONE who can also speak English, two can speak only French. But for every anglophone who can speak French, *fifteen* can speak only English. As Brimelow acutely points out, in an understatement, "They constitute an improbably large bloc . . . to be permanently reduced to the status of second-class citizens." He continues, "That the children of the majority should be required to bear the brunt of acculturation, particularly when their language is that of the entire continent, is a measure of the extent to which the minority has the moral initiative in Canada."[8] In 1981 there were about 809,000 anglophones living in Quebec who spoke English at home. The same year, there were about 666,000 francophones living outside Quebec, who spoke French at home. Yet we now have a situation in which full language rights have been suppressed for the English in Quebec — which has declared its official language to be French — at the same time as all other Canadians are being told their world must become increasingly bilingual, and they will receive second-class treatment in terms of their chances of gaining political power positions. As the journalist Richard Gwyn put it, they will "be disadvantaged in life, through no fault of their own. . . The central inescapable fact of bilingualism [is] becoming clear: it mean[s] loss of power for unilingual English Canadians."[9]

Why? Because the federal government in 1986 was the single largest employer in Canada, with some 222,000 in the civil service proper, and about 236,000 in Crown corporations.[10] On February 3, 1989, the *Globe and Mail* reported that of more than 1,300 federal public servants who failed the Language Knowledge Examination, about two-thirds were anglophones. They had trouble passing "because most of them don't get the chance to use French," said Joane Hurens, executive vice-president of the Public Service Alliance of Canada. As for the top ranks? When Trudeau was at the height of his power, 44 percent of his cabinet were francophones, including twelve of his top eighteen ministers, ranked in official order.[11] Today, the percentage of francophones in the federal civil service is already well beyond any "quota" percentage (22.8) in most important departments (see Chart 27, Chapter Seven). In Elections Canada, they represent 82 percent of staff; of the House of Commons staff, 65 percent; of the Public Service Commission, 82 percent; of CIDA (the Canadian International Development Agency, whose work was reviewed in Chapter Nine), 57 percent; of the governor general's staff, 68 percent; of the Secretary of State staff, 68 percent; and (wouldn't you know it!) of the office of the commissioner of official languages, 71 percent.[12] And still, the one part of the country where bilingualism is *not* promoted is Quebec. And though the English there are under "legislative attack," as Brimelow puts it (now outright oppression), in 1981 they only received 6 percent of the $21 million that went to "official-language minority groups." The other 94 percent went to French-language groups outside Quebec.[13]

What is the upshot of all this? It's getting worse, not better. Since Brimelow's book was published, the Supreme Court ruled Quebec's Bill 101 unconstitutional, because it suppressed fundamental language freedoms of the English and other minorities there. In response, Quebec used the Charter's "notwithstanding" clause to outlaw English or signs, thus flouting the wisdom of the Supreme Court of Canada — clear example of a province persisting in the *legal* suppression of rights Let us again recall Frédéric Bastiat's words from his seminal book, *Th Law*: "I cannot possibly understand how fraternity can be *legall* enforced without liberty being *legally* destroyed, and thus justice bein *legally* trampled underfoot." Quebec, through the use of the French style Charter we have all been obliged to accept, has *legally* trample justice underfoot for more than eight hundred thousand Canadian living in Quebec. So how bad will it get?

BILL C-72 — THE CREATION OF CANADA'S LANGUAGE POLICE

THE OSTENSIBLE PURPOSE of Bill C-72, passed into law by a majority o 129-9 on July 7, 1988, is to extend the laws relating to official language: and to ensure respect for the two languages. But as Kenneth McDonald writes in his study *A Solution to the Problem of Quebec*, "it's clear tha the purpose [of Bill C-72] is to expand the use of French far beyond th provisions of the Official Languages Act, which themselves went fa beyond those of the British North America Act."[14] Bill C-72 surpasses considerably the original provisions of the BNA Act, which "permitted" the use of English or French in Parliament, or the Quebec legislature and required their proceedings to be published in the two languages and said that "either" could be used in the federal courts, or the court of Quebec. Now, the two languages are to be "the language of work" ir "all federal institutions," and the officers and employees have the righ to use either. From now on, "all Crown corporations, courts, boards commissions, councils or departments of the federal government, the armed forces, the RCMP," will fall under Bill C-72.[15] As McDonald says from now on, "language skill, not professional merit, is to be the key tc promotion."[16]

It is very hard to believe that this has all happened in Canada, bu here are a few of the draconian provisions of Quebec's Bill 101, and Ottawa's Bill C-72, both prototypical instruments in the creation of the collectivist State, the latter enthusiastically supported by all three parties under a "Conservative" government. After reading this, you will not wonder that Amnesty International, an organization that serves as a watchdog on political repression around the world, has since the introduction of Bill C-72 vowed to "keep an eye" on Canada. Some highlights of Bill 101:

• French is the official language of Quebec, of its courts, and legislature. Only the French text of statutes and regulations is official.

• The Office de la langue française will determine appropriate knowledge of French of all civil servants.

• Company names, business publications, signs, and advertising are to be in French.

• The Office de la langue française has been established "to see that the French language becomes, as soon as possible, the language of communication, work, commerce and business in the civil administration and business firms."

• Members and staff of the Office cannot be prosecuted.

• A *Commission de surveillance* was established to deal with "failures to comply with this act." (The people will be spied upon.)

• The identity of someone complaining about an infraction cannot be revealed. (This means that the act encourages the French to spy on and report the English.)

• Those who contravene the act, are liable, in addition to costs, for fines of up to $500 (persons), or $1000 (corporations) on a first offence, and $1000 to $5,000 respectively thereafter. For carrying on business without a "francization certificate," a firm is liable for fines of up to $2,000 for each day.

As for Bill C-72? It basically places the offical languages commissioner above the law, throughout Canada. Neither he nor his staff are compellable witnesses, nor can they be pursued in the courts or sued for libel or slander. And the cabinet can make regulations "prescribing anything that is by this act to be prescribed . . ." — a wonderful bit of double-talk that basically means it can create new language regulations without leave of Parliament. In effect, all of Canada, not just Quebec, now has language police. As McDonald so clearly reminds us, "the law as it stands is forcing English speakers to learn French to get a job in Ottawa [or in Vancouver, for that matter — where there's a lot more demand for Chinese than for French] and forcing private businesses all over Canada to hire bilingual receptionists in case the local francophone association checks them out and reports them to the language police." (Anyone doing business with the government is subject to these regulations.) "Imagine," he continues, "trying to legislate languages, and making failure to speak or write one of them an indictable offence! The people who drafted it must be mad, the non-French MPs and senators who passed it supine and sycophantic."[17] It is especially oppressive when you consider that the largest minority in Ontario is Italian, in Saskatchewan Ukrainian, and in British Columbia, Chinese.

But the story is not ended. As Jane Jacobs so trenchantly observes in her book *The Question of Separatism,*

> *the issue of how to combine duality of French and English Canada with [a] federation of ten provinces remains insoluble because it is inherently insoluble. To adopt the theory that the country consists of two peoples highly unequal in numbers, and yet equal, or almost so, in their powers over the country as a whole, is to make federation unworkable.*[18]

I believe her judgement is currently being corroborated by the fact that after extensive efforts to francize Canada, Quebec is now quietly heading out of federation, if not officially, then practically and spiritually, at the same time that the rest of Canada — especially the West — tires of the hypocrisy, silliness, and legalized discrimination inherent in official bilingualism. The normalization and equalization of the French fact throughout Canada *had* to precede Quebec's exodus, because it was only this process that could create public awareness of its "distinct society" status, making an exit possible.

Thus ends the story, if not of the French takeover of English Canada, then certainly of a profound and it would appear lasting change in our way of life based on social engineering derived from the French model. Canadians need to wake up and study this crafty transformation of their entire society by a minority, then aggressively reconstitute the nation in a way that reflects what is still the majority culture.

IMMIGRATION: THE FINAL STEP IN THE HOMOGENIZATION OF CANADIANS

IN THE CLASH BETWEEN the two following quotations can be felt the tension between the elite of our collectivist government and the popular wisdom of the people, for which such elites normally have only scorn.

It doesn't matter where the immigrants come from.
(Pierre Elliott Trudeau, March 15, 1979, in Vancouver)

Do you . . . think the size and content of immigration should be permitted to change our ethnic and cultural balance?
(78% of Canadians answered "no" in a Gallup Poll released in June of 1987)

All peoples of the world have a natural fear of losing their culture — a threat normally posed only by external foreign forces. But if governing elites have an immigration ideology that differs radically from that of the people and strive to impose it on the people against their will, the foreign threat exists internally. I am not going to attack immigration in itself. I am going to attack foolhardy immigration policy. By now, the entire subject has become so politicized, the average Canadian so frightened of expressing an opinion, and the media so ready to pounce, that all reasonable dialogue has been shut down completely. Public opinion on immigration has been officially squelched. This attests to the power of the State and its minions to control public opinion, but it is the antithesis of democracy. Surely it is the people who should decide, and their elected representatives who should affirm the ethos and fabric of their society. Instead, the people's will is flouted. So we not only have an immigration problem, we also have a democracy problem. For what is at stake here is something far more important than the possibility of offending a newcomer to Canada. The basic question is, How open are we to self-determination through the encouragement of debate on the matters most crucial to our well-being? After all, despite what the government wants us to believe, is it just possible that the policy is wrong? Is it possible that Canada is asking for trouble? What has been going on with immigration over the past few decades, anyway? Let us review the matter briefly.

CONTROL VS. "UNIVERSALITY"

UNTIL THE END OF the 1950s, immigration policy that tried to plan, or *control* the flow of non-traditional immigrants to Canada in the interest of preserving some sort of traditional ethnic balance, went unremarked. Then, suddenly, with the advent of our government's growing fondness for egalitarianism — specifically after Tom Kent set to work fashioning Prime Minister Lester Pearson's 1967 decision, enthusiastically embraced by Pierre Trudeau, to open the country up to multiculturalism, and "universal" immigration — everything changed. Suddenly, the "control" method was regarded as racially "discriminatory." No one then objected that this was a loaded word. For a selective policy can be considered "discriminatory" only if you believe that all people and all cultures are the same. If you do not, then it was not discriminatory, it was rationally "preferential." Preferential in the same sense that a black man may normally prefer a black wife and black children to white ones. It is extreme intellectual lethargy to call this discrimination. But if you desperately want everyone to be colourblind, culture-blind, and value-blind, you will promote this Discrimination Illusion.

What I call the *control* policy was designed to ensure that the bulk of Canada's children would grow up among parents and people more or less similar to themselves, who spoke the same language and who were more or less rooted in the same Judeo-Christian religion, Graeco-Roman philosophical and legal tradition, and Anglo-European culture. Was it all that unreasonable to want to provide future generations with the same culture and environment that made the nation strong? And if not, why did we change a system that was working so well?

WHAT ARE PEOPLE AFRAID OF?

FIRST OF ALL, MOST of us are very moved by the experiences of immigrants who come to this country, work hard, and advance themselves and their families. Especially when we see a large percentage of our own population wailing about unemployment, or on the pogey, and then learn that many of them refuse to take hard physical jobs that immigrants gladly take, or for which we import foreign labour. The question has nothing to do with admiring deserving immigrants. It has everything to do with the people's fear of losing their connection with the familiar.

"UNIVERSALITY"

IN ORDER TO NEUTRALIZE this natural fear, the government hit upon the idea of "universality" — the idea that people all over the world are basically the same, and therefore, as Trudeau said, "it doesn't matter where the immigrants come from." The governing elite would like us to agree with this sentiment, and at first it sounds good. But it is just that, a sentiment. In the section on multiculturalism above, I tried to explain why it is a badly flawed result of Pollyanna thinking. As you will see, the "universality" approach was really another form of planning, of control disguised as humanitarianism. It was the government's way of changing our society to match its one-world dreams, to buy ethnic votes, and fend off any objection from the citizenry at the same time.

But we can test this idea for ourselves with a little thought experiment. *Let us suppose the government is right, and people are all the same*. Let us also agree that the three areas that generate the most fear are language, appearance, and religion. For these have to do with how we communicate with others, how we see ourselves reflected in our children, families, and in daily life, and with our most fervent relationship with the Divine. Let us question ourselves honestly to see if the universality theory holds up.

1. "Would it make any difference to you if 80 percent of those around you spoke an unfamiliar foreign language?" Although I very much enjoy foreign languages, I would have to answer "yes." For I would at first be interested, then quite uncomfortable. Then possibly a bit desperate in this situation.

2. "Would it make any difference to you if 80 percent of those around you were suddenly a different colour and/or had different racial features from you and your family?" I would have to answer "no," not if it was a limited experience, such as I had once living in Japan for six months, quite removed from any Westerners. For I always knew I could leave and come home. But if I had to stay in such a foreign community for life, I would feel quite forlorn. My answer would be "yes."

3. "Would it make any difference to you if 80 percent of those around you suddenly worshipped a God other than yours?" Again, this would be a fascinating situation at first, then downright nervewracking. The disappearance of many churches of my faith, its music, festivals, religious celebrations, and holidays, as well as the scriptural literature and ethical system derived from it, would in the long run be the most upsetting. My answer would be "yes."

If you answered "no" to these three questions, you are either a died-in-the-wool universalist, or you haven't had the experiences I've outlined. If you answered "yes," you cannot be a universalist. You will probably argue for some kind of control over immigration.

When put to the test in this way, the "universality" theory is so obviously badly flawed we can only conclude that either it has been concocted to popularize, and assist a lazy government out of messy racial situations, or more cynically, it is simply an extension of the egalitarian, one-worlder's philosophy that requires the eradication of differences — a policy introduced to make their theory more plausible.

I know that in real life we rarely encounter the extreme situations in my questions — but we *do* encounter them by *degrees*, and increasingly so in Canada's major cities. A person in downtown Toronto or Vancouver is more likely to answer "yes" strongly to all these questions. But logically, once we agree it's a matter of degree, then the idea of universality goes out the window. It cannot stand the test. Language, appearance, and religion *do* make a difference to people — a difference of degree, which is enough to frighten them about the extreme. So the question goes back to *control*. If two immigrants stood before you, each aspiring to take the one last spot, and equally qualified in all respects except that one believes like you, looks like you, and speaks your language, while the other has a foreign religion and language and is racially quite different — which would you choose? For since *any* immigration policy will introduce a difference to a culture — it will either fortify it or weaken it — the outstanding question to be answered, but which no one wants to raise, is, How *much* and what *kind* of difference should be introduced into any cultural setting by immigration policy?, since logically there is no such thing as no difference.

THE CULTURAL COMFORT ZONE

THE ANSWER IS, no one knows. But everyone has a relatively reliable intuition. From extensive travels, including some years spent living in the U.S.A. and observation of cultural migrations in and out of urban-suburban areas, I would have put the cultural comfort zone somewhere about 15 percent. Whenever an invading culture reaches about this percentage of the total, the majority gets restless. They intuitively feel threatened. It doesn't matter whether they *are* threatened or not. What matters is that they *feel* threatened. As marketing experts say, there are only two important things in life — reality and perception. And guess what — the perception *is* the reality! Once people start to *feel* their culture is threatened, racial strife increases, people relocate, and feelings of discrimination become common in those who have never before experienced such feelings. In this sense, *the government creates racism in the people* by restructuring society against its will in a way that *generates* racial attitudes. And it doesn't matter what the mix is. *All* cultures experience this, for a minority here is a majority back home (where there are other "minority" problems). What governments designing immigration policies have to determine is where the Cultural Comfort Zone lies, for otherwise they court social upheaval. I have discussed this briefly with Daniel Cappon of the Department of Environmental Studies at York University, a former health director for the inner city of Baltimore, according to whom very little research exists on this common situation. He told the *Globe and Mail* that

> *ten per cent is a critical mass. Under ten per cent they are well tolerated. Over ten per cent and the majority starts sweating, feeling that the neighborhood is invaded. . . . What often happens is that there is a displosion, an impact, when a minority moves in on a majority. Canada has opened the gates of immigration under the delusion that Canadians are superior beings, the false illusion that Canadians are somehow immune to racism. They aren't. The racial troubles are only beginning.*

Culture Canada has admitted that visible minorities now make up about 15 percent of the population in some Canadian cities (the *Globe and Mail* said 17 percent, Feb. 8, 1989).

I think it is time for our government to consider the possibility that it has made a mistake. For its universality policy is a cultural time-bomb deliberately placed in our luggage through the engineering of changes in the racial and cultural mix of immigrants over the past thirty years. The impact of changes of this magnitude would be felt in *any* majority culture. For the dynamics of cultural change affect every culture similarly. They would be the same if the minorities were green and spoke a computer language. Toronto, say, would be experiencing the same increase in racial "incidents" even if it were 85 percent black, with a mixed non-black minority rapidly growing in its midst. The human fears about continuity, similarity, and cultural comfort are the same for all peoples. For everyone affiliates backward, so to speak, with his own history and culture, not forward to an unknown, faceless, and confusing future. When people travel to foreign lands, they don't take along manifestos about perfect societies; they take photographs of loved ones, their own literature, mementos, and cherished knick-knacks, and they compare everything with "home." When, in a lonely moment, they encounter a familiar face, a smell, a reminder, they can be totally and powerfully overcome by memories of their past, their childhood, their roots. The French word *déraciné* is close to the English word "uprooted," but is a clearer rendering of this phenomenon, for it implies that our original roots are *cut off* — they remain forever in their original soil. Neither multiculturalism nor the immigration policy that feeds it can work, for human roots, human memory, and the need to affiliate with similarity are far more powerful forces than utopian theories proposed by governments that crave immigrant votes.

WHAT HAS THE GOVERNMENT DONE TO TRADITIONAL IMMIGRATION?

HERE IS A SIMPLE table to illustrate what the government has done since it assumed its one-world, universality approach. Traditional immigration is defined as from the U.K., Europe, the U.S.A., New Zealand, Australia, and South Africa (we can disregard the minimal non-white immigration from the U.S.A. and South Africa); non-traditional is from everywhere else. The figures are probably understated, because the Department of Immigration bases its statistics on "country of last permanent residence," not on cultural, racial, or religious affinity. For example, it would count ten black Africans (or ten white Africans) who moved here after residence in England as "British." Nevertheless, it's all we have to go on. You will see that without ever consulting the wishes of the Canadian people, a small government elite has totally reversed the trend.

Immigration in the Post-War Years, Under the "Control" Policy

YEAR AVERAGE:	TRADITIONAL	%	NON-TRADITIONAL	%
1946-1966:	125,000	92.7	9,900	7.3

After the New, "Universalist" Policy

YEAR	TRADITIONAL	%	NON-TRADITIONAL	%
1968	145,937	79.3	38,037	20.6
1973	100,448	54.5	83,752	45.5
1976	70,708	47.3	78,721	52.7
1987*	44,434	31.0	104,950	69.0

(Sources: All figures are from Department of Immigration statistics except that 1987 is calculated from Canadian Press figures, Feb. 26, 1988.)

In the last Liberal government's report to Parliament on immigration levels in May 1980, it echoed the same reality, that "European countries provided 88 per cent of all immigrants in the 1954-1958 period [but only] accounted for 37 per cent in the 1974-1978 period." It says that Asian immigrants went from 2 to 26 percent in the same period.

HOW WILL THIS CHANGE THE FUTURE OF CANADA?

DRASTICALLY, THAT'S HOW. And if that's what the people want, well and good. But my suspicion is that it is *not* what they want; certainly they are making this view consistently known when polled. But the government is not listening, because its mind is made up: Canada must be transformed according to the current one-world game plan, whether we like it or not. If this trend continues, the Canada we know today will be changed forever, as you can see from the charts below. My calculations are based on immigration figures obtained from Statistics Canada and were somewhat difficult to perform because of mixed data and methodology. The thought did not escape me that this confusion may be intentional because it will make impossible the future task of sorting out Canada's ethnic direction — already a difficult task. At any rate, this whole field is rife with pseudo-scholarship and wild predictions, but I don't think a career demographer would come up with results very different from mine — depending on his biases. So don't take this too seriously, but also remember: it merely reflects present trends, which may alter, and . . . it could be worse. Although, I have softened the trend somewhat to avoid the charge of alarmism, it still looks alarming to me!

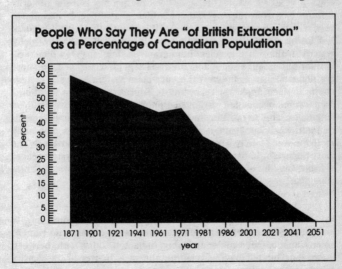

People Who Say They Are "of British Extraction" as a Percentage of Canadian Population

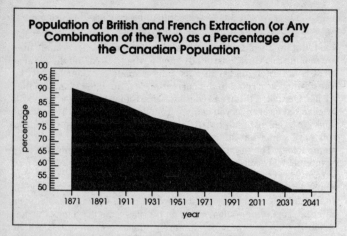

Population of British and French Extraction (or Any Combination of the Two) as a Percentage of the Canadian Population

THE MESS, AND THE MESS TO COME

WHO IS REALLY CALLING the shots? Not the people. Not the majority culture. Not even the government, which has so deeply ingratiated itself with the immigrant population of this country that it wouldn't dare risk losing votes. And most politicians, it turns out, think the "point system" we now use to select immigrants is "fair" (as Don Blenkarn, M.P. for Mississauga South, told me). So I sent for a copy of it, and here are my conclusions: the government's point system basically assigns points to each applicant according to education, specific vocational preparation, occupation, arranged employment, knowledge of official languages, and so on. But there are no criteria for culture, race, or religion. Each applicant is screened as if these aspects of human societies were totally irrelevant (even though they are obviously the most important to us, *and to most immigrants*). Such a system, eager to avoid any hint of discrimination, thereby introduces a systemic bias of its own.

THE POINT SYSTEM AS AN EGALITARIAN SIEVE

HERE'S HOW. JUST IMAGINE this "fair" point system applied, say, to foreign engineers, teachers, mathematicians, or·clerks, who want to enter Canada. Quite understandably, India and China with, between them, massive populations totalling almost a quarter of the world's people, could present more qualified applicants than most of the other countries put together. So the immigration official asked to use a fair point system could end up allowing vastly more applicants into Canada from India and China than from any other nation — just because more of them want in. This systemic bias, due not to any discriminatory motive, but to its opposite, will automatically discriminate against less populous nations. Or try this thought experiment: Imagine that *only* people completely alien to our culture, language, religion, and customs (the Chinese, say) are applying to enter Canada. Theoretically, in a sufficient number of years they could dominate every profession in Canada. In 250 years Canada could be a Chinese nation. If that's what we want, then let's get on with it. But if it's not, then let's say so and take steps to ensure it doesn't happen.

The dilemma I see is that Canada, in its weak-kneed, poorly thought-out wish to comply with the United Nations Charter on Human Rights, and with our own Charter, is confusing fairness in the treatment of those to whom we grant the *privilege* of entering Canada, with the *fairness* of the selection process by which they entered. These are two different things entirely. After all, *surely any nation has the right to defend itself against demographic capture, or, if you prefer, against passive racial or cultural take-over.* One way I can think of to stop it is to use quotas: any year's crop of immigrants must reflect the current racial, cultural, and religious composition of the nation. We currently have 1 percent Chinese? Then only 1 percent of the immigrants can be Chinese. Now, I don't like quotas for anything, but in the face of outsiders determining the fate of our nation by numerically over-whelming a "neutral" selection system, I'd use them. I might even argue that we should use them to redress the present trend. Otherwise, we may become subordinated to people and cultures unlike our own through reliance on a system designed to eliminate cultural bias!

By using only administrative criteria — a kind of egalitarian sieve — we indeed avoid the painful need to make cultural, racial, and religious decisions, but at the same time we surrender our ability to determine the future composition of our nation. Instead, its composition gets decided by the demographic forces of the outside world; by the desires of people quite different from us, who have no intention of changing, whom we pay to remain the same and who may even cherish the day when we become more like them in a kind of demographic capture of Canada. The result of this systemic bias is that "independent" (as opposed to "family class") traditional-source immigrants who cannot compete go elsewhere. In 1987, only about 5,800 immigrants came to Canada from the British Isles — one of our traditional source countries.

Upon enquiry as to why so few, I was told they were not applying. But around 28,000 went to Australia in the same year. However, the Canadian High Commission in London says that it receives more than 2,000 applications a month and *rejects* 80 percent out of hand. Australia gets the same, but rejects only 20 percent. So I conclude that our system and our reluctance to state our preferences and aggressively to seek out people who share our moral, legal, cultural, and racial heritage, have persuaded them to go elsewhere. Of course, the effect is cumulative. Once the word gets out, as it evidently has in the U.K., people simply stop applying to emigrate to Canada. But rest assured our government will do nothing unpopular with immigrants already here to alter this situation. For to a great extent, it is the immigrants themselves who are calling the shots on immigration policy in Canada, through the power of the ethnic vote, their lobbying organizations, and the "family reunification" program.

The 1982 report to Parliament on immigration levels said, "Family reunification has been and is one of the traditional foundations of Canadian immigration policy. [It is] intended to facilitate the *relatively uninhibited* reunification of Canadian citizens and [landed immigrants] with their close relatives from abroad." Well, the *idea* is a winner, because no one is publicly against families. Then Junior Immigration Minister Gary Weiner told us that the emotional bonds of family take precedence over qualifications and adaptability. The *result* is that immigrants already here determine the mix of immigrants to come, 80 percent of whom enter without regard to their merit. Employment and Immigration, in Hull, has informed me that of the up to 175,000 immigrants planned for 1990 (not including the refugee backlog), only 24,000, or 16 percent, will actually have to qualify under our point system. A full 84 percent — 147,000 — just walk through the door! For all we know they could be ignorant, illiterate, unqualified people. We don't know, because we don't ask. But we do know that non-traditional immigrants tend to have much larger families than those from traditional countries. So just imagine the multiplication of unscreened immigrants this implies.

Don Blenkarn told me that an average of *thirty* family members followed each family class immigrant to Canada. Further, although "independent" applicants are restricted to those who have confirmed jobs that cannot be filled by Canadians, family-class immigrants have no restrictions. According to Charles Campbell, formerly vice-chairman of the Immigration Appeal Board, who called Canada's immigration policy "a national disaster," the effect of such policy changes was that between 1973 and 1983 the number of unscreened, unskilled family-class immigrants doubled to 55 percent, while skilled immigrants dropped from 76 to 33 percent. Consequently, immigration dropped drastically from developed sources like the U.S.A., Europe, and the U.K. (from about 20,000 to 5,000 annually).

The effect of this distortion is exponential. It creates unbearable pressure on politicians and immigration officials, all fuelled by multi-cultural grants to ethnic lobby groups. At the insistence of immigrant groups here already, the government beefs up processing staff in the non-traditional source nations — New Delhi, India, by 1983 had become Canada's largest immigration post, with thirteen officers and thirty-four support staff. Recently, Canada shut down its embassy in Finland, a country with which Canada shares much, closed its consulates in Perth, Birmingham, Hamburg, Strasbourg, Marseilles, and Bordeaux, and cut back its staff at the High Commission in London. Thereafter, it opened consulates in Shanghai, Bombay, and Osaka.

Meanwhile, on December 30, 1987, the *Globe and Mail* reported what must be a world record. The newspaper tells the story of Harbhajan Singh Pandori, who came to Canada in July 1970. About thirty Sikh families were in Toronto at that time, he said. Two years later, he sponsored a brother. A year later, another brother. He went back to India to pick a bride and then began sponsoring his in-laws and the rest of his own family. "During the past 17 years, Mr. Pandori estimates that about 60 to 70 family members have followed in his tracks. If friends and neighbors are included, his connections stretch to a few hundred immigrants." On the purely personal level, we can only be happy for Mr. Pandori. He has used everything available to him to recreate in Canada the world he left behind — just as the assumptions in this chapter suggest any normal person would.

The question, quite apart from whether Mr. Pandori was right or wrong, is, Can this be good for Canada? Can Canada survive the aggressive, government-financed creation of hundreds of competing cultures on its own soil, especially when so many are drawn from Third World nations that are either Marxist in orientation, or fatalist in their economic ways, as was emphasized in Chapter Nine? After all, Canada's record with only *one* competing culture — the French — has been an ongoing struggle. The future is long, but it does not take a great leap of the imagination to see five or more French-type situations in Canada. Again, keep in mind that the largest minority in Toronto is Italian, not French; in Saskatchewan it is Ukrainian; in Vancouver, Chinese. What happens when their associations and lobby groups, government-funded and with full-time professional lobbyists, become as militant as the French and proceed against the majority culture for their equal "rights" under our (discriminatory) Charter? I predict that our judges will be juggling one culture's rights against another's until doomsday.

SOME OTHER PROBLEMS, AND A CONCLUSION

AT LAST, THE MULRONEY government has done *something* to stem the tide of queue-jumping "economic" refugees. Needless to say, Canada's refugee screening process has been, and I'm sure still is, a scandal. As Joe Bissett, executive director for immigration in the federal Employment and Immigration Department, says, "70% of refugees coming to Canada are bogus." Gerald Yetming, High Commissioner for Trinidad, says that "what we are having with [our] nationals coming to Canada is a claim for refugee status, not on the basis of political persecution but for economic reasons" (*Toronto Star*, Jan. 5, 1989). Most Canadians feel that priority should *not* be given to immigrants or refugees landing here illegally. (Obviously, it makes a sham of the whole process when honest people who go through normal channels are refused, while the dishonest are accepted as "refugees.") In a Gallup Poll of September 1, 1988, a full 79 percent said such persons should *not* have privileges under the Charter of Rights (they do). Feelings were strongest — up to 91 percent — in British Columbia, which for years has experienced a large influx of non-traditional immigrants. This higher percentage is just further evidence of greater social dislocation caused by higher non-traditional immigration.

A Drain On Canadian Resources

Phony refugee immigrants are a drain on Canadian resources. Often here for purely economic reasons, they are now instantly entitled to full welfare services, provincial medical services, and public schools. Since January 1989, they have been allowed to work, which of course bolsters their future claims for admission. Still, visas have not been required for refugees or visitors from many of the non-traditional source nations. On December 30, 1988, the *Globe and Mail* ran a story about how our schools were "overwhelmed by the task of teaching immigrant [and refugee] children." If they are overwhelmed trying to teach immigrants who are officially encouraged not to assimilate, but to preserve their own ways, then the children of existing citizens cannot be very well served, can they? Other articles describe how hospital staff cannot communicate with the sick immigrants — and pressure the medical staff to jump on the multicultural bandwagon. Nowhere is there mention of encouraging the immigrants to adapt to the core culture and learn its language!

In 1987, according to the Department of Immigration, more than 26,000 people claimed refugee status in Canada. Based on the standard used by the United Nations Convention on Refugees, *nearly 85 percent of the claims were found to be false.* Such scandals have been known for a long time. As long ago as 1981, the Liberal immigration minister Lloyd Axworthy, noting that we had taken in 75,000 refugees, said, "A lot of them are claiming they left for political reasons, but in fact it's economic." Well, what does that tell us? It tells us that these people are lying to us. If they are lying, we should send them all back home, if only to protect the integrity of our policy and the dignity and honesty of those who are applying through normal channels. Finally, no one is asking whether these are the penny-in-the-pocket type of immigrants that take a chance, work harder than anyone else, and succeed, or spongers and lazybones who come here for the instant benefits of the welfare State.

Why Do We Really Need Immigrants?

Even though we have a continuing record of unemployment, the government keeps bringing in immigrants who compete with citizens for jobs. After all, it's farcical to assume that an immigrant who comes here with a job already in hand (part of the point system qualification) will necessarily *stay* in that job. More likely, as time passes, he becomes a free-floating competitor for other jobs and therefore a threat to the unemployed already here. If the country cannot even generate enough jobs for its own citizens, why are we bringing others in? In 1980, with 1,000,000 unemployed, Axworthy was saying Western Canada would need 600,000 immigrants by 1990!

Last summer I sat on an airplane with a young man from the Caribbean island of Dominica, who smilingly told me he had earned close to $5,000 for two months, with free room and board, picking tobacco. Polish visitors working illegally here "Go Home Rich," says the *Toronto Star* (Aug. 14, 1988). And the federal government has a "farm labour" program that brings in 7,000 workers every summer from the Caribbean and Mexico for Ontario alone, who work at $7 per hour — while the rest of us cough up welfare and "unemployment" for Canadians who won't take these jobs. Something is amiss . . . are they unemployed, or unemployable?

As for the shrinking population, let's suppose the demographers are correct. Let's say that Canada is not growing (which it has been). My first response to this "problem" is, so what? There is no evidence that a country of fifty million is better off than one of twenty-five. Japan has had zero population growth for the past couple of decades and is doing just fine. Why can't we do the same? If we still want to grow despite this evidence of good economic health from zero growth, why replace or add population through immigration — especially immigration that threatens social dislocation? After all, the fact is that the immigrants, by and large, are not coming to Canada. They are coming to Toronto, Montreal, and Vancouver — already densely populated and ethnically tense urban centres, where crime is rising. Why do we want to fan such flames? Rather, why not develop a pro-family, tax-relief-based, "made in Canada" incentive to encourage young Canadians to have larger families and provide ways for them to avoid the crippling tax and expense levels that befall large families? A natural increase in family formation is what is required for growth in Canadian population, not ludicrously high tax rates to support welfare State policies that implicitly attack the family.

Our current tax policy attacks family formation in the sense that, everything else being equal, it costs John and Mary Doe a lot more to have one of them stay at home to raise their children than for both spouses to go out to work, and have the children raised by others. My point, simply, is that since tax policy will affect family formation one way or the other, we should design it to favour the creation of families by existing citizens. If that doesn't work, and we are convinced more population is needed (I'm not), then at least let's have the intelligence to attract immigrants who are compatible with our core culture in every way possible, and if not, then at least willing to assimilate to it, and if they wish to preserve whatever drove them to leave their native countries — to do so privately and at their own expense.

WHAT IS TO BE DONE?

MULTICULTURALISM

1. Ethnic groups lobbying for money from the State are like any other lobby group. They use the money to circumvent the political process. The government must stop funding all of them — left, right, business, radical, ethnic, all of them. Let them fight for what they want through

their democratically elected representatives, or through privately funded groups.

2. Immigrants to Canada should be instructed in the core heritage and culture of this nation, which is Judeo-Christian, Greco-Roman, and Anglo-European. And they should be expected to assimilate to that culture. This does not mean losing their own, which they are free to promote and protect, using their own resources, if they so desire. But it does mean their own culture is secondary.

3. The government must recognize that its "multicultural" policy is self-contradictory and that it is currently funding long-term social unrest by financially rewarding the development of cultural differences within Canada. Just as these lead to strife between nations, they will lead to strife between the "nations-within-Canada."

4. The government should reconstitute, publicize, and encourage schools to inculcate the key symbols of the core Canadian heritage before they are totally forgotten.

BILINGUALISM

1. Canada does not need any "official" languages. It is a free country, and the people ought to be able to speak whatever language they wish. We need a free language market, not government language police to terrorize people and fine them for posting signs on their own property in their own language.

2. But if we must have an "official" language, then let it be only one. We don't need more than one to run our federal or international governmental affairs. But let any province that wishes, have more official languages, to be decided by referendum. In effect, Switzerland has language-based provinces on this pattern that work very successfully.

IMMIGRATION

1. The government must consult the people through a democratic referendum on immigration to find out what they want. That should set the government's agenda. During the period of the referendum — say two years — all immigration should be halted: visitors' permits only. This way, majority opinion would be reflected in policy.

2. If the people want to protect their traditional heritage and avoid the sort of social dislocation that seems to come whenever non-traditional immigration hits a certain level — then they should. Otherwise, there will be strife, brought about by a haughty government through tax-financed social engineering of the most elitist sort.

3. If there is concern over zero growth, Canada should examine ways to stimulate growth in the Canadian family before resorting to immigration.

A government that imposes multiculturalism, bilingualism, and non-traditional immigration in a calculated attempt to bury Canada's traditional culture is guilty of subverting the ethos of the nation. These three programs are a veneer disguising cynical vote-grabbing from Quebec as well as from ethnic groups. They have had the effect of transforming Canada, in the space of two decades, into a collectivist nation designed to encourage a bureaucratic culture and eradicate our traditional heritage. Unless we learn the lessons of history, this can end only in intra-ethnic strife and militancy on our own soil.

16

Political Sleight Of Hand
The Charter And The Meech Lake Accord

France is a country that lives by the statute book.
For us the law, once written, is sacred. It can be
altered only in the most solemn circumstances.
Britain, on the other hand, is famous for its
pragmatism. Its law is that of custom and usage,
constantly adapting to new conditions.

Maurice Couve de Murville, French Statesman

AT SOME POINT, as civilized nations grope their way toward a satisfactory style of operation, one that combines sufficient protections for
the individual with sufficient leeway for the State to perform its role,
the most fundamental question must always be: *What is the role of the
State?*

Until that question is answered, we cannot say to what *degree*
individual rights ought to be restricted, if at all. In a Libertarian, or
Classical Liberal State, individual rights would mean everything, and
the State would have very little room to manoeuvre beyond the setting
of "rules of just conduct equal for all." In a socialist, or any other form
of collectivist State, the individual is utterly subordinate, as a matter of
national philosophy and law, to the State and the totality of collective
rights. The national debate on the relationship between individual and
collective rights, therefore, ultimately hinges on the permissible use of

force, or coercion. Under despotism, such coercion is designed to get the dictator and his elites what they want, regardless of the inherent morality or immorality of the policy. In a socialist nation or — not to split too fine a hair — a social-welfare State like our own, the coercion is justified by elites who are convinced a certain policy is moral and *good* for the people — *whether they want it or not*. Mandatory seat belts, mandatory pensions, mandatory health-care premiums, and welfare largesse paid for by mandatory high tax rates are examples of coercive humanitarian policies. The fact that the people could decide for themselves whether or not they want to risk dying in a car, to pay for their own health care or pensions privately, or believe that welfare should be only for the truly needy — is ignored in the effort of the State to control what it believes to be the well-being of the people, even as it designs such policies to attract votes.

In countries based on the English model, this struggle between individual and collective rights and the proportionality between them is normally worked out through deliberation of actual cases in the courts, the decisions from which then form a body of Common Law that is passed down from generation to generation, thus forming judicial precedents that keep pace with the changing times. In others, like France, the U.S.A., and now Canada, the principles defining this relationship are enshrined in a written Charter, or Constitution. How does a country like the U.S.A. resolve this clash between its "Charter" (actually, a Bill of Rights) and its Common-Law tradition? Very simply, its "Charter" defends Common-Law principles and individual freedom fiercely. Ours defends the State first. The Bill of Rights defends "life, liberty, and the pursuit of happiness"; we defend "peace, order, and good government."

In Chapter One, "A Question of Styles," I suggested that Canada, long a country based on English Common-Law traditions, yet with a large French presence, is still struggling with the conflict between these two styles of self-government. A July 22, 1989, article on government in the *Toronto Star* captioned its lead photo of the parliament buildings with this line: "Parliamentary Problems: Canada has seesawed between centralization and decentralization for more than 100 years." But such articles routinely ignore the moral underpinnings in this seesaw, to focus on the management problems involved in governing. This book has been an attempt to unravel this moral and ideological conflict. For the "English," or what I have called "bottom-up" style, is based on the notion that the most important fact of life is individual freedom and responsibility and that there is a bundle of natural rights we all possess by virtue of being born humans. These cannot be given to a person, or taken away, by a Charter, and from these grow other important rights such as the right to the enjoyment of private property, free association, and so on.

It was the English who were the first to entrench in the Common Law a clear legal and philosophical protection for such rights, and to argue for the creation of political institutions that would serve as inherent checks and balances on the power of the State to erode these precious rights. They are sometimes called "negative rights" because their importance lies in our inherent right *not* to be interfered with by others, particularly by government. Each individual, in this view, is really a kind of agent who adds to or subtracts from the moral fabric of society; the role of government, therefore, is not to control the people and manage their morality but to create an environment in which they can manage it themselves, under the same rules for all. The effect of this style is to create what I have called a "bonus system" in which the free play of individuality is allowed to flourish without hindrance from the State, or any desire on the part of the State to control social outcomes.

In contrast to this, the "French" style of government is collectivist, centralizing, and "top-down," rooted in the belief that people are basically unredeemed — and that, therefore, the way to create a virtuous society and keep anarchy at bay is through the creation of a Constitution imposed from above by a political elite to ensure that society is managed according to this elite's idea of the social good, for which a strong central government supplies the power. This is a quasi-utopian vision of society bent on moral perfection by force, if necessary. This French style inevitably results in an unofficial division of society into the governing elite and the governed, in which legislatures see themselves not as carrying out the people's wishes but as shaping those wishes, marketing them to the people, and then entrenching them in law as rights. The unintended consequence is always the weakening of self-reliance, a depression of the wealth-creating instincts of the people by removing incentives, and in general the creation of what I have called a "handicap system" in which equality of social outcomes, mostly through massive transfers of wealth from the productive to the unproductive, takes precedence over, in fact requires the suppression of, basic individual rights.

In place of the negative rights common to the English system, new "positive rights" are then invented that really constitute claims by individuals against the State for goods and services that the State promises to provide (the better to get itself elected). Such positive rights (thus termed because they have specific objects in mind) are provided to all, regardless of effort or merit, and because they can only be provided by the State's first taking from some to give unto others, such positive rights enshrined in a Charter form the basis for the handicap system.

Despite Canada's brave efforts to blend the two styles, *they are inherently mutually destructive.* That is why I have maintained throughout this book that any society must first of all decide what its belief system or its core values ought to be, before setting about entrenching these in any constitutional form. If this belief system, these values, are not clearly defined before they are written into a constitution, it would be better *not* to commit them to a constitution, for the result can only be a calcification of social confusion. It's a bit like setting out to make a plaster sculpture. If you know clearly what you want it to look like, you can finish the whole thing nicely before it dries. But if you don't, the plaster hardens halfway through the process, and then you're stuck with it. From then on, you can only chip away, or stick other bits of plaster on to make the thing look acceptable.

The result of this irresolution has been a struggle for the constitutional supremacy of one or the other of these visions that has been ongoing ever since the battle on the Plains of Abraham. After generations of rule under the English style, Pierre Elliott Trudeau came to power and began to change everything. While English Canada slept, he slowly transformed Canada into a "French"-style nation. He did this firstly through insistence on his official-bilingualism policy, which had the again unperceived effect of placing French Canadians in every important government post possible, and shaking out English bureaucrats. In this way, the French minority in Canada (22.8 percent of the population) got its hands on 28 percent of the government jobs, including a disproportionate share of the important ones (often more than 60 percent).

But most significantly, he altered us by superimposing the Charter of Rights and Freedoms on Canada, which was in immediate and inherent conflict with the whole system of English Common Law. It was the "top-down" system smothering the "bottom-up" system; ultimately, it was the handicap system swallowing the bonus system — and therefore all the values underlying it as outlined in Chapter Four. It was, very simply, the declaration of the priority of State's rights over individual rights at every turn. For although the Charter appears ostensibly to defend the individual against the State, it in fact presupposes the huge State required to satisfy all the uniform positive rights guaranteed in the Charter itself — a greatly expanded, far more centralized and expensive government, the effect of which can be seen in the charts in Chapter Seven. This was the vision of Canada Trudeau and his "Liberals" worked so hard to fashion for Canada. It was also the vision they recognized would be so threatened by the "notwithstanding" clause (section 33) by Brian Mulroney's Meech Lake Accord and by other similar constitutional compromises that flow from the Charter.

With this scenario now unravelled, we can turn to some of the specific aspects of the constitutional contradictions we have allowed to harden into law, by way of asking some fundamental questions. How did the 1982 Constitution and the Charter come about? Do we really need a Charter anyway? What is the effect of the Charter and the Meech Lake Accord on Canada, its style of government, and its belief system? Can the two styles of government really be forced to cohabit in the same constitutional house?

A TRAVESTY OF DEMOCRACY

LESS THAN A DECADE later, we seem to have forgotten what a travesty of the democratic process the passage of our Constitution Act was until, with the Meech Lake Accord, we saw a re-enactment. None of the ten First Ministers who signed the 1982 accord had a mandate from electors to change our Constitution. And the eleventh — Quebec's René Lévesque — did have such a mandate, but was left out of it. So when Senator Lowell Murray declares that the Charter of Rights and Freedoms "commands the respect and support of many Canadians," we wonder how he arrived at this conclusion. In a classic example of top-down government, Canadians were never asked. The Meech Lake meeting was the same. It was a secret back-room gathering. So, in 1981-82, was the introduction of the "notwithstanding" clause. According to University of Ottawa law professor Anne Bayevsky, "There was no public debate of the merits or drawbacks of using a notwithstanding clause in this way, it was all done behind closed doors" (*Toronto Star*, Jan. 28, 1989).

This was a classic case of the government vs. the people, resulting in a document that had no mandate and no prior public discussion. The reason for this is straightforward. Public debates and referendums such as the Swiss enjoy *prevent the political class from structuring society against the interests of the people*, or from taxing them and spending their money in unrestricted ways. But in an elitist government, every effort is made to avoid such direct democracy. Inquiries are held, royal commissions are struck, standing committees and task forces established. But none of these constitutes a device with any *democratic power* over the government. It can, as it so recently did with the Kierans Task Force Report and the Forget Report, dismiss them with great regularity. All these devices are the opposite of democratic: they are bureaucratic strategies to diffuse dissent. To change this sad state of affairs, Canada must seriously consider the use of plebiscites (for public opinion), referendums (which make such opinion binding on government), and citizen "initiatives" (issues which, at the insistence of the people, must be voted on).

Are The Common Law And The Charter In Conflict?

Perhaps a distinction from everyday life will serve to illustrate the difference between the *prohibitive* and *imperative* concepts attached to rule by Common Law, and rule by Charter, for in a curious way, the Charter has made us less free. Prohibitive laws like "keep off the grass" are normal and acceptable because they leave us alone in our freedom, which except for all such laws, is natural and boundless. Two responses. First, it is insulting when a government Charter suddenly declares that henceforth something we have done all our lives such as walking in the country is now a "right." After all, I was born free, and my freedom *preceded* the existence of the government; I have only asked it to protect my freedom. So how does the government suddenly give itself the right to *confer* a freedom upon us, like a landlord giving us bread? Very simply, it decides to *appropriate* the rights and freedoms we already have, simply by declaration, and then to turn around and generously *bestow* them upon us. In this way, a freedom that we ourselves formerly controlled is now under the control and definition of government. The process of conceding government this right is like yielding up our earthly bread so that the government can convert it into heavenly bread for us. It's an illusion. It is therefore very dangerous for any people to accept unquestioningly the idea that a government is *able* to grant it freedom, *because a freedom granted by government is a freedom that may be revoked.*

Second, in *defining* our freedoms, the government has *limited* them. Under the Common Law, I could do absolutely anything I wished that was not prohibited by the law. Now I have only a specific, limited number of freedoms, and such finite declared freedoms now form our fetters, for to travel outside their narrow and imprecise definitions I must ask legislators and judges to tell me whether in doing so I will still be free. My freedom, which heretofore had never been in question, is now something bound by whatever definition the government of the day decides to give it. Judges under this system are asked not simply to interpret the Common Law — a task for which they were trained — but to become the moral philosophers of the nation, a task for which they are not trained; neither is anyone else, for that matter. That's why we will always need juries.

How Shall We Choose Our Judges?

THE COMMON-LAW PRECEDENT was an august body of law understandable by anyone as a simple set of prohibitions transgressed at the risk of punishment. It was the perfect embodiment of the bottom-up system of values and institutions. But the switch from this simple system to the top-down system relying on arcane theoretical interpretations of intellectual concepts by judges is a danger to all Canadians. After all, a judge is a human being who will be tempted to define freedoms according to his political instincts. This is especially dangerous because section 1 and the "notwithstanding" clause of our Charter (section 33) basically give the government the right to bend society to its will by allowing itself to breach the very same rights it has so generously bestowed upon us. (Quebec's language legislation is an example.) This will inevitably lead to what Michael Mandel in his recent book by the same title refers to as "the legalization of politics." On the other hand, the "notwithstanding" clause is a kind of protection for the electorate against the whims of judges, and clearly allows elected representatives to have the last word on Charter matters, by defection, so to speak.

Under the Meech Lake Accord, the premiers of each province will have a say in who our judges are, which at least has the virtue of equalizing the sin of patronage provincially. If our rights are to be breached, then let us at least have a judge or two from home! More seriously, a formal public process of examining judges selected from a list submitted by the provinces would inject a strong measure of fairness and national representation into a process which in the transition from a Common-Law to a Charter-based country has changed from important to crucial. The more important judges become, the more important it becomes to know the judges!

Finally, there is a further ray of hope. Mr. Justice William McIntyre of the Supreme Court of Canada ruled that the Charter should not apply to disputes in the private sector, where the Common Law can be successfully applied. Upholding this ruling would have the effect of limiting collectivist government, thus preserving the English-individualist system to some degree, and preventing the "constitutionalizing" of private legal disputes. Such a division of systems is desirable, because it would mean that tradition and the Common Law would protect us from each other, and the Charter would protect us from government (except in cases like Quebec's). But the two systems clash, and at any rate the continued presence of a written Constitution that says it is "the supreme law of Canada" (section 52 (1)) is pretty well guaranteed to perpetuate claims for individual and collective "rights" by a whole stream of litigants in an increasingly litigious society. In the criminal-justice system, for instance, the Charter has proved to be a windfall benefit to criminals and their lawyers, and a real danger to society (section 24(2)).

DO WE HAVE THE RIGHT TO OWN PRIVATE PROPERTY?

ALTHOUGH SOME MAY HOLD that our right to own private property is still protected by the Common Law, Canadians are uneasy because, to speak plainly, this right was intentionally omitted from the 1982 Constitution Act through a backroom deal between Pierre Trudeau and Ed Broadbent. But the right to own and enjoy private property is especially important in a free society, for this is the poor man's last bastion of defence against the power of the State. (See Chapter Four.) Without this right, we cannot truly be said to be free, for if we do not own our bit of land, our shoes, our loaf of bread, the work of our hands, our speech, we have nothing for which to be responsible and nothing to exchange with others in any contract. Without the right to own and enjoy property, freedom simply has no practical value because everything not already legally belonging to the State is vulnerable to being taken by the State, and we have no grounds for defence against such a taking. The ultimate aim of socialism is the abolition of the basic concept and right of private property. This most important step in clearing the way for genteel socialism has been achieved in Canada without our consent, and without a fight. It is an expressed aim of the socialist party, the NDP, and of the National Action Committee on the Status of Women in their wish to nationalize industry. This is not only a disentitlement of the common man, but also a threat to the fundamental process of wealth creation for this nation.

Had the same omission occurred in the United States (Article 5, U.S. Constitution), the people would be marching in the streets. If we must have a Charter, then we must insist on protecting our fundamental political and economic freedoms by entrenching in our Constitution the right to own and enjoy private property. Our government eliminated this provision in order more easily to expropriate private property and control resources, but there was never any discussion or disclosure of this intent. Alexander Kerensky, Prime Minister of the Russian Provisional Government in 1917, until he was ousted by the Bolsheviks, knew something of terrorism. He confided to a close associate, a friend of John Carrothers of Mill Valley, California, some sobering thoughts. "The ownership of private property is the most important of all human rights," he said. He described in vivid detail the consequences to a man and his family when they were ordered out of their own home. Their furniture, farming tools, house, and land were confiscated. Money in the bank was no longer theirs. In order for him and his children to eat, the man would do anything the Communist bosses ordered. He was a slave. No action was needed to effect this except the confiscation of private property (*National Review*, Feb. 18, 1983).

REVERSE DISCRIMINATION: THE FOUNDATION OF AN ORWELLIAN CONSTITUTION

WHILE THE CHARTER FORBIDS Canadians to discriminate on a variety of grounds, it allows the government to discriminate on those very same grounds whenever it pleases, particularly under the iniquitous section 15(2), which permits and even encourages the government to engage in engineering social results in the interests of egalitarianism, or to right perceived historical wrongs. A proper constitution should protect equal opportunity for all, without distinction, but our Charter goes far beyond this. It is not satisfied merely to guarantee equal conditions but attempts to force equal results, or outcomes, regardless of the inherent differences between individuals and their situations, characters, motivations, or skills. These so-called "affirmative action" provisions of our Charter are an embarrassing hypocrisy that reserve one moral law for the government and another for the people. By using such a section, the government perverts the rule of law to its own end, which is the centralist control of social outcomes through more government intervention and more policing of our daily lives. It confers positive rights on some, but denies them to others. Section 15(2) and all similar clauses should be eliminated from the constitution of any free and democratic nation, simply because a constitution should protect the people's rights against government, not the government's right to bend the people to its will. Interestingly, the more strictly "constructionist" Supreme Court of the U.S.A. is now softening and reversing such decisions on the grounds that discrimination, whether by an individual or by the State, cannot be defended in the law.

Eliminate The Meech Lake Veto

Constitutional sins against our basic political and economic freedoms were already sufficiently disappointing, but now the Meech Lake Accord has enshrined such faults — and enshrined them in perpetuity, simply by declaring that, henceforth, all ten provinces must unanimously approve constitutional changes, giving any one province absolute power over the majority. Besides being offensive to the democratic spirit, the veto prevents improvement of the Constitution, thus setting in stone a multitude of unwise provisions granting the State social-engineering powers. This should be prevented by returning to the original amending formula requiring assent by seven of ten provinces having between them fifty percent of the Canadian population (or, say, seventy percent, if we want to be tougher). The referendum is an even better method. (See Chapter Seventeen.)

While this reversion to the original amending formula would permit future improvement (or damage) to our Constitution, the "opting out" provisions of the Meech Lake Accord have the parallel and salutary effect of making centralized control of social policy more difficult for the federal government. Those suspicious of central government control would ordinarily applaud this provision on the grounds that it ought to make provincial government more responsive even as it dilutes the central authority. However, the central government still holds the purse strings. The concept of Canadian federalism is underwritten by such purse-string coercion.

Checks And Balances: The Need For A Triple-E Senate

Unlike the u.s. system of government, with its complex checks and balances of power, our system doesn't give us the protection of an elected "Second House" to ensure that majority governments are not prodigal with their powers. Our Senate's right of veto can never be more than mere lip service to the idea of checking government until senators are elected. Currently, the Canadian taxpayer votes once every four or five years with the knowledge that, once the election is over, and owing to the lack of a true Senate, the leader of the winning party will become, in Lester Pearson's phrase, "the nearest thing to a dictator — if he wants to be one."

What this country therefore ought to have is an elected, equal, and effective ("Triple-E") Senate, which would offset the present domination of the House of Commons by Ontario and Quebec and provide the people of this nation with at least some hope of protection against unwise legislation. Senators ought to be provincially elected, with an equal number from each province. Such a Senate, with a veto over Commons legislation, would prevent narrow federal patronage, force the two chambers to arrive at mutually agreeable compromises, and give all provinces a more thorough sense of involvement in directing the fortunes of this nation.

SPENDING LIMITS: LET'S STOP STEALING FROM OUR CHILDREN

THE BRITISH NORTH AMERICA ACT, now renamed the Constitution Act of 1867, gave Canada's provinces exclusive direct taxing powers to raise revenue for provincial purposes, and to borrow "on the sole credit of the province." Prime Ministers Pearson and Trudeau undermined that wise provision when they enticed the provinces into so-called "shared cost" programs such as education and medicare. (The provinces alone could not afford the enormous costs of the coming welfare State, and thus welcomed the enormous taxing power of the federal government.) Thereafter, the provinces were no longer restricted by their own credit ratings but were free to "borrow" money by proxy, through transfer payments from a federal government that "created" it through the Bank of Canada. In this way, the government has circumvented the BNA Act, which restricts the provinces to borrowing solely on their own credit.

Funds so created amount to "fiat" money, which is not linked in any way to economic growth or hard assets, and contributes directly to inflation. Through such borrowing for collectivist causes, under the pretence that "we owe the money to ourselves," Canada has promised programs and "entitlements" that have raised our total federal, provincial, and local debt to more than $550 billion — a level that, proportionately, is twice the size of the U.S. debt — or about $85,000 per family of four! (Note that since the last election, the "universality" principle underlying all this has been slowly crumbling.)

We should emulate the Gramm-Rudman Act of the U.S., which

mandates a balanced budget in five years. Although a 1984 Gallup poll showed that 71.6 percent of Canadians want the government to balance its budget every three years, nothing has been done. Canadians need such a law to protect them against government's overspending. Furthermore, our budget should be balanced not by raising taxes, but by cutting government spending at all levels — a rational expectation horribly abused by the government's proposed new 9 percent goods and services (GST) tax due for January 1991, in *addition* to increased government spending! (They may start at 7 percent, but they'll soon hike it to 9.) As the renowned privatization expert Dr. Madsen Pirie has shown so successfully in Britain, it's almost impossible simply to cut government spending — the government itself must be cut. The best way to do this is to shut off the money pump, for a government with less money is a government with less the power to aggrandize itself and control us.

Finally, the vexing matter of doling out tax dollars to provinces that opt out of federal programs under the Meech Lake Accord is fraught with possibilities for creative abuse, and must be clarified. A better solution, consistent with the English individualist concept, would be to reduce the tax transfer rate of provinces that opt out (that is, the tax money they collect on Ottawa's behalf) and let them keep more of it to solve their own problems directly. As things are now, they send tax money to Ottawa for "processing" by federal bureaucrats, who then send a smaller amount back in the form of services which the province might not have wanted, or could have arranged at a lesser cost. Should we worry that this would "Balkanize" Canada? That medical services in one province might be different from those in another? I say, well and good. This approach has not hurt Switzerland's twenty-three cantons one bit. In that country, funds and standards are controlled locally, and each canton competes with all the others for excellence. Such competition between provinces in Canada is just what is needed to render high-quality, low-cost government services.

"Multiculturalism," "Bilingualism," And The "Distinct Society"

The great institutions of Canada are British in origin and have served this country well. While a controlled multi-ethnic inflow of immigrants is desirable, it must be balanced with the preservation of our traditional European heritage so that the great strength Canada has gained from this heritage is not lost. Productive immigrants have always made a major contribution to this nation. Any immigrant ethnic group will naturally retain cultural links with the past, but we should expect this to be within the context of a wider recognition of and assimilation to our central national heritage. Government's role should be to protect this heritage, not to institutionalize, promote, or finance cultural differences. An official "multicultural" policy, protected by a Constitution, as we saw in Chapter Fifteen, is a recipe for no cultural policy at all. It will surely result in many Charter-based attacks on our central heritage and institutions, further weakening the ties that bind. (Under way already are many such attacks, such as on the R.C.M.P. to allow turbans.)

As for constitutionally protected "official bilingualism," history shows that one language tends to unify, and more than one to divide. While we are bound to respect our original deal with Quebec under the BNA Act to provide French and English services in Parliament, the Quebec Legislature and courts, and the federal courts, common sense suggests that Canada needs only one official language to run its governments and foreign policy. However, any province of Canada that wishes to have more than one official language should be allowed by referendum to have as many as it wishes. But an "official bilingualism" policy is logically absurd in the sense that if such a policy were ever fully realized and all Canadians became bilingual — why would we need two official languages? Again, Switzerland gets along just fine with cantonal language regions of the kind I am proposing, of which it has five.

Even worse, the "distinct society" clause in the Meech Lake Accord patronizes Quebec and amounts to a licence for a nation state, as witnessed in January 1989, when Premier Bourassa used the "notwithstanding" clause to defend his province's oppressive language laws. Even though the "distinct society" clause was intended to be merely "interpretive," its extreme vagueness handed Quebec the means to become even more unilingual, while continuing to enjoy all the benefits of federal largesse. Currently, Quebec is lobbying for the right to enter into foreign treaties (and Ontario apparently wishes to do the same) — historically solely a federal right.

Meanwhile, English Canada is slowly being forced to institute the right to French-language services for a French-speaking minority outside Quebec that is smaller than the unprotected English-speaking minority inside Quebec, which is being openly discriminated against. Francophones often claim that anglophones in Quebec enjoy more "privileges" than francophones elsewhere in Canada. In fact, Quebec did not secularize its education system until the 1960s; English Canadians in that province had long since established and financed their own educational system, of which the prime example is McGill University.

The "distinct society" clause, an obvious and constitutionally protected double standard, will prove to be a weeping sore for the body politic of Canada in the future, by entrenching the otherness of Quebec and encouraging it to become a nation state. One distinct society is a recipe for separation; ten equally distinct societies under a limited federal umbrella, a recipe for harmony.

In the sense that our Constitution creates and protects any group of citizens or any one society at the expense of others, it sows the seeds of discontent. The Meech Lake Accord should be altered to ensure that all its provisions are subject to the provisions of the Charter of Rights and Freedoms, thus rendering the "distinct society" clause more or less cosmetic. The "notwithstanding" clause would then be the only way out.

THE "NOTWITHSTANDING" CLAUSE

THIS CLAUSE (SECTION 33) of our Charter of Rights and Freedoms (sometimes called the "override" clause) has the effect of legally limiting our freedoms or promoting them, according to *how* it is used. For that matter, our entire Charter is qualified by the sense of "reasonable limits" of whoever holds the reins of power when an act of Parliament is passed. This is because section 1 of the Constitution Act, 1982, says: "The *Canadian Charter of Rights and Freedoms* guarantees the rights and freedoms set out in it *subject only to such reasonable limits* prescribed by law as can be demonstrably justified in a free and democratic society." The government giveth, and the government taketh away! It's a sleight-of-hand phrase designed to give legislators the ultimate right over your rights — which is to tell you that you have no rights at all! This is what Mandel meant by the phrase the "legalization of politics."

Section 33 of the Charter is just a magnification of the same idea, for it basically says that any legislature can pass a law that denies individual rights, "notwithstanding" the fact that the Charter has given us those rights. In other words, no one's rights are absolute in Canada. They can be abridged or denied by Parliament, or by any provincial legislature if so desired. So I say Canadians do not have a Charter of

Rights and Freedoms. They have a Charter of "qualified" Rights and Freedoms. Their legislators have ultimate power over their freedoms and over the Charter itself, because they are allowed to sidestep, or "override" it. In Quebec, we saw a demonstration of this as Premier Bourassa stripped 800,000 Canadian citizens of a fundamental expression of their language rights. Normally a citizen would be protected against such a thing either by the Common Law, as in Britain (and in Canada before the Charter), or by an absolute Charter right, as in France or the U.S.A.. But with a notwithstanding clause, there is obviously no such protection.

The question may be asked, then, is it a good thing or a bad thing to have a "notwithstanding" clause? The answer is that it depends on your point of view. It depends on whether you would like politicians or judges to decide on the fate of your freedoms. *With* a "notwithstanding" clause, elected politicians can easily modify or eliminate your Charter freedoms. (Bourassa did just that.) *Without* a "notwithstanding" clause, disputes go to the courts, where judges can easily modify or eliminate your freedoms. As *Toronto Star* columnist Susan Kastner wittily wrote (July 22, 1989):

> *You charter your rights,*
> *I'll charter my rights;*
> *If my rights meet your rights*
> *And get into fistfights,*
> *You don't wanna budge?*
> *Well, here come the judge.*

Are we safer with or without the "notwithstanding" clause? Again, it depends. If judges make bad decisions, we cannot easily get rid of them. We have to wait until they die and then fight to appoint judges more to our political liking. At least you can throw out a bad elected politician. On the other hand, judges are not normally swung by votes, nor by short-term political considerations; their judgements draw from accumulated precedents of the past. So the best solution, from my point of view, is:

1. Get rid of the the French-style formal Charter of Rights and Freedoms and go back to what built this country in the first place — an English-style Common Law, which has the tremendous merit of flexibility as well as legal precedent, is not dependent on theoretical abstractions, and, importantly, *assumes rights and freedoms are inherent,*

not conferred by governments. This is the best protection against government. *Failing this* — if we decide to continue forsaking our heritage, by imposing the French model . . .

2. Let's keep the formal Charter of Rights and Freedoms, but let's get rid of the "notwithstanding" clause as well as the caveat in section 1, thus converting our rights into *absolute* rights (thus elevating their status to those of the "natural" rights under the Common Law).

However,we then need a way to alter our Charter and control judges and legislators.

3. In order to prevent rule by judges, and yet also to avoid precipitate modification or suspension of rights by politicians, we should provide for amendments to the Constitution and the Charter by a majority of 7 of 1O provinces representing more than 5O percent of the Canadian people (or a higher percentage if we wish to make it more difficult). We could also simply submit any proposed changes to a referendum. This would have the salutary effect of permitting change to constitutional rights, but only slowly, and with great difficulty. This system would have the merit of preventing any legislature or Parliament from overriding fundamental individual rights and freedoms without having first persuaded a great majority of the people that this was in their interests. And it would bridle judges by forcing them to interpret the law as closely as possible to its intended meanings (for our protection).

Fixing The Constitution

CANADA MUST CLEAN UP its constitutional document, the first, all-important step being to decide which style of government is really wanted. We must finally admit that more forced equality requires more government, and absolute equality, absolute government. The Meech Lake Accord was a positive, if flawed, step in correcting this, for at least it will have the effect of weakening central power.

Once the dangerous option of absolute government is soundly rejected, we must resolve to reduce the size and influence of government itself. Rule by a political elite must be ended. A true process of public self-examination and self-creation must be established through public forums, leading to a simple, binding, and fair Constitution that would protect the political and economic freedoms of all Canadians equally, one that will not *regulate* our work, our pleasures, and our freedoms, but *protect* them.

Such a Constitution would openly recognize the inherent incompatibility between the two basic methods for achieving freedom, virtue and authority, and would spurn collectivism, social engineering, and the coercion this requires. It would recognize that the welfare State into which Canadians have been manoeuvred has been an expensive failure, destructive of the ethos and spirit of this nation. We ought to dismantle it, and reverse the irresponsibility and dependence it has engendered.

Unfortunately, such a constitutional vision would be opposed at every stage by the large New Class of politicians, bureaucrats, unionists, teachers, professors, journalists, and all special-interest groups including businesses, that benefit from the biases and privileges inherent in our current Constitution. It would therefore require a party and a leader committed to such fundamental principles to bring such changes about, perhaps combined with enough concerned citizens prepared to contribute their own time and money. Such a group would have to prepare the first draft of "Constitution 2000," which would then serve as a focus for public debate leading to a document embodying a true sovereignty of the people instead of the elite.

Unlike our present drab document, Constitution 2000 should be written in language intended to inspire the citizens of this nation with a strong sense of the sanctity of their political and economic freedoms, their civic responsibility to nurture them, and the potential for individual self-realization within a nation that proudly protects such freedoms. The goal of creating Constitution 2000 would be a stimulating challenge for all Canadians, an opportunity once and for all to eliminate the deeply institutionalized conflicts of principle so damaging to this nation — conflicts which, if continued, are sure to bring it down.

17

A Call to Action
We Can Regain
Popular Democracy

THERE ARE SIMPLE, CLEAR solutions — not without challenges of implementation — to the trouble with Canada. If Canadians really want to
take the future of this nation into their own hands, to fulfil the vision
of a truly free, popular, bottom-up democracy to replace the top-down
system we now have, there is a way. But it will have to be carried out
with a thoroughgoing faith in the core values I have discussed in every
chapter of this book: the importance of human freedom and responsibility; the crucial role of private property and how it empowers free
people to control their own destinies; the fundamental belief in self-
reliance that arises from this; and the corresponding belief that through
hard work, honesty, and striving for betterment, the best society will
always arise, based on the idea that each individual is an active moral
agent in the creation of a viable community. Perhaps most important
of all: this can only work if everyone operates under exactly the same
rules, *with no exceptions* — including for government itself.

These core beliefs in the virtue of private persons must, in turn, be
protected by a fierce, deep-seated mistrust in the prospect that those
in the public sphere to whom we have surrendered life's important
tasks can ever create a truly viable, harmonious society. For the expectation that they will do so springs from human laziness and a fatal
relinquishment of the most crucial personal, familial, and community
tasks. So we must first, and at every turn, resist this natural tendency

to surrender such duties to others, who only too happily accept them in return for control over our lives and more power and security in their own. In our own best interests, we must promote moral-cultural beliefs to prevent this surrender, and we must put in place political and legal instruments to protect us from domination by any elite and the consequent moral and social decay that will otherwise always ensue. This requires not a revolution but a great love of principle, truth, and one's country.

Everything I am about to suggest can be carried out without the need to eliminate any of our valuable political institutions. The object, rather, is to enhance them. Specifically, we must: depoliticize Canada; modify our political institutions; and impose financial restraints on government.

DEPOLITICIZING CANADA

THE PROBLEM

POLITICS IN CANADA and most other democracies is a highly charged, Hollywood-style power struggle. Its focus is *not* primarily on the creation of a good nation or on the ideal mix of freedom, virtue, and authority. Rather, it is about how political "stars" and their political machines struggle for control of political life itself, all the while *appearing* to have only our best interests at heart. Nevertheless, the result of all *political-auction* systems can only be a dissolute one, for at least half the government's energy is spent not in serving the people but in serving the political machinery that keeps the reigning party in power. For example, in 1990 Ottawa will spend $9 million of our money on advertising, to convince us that its new Goods and Services Tax is a good idea. Spending our money to convince us it needs more of our money? This is cynical in the extreme. It's more "prostitution politics," essentially a demeaning display to which we are subjected — heavily once every four or five years — in which professional politicians "work" the electorate, vying for the right to grab ever greater amounts of the taxpayers' money and, after taking government's commission, redistributing it to (some) others in ways they believe will win more votes. How cleverly they do this will determine whether or not they stay in power. How, under our system, could it be otherwise? What we have allowed them to do is to conduct an advanced auction in extracted goods. How can any self-respecting people be proud of this grovelling deception and caterwauling in the name of democracy? Is this what

Athens had in mind? Is this what the founding fathers of the United States and Canada had in mind? I think not.

How, then, can we change the system?

THE SOLUTION

FIRST, WE MUST muster the national will to *depoliticize* Canada. We must *demand* that popular democracy be entrenched in our parliamentary system once and for all so that politicians will be forced truly to do *our* will, instead of we doing *theirs*. Isn't this what democracy is supposed to be? Or is this a crazy, utopian idea? Am I guilty of spinning unattainable dreams, just like the socialists? Not at all. For there is a real, live, warm-blooded successful example at work in the world today. No untried theories are necessary, for I am speaking of the *popular democracy* of Switzerland, and I heartily recommend we copy them, almost word for word.[1]

Here's how the Swiss have managed to bring the democratic monster to heel, forcing their politicians to serve the people. It's inspiring!

But first, some facts. Switzerland is a small country of fewer than seven million people, with very few natural resources, a harsh climate, and 25 percent of its land area covered by mountains, many impassable. It has four official language groups, many ethnic sub-groups, and large regional economic disparities. To anyone, this would read like a recipe for disaster. But it's not, for the Swiss enjoy:

- The highest standard of living in the world over the past fifty years.

- Very low unemployment (never more than 1.5 percent, only 0.7 percent in 1986).

- Inflation never higher than 4 percent.

- Interest rates about 6 percent.

- Extensive high-quality health and educational services (health services provided mostly through private insurance, and user fees).

- Generous social services for the truly needy, especially the handicapped.

- World-class public transportation — and the trains are clean and on time!

• In proportion to population, Switzerland has the *smallest* civil service in Europe, the *lowest* tax rates, and the *smallest* national budget.

And on it goes: enough stories of political, economic, and cultural success to make you wonder what we've been doing all these years.

HOW HAVE THE SWISS DONE IT?

1. *Devolution of power.* The Swiss have learned that if democracy is to be meaningful it has to be a bottom-up system of popular government, with teeth in it. Government of, by, and for the people; not of, by, and for the government. The Swiss are not content with mere "parliamentary sovereignty" like ours, in which all power is delegated to their representatives (soon developing into a governing elite that opposes their wishes). Rather, they insist on a "popular democracy," which is the reverse. They have been determined to arrest the tendency inherent in any government to become a top-down system. So the phrase "devolution of power" means *pushing the power down as close to the people as possible*, thus ensuring that the top levels are not too strong. This works in Switzerland, and it would create freedom, responsibility, and harmony in our own fractured nation. Even Australia, a former British colony as was Canada, has adopted some of the most important measures to be discussed here.

2. *Self-governing cantons, or provinces.* Switzerland is divided into provinces (cantons), like Canada. They have 23 of them. But their provinces are basically self-governing and look after *everything* for their residents, except for certain national matters dealt with by seven federal departments. Each canton has its own laws, courts, constitution, parliament, medical systems, schools, welfare and other government services, distinctness, culture, and, of course, language(s). (In fact, many cantons were originally organized around language groups.) But if any canton wants to add or subtract a new official language, it just votes for it. There is no obligation on anyone to speak or use any other language. The Swiss, therefore, have relative language harmony. If you don't like French, or Italian, or German, you just move to another canton and get on with your life.

So the chief principle underlying Swiss life is that all important political, economic, social, and cultural matters must be dealt with *at the political level closest to the people*. (Ironically, much of their desire to have things this way sprang from admiration of the founding principles of American democracy — now so threatened there.) Some cantons still have general meetings where, by a show of hands, their leaders are elected publicly (as did our own settlers in earlier times, before they surrendered political control to professional politicians). In short, the political environment is decided right there, in each small town, not hundreds or thousands of miles away in some capital city. Such is the devolution of power in Swiss life.

Unfortunately, whereas Switzerland and Australia have specified very narrow *federal* powers, leaving all else to their provinces, Canada has done the reverse. We have specified narrow *provincial* powers and left the federal government all but unfettered — a poor choice of systems.

So how do Swiss provinces hang together as a nation if they are all like separate states? The answer is: by an act of will — which, in the long run, is all that can or ought to hold any nation together. They all agree on the necessity for *seven* federal functions that serve the common good, and that's it. By law, *no more ministries can be created without the specific permission of the people.* In Canada, unfortunately, the functions of our federal government are *almost unlimited.* The result? Our present federal Cabinet has 39 members! It oversees 28 full departments, and 15 "sub-departments." In addition, there are 28 "parliamentary secretaries" to assist in these machinations. All these people have relatively unlimited powers to dream up all sorts of expensive new ways to affect or control the lives of Canadians.

Now here's what the Swiss people allow *their* federal government to do. The seven ministries are: Justice and Police; National Defence; Interior; Finance; Economic Affairs; Transport and Energy; and Foreign Affairs.

That's it. Seven truly national functions. Seven ministries. Seven cabinet ministers. If Canada had this eminently sensible system, we would be able to shut down more than *21 federal ministries* and reduce the size of our federal government by perhaps a hundred thousand civil servants! Just multiply that number times the average salary and . . . that's right, it's billions per year — and I haven't included rents for office space, indexed pensions, travel, perks, and so on. (True, the provinces would pick up some of these costs — but not all, for they would control them better, each in its own way, and our costly federal-provincial duplication of ministries would be eliminated.)

3. *Taxing power.* Perhaps the strongest underlying reason for the development of auction politics and the collectivism it encourages is the taxing power. For even where Ottawa has not had specific authority for particular programs, it has used the taxing power to bribe provincial consent. So another extremely effective method to restore popular

democracy is this: *you make central government utterly dependent on the will of the people by removing its power to tax them directly.* (The Swiss do pay some federal tax directly — about 5 percent.) How, then, would Ottawa get its money? Very simply, the provinces would be constitutionally bound to agree on how much to give it — an equal percentage of Provincial Domestic Product would seem the easiest measure. In turn, the people decide how much to give their own provinces — so there you have direct popular control: a nightmare, I am happy to say, for social engineers.

At the same time, like Switzerland, you remove the power of the federal government to "redistribute," or to subsidize one canton-province at the expense of the other. Each stands on its own merits. Will some regions be different — less, or more, well off than others? Of course. But because total political, economic, and cultural freedom are preserved for all, people can live anywhere they like. The Swiss don't believe it is the government's function to equalize outcomes for everybody, because all individuals are different, as are all regions. What is important is having the same rules.

So this leaves the question: How do the people control the provinces? The answer is that they do it through entrenched "people power."

4. *Referendums and intitiatives.* The Swiss *vote on everything.* By law, all federal and cantonal legislation must be submitted to a public referendum for direct approval by the people (called an "obligatory referendum"). You could never have a situation in Switzerland where, as here, 8O percent of the people want less government spending, but parliament votes it up; or the people don't want to dish out money to interest groups, but the government does it anyway. Unthinkable for a Swiss! For the Swiss go to the polls an average of four times per year and vote on an average of five issues per time, *specifically to control their leaders.* This procedure acts as a powerful brake on the ambitions of social engineers, for the Swiss are proud that they generally say "no." You can therefore assume there isn't much new legislation created in Switzerland, because politicians won't go to the effort if they know in advance the people may reject it. Now isn't that a healthy political climate? In short, you couldn't create a Government vs. The People chart like the one in Chapter Seven of this book, for in Switzerland the people *are* the government. By gathering 5O,OOO signatures, they themselves can change legislation (called an "optional referendum") or even force the government to put issues to a referendum (called a "popular initiative," requiring 1OO,OOO signatures).

As early as 1885, A.V. Dicey, perhaps the most famous and influential of writers on constitutional matters, described the Swiss referendum system as "the people's veto."

> *Though . . . party spirit occasionally runs high in Switzerland, party government is not found there to be a necessity. The evils, at any rate, attributed to government by party are either greatly diminished or entirely averted. The Caucus and the "Machine" are all but unknown. The country is freed from the unwholesome excitement of a Presidential election, or even of a general election, which, as in England, determines which party shall have possession of the government. There is no notion of spoils, and no one apparently even hints at corruption.*[2]

In our highly computerized societies, such mass referendum techniques as the Swiss people enjoy would be relatively simple to organize. The purported difficulty of implementation — an excuse frightened politicians usually trot out for resisting such methods of popular democracy — is no excuse today. Nor can we accept Prime Minister Mulroney's lame reasoning, uttered during the 1989 First Ministers' Conference, that referendums "are not the Canadian way." For in reality what terrifies politicians is the loss of direct control over the people, and the right to engineer society.

5. *Getting rid of the personality contest.* Another great feature of the Swiss system is that it totally neutralizes the Hollywood-style electoral races we suffer through by eliminating the role of president or prime minister. *The office simply doesn't exist.* In more than three hundred years, the Swiss have never had a president or prime minister! Instead, each of the seven federal ministers mentioned above serves on the seven-seat cabinet, and each takes a turn — for one year only — as chairman. Thus, there is nothing to race for. The cabinet is expected, as a team, to manage the government, with no false sense of glory attached to that task. Popularity, in short, is not an issue. But competence is, because government, in the Swiss people's view, is an instrument of the will of the people; its role is to carry out their wishes. Thus political life in that country is generally harmonious.

6. *Making government competitive.* A key feature of the Swiss system is that each province ends up *competing* with all the others to provide the highest-quality government services at the lowest cost. The result of this is that all Swiss cantons generally have very low tax rates (the Swiss pay about 20 percent on average: about 15 percent to the canton and 5 percent to the Confederation), and all have top-drawer

social services and education and health programs. Inter-cantonal competition ensures this — as does the people's control over spending. In effect, this system all but privatizes the supply of government services.

7. *All taxes are visible.* Another key to the Swiss system is that taxes are not hidden, as many are here. (About 25 percent of the average Canadian's taxes are hidden in the prices of things we buy — about 5 percent of taxes are so hidden for Americans.) Nor do the Swiss have their income taxes deducted from their paycheques. They get a *tax bill* once a year instead, spelling it all out. Now there's a way to drive home to Canadians the direct cost of their social-welfare State! As an added twist on this for Canada, I would insist that such a bill should include a line showing exactly how much of my taxes were being used to pay debt. Let's have honesty in taxation! Many European countries already send annual tax bills. There is a cost to switching systems, of course (the financing costs of the one-time loss in cash flow), but this is not as great as the cost of not switching. Failing this, an *itemized* tax receipt detailing the precise, specific use of tax dollars would create awareness of government profligacy. For the one system is open and fully disclosed, and the other hidden and deceptive. As for the problem of citizens not paying annual tax bills? Prison terms and garnishee provisions seem to take care of that.

MODIFYING OUR POLITICAL INSTITUTIONS

THE PROCESS BY WHICH Canadians obtained their constitutional package of 1980-82 was an abhorrent sham. It was a direct expression of top-down manipulation of the rights and freedoms of Canadians by a small political elite, none of whom had the slightest mandate from the people to alter the fundamental laws and values by which they lived. That package was imposed on the people (as was the Meech Lake Accord) and is unworthy of a great nation. In fact, it ensures we will never become one. For it is a document that embodies the political philosophy of a whole statist era and its vision, not of how best to free Canadians to control their own destiny within a popular democracy, but of how government itself can best control Canada.

So we now have top-heavy rule by parliamentary sovereignty (now further complicated by an abstract judge-dependent Charter of Rights and Freedoms that hovers over Parliament) with no recourse other than a change of political party at five-year intervals for a re-enactment of the same scenario. As I said, it was a sham. We have a mess on our hands. But what can be done? How can our Constitution be made legitimate? Here's a way to acccomplish that task:

1. We keep our present Constitution until, through a constitutional convention called for this sole purpose, there is agreement on a better one. We then make it official by direct referendum (or send it back for improvement). Such a convention would be composed of a representative body of ordinary Canadians (perhaps selected at random, like a jury). But let us debate our own Constitution, for goodness' sake — and keep the manipulating politicians out of it! This doesn't imply throwing out the good in it. It means getting rid of the bad — not a large job. Most of all, it means making it ours. For there would be no new Constitution until it was put to the people, and the people must always have the choice to say "it's not good enough yet."

2. Ensure that the principles of a free and democratic society are included in the Constitution (as outlined above).

3. Incorporate the idea of a confederation of states (provinces), like Switzerland's, with seven strictly limited federal functions. Let the people control the government, not the other way around.

4. Eliminate all "distinct society" clauses on the grounds that each province will be naturally distinct and allowed to grow, each in its own way, with complete freedom of movement, languages, culture, etc., between provinces, and forbid any socialist-style equalization.

5. Enshrine in the Constitution a sanction against government's doing anything that a citizen is not allowed to do. That is, make sure all government is subject to the rule of law, and not above it, as it sometimes is now. (Examples are reverse discrimination measures under section 15, the *droit administratif* in Quebec, the privileged immunity of language commissioners, etc.) It is only through insistence on submission to the rule of law by all citizens equally, and the corresponding insistence on individual freedom and therefore responsibility for one's actions that makes a free civil society possible.

6. If the people want to keep a Charter, then let's get rid of the "notwithstanding" clause (section 33), thus preventing government from skirting constitutional provisions, as Premier Bourassa did recently. (This clause is a kind of Canadian *droit administratif* loophole,

an instance of the French style eroding the English style of governance, for it permits the government to override the rights of the people.) But at the same time, so that the people can control the government, we must *include* the right of the people to alter their own Constitution by *referendum* — thus protecting them from unwise judges and ensuring that the will of the people is always sovereign.

7. Ensure that all political bodies, including the Senate, are elected.

IMPOSING FINANCIAL RESTRAINTS ON GOVERNMENT

A GOVERNMENT WITH LESS money is a government with less power, so we must:

1. Remove the right of the federal government to tax citizens directly. Its money should be voted to it by consent of the provinces.

2. Disallow tax deduction at source from paycheques. All taxes must be visible, and citizens must get a clearly marked tax bill once per year. Also, all income taxes should be indexed for inflation, to prevent the "bracket creep" that forces people into higher tax brackets (alternatively, a "flat tax" removes this problem).

3. Force all levels of government to set aside regular amounts to settle their debts, and force them to submit to balanced-budget legislation if required by the people — or face a referendum for expulsion. An easy standard might be that two years of continuous deficits triggers such a referendum automatically. (America has somewhat the equivalent in the Gramm-Rudman Act.)

4. Sell off Crown corporations at a faster rate than we are now doing through a broad distribution to employees and the general public (thus making it difficult for any government to take them back). Such a program does not prevent a government from rightly setting the *terms of contract* for such companies. For example, if Canada Post is put on the block but a legitimate fear is that unprofitable routes will be folded, government simply has to include servicing of such routes in the contract of sale. Government should legislate such terms for certain "public good" companies, but not operate them. The result would be better service, at half the cost.

5. Introduce a "flat tax" as the Americans call it (often called a "single tax" here — not as apt a term). Research, especially by Robert Hall and Alvin Rabushka of Stanford University, California, has shown that a flat tax (meaning that all taxpayers pay the same percentage of their income), in addition to its obvious simplicity, actually creates more revenue for government, or, at the least, is neutral. It has the additional merit of ending the discriminatory "progressive" income tax, and — a sure sign of its success — it makes tax planners, lawyers, and supervisors more or less obsolete, freeing them to do more productive work. With the flat tax, there are no more "loopholes," no more "shelters" for businesses or individuals, no corporate tax (it's really a consumer tax), no more resentment, no need for a GST. Just basic fairness for everyone, equally. Everyone — except the truly needy who get tax credits — pays, period. Dennis Mills, Liberal M.P. for Broadview-Greenwood in Toronto, is pushing this conservative idea hard. I hope he will be heard.

WHAT CAN THE ORDINARY CITIZEN DO?

1. Write to your Member of Parliament, c/o the House of Commons, Ottawa, Ontario K1A OA6 (no stamp required).

2. Write to your Member of the provincial legislature (stamp required).

3. Write to your local newspaper(s), with copies to a goodly list of influential citizens and local politicians. You can build your list gradually. This really concerns politicians, who will wonder what others are thinking of your point of view. Short letters are more likely to be published. Even if your letter is not published, you can be sure it is being read, and thus is contributing to a body of opinion, making it easier for the next letter to get printed. Media and political types *do* listen.

4. Participate in radio call-in shows.

5. Be sure to express your opinion to friends and acquaintances — this has a growing effect.

6. When you hear of some new proposal to tax the people and spend more government money, ask yourself why the thing proposed couldn't be done by individuals and their families, or communities themselves,

or contracted out, or insured privately. Most of all, ask whether it is good for Canada.

7. When you send in cheques for property taxes, always send a letter (with distributed copies) to the mayor, councillors, and so on, asking the municipality to economize by eliminating redundant wasteful services, or contracting out government services to the private sector.

8. When you receive fund-raising letters from political parties, write back and tell them your views.

9. Campaign personally in small and large ways for true popular democracy in Canada, as described above.

10. In every way possible, argue to rid Canada of its present top-down system, one that regards the people like children, unable to make important decisions in their own best interests, and for the creation of a popular, bottom-up system in which the wisdom of the people in the creation of their democracy is respected and protected.

Great nations spring from great principles. My fondest hope for this book is that it will help Canadians understand that those principles can work only if they spring from the hearts and minds of each individual Canadian. To surrender our destiny to others, even if they appear to have the best of intentions, is to be controlled by them — with predictably inimical results.

It is time for Canadians to take back that control.

Notes

Chapter One: A Question Of Styles

1. I am indebted to Irving Kristol's fine treatment of the differences between the French and Anglo-Scottish Enlightenments in his essay "Adam Smith and the Spirit of Capitalism," in *Reflection of a Neoconservative* (New York: Basic Books, 1983), p. 139; also, to Alain Peyrefitte's elaboration of these differences in *The Trouble With France* (New York: Alfred Knopf, 1981), the title of which was an inspiration for the present book. This chapter was first presented as an address to the Student Law Society of the University of Western Ontario, autumn, 1987.

2. Paul Johnson, *A History of the English People* (London: Weidenfeld and Nicolson, 1972), p. 9.

Chapter Two: The Popular Illusions

1. Michael Novak, *The Spirit of Democratic Capitalism* (New York: Simon and Schuster, 1982), p. 123.

2. Max Singer, *Passage to a Human World* (Indianapolis: The Hudson Institute, 1987), p. 59.

3. Statistics Canada, *Charting Canadian Incomes*, 1951-1981.

4. Charles Murray, *In Pursuit of Happiness and Good Government* (New York: Simon and Schuster, 1988), and *Losing Ground* (New York: Basic Books, 1984). The U.S.A. has a large and highly respected group of anti-statist intellectuals like Novak, Murray, Epstein, Berger, and Gilder, whereas most professional economists in Canada work for the government at some level and either argue in support of it, or avoid speaking out against it, for career reasons.

5. Murray, *Losing Ground*, p. 273

6. Henry Hazlitt, *Man vs. the Welfare State* (New York: University Press of America, 1983), p. 107.

7. Hazlitt, *Man vs. the Welfare State*, p. 107.

8. Sally Pipes and Michael Walker, *Tax Facts* (Vancouver: The Fraser Institute, 1988), p. 28.

9. Hazlitt, *Man vs. the Welfare State*, p. 106.

Chapter Three: Democratic Capitalism

1. Nathan Rosenberg and L.E. Birdzell, Jr., *How the West Grew Rich: The Economic Transformation of the Western World* (New York: Basic Books, 1986). I am indebted to the authors for much of my commentary on early and developing capitalism.

2. Jane Jacobs, *Cities and the Wealth of Nations* (New York: Random House, 1984), pp. 182 ff.

3. The Anti-Slavery Society (180 Brixton Road, London, England, SW9 6AT) has been in existence since 1839. It documents and publicizes the incidence of "slavery" around the world. Notwithstanding quibbles about definitions, its findings clearly show that many countries currently practise a variety of forms of child labour (India, Pakistan, Brazil), child and adult labour-bondage (India in particular), and the selling, trading, and kidnapping of children.

4. W.H. Hutt, "The Factory System of the Early Nineteenth Century," in *Capitalism and the Historians*, ed. F.A. Hayek (Chicago: University of Chicago Press, 1954), p. 168. Hutt, and others in this volume, give a sober critique of distorted history.

5. *The Norton Anthology of English Literature*, ed. Abrams et al. (New York: W. W. Norton, 1962), p. 4

6. Michael Novak, *The Spirit of Democratic Capitalism*, p. 17.

7. See T.S. Ashton, "The Treatment of Capitalism by Historians," in *Capitalism and the Historians*, pp. 31 ff. See also Paul Johnson's "Karl Marx: Howling, Gigantic Curses," in *Intellectuals* (New York: Harper and Row, 1988), Chap. 3. He succinctly characterizes Marx as a tyrannical, disorganized, intellectual cheater, who systematically excluded objective facts and all countervailing evidence in his angry campaign to discredit capitalism.

8. Ludwig von Mises, *Human Action* (Chicago: Yale University Press, 1963), pp. 617 ff.

9. Peter L. Berger, The Capitalist Revolution (New York, Basic Books, 1986), p. 37.

10. Sven Rydenfelt, *A Pattern for Failure: Socialist Economies in Crisis* (New York: Harcourt Brace Jovanovich, 1984).

CHAPTER FOUR: THE BONUS SYSTEM

1. Max Singer, *Passage to a Human World* (Indianapolis: The Hudson Institute, 1987).

2. Julian Simon, *The Ultimate Resource* (New Jersey: Princeton University Press, 1981). Simon's work was perhaps the first seriously to question the work of "environmentalists" and their anti-capitalist campaign.

3. A thorough overview of these North-South differences is given in Michael Novak, *Will It Liberate?* (New York: Paulist Press, 1986), and also in Alain Peyrefitte's *The Trouble With France*. Peyrefitte expands on the French vs. English modes of governance and compares their effects on whole continents like backward South America and modern North America. Novak focuses on the well-intentioned but tragically wrong-headed social assumptions of Roman Catholic clerics who espouse "liberation theology," particularly in South America.

4. Rydenfelt, *A Pattern for Failure*, p. 38. Since the publication of this study, "glasnost" has appeared and, though halting and far from having run its course, is at least openly recognizing the many advantages of private ownership.

5. Robert Hessen, *In Defense of the Corporation* (Stanford: Hoover Institute Press, 1979). I am indebted to Hessen's book for my treatment in this section.

6. Raymond D. Gastil, *Freedom in the World* (New York: Freedom House, 1988). This volume includes an exhaustive ranking of nations by degrees of freedom, including civil rights, political rights, social progress, voting rights, and elections.

7. Don Lavoie, *National Economic Planning: What Is Left?* (Cambridge, Mass.: Ballinger Press, 1985), p. 43.

8. Paul Johnson, *Intellectuals*, p. 58.

9. Peter L. Berger, *The Capitalist Revolution*, p. 109.

10. Rosenberg and Birdzell, *How the West Grew Rich*, p. 118.

11. Paul Johnson, *Modern Times: The World From the Twenties to the Eighties* (New York: Harper and Row, 1983), p. 14.

12. Michael Novak, *The Spirit of Democratic Capitalism*, p. 64.

13. *Ibid.*, p. 64.

14. F.A. Hayek, *The Counter-Revolution of Science* (Indianapolis: Liberty Press, 1952), p. 249.

15. Even though newly capitalist Asian societies would seem to contradict this view, there is, as Peter Berger suggests, evidence of ever greater individuation with the increasing influence of Western ideas in all economically successful Asian nations. (See Berger, *The Capitalist Revolution*, pp. 168-69.)

16. Roland Huntford, *The New Totalitarians* (New York: Stein and Day, 1972), p. 279.

17. Bryce Christensen, "The Costly Retreat From Marriage," in *The Public Interest*, no. 91, Spring 1988, p. 59.

18. George Gilder, *Men and Marriage* (Louisiana: Graetna, 1986), p. 92.

19. Joseph A. Schumpeter, *Capitalism, Socialism and Democracy* (New York: Harper and Row, 1952), p. 61.

20. Boethius, *The Consolation of Philosophy* (New York: Bobbs Merrill, 1962), Book II, Prose 5, p. 31.

21. Igor Shafarevich *The Socialist Phenomenon* (New York: Harper and Row, 1980), pp. 262-63.

CHAPTER FIVE: THE HANDICAP SYSTEM

1. The Socialist International was founded in London in 1864 by Karl Marx (called "The First International"). It has suffered a series of dissolutions and rebirths, most recently in 1951, in Frankfurt, Germany. By its own description, "its ideology is based on the principles of democratic socialism, expressed in the Declaration of Principles formulated in the Frankfurt Program of 1951, and revised in Oslo in 1962."

2. Joseph A. Schumpeter, *Capitalism, Socialism and Democracy*, p. 168.

3. Thomas Sowell, *Marxism* (New York: William Morrow, 1985), p. 156.

4. G.D.H. Cole, spoken when he became chairman of the Fabian Society in 1941 (Encyclopaedia Britannica, 1946, Vol. 20), p. 890.

5. Don Lavoie, *National Economic Planning*, p. 216.

6. Lavoie, *Ibid.*, p. 216.

7. Lavoie, *Ibid.*, p. 217.

8. F.A. Hayek, *The Counter-Revolution of Science*, p. 249.

9. Colin Campbell, *Governments Under Stress* (Toronto: University of Toronto Press, 1983). An excellent review of Campbell's book appeared in *Alberta Report*, April 2, 1984; but apart from such brief appearances, the public is woefully unaware of Canada's bloated bureaucracy.

10. Robert Owen, *A New View of Society* (New York: Everyman's Library, 1963), p. 24.

11. F.A. Hayek, *The Counter-Revolution of Science*, p. 311.

12. These remarks on Saint-Simon by Kolakowski, Halévy, and J.S. Mill are from Don Lavoie's *National Economic Planning*, Chap. 7, note 5, p. 242.

13. "Tax Freedom Day" is calculated by province and nationally every year by the Fraser Institute, in Vancouver. A summary is available in *Fraser Forum* (Vancouver: The Fraser Institute, June 1988), p. 20. A similar study is done for the U.S.A. by the Tax Foundation Inc., and was printed in summary in the daily *USA Today*, May 5, 1989.

14. F.A. Hayek, *New Studies in Philosophy, Politics, Economics and the History of Ideas* (Chicago: University of Chicago Press, 1985), p. 20.

15. F.A. Hayek, *The Road to Serfdom* (Chicago: University of Chicago Press, 1972), p. 30.

16. Quoted in Novak, *The Spirit of Democratic Capitalism*, p. 368.

17. John Metcalf, "Freedom From Culture," in *Fraser Forum* (Vancouver: The Fraser Institute, January 1988), p. 6.

18. Lavoie, *National Economic Planning*, p. 52.

19. *Ibid.*, p. 54.

20. *Ibid.*, p. 56.

21. *Ibid.*, p. 56.

22. *Ibid.*, p. 56.

23. *Ibid.*, p. 57.

24. *Ibid.*, p. 58.

25. *Ibid.*, p. 58.

26. *Ibid.*, p. 66.

27. *Ibid.*, p. 69.

28. *Ibid.*, p. 73.

29. Milton Friedman, *Friedman on Galbraith, and on Curing the British Disease* (Vancouver: The Fraser Institute, 1977), p. 57.

30. Douglas Auld and Harry Kitchen, *The Supply of Government Services* (Vancouver: The Fraser Institute, 1988), pp. 83 ff.

31. Sven Rydenfelt, *A Pattern for Failure*, p. 44.

32. James M. Buchanan, *Cost and Choice* (Chicago: University of Chicago Press, 1969), p. 96.

33. *Ibid.*, p. 100.

34. Jacobs, *Cities and the Wealth of Nations*, p. 182.

35. *Ibid.*, p. 189.

36. Conrad Black, "The Future of Conservatism in Canada," in *Fraser Forum* (Vancouver: The Fraser Institute, 1988), August, p. 7.

37. Jacobs, *Cities and the Wealth of Nations*, p. 191.

38. *Ibid.*, p. 192.

39. *Ibid.*, p. 192.

40. *Ibid.*, p. 194.

41. *Ibid.*, p. 194.

42. *Ibid.*, p. 202.

43. Eric Brodin, "Sweden's Welfare State," in *The Freeman* (Irvington-on-Hudson: The Foundation for Economic Education), December 1980.

44. Eric Brodin, in *The Freeman*, March 1987.

45. Roland Huntford, *The New Totalitarians*, p. 326.

CHAPTER SIX: THE POLITICAL PARTIES

1. Gordon Graham, *Politics in Its Place: A Study of Six Ideologies* (Oxford: Clarendon Press, 1986), p. 79.

2. "Liberalism Thriving Here, Canadians Insist," *Toronto Star*, April 2, 1989.

3. Peter Brimelow, *The Patriot Game* (Toronto: Key Porter Books, 1986), p. 49.

4. Graham, *Politics in Its Place*, pp. 180-81.

5. Russell Kirk, *The Conservative Mind* (Chicago: Regnery Books, 1986), p. 28.

6. Quoted in Kirk, *The Conservative Mind*, p. 31.

7. Brimelow, *The Patriot Game*, p. 18. See also Nicole Morgan, *Implosion: An Analysis of the Growth of the Federal Public Service in Canada, 1945-1985* (Montreal: The Institute for Research on Public Policy, 1986).

8. Brimelow, *The Patriot Game*, p. 49.

9. *Ibid.*, p. 144.

10. Peter Foster, *Other People's Money* (Toronto: Collins, 1983), p. 91.

11. "Resolutions Reference: Convention 1987 Supplement," subtitled "Taking the Future On." Available from the New Democratic Party of Canada.

CHAPTER EIGHT: THE GREAT WELFARE RIP-OFF

1. George Gilder, *Wealth and Poverty* (New York: Basic Books, 1981), p. 111.

2. *Ibid.*, p. 110.

3. *Ibid.*, p. 111.

4. Murray, *Losing Ground*, p. 111.

5. *Ibid.*, p. 46.

6. Gertrude Himmelfarb, *The Idea of Poverty* (New York: Vintage, 1985), p. 399.

7. Murray, *Losing Ground*, p. 182.

8. *Welfare in Canada* (Ottawa: National Council of Welfare, 1987).

9. Murray, *Losing Ground*, p. 191.

10. *Ibid.*, p. 146.

11. Michael Walker, "The Mismeasurement of Poverty in Canada" (Vancouver: The Fraser Institute, 1986).

12. *1988 Poverty Lines: Estimates by the National Council of Welfare* (Ottawa, April 1988), p.2.

13. John C. Goodman, "Privatizing Government Health Care Programs," in *Policies and Prescriptions* (New South Wales, Australia: The Centre for Independent Studies, 1986), p. 183.

14. Murray, *In Pursuit of Happiness and Good Government*, p. 122.

15. Abrar Hasan and Surendra Gera, *Job Search Behaviour, Unemployment, and Wage Gain in Canadian Labour Markets* (Ottawa: Economic Council of Canada, 1982), p. 50.

16. Murray, *Losing Ground*, p. 149.

17. *Ibid.*, p. 150.

18. *Ibid.*, p. 153.

19. Barrington Moore Jr., *Authority and Inequality Under Capitalism and Socialism* (Oxford: Clarendon Press, 1987), p. 9.

20. Harmon Zeigler and Thomas R. Dye, "Freedom vs. Equality," in *Critical Review*, vol. 2, nos. 2 & 3, Spring-Summer 1988, p. 190.

21. *Ibid.*, p. 197.

22. Murray, *Losing Ground*, p. 228.

CHAPTER NINE: FOREIGN AID

1. Quoted in Melvyn B. Kraus, *Development Without Aid: Growth, Poverty, and Government* (New York: McGraw Hill, 1983), p. 159.

2. Karl Brunner, ed., *The First World and the Third World* (Rochester: University of Rochester Policy Center, 1978), p. 8.

3. *Ibid.*, p. 193

4. *Ibid.*, p. 26.

5. *Ibid.*, p. 140.

6. *Ibid.*, p. 140.

7. Peter T. Bauer, *Reality and Rhetoric: Studies in the Economics of Development* (Cambridge, Mass.: Harvard University Press, 1984), p. 46.

8. *Ibid.*, pp. 49-50.

9. *Ibid.*, p. 51.

10. *Ibid.*, p. 3.

11. In Karl Brunner, ed., *The First World and the Third World*, p. 143.

12. Peter T. Bauer, *Equality, the Third World, and Economic Delusion* (Cambridge, Mass.: Harvard University Press, 1981), p. 70.

13. *Ibid.*, p. 100.

14. *Ibid.*, p. 113.

15. *Ibid.*, p. 100.

16. Sven Rydenfelt, *A Pattern for Failure*, p. 94.

CHAPTER TEN: RADICAL FEMINISM

1. The "family wage" concept has been the focus of renewed interest among social scientists lately. Two useful studies are Bryce Christensen, ed., *The Family Wage: Work, Gender, and Children in the Modern Economy* (Rockford, Illinois: The Rockford Institute, 1988); and David Popenoe, *Disturbing the Nest: Family Change and Decline in Modern Societies* (New York: Aldine de Gruyter, 1988). This important book traces the origins and changes in the family from mediaeval times to the present, then uses Sweden as a bellwether nation that has gone down the path of family destruction farther and sooner than the rest of us that follow.

2. Michael Levin, *Feminism and Freedom* (New Jersey: Transaction Books, 1987), p. 12. Readers will find this book to be a rigorous treatment and exposure of the philosophical and moral inadequacies of radical feminism.

3. *Ibid.*, p. 26.

4. *Ibid.*, p. 20.

5. Eleanor Maccoby and Carol Jenkins, *The Psychology of Sex Differences* (Stanford, California: Stanford University Press, 1974), vol. 1. This volume is basically a thorough survey of the entire field of sex-differences research. Their treatment of each area is suffused with an open and honest feminist bias (that there are no inherent differences between males and females); this creates a constant tension throughout the book due to their desire for scholarly objectivity. Both scholars conclude that there are indeed inherent, genetically controlled differences.

6. Levin, *Feminism and Freedom*, p. 70

7. George Gilder, *Men and Marriage* (Gretna, Louisiana: Pelican Books, 1986), p. 20.

8. See Steven Goldberg, *The Inevitability of Patriarchy* (London: Temple Smith, 1977).

9. Gilder, *Men and Marriage*, p. 23. A more scientifically detailed and fascinating description of the processes whereby we all begin life as females — but some, approximately half, turn into males — can be found in the *Stanford Magazine* (Stanford, California, winter 1985). The article is

adapted from another Stanford publication, *Hormones: The Messengers of Life*.

10. Gilder, *Men and Marriage*, p. 24.

11. Levin, *Feminism and Freedom*, p. 91.

12. Gilder, *Men and Marriage*, p. 140. Sources are U.S. Department of Labor, and Bureau of Labor Statistics.

13. *Ibid.*, p. 141.

14. Brigitte Berger, "At Odds With American Reality," in *Society* (New York: Rutgers University, 1985), July-August, pp. 77-78.

15. Gilder, *Wealth and Poverty*, p. 130.

16. Gilder, *Men and Marriage*, p. 142.

17. *Ibid.*, p. 143.

18. Sam Staley, "Women and the Market," *The Freeman* (Irvington-on-Hudson: The Foundation for Economic Education, April 1987), pp. 143-46.

19. Cited in Gilder, *Wealth and Poverty*, p. 142, from *The State of Small Business: A Report to the President* (Washington D. C.: Government Printing Office, 1984), Appendix A: "Women-Owned Businesses," p. 347.

20. Gilder, *Men and Marriage*, p. 142.

21. *Ibid.*, p. 147.

22. *Ibid.*, p. 147.

23. *Ibid.*, p. 65.

24. *Ibid.*, p. 77.

25. Allan Carlson, "Charity Begins at Home," in *Chronicles* (Rockford, Illinois: The Rockford Institute), August 1988, pp. 12-15.

26. Gilder, *Men and Marriage*, p. 78.

27. *Ibid.*, p. 5.

28. *Ibid.*, p. 10.

29. *Ibid.*, p. 13.

30. *Ibid.*, p. 14.

31. Walter Block, "Economic Intervention, Discrimination, and Unforeseen Consequences," in *Discrimination, Affirmative Action, and Equal Opportunity* (Vancouver: The Fraser Institute, 1982), p. 112.

32. *Ibid.*, p. 51.

33. *Ibid.*, p. 50.

34. See Gilder, *Wealth and Poverty*, p. 279, note 8; also, "Earnings of Men and Women," in *Statistics Canada* report, 1987.

35. Jane Orient, "Comparable Worth vs. Civil Liberty: Are Feminists Pro-Choice?" in *The Freeman* (Irvington-on-Hudson: The Foundation for Economic Education), June 1985, pp. 332-33.

36. Morley Gunderson, "Discrimination, Equal Pay, and Equal Opportunities in the Labour Market," in *Work and Pay: The Canadian Labour Market*

(Ottawa: Ministry of Supply and Services, 1985), p. 238.

37. Charles Krauthammer, "From Bad to Comparable Worth," in *Regulation* (Washington D.C.: American Enterprise Institute, 1984), pp. 32-33.

CHAPTER ELEVEN: MEDICAL MEDIOCRITY

1. John Goodman, *National Health Care in Great Britain: Lessons for the U.S.A.* (Dallas: The Fisher Institute, 1982), p. 16.

2. Paul Starr, *The Social Transformation of American Medicine* (New York: Basic Books, 1982), p. 26.

3. *Ibid.*, p. 216.

4. Monique Begin, *Medicare: Canada's Right to Health* (Montreal: Optimum Publishing, 1987), p. 25.

5. John Goodman, "Rationing Health Care: An International Perspective," in *Policies and Prescriptions: Current Directions in Health Policies* (New South Wales, Australia: The Centre for Independent Studies, 1987), p. 89.

6. A.F. Gonzales, "Britain's NHS: a Sick Joke?" in *Canadian Doctor*, 44: 1978, p. 36.

7. Pierre Lemieux, "Socialized Medicine: The Canadian Experience," in *The Freeman* (Irvington-on-Hudson: Foundation for Economic Education), March 1988, p. 99.

8. Malcolm C. Brown, *Caring for Profit* (Vancouver: The Fraser Institute, 1987), p. 71.

9. Jane Orient, "Who Will Control Medical Care?" in *The Freeman* (Irvington-on-Hudson: Foundation for Economic Education), March 1986, p. 110.

10. *Ibid.*, p. 113.

11. John Goodman, in *Policies and Prescriptions*. See also John Goodman, Gary Robins, and Aldona Robbins, "Mandating Health Insurance," a study by the National Center for Policy Analysis (Dallas), report no. 136, Feb. 1989.

12. Victor Fuchs, *Who Shall Live? Health and Economics and Social Choice* (New York: Basic Books, 1983), p. 28.

13. In *Policies and Prescriptions*, p. 8.

14. *Ibid.*, p. 18.

15. John Goodman, *National Health Care in Great Britain*, p. 57.

16. *Ibid.*, p. 58.

17. *Ibid.*, p. 57.

CHAPTER TWELVE: THE CRIMINAL-JUSTICE SYSTEM:

1. James W. Wilson and Richard Herrnstein, *Crime and Human Nature: A Definitive Study of the Causes of Crime* (New York: Simon and Schuster, 1985).

2. *Ibid.*, p. 516.

3. *Ibid.*, p. 518.

4. *Ibid.*, p. 519.

5. David Daubney, M.P., Chairman, *Report of the Standing Committee on Justice and Solicitor General on Its Review of Sentencing, Conditional Release and Related Aspects of Correction* (Ottawa: House of Commons, Aug. 17, 1988), issue no. 65, p. 52.

6. Wilson and Herrnstein, *Crime and Human Nature*, p. 529.

7. *Ibid.*, p. 492.

8. *Ibid.*, p. 494.

9. *Ibid.*, p. 495.

10. C.S. Lewis, "The Humanitarian Theory of Punishment," in *Res Judicatae*, vol. 6, 1956, pp. 224-30.

11. *Ibid.*, p. 225.

12. *Ibid.*, p. 498.

13. *Ibid.*, p. 498.

14. *Ibid.*, p. 453.

15. *Ibid.*, p. 473.

16. Stanton Samenow, *Inside the Criminal Mind* (New York and Toronto: Random House, 1984). These excerpts are from Chap. 2: "Basic Myths About Criminals."

CHAPTER THIRTEEN: PULPIT SOCIALISM

1. See especially Michael Novak, *Will It Liberate?* (New York: Paulist Press, 1986), for a thorough treatment of liberation theology.

2. Paul Heyne, "Concepts of Economic Justice," in *Morality of the Market: Religious and Economic Perspectives* (Vancouver: The Fraser Institute, 1982), p. 478.

3. Novak, *Will It Liberate?*, p. 50.

CHAPTER FIFTEEN: THE SILENT DESTRUCTION OF ENGLISH CANADA

1. Peter Brimelow, *The Patriot Game* (Toronto: Key Porter Books, 1986), p. 142.

2. *Ibid.*, p. 143.

3. *Consensus*, a Newsletter of the National Citizens' Coalition, vol. 14, no. 2, April 1989, p. 4.

4. Quoted in Kenneth McDonald, *A Solution to the Problem of Quebec* (being offered to publishers at this date), p. 14.

5. Brimelow, *The Patriot Game*, p. 95.

6. APEC (Alliance for the Preservation of English in Canada), pamphlet, p. 2.

7. Peter Brimelow, from Introduction to APEC pamphlet (note 6).

8. Brimelow, *The Patriot Game*, p. 82.

9. *Ibid.*, p. 85.

10. *Ibid.*, p. 85.

11. *Ibid.*, p. 54.

12. "Can Canada Survive Its Language Crisis?", an address by Nicholas J. Patterson, the Canadian Development Institute, to the third annual meeting of *US English*, of Washington, D.C., April 15, 1989.

13. Brimelow, *The Patriot Game*, p. 93.

14. McDonald, *A Solution to the Problem of Quebec*, p. 69.

15. *Ibid., p. 69.*

16. *Ibid., p. 70.*

17. *Ibid., p. 71.*

18. Jane Jacobs, *The Question of Separatism: Quebec and the Struggle for Sovereignty* (New York: Random House, 1980), p. 89.

CHAPTER SEVENTEEN: A CALL TO ACTION

1. I am indebted to Leon Louw and Frances Kendall for their book *South Africa, A Solution* (Amagi Publications, Ciskei, South Africa; 1986), which is the first complete blueprint for the application of Swiss-style popular democracy to another nation. Also, to Richard Tafel, a lawyer in North Bay, Ontario, who published a series of newspaper articles summarizing his investigations and personal trips to discover the nature of Swiss democracy.

2. A.V. Dicey, *Introduction to the Law of the Constitution* (Indianapolis: Liberty Classics, 1982), p. 386. This famous book was first published in 1885 and has served as the foundation for explication of constitutional law ever since.

Selected Bibliography

Bastiat, Frédéric, *The Law*, Irvington-on-Hudson, New York: The Foundation for Economic Education, 1981.

Berger, Peter L., *The Capitalist Revolution*, New York: Basic Books, 1986.

Bauer, P. T., *Rhetoric and Reality*, Cambridge, Massachusetts: Harvard University Press, 1984.

Brimelow, Peter, *The Patriot Game*, Toronto: Key Porter Books, 1986.

Fraser Institute, The (All publications), 626 Bute St., Vancouver, B.C., Canada.

Friedman, Milton and Rose, *Free to Choose*, New York: Harcourt Brace Jovanovich, 1980.

Gilder, George, *Men and Marriage*, Gretna, Louisiana: Pelican Publishing, 1986.

Gilder, George, *Wealth and Poverty*, New York: Basic Books, 1981.

Hayek, Friedrich A., *The Road to Serfdom*, Chicago: University of Chicago Press, 1944.

Huntford, Roland, *The New Totalitarians*, New York: Stein and Day, 1972.

Kristol, Irving, *Reflections of a Neoconservative*, New York: Basic Books, 1983.

Lavoie, Don, *National Economic Planning: What Is Left?* Cambridge, Massachusetts: Ballinger Press, 1985.

Levin, Michael, *Feminism and Freedom*, New Jersey: Transaction Books, 1987.

Novak, Michael, *The Spirit of Democratic Capitalism*, New York: Simon and Schuster, 1982.

Murray, Charles, *Losing Ground*, New York: Basic Books, 1984.

Murray, Charles, *In Pursuit of Happiness and Good Government*, New York: Simon and Schuster, 1988.

Rydenfelt, Sven, *A Pattern for Failure*, New York: Harcourt Brace Jovanovich, 1984.

Samenow, Stanton E., *Inside the Criminal Mind*, New York: Random House, 1984.

Wilson, James Q., and Herrnstein, Richard J., *Crime and Human Nature*, New York: Simon and Schuster, 1985.

Index